The Tyser Legacy

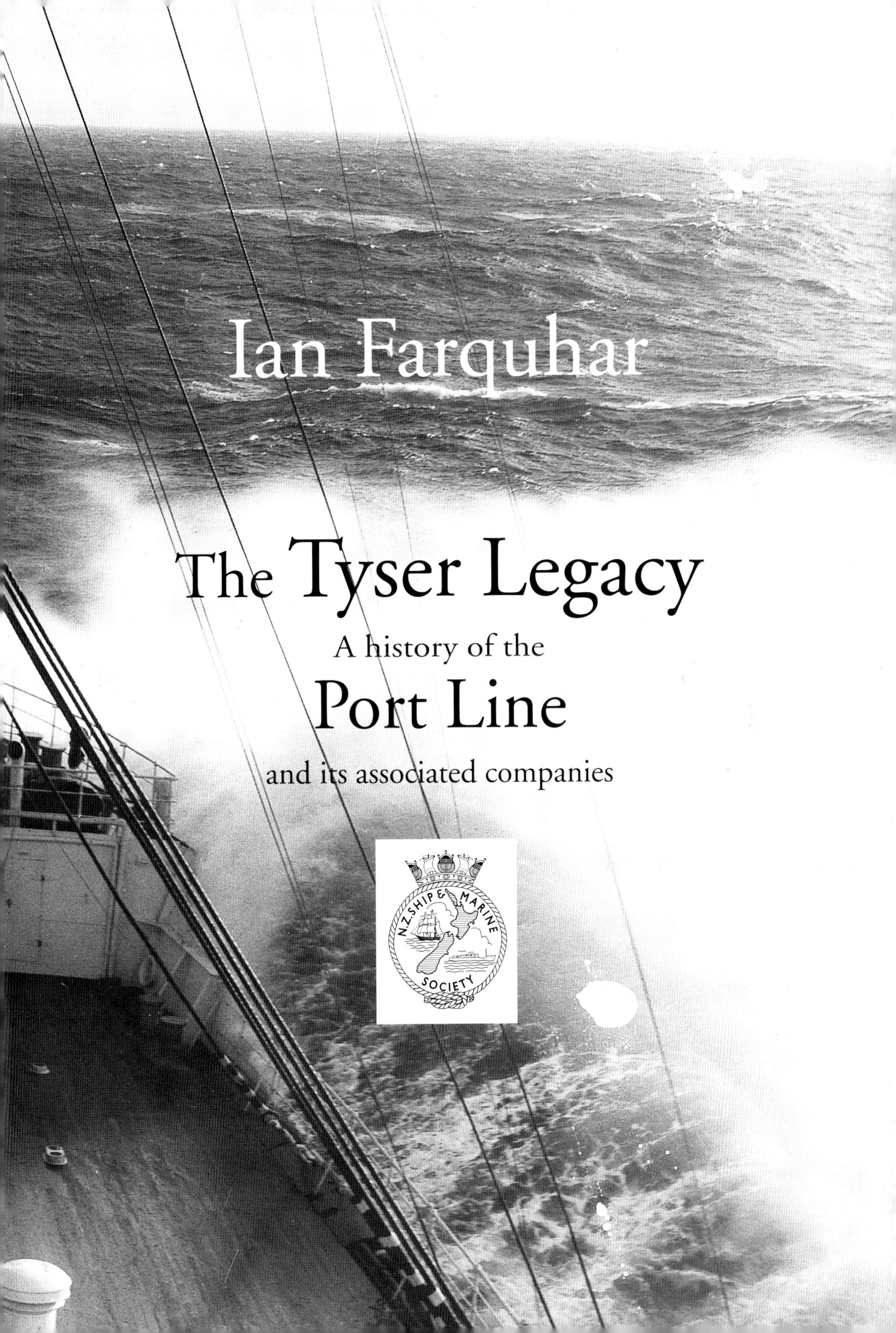

Ian Farquhar

The Tyser Legacy

A history of the Port Line

and its associated companies

N.Z. SHIP & MARINE SOCIETY

Dedicated to my wife Shirley

Endpapers:
Sister ships *Port Auckland* and *Port Brisbane* pass each other in the Rangitoto Channel, Auckland on 9 July 1949. WEEKLY NEWS
Title page:
The *Port Alma* punches her way north on a coastal passage from Wellington to Auckland in 1953. V.H. YOUNG & L.A. SAWYER

First published 2006
New Zealand Ship & Marine Society (Inc)
P.O. Box 5104
Wellington 6145
New Zealand
www.nzshipmarine.com

ISBN: 0 9597834 1 5

Edited by Gavin McLean

Designed by Graham Stewart, Bookprint Consultants, Wellington

Printed in China by Bookprint International Limited, Hong Kong and Wellington, New Zealand

Contents

Port Alma on passage Wellington to Auckland in 1953. V.H.YOUNG and L.A. SAWYER

Preface

Previous histories of Port Line and its forebears, published in 1964, 1985, 1990 and 2004, and numerous articles about the company, have tended to infer that the four British family shipping companies – Tyser, Milburn, Corry and Royden - amalgamated as equals in 1913 to subsequently form the Commonwealth and Dominion Line Ltd (Port Line Ltd from 1937). More detailed research into the origins of the company clearly show that Tyser and Company made the running throughout. It was Tyser that gained the first meat and wool contracts from New Zealand and Australia to England; it was the Tyser Line that developed the New York/Australasian service, and it was the Tyser interests that enhanced the fortunes of all four lines on the Australian-UK-Europe service by creating the Australian Union Line in 1905 and later negotiating the contract with the Victorian government for the carriage of migrants. It was also Tyser and Company that influenced the other three lines to unite as one strong group from 1913.

From 1889 and 1891 respectively, the Corry and Royden families provided capital in the form of steamers which were operated on commission by the Tyser Line network, while Wm. Milburn's Anglo-Australasian Steam Navigation Company benefited from participation in the Australian Union Line from 1905 to 1914. The identity of the Corry and Royden ships was always submerged in the advertising as they were described as Tyser Line vessels. This analogy is confirmed by Tyser family interests holding 48 per cent of the shares in the Commonwealth and Dominion Line on its formation. The Milburn shareholding of 27 per cent reflected the number of ships taken over by the new company and the trade share the company had built up on the England/Australia/England service from 1883. The Corry and Royden families held only 13 per cent and 12 per cent respectively in the company appropriate to their role as financiers in the supply of ships.

The important element in the success of the Commonwealth and Dominion Line/Port Line was the pool share in the various trades that Tyser and Company had vigorously fought to secure in the 28 years prior to 1914. Enshrined within Conference agreements, the strict regimes and rules practiced between the various lines meant that the Commonwealth and Dominion Line/Port Line was restricted to expansion only as trade developed, and in the same ratio to the other lines within the various Conference groupings. In the New Zealand/UK trade, the Conference Lines (Shaw Savill & Albion Company, New Zealand Shipping Company, Port Line, and Blue Star Line from 1933) held exclusive contracts with the various New Zealand producer boards and the tightly controlled system, which locked in all other shippers, remained in place for 75 years – a situation unique in world trade. Previous histories have contained few references to the significance of these pooling agreements and the security they provided, as well as the complacency they also generated within each company in the cartel. The history of the C&D/Port Line cannot effectively be told in isolation, as the company was inextricably linked to the Conference requirements of each trade and to the partner lines in the various liner services.

As the trades and handling methods changed from the 1960s this record also provides, for the first time, a more detailed insight into the operations of Port Line associated concerns such as the Montreal Australia New Zealand Line Ltd (1936), Crusader Shipping Company Ltd (1957), Associated Container Transportation Company (Australia) Ltd, (ACT(A) (1967), Atlas Line (1967), Compass Line (1969) and the ACT(A) interest in the Pacific Australia Direct Line (PAD) (1969).

The MANZ Line was a partnership between the New Zealand Shipping Company, Port Line and Ellerman and Bucknall Steamship Company and in 1936 it acquired ten ships and the rights of the Canadian Government Merchant Marine service from Canada to Australia and New Zealand. Throughout its history it was in most years a profitable adjunct to the main line trades between Australia/New Zealand and the UK and Continent.

Crusader Shipping Company was set up by the four British lines in the New Zealand/UK trade in 1957 to foster development services around the Pacific basin to assist New Zealand exporters in establishing new markets. It was clear that in time there were going to be quotas on the amount of frozen meat and dairy produce that could be sent to the UK and Continental Europe. The four lines, Shaw Savill & Albion Company, New Zealand Shipping Company, Port Line and Blue Star Line, each had a quarter-share in the company, and management was with Shaw Savill & Albion. Crusader made a loss in every year of its history, although the shareholders would receive income from charter hire of their vessels. Port Line sold its shares to the other three companies and withdrew from the business in 1972.

The Atlas Line in 1967 was a joint venture between the Port Line, Blue Star Line and Ellerman Lines to mount a service from Australia to the Far East, in order to establish some 'rights' in that trade, if and when container services were later developed over the route. It was a short, sharp, costly foray which achieved its purpose but subsequent events prevented the lines participating in the container service. The Atlas Line service only lasted four months.

Compass Line was established by Blue Star Line and Port Line to develop a conventional service to and from Australia and South Africa, following the withdrawal of conventional shipping and the advent of direct container services between the UK/Europe and Australia. The first sailing took place in October 1969 but the large refrigerated ships employed were not entirely suitable for the service and there was an imbalance of cargo between South Africa and Australia. The Compass Line was never profitable and Port Line withdrew in 1971.

The Port Line parent company, Cunard Steam-Ship Company, was a 20 per cent shareholder in Associated Container Transportation Company Limited (ACT), when it was formed in January 1966. The other four shareholders were Ben Line Steamers, Blue Star Line, T&J Harrison, and Ellerman Lines. When it came to developing a container service from United Kingdom and Europe to Australia and also from the East Coast of North America to Australia and New Zealand, the three lines involved, Port Line, Blue Star Line and Ellerman Lines, set up a separate company in 1967 called Associated Container Transportation Company (Australia) Limited (ACT(A) with Port Line and Blue Star Line each holding 42.5 per cent of the shares, and Ellermans, the remaining 15%. It was ACT(A) that also took a third share in the Pacific Australia Direct roll-on, roll-off service (PAD) to and from the Pacific Coast of North America to Australia. The other parties were the Transatlantic Steam Ship Company of Gothenburg and the Australian National Line. The first ACT(A) container service from UK/Europe commenced in March 1969, and from East Coast of North America in July 1971, with the first sailing in the PAD service coming south from the west coast of North America in March 1971. Up to 1986 ACT(A) was profitable for its shareholders. In 1977 and again in 1978, Port Line Ltd paid the highest dividends in its history. As most of the conventional ships had been sold or transferred out of the Port Line fleet by this time, these dividends were largely generated by the profits on charter hire of the ACT(A) container ships with Port Line receiving 42.5 per cent of the surplus. PAD continually struggled to make a profit and ACT(A) was quite happy to withdraw from the arrangement with the Swedish company when the 15-year agreement expired in 1986.

ACT(A)'s financial position deteriorated in the late 1980s and the company was sold to P&O Containers Ltd. in 1991. P&O Containers absorbed the main line trade into its own schedules with Blue Star Line buying back the services from the East and West Coasts of North America to Australia and New Zealand. Blue Star Line subsequently sold these to P&O Nedlloyd in 1998. However the 1991 purchase of ACT(A) by P&O Containers marked the end of the shipping services originally established by the Tyser Line in the latter part of the 19th century. Port Line Limited still exists today (2006), but only as a dormant company initially within the P&O group, then P&O Nedlloyd and eventually A.P. Moller-Maersk. The Tyser shipping legacy, which the Commonwealth and Dominion Line/Port Line and its associated companies had maintained and developed since 1914, has gone forever.

In recording the history of Port Line I have endeavoured to expand on the research of past histories by being more specific with detail in covering dates of events of significance, and also to eliminate errors carried forward from previous publications. The final result may be more definitive than others, but overall it is intended to be a business history, providing explanations and comment on circumstances and events affecting the fortunes of the company, the specific trades, and the other partner lines involved. The story of Port Line weaves through these elements and many of those who were at sea with the company, or have had a keen interest in it, may gain a broader perspective of the ramifications of running a liner company within the constraints of shipping conferences.

Ian Farquhar
Dunedin
2006

Acknowledgements

My interest in the Port Line and its associated concerns has been boosted by my involvement with the company's ships as a shipping agent, and making many friendships with company personnel, both ashore and afloat, over a 42 year period from 1949 to 1991. The desire to delve more deeply into the history of the company and its forebears intensified more recently when I felt that soon there would be few around who would remember the company and its immaculate ships.

Much of the resource material has come from my own records accumulated over many years, plus research undertaken on the Port Line archives held within the Cunard Steam-Ship Company records in the University of Liverpool, and I appreciate the assistance provided to me by Mrs Maureen Watry and Miss Lorna Williams of the Sydney Jones Library. Most of the additional research has been undertaken at the Mitchell Library, Sydney, the Hocken Collections and Otago Settlers Museum in Dunedin, as well as the Alexander Turnbull Library in Wellington.

In addition I have welcomed the support of former Port Line staff and would like to thank Brian Barlow (company secretary 1974-91), David Gill (Port Line, managers' office London 1950-68, Blue Star Port Line Management 1968-69, ACT(A) 1969-91), Captain David (Joe) Sinclair (sea staff 1943-79), Ron Conolly (engineer with Port Line from 1955, came ashore in 1965 and was technical services manager when transferred to Cunard in 1981) and John Fleck, former chief engineer and engineer superintendent. I have also been grateful for the information and ideas which have flowed forth from the members of the Vintage Port Association and the Vintage Port website. Captain Tony Braithwaite, as Chairman of Vintage Port, Cyril Simmons, as Secretary, both in London, and Don Ramsey in Dubai, moderator of the website, could not have been more helpful. The list of senior personnel developed by Captain A.G. Russell in *Port Line* (1985) has been updated and expanded.

Several key people have been my mentors in kindly reading my drafts and offering constructive criticism, technical assistance and other ideas to improve the overall coverage of the material as well as tightening up on the accuracy of the texts. In this respect, Captain Ifor Owen, of Wellington (former Blue Star Port Line superintendent, London and then a superintendent with Blueport ACT in New Zealand), Wm. A. Schell of Holbrook, Mass., USA, and Nigel A. Kirby in Lyttelton, have been very generous with their time. Quite a number of other people have helped with specific queries and my warm thanks go to Brian Angers, UK; John Beckett, Waikouaiti, Otago; Bob Blackwood, London; Louis Bosschaart, Netherlands; Captain Tony Braund, Liverpool; David Burrell, Cumnock, Scotland; Michael J Cairns, (Tysers), London; Frank Clapp, Victoria, B.C; Denham Cook, Christchurch; Rex Cox, Hobart; Ken Curnow, Auckland; Howard Dick, Melbourne; John Dobson, Newcastle upon Tyne; David Finch, Katoomba; John Fleck, Wellington; Rodney Hazlitt, Billinghurst, UK; Syd Heal, Vancouver; Richard Henshaw, Christchurch; Antonia Johnson, UK; Ron

King, NSW; Arnold Kludas, Hamburg; Rob McKinney, Timaru; Matti Pietikainen, Helsinki; Captain Mike Pryce, Wellington; Mrs Shirley Richardson, Winnipeg; Robert Ross, UK; Mrs Vonda Sandtmann, Napier; Tom Stevens, Melbourne; Captain Mike Thwaite, Donaumunster; Arthur Turnbull, Christchurch. Ian Weatherston, UK and Doug Wright, Port Chalmers.

I again thank the New Zealand Ship and Marine Society for kindly undertaking to publish this material and special thanks must go to the Society's publications editor, Gavin McLean, and his production team, as well as national president and secretary, Captain Michael Pryce.

Finally to Shirley, my wife and friend of 46 years who has also been induced to share my interest in ships, I can only say that without her support I could not have accomplished so much in my study of maritime history. She also enjoyed being associated with many Port Line personnel when they came to our home in the 1950s/70s and her pavlova cake recipe was activated on many occasions.

A considerable portion of this text is being published for the first time, and although every effort has been made to achieve accuracy, I would welcome any corrections or additional details and any information of this nature can be sent to Ian Farquhar, R.D.2, Dunedin, New Zealand.

Illustrations

All the illustrations have come from the author's collection, unless otherwise specified, with the name of the photographer(s) listed. Names after each photograph indicate the name of the original photographer where this is known. Most of these illustrations are now held by specific archives around the world but many of the prints used were obtained directly from the photographers or collectors prior to their collections being archived. For the interest of readers, material from F.C. Gould (1842-1912) and his son F.S. Gould (1867-1948) of Gravesend is now held by the National Maritime Museum, Greenwich, UK; B. Fielden by John and Marion Clarkson, Preston, UK; A. Duncan (British ships) by Ships in Focus Publications, UK; Allan C. Green, Melbourne by the State Library of Victoria; D.A. de Maus, Port Chalmers, and G.C. Heron, Wellington, by the Alexander Turnbull Library in Wellington and Douglas Jones, Lyttelton by the Wellington Museum of City and Sea, Wellington. Plates and negatives credited to Wm. Livermore, Sydney, F.E. Wear, E. Fluck, and W. Burch, Adelaide, and E.A. Phillips, Dunedin, are in the Hocken Collections in Dunedin, the second largest cultural research library in New Zealand.

More modern material has kindly been supplied from the Bain-Wright Collection (Garry Bain & Doug Wright, Port Chalmers); Ian Edwards, Sydney; Freeman-Priest and Rex-Priest (J.Y. Freeman, Adelaide & Sydney. Lindsay Rex, Hobart and Melbourne) & R.A. Priest, Melbourne); Nigel J. Kirby, Lyttelton, I.G.B. Lovie, Napier, Peter Stacey, Wellington and V.H. Young & L.A. Sawyer, (Vic Young, Wellington). I would also like to thank Matheson Beaumont for his specialist computer skills in enhancing old and faded photographs.

Chronology of significant dates in the history of the Port Line Ltd, associated companies and predecessors

19.07.1809	Birth of George Dorman Tyser, founder of the Tyser shipping interests.
29.06.1839	G.D. Tyser, while working with T. Haviside & Co, London, signed the charter party, on behalf of the owners, for the voyage of *Aurora*, the first migrant ship to come to New Zealand (arrived Wellington 22.1.1840).
1873	G.D. Tyser & Co established by G.D. Tyser and his two eldest sons, G.W. Tyser and W.H. Tyser. (Renamed Tyser and Co from 1886).
7.05.1883	*Chollerton* sailed London for Adelaide, Melbourne and Sydney – first sailing of Wm. Milburn's Anglo-Australasian Steam Navigation C o service.
12.08.1883	*Teddington* berthed Adelaide, the first Anglo-Australasian Steam Navigation Co vessel to arrive in Australia (sailed London 9.6.1883) as *Chollerton* lost her propeller and had to proceed Bombay under sail for the spare to be fitted.
12.11.1883	The first Port-named ship of the Anglo-Australasian Steam Navigation Co, *Port Jackson*, sails from Plymouth for Australia. Followed by *Port Phillip* from London on 15.12.1883.
20.04.1887	Tyser & Co form Colonial Union Line Ltd to provide a steamship service from Australia and New Zealand to London, essentially to carry frozen meat for Nelson Bros. (Initial capital £50,000, increased to £75,000 14.11.1888)

The *Port Phillip* was the second 'Port' steamer for the Australian trade. She sailed from London on 15 December 1883 on her maiden voyage. She is flying the house flag of the Anglo-Australasian Steam Navigation Company; the extensive yards on her masts indicated that her steam power was supplemented with sail on the long ocean hauls. F.C. GOULD & SON

24.07.1887	*Balmoral Castle,* sailed London for Australia and New Zealand, the first sailing of the Colonial Union Line. (Sailed Napier for London 10.11.1887)
13.03.1888	Death of company founder, G.D. Tyser.
14.05.1888	Death of John Henry Flint of the Colonial Line of Australian Packets gave Tyser & Co four shares in the Associated Australian Owners and Brokers conference.
20.09.1888	First advertisement for Tyser & Co acting as brokers for New Zealand Shipping Co (NZSCo) for sailings to Australia and New Zealand.
07.09.1889	Tyser Line Ltd formed in London (capital, £100,000) to acquire the assets of the Colonial Union Line Ltd, with Tyser & Co being appointed managers.
23.08.1889	*Star of England* sailed London for Adelaide, Melbourne, Sydney, Rockhampton, Gisborne and Napier, commencing the link between the James P Corry 'Star' Line and Tyser & Co.
15.10.1890	Tyser and Co dismissed as brokers for NZSCo in favour of J.B. Westray & Co Ltd.
12.03.1891	The first steamer built for the Tyser Line, the 4,583 ton *Hawkes Bay* sailed Antwerp, via London, for Australia.
29.09.1891	The chartered steamer *Indra* sailed London for Australia, marking the commencement of a long association between Royden's 'Indra' vessels and the Tyser Line, with Sir Thomas Royden joining the Tyser Line board in 9.1892.
25.07.1893	Tyser & Co reach agreement with the NZSCo and Shaw Savill & Albion Co Ltd for the regulation of the outward trade from London to New Zealand.
06.12.1893	Tyser Line concludes an agreement with James P. Corry for that company to purchase the refrigerating machinery and insulation in the *Star of Victoria* and *Star of England* from the commencement of voyage seven. Thereafter Corry vessels were operated on a commission basis with Tyser Line, and this arrangement also extended to vessels of the Royden Line.
06.12.1893	The Australian Conference 'DAVIS' and Tyser & Co finalise an agreement on the number of outward sailings the Tyser Line will have in the London/Australia trade.
25.09.1898	The chartered steamer *Queen Margaret* sailed New York for Australia and New Zealand to inaugurate the Tyser Line service from New York to Australasia.
06.04.1900	Agreement signed between Tyser & Co, James P. Corry, and T.B. Royden & Co to pool all freights for vessels of the three lines employed on the various Tyser Line services.
04.02.1904	*Indralema* sailed Liverpool for Australia and New Zealand, inaugurating

	Tyser Line service from West Coast UK ports.
11.05.1905	Tyser Line board approves arrangements made with Gibbs, Bright & Co, Sydney and W. & A. McArthur Ltd, Sydney for the establishment of a new shipping line to provide a weekly service from Australia to UK/Europe during the wool season.
26.05.1905	First advertisement for Australia Union Line service from Australia to South Africa/England/Continent with Tyser and Co, Gibbs, Bright and Co, and W. & A. McArthur Ltd, Joint Agents.
29.06.1905	The first Australian Union Line sailing with the *Star of Victoria* leaving Melbourne for Durban, East London and Cape Town. *Indraghiri* sailed Melbourne for London on 2.7.1905, the first AUL sailing to England.
06.11.1905	*Port Albert* sailed Sydney, the first Australian Union Line sailing from Australia for Wm. Milburn's Anglo-Australasian Steam Navigation Co, followed by *Port Caroline* from Melbourne on 7.11.1905.
20.04.1907	*Hawkes Bay* sailed New York for Australia, marking the first sailing of United Tyser Line, a partnership between Tyser Line Ltd (50 per cent) and two German companies – Deutchse Dampfschiffahrts-Gesellschaft "HANSA", Bremen and the Deutchse-Australische Dampfschiffs-Gesellschaft, Hamburg (50 per cent).
01.06.1907	*Itzehoe*, the first German vessel under the new United Tyser Line, sails New York for Australia.
30.06.1908	Death of William Haviside Tyser, second son of G.D. Tyser.
23.01.1912	Tyser & Co, Wm. Milburn and Co, and P&O Branch Service sign agreement with agent-general for Victoria to carry 24,000 migrants from London to Melbourne in the period 1912-1914.
12.06.1912	*Makarini* sailed London for Melbourne, the first of seven ships fitted with dormitory accommodation for migrants. Followed 1912-14 by *Indrapura, Port Lincoln, Port Macquarie, Hawkes Bay, Star of Victoria* and *Star of England.*
16.04.1913	Tyser & Co sign agreement with NZSCo and Shaw Savill & Albion for sharing of the trade to and from the UK and New Zealand.
31.12.1913	Tyser & Co, Tyser Line Ltd, Wm. Milburn & Co, James P. Corry and T.B. Royden agree to amalgamate Australian and New Zealand trade interests effective 1.7.1913, with interest at 5 per cent on capital utilised in the period 1.7.1913-1.1.1914 and the ships involved to be valued at cost, less depreciation at 5 per cent per annum. The proposed new company to also acquire the whole of the Tyser & Co shipping business.
23.01.1914	Commonwealth & Dominion Line Ltd, registered in London as an amalgamation of Tyser & Co/Tyser Line Ltd, James P. Corry 'Star' Line and segments of the fleets of T.B. Royden & Co and Wm. Milburn & Co

	– the new company to have a fleet of 25 steamers of which 8 were from Tysers, 5 from Corry, 3 from Royden and 9 from Milburn.
12.03.1915	C&D Line concludes agreement with Gibbs, Bright & Company to act as principal agents for the Line at Australian mainland ports.
08.06.1916	The Cunard Steam-Ship Co Ltd, Liverpool acquires all the ordinary shares of the C&D Line Ltd. The company continued to trade separately as the Cunard Line Australasian Service-C&D Line Ltd
09.05.1917.	Contract signed for new Wellington office building, jointly owned and used by the C&D Line Ltd, and the NZSCo.
18.12.1917	*Port Darwin* ran trials – first ship specially built for the C&D Line Ltd.
04.02.1919	Death of Sir Montague Nelson. Director Tyser Line 1892-1914, C&D Line 1914-19.
26.11.1920	A pooling agreement concluded with the British lines in the Australian/UK/Europe trade.
24.12.1920	The lines in the New Zealand trade – Shaw Savill & Albion, NZSCo and the associated Federal Steam Navigation Co Ltd, and the C&D Line Ltd sign an agreement (known as the BENMACOW agreement)to promote the efficiency and economy of an integrated liner service to and from New Zealand/UK and subsequently enter into contractual arrangements for the service with the New Zealand producer boards.
24.1.1921	George William Tyser, elder son of G.D. Tyser, and brother of the late W.H. Tyser, dies.
23.11.1922	The death of Charles T. Milburn, the last Milburn family member on the board of the C&D Line.
27.05.1925	*Port Dunedin* delivered – the first motor ship built for the company – thereafter all subsequent vessels built for it were motor ships.
09.06.1926	Sir William Corry died, a director of Tyser Line 1892-1915 and the C&D Line 1914-26. Also on the Cunard Steam-Ship Company board 1916-1926.
03.10.1933	*Port Chalmers* launched – first ship in the fleet to be specially equipped to carry chilled beef in quantity. Also the first vessel with sections of the vessel being welded rather than the traditional riveted construction.
13.10.1933	*Tuscan Star* sails London for New Zealand, the first Blue Star Line vessel to enter the New Zealand trade on a regular service.
24.01.1935	Brine grid cooling for refrigeration improved with forced air cooling in *Port Wyndham* delivered 24.1.1935.
12.12.1935	C&D board approve company becoming known as Port Line but the legal name of the company not changed to Port Line Ltd until 11.11.1937 with approval from the Board of Trade 18.11.1937.
08.06.1936	C&D Line Ltd, in conjunction with Ellerman & Bucknall Steamship

Co Ltd, and NZSCo, sign agreement to form Montreal Australia New Zealand Line Ltd (MANZ Line) to take over 10 former Canadian Government Merchant Marine vessels to provide regular service from Canadian ports to Australia and New Zealand. *City of Batavia* had sailed 22.5.1936 for Australia, as the first MANZ Line sailing.

20.1.1937 *Port Jackson* delivered, first ship in the fleet to be completely fitted out with forced air cooling in the refrigerated compartments. Also first vessel in the fleet to carry a bow plaque with the Port Line house flag, a practice followed for subsequent new-builds.

05.05.1944 Walter P. Tyser died, son of G.W. Tyser, and the first chairman of the C&D Line/Port Line 1914-1939.

12.11.1946 *Port Napier* launched, the first Port Line ship to be fitted with Birmabright aluminium sheathing in her refrigerated compartments, and at the time the largest refrigerated ship in the world.

28.02.1949 *Port Brisbane*, delivered: her cargo handling gear incorporated a 3-ton electric deck crane.

03.03.1949 Queen Elizabeth, accompanied by Princess Margaret, visited *Port Brisbane* in King George V dock, London – the first reigning Queen to inspect a cargo ship since the days of Queen Elizabeth the First.

01.06.1949 Port Line took delivery of *Port Vindex*, the only vessel owned by the company not to be named after a port in Australia, New Zealand or Canada, but in recognition of her service in World War II as the escort aircraft carrier H.M.S. *Vindex.*

06.11.1950 Death of Lord Royden, who joined the board of the C&D Line 1914 as Thomas Royden, later Sir Thomas Royden, then Baron Royden of Frankby (1944) and remained on the board until his death. He was a director of Cunard Steam-Ship Co Ltd 1905-50.

12.05.1953 *Port Campbell* arrived Briton Ferry, UK for demolition – the last coal-burning steamer in the fleet.

22.11.1957 Launching of *Port Invercargill* at Harland and Wolff, Belfast, accomplished by radio telephone impulse from sponsor in Sydney, Mrs. D.F. Middleton.

22.11.1957 Port Line Ltd, along with Shaw Savill & Albion, NZSCo and Blue Star Line, register Crusader Shipping Co Ltd to develop refrigerated cargo services from New Zealand ports to Japan, West Coast of North America, West Indies and the north Pacific coast of South America, each company having a 25 per cent shareholding; Shaw Savill & Albion managers.

09.11.1962 *Port Nicholson* delivered, the largest (13,847 grt) vessel yet built for Port Line; also the largest refrigerated cargo vessel in the world (603,810 cubic feet 17,100 cu metres) of insulated space.

11.01.1966 The Cunard Steam-Ship Co Ltd, parent company of Port Line Ltd, joins with The Ben Line Steamers, Blue Star Line Ltd, The Charente Steam-Ship Co Ltd, and Ellerman Lines Ltd to form Associated Container Transportation Co Ltd (ACT) to develop container services over existing trade routes.

05.06.1967 *Port Invercargill* trapped in Great Bitter Lakes. Suez Canal during six day war between Israel and Egypt. Declared a constructive total loss 19.2.1969 but not removed until 30.5.1975.

23.08.1967 Port Line, Blue Star Line and Ellerman & Bucknall Steamship Co form subsidiary company – Associated Container Transportation Co (Australia) Ltd (ACT(A) to mount container services from U.K/Europe and East Coast North America to Australia and New Zealand.

01.09.1967 *Rockhampton Star* commences loading at Adelaide, the first northbound cargo for the Atlas Line.

08.09.1967 Port Line, in partnership with Blue Star Line, Ellerman & Bucknall Steamship Co, register Atlas Line (Australia) Pty Ltd, a company set up to develop a regular liner service from Australia to Japan. The service terminated four months later following agreement with the competing British lines.

09.10.1967 *Port Chalmers* launched, the largest refrigerated cargo liner in the world with 606,940 cubic feet (17,186 cubic metres) of refrigerated space. Refrigerated capacity was later increased to 663,170 cubic feet (18,781 cubic metres)

11.03.1968 Blue Star Port Lines (Management) Ltd formed by Port Line and Blue Star Line, to provide a management company for the joint conventional fleets – the arrangement terminated for husbandry and operation of the ships from 1.1.1972.

18.10.1968 *ACT 1* launched, first containership for ACT(A) service from U.K./Europe to and from Australia.

22.03.1969 *ACT 1* sails Rotterdam for Australia on maiden voyage for ACT(A).

22.04.1969 ACT(A) signs agreement with Australian government for the Australian National Line (ANL) to operate a joint container serviceas ACT(A)/ANL between U.K./Europe to and from Australia. The agreement subsequently extended to a similar arrangement in the trade to and from Australia to East Coast North America.

05.08.1969 Blue Star Line Ltd, Ellerman Lines and Port Line Ltd, sign a 15 year agreement with Rederiaktiebolaget Transatlantic, Gothenburg to operate RORO ships between the West Coast of North America, Hawaii, Australia and New Zealand under the Pacific Australia Direct (PAD) line.

14.08.1969 Letter of intent given by the three lines to Eriksbergs, Gothenburg for the construction of RORO ship for the PAD service, with delivery

	July 1971.
22.10.1969	*Port Melbourne* sails from Durban for Melbourne via Lourenco Marques, on first sailing to Australia of Compass Line service, jointly operated with Blue Star Line. Port Line withdrew from the service in March 1971.
26.02.1971	*ACT 3* launched, first ACT(A) containership for PACE service between Australia/New Zealand and East Coast of North America.
06.05.1971	*Dilkara* launched, the ACT(A) RORO ship specially built for the PAD service between West Coast of North America to and from Australia.
24.07.1971	*Port New Plymouth* sails Auckland for Galveston, the last conventional Port Line ship to load in New Zealand for East Coast North America.
25.08.1971	Final Cunard Steam-Ship Company Ltd board meeting prior to company's acquisition by property and investment company, Trafalgar House Investments Ltd.
29.09.1972	Port Line withdrawal from Crusader Shipping Co Ltd, becomes effective.
25.11.1978	*Port Caroline* sails Mount Maunganui for Avonmouth, the last direct conventional sailing on the main line trade, commenced by Tyser & Co with *Balmoral Castle* in 1887. (A later conventional sailing of *Port Nicholson* in March 1979 was to Mediterranean ports thence Avonmouth).
10.1986	By mutual agreement, ACT(A) withdraws from the PAD service and *Dilkara* delivered to Taiwan shipbreakers 2.12.1986.
01.07.1987	Trafalgar House Investments purchase 15 per cent share of ACT(A) owned by Ellerman Lines, which with the 42.5 per cent held by its subsidiary Port Line Ltd, took their interest in ACT(A) to 57.5 per cent.
03.04.1989	ACTNZ, a wholly owned subsidiary of ACT(A) purchases the trades, pool shares and vessels of the Shipping Corporation of New Zealand Ltd from the N.Z. government.
30.09.1991	P&O Containers Ltd purchases container interests of Cunard Ellerman Lines, the takeover operationally effective from 11.10.1991, with P&O on-selling the American trades to Blue Star Line Ltd. The purchase thus included Port Line Ltd and any remaining Port Line links with the Australasian trades.
20.04.1998	P&O Nedlloyd announces the takeover of Blue Star Line container services which completes the absorption of the remaining remnants of the four former British Conference Lines in the New Zealand trade.

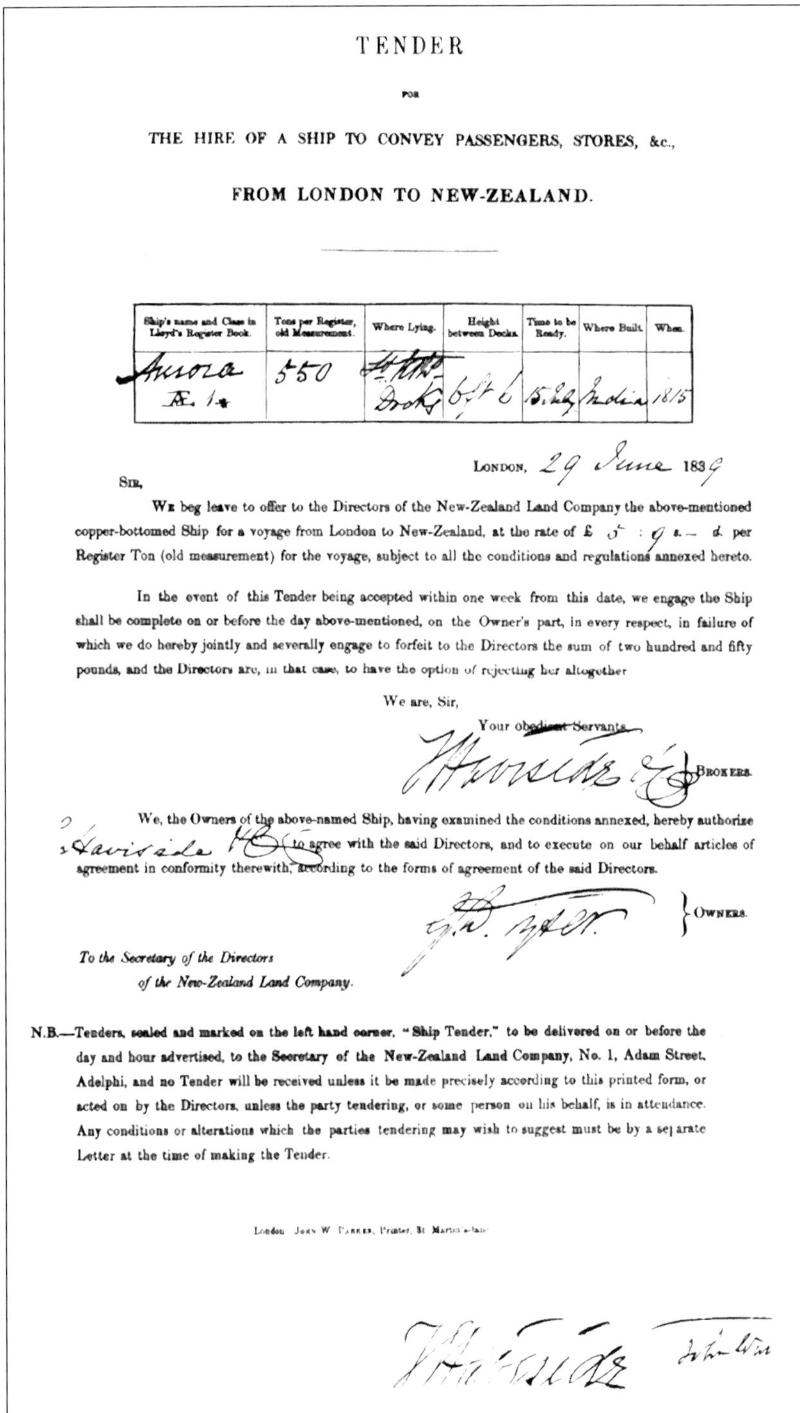

TENDER

FOR

THE HIRE OF A SHIP TO CONVEY PASSENGERS, STORES, &c.,

FROM LONDON TO NEW-ZEALAND.

Ship's name and Class in Lloyd's Register Book.	Tons per Register, old Measurement.	Where Lying.	Height between Decks.	Time to be Ready.	Where Built.	When.
Aurora Æ. 1	550	Docks	6 ft 6	15. July	India	1815

London, 29 June 1839

Sir,

We beg leave to offer to the Directors of the New-Zealand Land Company the above-mentioned copper-bottomed Ship for a voyage from London to New-Zealand, at the rate of £ 5 : 9 s. – d. per Register Ton (old measurement) for the voyage, subject to all the conditions and regulations annexed hereto.

In the event of this Tender being accepted within one week from this date, we engage the Ship shall be complete on or before the day above-mentioned, on the Owner's part, in every respect, in failure of which we do hereby jointly and severally engage to forfeit to the Directors the sum of two hundred and fifty pounds, and the Directors are, in that case, to have the option of rejecting her altogether

We are, Sir,

Your obedient Servants,

T. Haviside & Co. Brokers.

We, the Owners of the above-named Ship, having examined the conditions annexed, hereby authorize Haviside & Co to agree with the said Directors, and to execute on our behalf articles of agreement in conformity therewith, according to the forms of agreement of the said Directors.

G.D. Tyser } Owners.

To the Secretary of the Directors of the New-Zealand Land Company.

N.B.—Tenders, sealed and marked on the left hand corner, "Ship Tender," to be delivered on or before the day and hour advertised, to the Secretary of the New-Zealand Land Company, No. 1, Adam Street, Adelphi, and no Tender will be received unless it be made precisely according to this printed form, or acted on by the Directors, unless the party tendering, or some person on his behalf, is in attendance. Any conditions or alterations which the parties tendering may wish to suggest must be by a separate Letter at the time of making the Tender.

London: John W. Parker, Printer, St. Martin's-lane

T. Haviside

While working with London shipbroker, T. Haviside & Company, G.D. Tyser signed the charter party, on behalf of the owners, for the *Aurora*, the first migrant ship to come to New Zealand in 1840. Haviside owned 24 and Tyser had 20 of the 64 shares in the ownership of the vessel. REV. W.C. COMBER COLLECTION

CHAPTER 1

Tyser establishes a foothold

Last century Port Line Limited was one of the finest cargo liner companies employed in the main line trade between Australia, New Zealand and United Kingdom/ Europe. For over 50 years it held more than 20 per cent of the trade between New Zealand and Great Britain and around 15 per cent of the liner trades from Australia to UK/Europe. It was also a significant carrier between Australia and New Zealand to and from the East Coast of North America, until all its trade shares were submerged into ACT(A) – Associated Container Transportation Company (Australia) Limited as container vessels steadily replaced conventional cargo ships from 1969. The company operated one of the largest fleets of refrigerated cargo liners in the world. Vessels of its fleet of some 30 immaculately maintained, grey-hulled cargo liners were regularly seen in most ports in Australasia between 1914 and the 1970s. Throughout its history Port Line operated within shipping conferences on all its trades, and in the New Zealand trade particularly, the protection the pool share provided within the cartel, and so fiercely protected, created a monopoly within the New Zealand/United Kingdom/Europe service which was unparalleled in any other conference line setting anywhere in the world. The enduring relationship between British shipping lines and the New Zealand producer boards locked every other shipper in to the levels of service and freight structure offered. But the very protection and security afforded by operating within a group of lines created a complacency which eventually took its toll on the fortunes of Port Line itself.

The initial success of the line owed most to the efforts of London ship and insurance broker, George Dorman Tyser, two of his sons and two grandsons, who between 1881 and 1914 fought their way into the tightly defended liner trades between London and Australasia. Tyser was the third son of Robert and Maria Tyser and was born 19 July 1809. He married Maria Moule on 16 September 1835 and they had a family of five boys and three girls. The two eldest sons went into business with their father and the fourth son, Charles Robert distinguished himself as a judge in Cyprus and was knighted for his services.

G. D. Tyser entered the shipping business of T. Haviside & Co, London shipbrokers. The company concentrated in chartering sailing ships for direct voyages from London to Bombay, and to a lesser extent, Calcutta. In addition they 'fixed' ships and cargoes for voyages to any part of the world. Tyser had an early link with New Zealand in that on 29 June 1839 he signed the charter party, as owner's broker, for the *Aurora* (1815,

550), the first migrant ship to come to New Zealand (arrived Wellington 22 January 1840); he had 20 shares in the ship. T. Haviside & Co continued chartering ships to Bombay right through until 1878 and these vessels included a few steamers as well as the sailing ships. The close relationship between Haviside and Tyser was such that George Tyser's second son, born in 1844, was named William Haviside Tyser.

Apart from the association with Haviside, G. D. Tyser started buying shares in sailing ships. The first vessel he owned was the *Northumberland* and two years later in 1861 he took delivery of the *Bombay*, the first ship built to his order. Between 1859 and 1883 Tyser owned or held shares in 12 sailing ships. In each case he generally spread the risk by owning the majority of the 64 shares, leaving around 25 per cent of the remaining shares to be held by friends or family. With most of the early ships, Sir Thomas G. A. Parkyns of Ruddington, eight kilometres south of Nottingham, was a regular holder of small parcels of shares and in later years this link extended to his son, Sir Thomas F. M. Parkyns, the 7th baronet, who was a director of the Colonial Union Line from 1888 to1890 and the Tyser Line Limited from 1890 to 1915. Again this close friendship and long association with the two generations of Parkyns was further linked when G. D. Tyser's eldest son, George William, married Annie Parkyns in September 1864. Their first son was named Walter Parkyns Tyser.

Some of the ships were chartered for voyages to New Zealand with immigrants. *Northumberland* made a 114 day passage to Auckland in 1861. Shaw Savill took the *Bombay* for four voyages between 1862 and 1863. On her third voyage in 1863 she encountered very heavy weather about ten days out from Auckland with 400 passengers and was virtually dismasted. She was fortunate to secure a tow from the Circular Saw Line barque *Constance* (1858, 351), and with further assistance from HMS *Curacao* on the last day out of Auckland, finally reached port. Repairs took four months. The area south of Auckland, known as Bombay, takes its name from this ship.

The *Berar* was also chartered by Shaw Savill and made one migrant voyage in 1873 and two more during 1873-5. *Howrah* was chartered for three New Zealand voyages between 1874-6. Two other Tyser sailing ships, *Himalaya* and *Trevelyan* were sold to Shaw Savill in 1874 and 1873 respectively. The *Himalaya* made a total of 24 voyages to New Zealand, either under Tyser or Shaw Savill, while the *Trevelyan* made six round voyages and was lost on her seventh in 1888 when she went missing with all hands off the southern coast of South Africa while on passage from Glasgow to Port Chalmers. *Northumberland* made four migrant voyages to Australia between 1850 and 1864, and other Tyser sailing ships such as *Trevelyan, Himalaya, Berar, North* and *Lightning* all made voyages to Adelaide, and or Melbourne, between 1865 and 1876.

In 1873 Tyser took two sons, George William Tyser and William Haviside Tyser, into partnership, trading as G. D. Tyser & Company. In 1881 Tyser & Co joined with three other brokers and formed the Alliance Line of Clipper Packets to trade to Australia. The established lines in the trade finally forced the Alliance consortium

The 1,042 ton iron ship *Trevelyan* was built for G.D. Tyser in 1863. She was sold to Shaw Savill for the New Zealand trade in 1873. Converted to a barque in 1885, she is shown here at Export Wharf, Port Chalmers, and in 1888 she went missing off the African coast. DE MAUS, ALEXANDER TURNBULL LIBRARY

out, and it was agreed that they would not load ships to Australia for two years. The following year Tyser & Co joined with London shipbrokers, J. B. Westray & Co, Alexander Howden & Co, Charles Howard & Co and McDiarmid, Greenshields & Co to form the International Line, trading with chartered ships to South Africa. The company also gained a contract from the South African government to carry migrants. This line was more successful and gained a pool share when the first South African Conference was formed in September 1883. The trading rights secured by Tyser were modest but they enabled the company to remain in the trade as a broker for many years.

The company also invested in other ventures, mostly short-lived, such as the Island Steam Shipping Co Ltd, formed in June 1883. A steamer was ordered from Doxfords but six weeks later, the directors, led by W. H. Tyser, as chairman, decided that with the shipyard full of work, costs were high, freights were low and trade dull, so the order was cancelled. The company never emerged as a steamship owner. In 1885 Tyser was the leading figure in securing support from several major shippers to form the Merchant Line of Packets to Australia. Tyser attempted to obtain cheaper rates of freight for the merchants involved and strongly attacked the established Australian lines, who were operating in a conference grouping called the 'Davis' pool. The shipowners secretly met on the premises of a Fen Court, Fenchurch Street shopkeeper named Davis where they discussed freight rates, service scheduling and other collective matters relating to the trade. The group had been formed by eight London shipbrokers in 1876 under the name of Associated Australian Owners and Brokers. To encourage shipper loyalty Associated Brokers offered a deferred rebate to exporters undertaking to ship all their cargo on vessels controlled by the group. Outsiders generally called the group the 'Shipping Ring'. By 1885 the Associated Brokers group comprised these London brokers: Anderson, Anderson & Co, Allport & Hughes, C. Bethell & Co, F. Green & Co, John Henry Flint of the Colonial Line, J. Gavin Birt & Co, Houlder Bros and Co, J. Potter & Co, George Thompson & Co and Trinder, Anderson & Co.

All the firms required shippers to sign an agreement undertaking to ship their cargoes solely in vessels loaded by this group of brokers. Failure to do so would result in higher rates being charged and there would be no rebates paid. In a letter to *The Times* of London on 3 December 1885, Tyser & Co made the company's independence of the 'Shipping Ring' clear. The company said 'we are publicly pledged by our circulars, of which we enclose copies, not to enter the 'Ring', and we offer to accept fair rates, as arranged by a committee of representative shippers with ourselves. We may add that nothing that the 'Ring' can do will move our resolution, and whether our contest with them continues for two months or two years is not now material; we are bound to the venture. We have provided a fighting fund of £20,000, our hearts are hardened, and we neither ask nor expect any quarter, but we intend to load ships to Australia independently of the 'Ring'.'

Tyser & Co also criticised the 'Ring' accepting cargo from continental shippers for shipment through London to Australia at a through rate of 50/- a tonne, whereas British shippers, were charged 60/- a tonne. The attempt by the 'Ring' to secure continental cargoes was at the expense of English manufacturers. In a further letter to *The Times* on 14 December 1885, W.H. Tyser commented that he personally regarded 'shipping rings as the sole hope of idle men and rotten concerns, whom they prop up at the expense of industrious men and sound commercial undertakings'. The 'Ring' offered some freight concessions, but the Australian trade shippers considered them valueless, and while Tyser & Co kept up the pressure on the other lines, shippers were also becoming upset at the continuing variations in the freight rates and were anxious for stability to return to the trade. Tyser & Co's main supporter was a wealthy 29-year old London shipbroker, John. H. Wackerbarth, and although they had some victories over the 'Ring', the Merchant Line survived only a very short time. In 1886 G.D. Tyser retired and he died in London on 13 March 1888. The style of the company was changed to Tyser & Co in 1886.

His sons were determined to break into the Australian trade and continued to wage freight wars with the Shipping Ring. At this time they had given little thought to the New Zealand trade, which was even more tightly controlled by Shaw Savill &

Albion Co and the New Zealand Shipping Co. The partnership of Robert Ewart Shaw and Walter Savill dated from 1858, and in 1882 they had merged with the wealthier Albion Line of Glasgow to form the Shaw Savill & Albion Co. Christchurch businessmen had enthusiastically formed the New Zealand Shipping Co in 1873 solely for the purpose of attacking the Shaw Savill monopoly but within a year the two lines had agreed to rationalise their services and maintain the same freight rates. When the New Zealand Shipping Co ordered five steamers for the trade and won a government mail contract, it elected to share the business with Shaw Savill & Albion, and the two lines had kept the New Zealand trade to themselves ever since, apart from one farmer, John Reid of Elderslie, near Oamaru, who chartered his own ship. The monopoly they enjoyed tended to make them autocratic and arrogant. They decided which ports in New Zealand they would use and applied a surcharge on shipments from so-called 'outports' like Napier and Bluff. In 1884 it was estimated that over 20,000 sheep from the Hawke's Bay area were driven to Wellington for killing and shipment. Shippers were further antagonised in 1886 when the two companies increased freight rates at a time of depressed farming returns.

Napier was a port supporting an affluent area of farming, and William Nelson, trading as Nelson Bros Limited, established the first freezing works in 1883-84 at Tomoana. He had initially built a meat preserving plant at Tomoana in 1881 but quickly saw the potential for a frozen meat trade following the successful voyage of the sailing ship *Dunedin* (1874, 1,320) from Port Chalmers to London in 1882. Frederick and William Nelson had arrived in New Zealand in 1863 in the ship *Devonshire* (1848, 807). They subsequently purchased land for a sheep station at Kereru in the Hawke's Bay. As William Nelson developed the plant for processing sheep for export, he had the foresight to realise the need for a selling organisation in London and another brother, Edward Montague Nelson, set this up. In addition, extensive cold storage facilities were developed and Nelson Bros also owned its own wharf on the Thames. William Nelson was anxious to secure a reliable and economical shipping service from Napier to London, away from the monopoly exercised by the two established lines. He asked Robert Dobson, the Napier accountant handling his work, to go to London to see if other shipping lines might be interested in calling direct at Napier, and who would carry meat and general cargo at lower rates of freight than that charged by the other two lines. Dobson approached two London shipowners – D. Bruce & Co and Tyser & Co. Dobson gave an undertaking that in return for an agreement to provide a monthly service from Napier, Nelson Bros. of the Tomoana freezing works would ship a fixed number of carcasses annually, and supply as much wool and tallow as it could for a period of four years. Tysers agreed to provide the service and at a rate of freight one farthing per pound lower than the established lines. Even though Tysers offered a reduced freight, it was estimated in 1885 that New Zealand Shipping and Shaw Savill & Albion were charging freights, which were

20-25 per cent more expensive for wool than similar rates from Australia to London and 20 per cent more costly for mutton.

On 20 April 1887 Tyser & Co formed the Colonial Union Line Ltd with a nominal capital of £50,000. On commencement 40,000 ordinary shares were paid up to 16/6 and 100 founders' shares were fully paid up, and of these, the Tyser brothers held 70 per cent. The remaining shares were held by fellow London shipbrokers, H. Clarkson & Co, Wright Bros. and Shaw Busby & Co. The directors were G. W. Tyser, W. H. Tyser, H. Benham, T. M. F. Parkyns, R. W. Shaw and W. Wright. In a letter to Robert Dobson in May 1887, W. H. Tyser wrote, 'we know that some heavy fighting is likely to ensue and provided you stand by us, we shall develop and arrange a series of cargo boats and we look forward in the course of the next two seasons, if not before, to be able to offer you freight for your meat in lots of 900 tons at 1d. per lb. for a permanency'.

In London, Tyser & Co set about providing ships for the service. All were dry-cargo vessels chartered from various owners and subsequently fitted out with refrigerated machinery and insulated holds at Tysers' expense. The average refrigerated capacity was sufficient for about 30,000 carcasses, which in those days averaged nearer 60 lbs each, compared to the much smaller lamb carcasses developed in later years as the standard for the New Zealand trade.

When it came to providing the refrigerating machinery, Tysers found that the two existing suppliers of refrigerating plant to Shaw Savill and the Shipping Company – Bell-Coleman and Haslam – had agreed not to supply machinery to competitors of the established lines. A. S. Haslam (later Sir Alfred) of Haslam Foundry & Engineering Co, Derby, in a letter, two years earlier, to a meat industry conference in Christchurch on 3 March 1885, had tried to justify his stance by saying that the indiscriminate supply of refrigerating machinery to a host of other companies would have brought 'disaster to the shipping companies, the sheep growers, and the freezing companies'. He went on to say, 'had we fitted up all the vessels which we had the opportunity of doing it would have paid us a handsome profit. The ship-owners (Shaw Savill & Albion/N.Z. Shipping Company) however, preferred to give us an allowance and thus pay us to restrict the manufacture of our machines.'[1] At this time Haslam had also taken over Bell-Coleman.

Tysers turned to J. & E. Hall, who in the early months of 1887, promptly equipped the steamers *Ashleigh Brook, Bayley* and *Balmoral Castle.* Tysers also chartered the steamer *Selembria* which had been already fitted with refrigeration in 1883 and *Balcarres Brook*, a general cargo carrier. Prior to her New Zealand voyage, *Selembria* had made a voyage to the Falkland Islands to load 30,000 carcasses of mutton for the Falkland Islands Meat Co. The design and development of specialist on-board refrigerating machinery was very much in its infancy and in November 1887, Haslam & Co was suing J. & E. Hall for infringement of patent rights. While the case was proceeding there was concern that if the verdict had gone against Hall, the company would not have been able to proceed with the Tyser contract. Fortunately the court decided that the attempts by Haslam, working in concert with Shaw Savill & Albion Co and New Zealand Shipping Co to secure a monopoly of the frozen meat trade had overstepped the boundaries of free trade and the waiting vessel, *Selembria,* was allowed to sail. Halls continued to provide refrigerating machinery to Tyser & Co, later the C&D Line, then Port Line, right through to the last vessel built for Port Line in 1968!

The first Colonial Union Line steamer to New Zealand, the *Balmoral Castle* (1876, 2,846), left London for Sydney and New Zealand on 24 July 1887. From Sydney she crossed the Tasman to arrive at Auckland on 8 October 1887 to discharge 900 tonnes of London cargo and to start loading her homeward cargo. She also loaded Wellington, Bluff, Lyttelton and Napier before leaving for London via Cape Horn and Rio de Janeiro. She sailed from Napier on 10 November and carried 22,089 carcasses of mutton, 176 quarters of beef, 410 kegs and 4 cases of butter, 1,268 sides of bacon, 1 box hams, 67 cases cheese, 120 cases preserved mullet, 3 casks oysters, 298 cases of kauri gum, 12 bales of basils, 1,262 sacks of cocksfoot seed, 203 sacks wheat, 7 logs and 10 pieces of timber, 173 casks and 13 kegs of tallow, 157 bales of sheepskins, 1,991 bales of greasy and scoured wool, 72 bales rabbit skins and some packages of general cargo and effects. Her frozen cargo out-turned in prime condition. Tysers then brought in the *Balcarres Brook* (1883, 1,874) and she loaded wool and general cargo at Sydney, Auckland, Gisborne and Napier for London. *Ashleigh Brook* (1882, 2,621) took the third sailing.

The fourth vessel, *Selembria* (1886, 2,907), had an unhappy first voyage on the Tyser berth. She sailed from Napier on 1 March 1888 and shortly after she had rounded Cape Horn, a fire developed in her bunkers and she had to put into Montevideo with her engines disabled. Some 12,000 carcasses were damaged and had to be sold quickly for 2.5 pence each. More had to be jettisoned at sea, and on arrival in London the balance of the cargo was condemned, with the exception of 3,000 carcasses. The twin-funneled, three-masted *Bayley* (1886, 2,396) completed the loading of the first five ships introduced to the new service, sailing Napier for London via Wellington and Rio de Janeiro on 27 February 1888. As Napier was a roadstead port it was more economical for the ships to proceed to Wellington and go alongside there to take in the 700/800 tonnes of coal needed for the voyage to Rio de Janeiro. The final vessel of the first group of Colonial Union Line charters was the *Worcester* (1887, 2,908) which loaded general cargo only at Sydney, Auckland, Napier, Wellington, Port Chalmers and Lyttelton, sailing for London on 4 June 1888.

The company had also agreed to charter sailing ships to lift wool and general cargo until it had sufficient steamers on the berth to cover general cargo requirements. The first to arrive at Napier was the ancient iron sailing ship *Herschel* (1857, 814) on

The first sailing ship to load on the Colonial Union Line berth was the iron barque *Peru*. She loaded 3,235 bales of wool at Napier for London in November 1887 and was 115 days on the passage. MONTEREY MARITIME MUSEUM

18 October 1887. Owned by R. M. Sloman of Hamburg, she brought out from Hamburg, 5,262 casks of cement for the Napier Harbour Board on a passage lasting 133 days. Nat Kettle, the Colonial Union Line agent, called the *Herschel* a 'rotten old tub', and it took some persuasion to get approval from Lloyd's Surveyor for her to load, as she needed repairs following the voyage from Hamburg.[2] By the time she had completed discharge there was far more wool awaiting shipment than she could handle and the company was desperate to obtain another ship. The iron barque *Peru* (1876, 710) was already in port and was being advertised to load on the NZSCo berth. However with the overwhelming support for the Colonial Union Line, she may have had to wait months for a cargo, so she was re-chartered to the Colonial Union Line and sailed from Napier for London on 22 November with a cargo of 3,235 bales of wool and 14 bales of skins valued at £39,803. *Herschel* followed on 17 December with 3,030 bales of wool, 128 casks of tallow and 19 bales of skins. The growing regularity of the steamers meant that there were only a few more sailing ship fixtures from Napier with the *Lurline* (1877, 801) sailing on 18 February 1888, and the *Linlithgowshire* (1877, 1,425) on 8 April 1889. With 3,819 bales of wool, 810 pockets of wool, plus some casks of tallow and general cargo, the cargo of the *Linlithgowshire* was the largest to have left Napier.

An upsurge in wool volumes in 1899 saw Tyser and Company charter the iron ship *Brambletye* and she loaded a full cargo of wool at Napier which she delivered to London 129 days later. She was the last sailing ship chartered by Tysers for the New Zealand trade. MONTEREY MARITIME MUSEUM

No further sailing ships were chartered until 1897 when the iron barque *Belle of Arvon* (1876, 964) sailed from Napier for London on 24 December 1897 and she was followed by the *Beechwood* (1875, 815) from Gisborne on 3 January 1898. They arrived at London on 11 April and 7 April respectively. Next season the iron ship *Brambletye* (1876, 1,558) was chartered to load wool and general cargo at Napier. She sailed from that port on 20 January 1899, and arrived at London 30 May 1899, the last sailing ship employed by Tyser and Co in the New Zealand service.

The Napier agent for the line was the partnership of F. W. Williams and N. Kettle (restructured as Williams & Kettle Ltd in 1891). Fred Williams and Nat Kettle had joined in partnership in 1885 as stock and station and commission agents. The other agents at the main New Zealand ports were Heather, Roberton & Co in Auckland, (general merchants/kauri gum exporters), W. M. Bannatyne & Co, Wellington, (importers and general merchants) Kinsey, Barns & Co, Christchurch, (shipping & insurance brokers), Keith Ramsey (shipping agent) in Dunedin and Hugh Carswell (stock and station agent) in Invercargill.

Nat Kettle made it clear to Shaw Savill & Albion that it only had itself to blame for the presence of Tysers. In a letter to Captain John Leslie, the Shaw Savill & Albion representative to New Zealand, he wrote, 'I can assure you that it is no fault of mine or my firms that we are not working with your company... it is a long story this freight question, and I think your company acted very unwisely in the first place when they refused to accept the guaranteed contract which the farmers of Hawke's Bay offered them. Your company made a sad mistake when they insisted on raising the freight on meat by one farthing per pound in 1886 when prices were low and most of the sheep farmers were at their wits end to know how to meet their engagements, and the affairs of the colony were in a most depressed state'. Kettle went on to tell Leslie that there was a feeling in New Zealand that his company's affairs were not as well managed as they should be. 'There seems to be a feeling of distrust, and the want of a head to whom one can refer, and who has the power to act'.[3]

When other meat companies learned of the Colonial Union Line contract with Nelson Bros, some approached Tyser & Company to influence calls at other ports in New Zealand. The Southland Frozen Meat and Produce Export Co, which had opened a works at Bluff in 1884, signed a two year contract for the ships to call at Bluff four times a year right from the first loading of the *Balmoral Castle* in 1887. A similar contract was made with the Canterbury Frozen Meat Company for shipments of meat from that company's Belfast works through the port of Lyttelton. In order to capitalise on the growing numbers of sheep becoming available in the Gisborne area, William Nelson opened a freezing works at Taruheru, Gisborne, in 1889. There was limited cold storage space at the plant, and Nelson Bros sent out the old sailing ship *Prince of Wales* (1850, 536) which had been employed as a freezer hulk in the Thames. She reached Gisborne in November 1889 and was able to freeze down about 200 carcasses a day. The first Colonial Union Line vessel to load at Gisborne was the *Star of England,* which sailed from there on 8 December 1889. She then came on to Napier where she loaded her coal for the voyage home from the coaster *Omapere* (1882, 601 tons) and sailed direct from Napier for London. Later loadings at the Gisborne roadstead invariably called at Napier first to pick up the lumpers (waterside workers) who would load the cargo and then the vessel would return them to Napier. In 1891 the *Prince of Wales* was sent to Picton where the Christchurch Meat Co, in association with William Nelson, opened a freezing works at Blenheim.

In Australia arrangements were also concluded with major Australian wool buyers, Ostermeyer, Dewez and von Rompaey, Masurel Fils, Wenz Co and Hicks, Martin and Drysdale, for special wool contracts similar to the one with Nelson Bros, and with the Central Queensland Meat Export Co at Rockhampton for the carriage of frozen meat.

Of the first vessels *Balmoral Castle* made seven round voyages, *Bayley* eight, *Ashleigh Brook* six, *Selembria* two and *Balcarres Brook* and *Worcester* one each. *Bayley* was also briefly employed as a meat store ship in London for Nelson Bros in 1892. The newly-built Norwegian steamer *Herman Wedel Jarlsberg* (1890, 3,000) was chartered for the Australian trade in October 1890 and the company also chartered

Buckingham (1891, 2,879) in 1891. *Ashleigh Brook* was totally wrecked on Boom Point, Dassen Island, near Cape Town on 24 May 1890 while on passage ballasting from Cardiff to Rockhampton. *Selembria* was later renamed *Wicklow* and was wrecked at Calais on 7 January 1893 while on a voyage from Buenos Aires to Dunkirk. Considering that all these vessels were only general cargo vessels fitted with refrigerating machinery, and were slow speed tramps, the schedules were performed remarkably well. The ships invariably loaded out from London with cargo for Adelaide, Melbourne and Sydney and New Zealand, took coal at Newcastle, then on to Rockhampton to load and across the Tasman to Auckland and Wellington to complete the discharge. They loaded at Napier, Lyttelton, Bluff and Wellington. In August 1890 a contract was signed with the Otaihape Farmers Meat and Produce Co Ltd at Castlecliff and from August 1891 Tyser Line ships made direct calls at the Wanganui roadstead to load frozen meat, wool and general cargo, the first cargo being taken by the chartered steamer *Duke of Sutherland* (1873, 3,116). Arrangements were also made in 1891 with Wm. Milburn & Co in London for its vessels fitted with refrigerated space to lift 300-ton parcels of frozen meat from Rockhampton, lightered to the Keppel Bay anchorage.

The head office in New Zealand for the Tyser Line was in Napier and Robert Dobson, the accountant who had negotiated with the company in London for the service, was appointed secretary. Captain Richard Todd became marine superintendent. Born at Dundee in 1844, he had obtained his master's certificate in London in 1868 and had commanded the barques *Malay* (1862, 328) from 1868 to 1873, and *St. Leonards* (1864, 1,054 from 1873-1883. He served with Shaw Savill for some years and his last command was the sailing ship (formerly an auxiliary steamer) *Northumberland* (1871, 2,170) which was wrecked at Napier in extreme weather conditions on 11 May 1887. When Dobson died in June 1893, Captain Todd was appointed colonial superintendent for Tysers in New Zealand. He travelled around the ports and was instrumental in giving Tysers a high profile in New Zealand. He was active in keeping the wider community informed through newspaper publicity, solely concentrating on Tyser business and seldom commenting or criticising the other shipping lines in the New Zealand trade.

By 1888 the Tyser Line had a firm presence in New Zealand, forcing the New Zealand Shipping Co and Shaw Savill & Albion to work more closely together, and to set up a pooling agreement for the cargoes they carried. Writing to Walter Savill in London, J. M. Ritchie, the senior agent for the line in New Zealand, wrote that, 'the Tyser Line is playing havoc with the whole trade. In spite of unpunctuality and breakdowns, the whole community serves to look upon them as having not only the possibility of carrying meat at a penny a pound, and from the outports too, but also the possibility of steamers loading general cargo without meat'.[4] In a later letter Ritchie commented that 'Dobson is a fine straightforward smart fellow and most agreeable to work with'.[5] The Tyser contract with Nelson Bros was renewed in 1891 and it was clear the New Zealand business was developing a permanency. In early 1892 Ritchie reminded Captain Leslie that 'Tyser is the Frankenstein and though he seems to have a faculty for spontaneous generation and might have appeared on the New Zealand scene in spite of you (Shaw Savill & Albion), yet it is not too much I think to declare that in New Zealand he is of your own (S.S.& A) creation'.[6]

Tysers had J. & E. Hall install refrigerating machinery in the former lighter *Vlissingen* (1872, 221) in 1886 and she was employed in the transport of meat from Britain to the continent. When the contract with Queensland was obtained she was sent out to Rockhampton to act as a meat lighter. She was the only vessel actually owned by the Colonial Union Co Ltd. However, her refrigerating machinery could not cope with the heat of the Queensland summer and had to be improved. *Vlissingen* was also too small and Tyser and Co arranged with the Melbourne-based company, McIlwraith, McEacharn Limited, to fit up its steamer *Leichardt* (1865, 690) with refrigerated capacity for 350 tonnes of frozen meat. *Leichardt* superseded *Vlissingen* in 1891 and the latter vessel was sold to Andrew McIlwraith. He immediately on-sold her to a subsidiary, Walter Reid & Co Ltd of Brisbane in 1895, who continued to employ her as a lighter transporting general cargo to and from ships in Keppel Bay. *Vlissingen* finally foundered in the Fitzroy River on 13 June 1898 after being in collision with the *Leichardt* and breaking her back. In order to meet their growing commitment to Nelson Bros Tysers chartered the steamer *Raven* (1883, 1,648) from the General Steam Navigation Co of London following the departure of *Vlissingen* and in 1887 equipped her with J. & E. Hall refrigerating machinery so that she could carry 3,000 carcasses of meat from London to Antwerp. Tyser & Co had maintained an office in Antwerp for some years and subsequently built a cold store there.

In 1873, 43-year old John Henry Flint, had commenced dispatching sailing ships to Australia under the name of The Colonial Line of Australian Packets. Three London loading brokers were also involved – Gellatley, Hankey, Sewell & Co, McDiarmid, Greenshields & Co and Alexander Howden & Co – and within a year the line was chartering steamers for the service. Regular dispatches continued until 1886. The sailings lapsed when Flint became seriously ill and Tyser & Co took over management of the Colonial Line. Flint died on 14 May 1888 and Tysers secured four of the 16 shares which the Colonial Line had held in the Australian conference called 'Davis'. This modest entitlement allowed Tysers a legitimate 'right' to load steamers for Australia but insufficient to provide a regular service of reasonable frequency. Tysers thereafter continued to nibble away at the outward cargoes from London to Australia and New Zealand and remained a continuing annoyance to the Associated Brokers Group who were the members of the Australian conference group of lines. The NZSCo offered Tyser & Co the brokerage of its London business to New Zealand in the hope that this would divert it from working against the interests of the conference. Tysers took up the contract in September 1888.

At this time the NZSCo was heavily in debt and eventually E. S. Dawes of shipbrokers Gray, Dawes & Co purchased the debts of Sir William Pearce, the shipbuilder who had equipped the company with five new steamers. This saved the company but transferred control from Christchurch to London. There were other worries for the Lines when McIver Bros of Liverpool announced plans in July 1891 to build ships for the New Zealand meat trade. A prospectus was issued for the Imperial Trading Co Ltd with an intended capital of £1 million. Despite their differences, this was war, and all the lines in the New Zealand trade, including Tyser, came together to chase away the newcomer (which in any case failed to secure the capital it needed).

The Colonial Union Line had increased its paid-up capital in November 1888 and one of the new major shareholders was the British India Associated Steamers Ltd, in which E. S. Dawes was a director. Holding 20 per cent of the capital, the new shareholder was going to be far more influential than Tysers would like and the brothers moved to wind up the Colonial Union Line and register a new company called Tyser Line Limited on 7 September 1889. The capital was set at £100,000 in 99,900 ordinary shares of £1 and 100 founders' shares. The Tyser brothers controlled 88 per cent of the founders' shares and 50 per cent of the paid up capital with the remaining support from the three broking firms involved with the Colonial Union Line. The shareholders in that company were offered 5 per cent debentures in exchange for their Colonial Union shares. Tyser and Co was appointed manager of the Tyser Line Ltd.

A meeting of shareholders approved the winding up by 17 votes to two but E. S. Dawes, on behalf of British India Associated Steamers, took out an injunction against the decision, presumably to delay and hamper the Tyser New Zealand service, as any delays would stretch the company's financial resources. An additional smoke screen was created by accusing the directors of misrepresentation, concealment, and suppression of facts and stated that actions of a majority of the shareholders would operate as a fraud on the minority. Dawes pursued his case right to the High Court, but again lost and in August 1890, Tysers triumphantly telegraphed Dobson in Napier, 'most exhaustive smashing judgement given in our favour – Petition is refused with costs'.[7]

But Dawes, by now in full control of the New Zealand Shipping Co, kept the pressure on Tyser and Co, which was continuing to undermine the existing companies and was accepting cargo for its steamers at the lower sailing ship rates. It had also extended its frozen meat liftings by buying shares in, and arranging a contract with, the Otaihape Farmers Meat and Produce Co Ltd at Castlecliff, Wanganui. This upset the NZSCo which had hoped to obtain this business. In accepting the brokerage of the Shipping Company vessels, Tysers had undertaken to restrict its outward loadings from London and it became clear the company had paid little attention to this aspect. On 15 October 1890, the NZSCo dismissed Tysers as its London brokers and placed the business with J. B. Westray and Co, a partnership between E. S. Dawes, his son, W. C. Dawes, and J. B. Westray. Then it initiated proceedings against Tysers for mismanaging its business. In reply Tysers moved to sue the Shipping Company and claim damages for the loss of the agency. Tysers had moved into New Zealand Shipping Company premises and had kept possession of the books and other files, which the Shipping Company not unnaturally wanted back. Three years of litigation ensued but Tysers never regained the brokerage. The company received strong support when it charged sailing ship freights on its steamers. Tysers always undercut the other lines and the NZSCo and Shaw Savill & Albion continuously had to reduce rates to maintain their liftings. By April 1893 it was reported that under pressure from the shippers, the London brokers in the Australian trade had opened talks with Tysers in an effort to restore stability to the trade.

The Tyser Line continued to cement its relations with the various shipping conferences and in June 1893 the Australian conference 'Davis' approved, for a period of five years, 12 outward sailings a year from London to Australia. A subsequent agreement in July 1893 for the New Zealand trade approved loadings for Auckland and Wellington, but the tonnage to New Zealand was restricted to 1,200 tonnes a month and no cargo at all to Lyttelton and Dunedin. The purpose of the latter restriction was to protect sufficient volumes for Shaw Savill & Albion and NZSCo to ensure the viability of direct calls at the two South Island ports. In December 1893 more formal arrangements were finalised with the other lines in the Australian trade.

In London W. H. Tyser had become known as 'The Terror of the Rings' and satirical verses about his activities appeared in shipping journals. In the book *Westrays*, a history of J. B. Westray & Co, author Alan Fagg wrote that 'there is little doubt that Tyser, while enjoying membership of groups comprising respectively the Australian and New Zealand shipping companies, was dispatching ships in competition, hence the stern measures taken against him. While battling with his contemporaries in one trade, he was hand in glove with them in another'. Prior to gaining the outward sailings in 1893, Tyser and Co had continued to expand its homeward cargoes from New Zealand and Australia and had also independently loaded ships from London, forcing the other lines to match its freights. The various shippers were therefore more than happy that Tysers had been admitted into the 'Davis' pooling agreement as it meant that a degree of stability would return to the trade.

On 6 March 1889 the Colonial Union Company chartered two new steamers from the James P. Corry 'Star Line' of Belfast. In 1880 Corrys had opened an office in Fenchurch Avenue, London and enjoyed friendly associations with Tysers. The first steamer, *Star of Victoria,* had been completed in 1887 and the second, *Star of England,* came into service in 1889. The *Star of Victoria* had initially been chartered out for voyages to India, but both had refrigerating machinery added in 1889 when they entered Tyser service. The *Star of England* sailed from London to Melbourne on

The first steamer built for James P. Corry was the *Star of Victoria* in 1887. Two years later she was fitted out for refrigerated cargo and spent the next 22 years on Tyser Line services. WM. LIVERMORE

23 August 1889 and the *Star of Victoria* followed on 19 October. After six voyages, the Corry Line agreed to purchase the refrigeration equipment and came to an agreement with Tysers to operate its ships on commission – an arrangement that proved very satisfactory over subsequent years as Tysers just kept absorbing new *Star* ships into their services. The association with the Corry 'Star' Line was such that every steamer the company built was immediately placed on a Tyser berth. The Star Line steamers were smartly painted with black hulls and white upper works, with the same buff funnel and black top as the Tyser Line vessels. The house flag was a red heart on a white background with two red broad horizontal stripes top and bottom.

The shipowning activities of the Corry family had begun in the middle of the nineteenth century following the establishment of a family timber business in Belfast. Initially a partnership between John Corry and William Montgomery from 1814, the business became known as James P. Corry & Son from 1851 and by this time the company was also well established as building contractors. As the firm expanded, Robert Corry, a son of the founder, had decided to charter ships to bring in timber from Canada, and eventually moved to ownership. Between 1845 and 1859 the company was part-owner or charterer of a number of sailing ships. From 1859 Corry & Son built its own fleet of ships, the first being the *Jane Porter* (1860, 953), completed in 1860 at the Belfast shipyard of Harland & Wolff. The association with this yard continued with a further 11 ships being built, all named with the prefix of *Star of......* Most ran from London to Calcutta with coal, and returned home with jute. It was only the occasional Corry sailer that ventured into the Australian trade. One of these, *Star of Italy* (1877, 1,644), went out from London to Melbourne in 78 days with a subsequent homeward passage of 79 days, proving her to be something of a flyer. From 1879, Workman Clark and Co opened a shipyard in Belfast and as members of the Corry family married into the Workman family, Workman Clark became the shipbuilders for Corry's, moving from sailing ships to steamers in 1887.

In 1890 Tyser & Co became involved in the carriage of frozen meat from the Falkland Islands to London. Three earlier shipments from 1888 had been handled by the Falkland Islands Co, but heavy losses were made. From 1890 London-based Spearing & Waldron Ltd decided to carry on the export of stock. The Waldron family had long been associated with breeding sheep on the island, and the principal of the firm, Walter G. Waldron, asked Tysers to provide a ship equipped with refrigerating machinery. Tyser and Company chartered the iron sailing ship *Hengist* (1860, 1,161) and she became the sixth vessel that J. & E. Hall fitted out for the company. Her six round voyages between 1890 and 1894, carried a total of about 100,000 carcasses. *Hengist* loaded at the ports of San Carlos, on the eastern side of the islands and Port Howard on the west. There were no shore facilities and a platform was placed over two lifeboats from the ship. The mutton carcasses were brought out by lighter, placed on the platform and then transferred to the holds of the *Hengist* and frozen down on board. The quality of the Falkland Island sheep was nowhere near that of New Zealand and the sale of the mutton only netted between five and seven shillings per carcase for the farmer. It was also difficult obtaining sufficient sheep to make up a viable shipload. Spearing and Waldron was the main supporter of the service with other individual farmers taking the risk to ship on their own account. By February 1893 Tyser & Company was making a substantial loss on the Falkland Islands service and the contract was cancelled in July. In addition to *Hengist*, the *Selembria, Star of Victoria* and *Bayley* also loaded meat in the Falklands.

Hengist was owned by The Ship Hengist Co Ltd of Liverpool and when this company failed in 1893, London shipbroker Owen Spearing acquired her to protect the trade, placing her in a new company called The Straits of Magellan Frozen Meat Co Ltd. However, she stranded at West Dungeness, Straits of Magellan 10 May 1895 and subsequently became a total wreck. Following the loss of their vessel, Spearing and Waldron abandoned the Falklands trade and developed facilities at Punta Delgado for the export of Patagonian mutton which was carried by the regular liners in the South American trade.

Tysers took long-term charters of two vessels from the firm of William Ross & Co of London in 1890 and had J. & E. Hall fit refrigerating machinery. These were the *Celtic King* (1890, 3,738) and *Maori King* (1890, 3,807), the latter being described

The *Celtic*, formerly the *Celtic King*, which was on charter to the Tyser Line in the early 1890s, is shown in Sydney harbour some years later in her role as a refrigerated supply ship for the United States Navy. WM. LIVERMORE

as the largest refrigerated ship in the world. Ross had died on 17 October 1889 and as both ships were mortgaged, the mortgagor decided to sell them in 1893 to Allport & Hughes. Tysers claimed that they had the use of the ships for the term of their charter, but in a test case, involving only the circumstances of the *Celtic King* in January 1894, it was ruled that the registration certificate was part of the sale documents.[8] Tysers were then deprived of the use of the vessels and the judge advised them to proceed against the estate of William Ross if they wished to recover damages. This they did, and obtained £9,923 from the Ross estate in 1895. The two vessels subsequently became the first two steamers in the fleet of the Federal Steam Navigation Company when Allan Hughes formed it in 1895. Both the Federal Line and Allan Hughes were to figure largely in the business affairs of the Tyser Line and the Commonwealth & Dominion Line in later years.

Tysers ordered a steamer from Wm Doxford & Sons, Sunderland in 1890 and she entered service in 1891. Appropriately named *Hawkes Bay,* she had distinctive lines, with joggled plating, and a clipper bow, complete with figurehead. She also carried yards and a full set of sails to supplement her speed when the wind conditions were favourable. The first and second holds were fully insulated with a capacity for about 85,000 carcasses of frozen mutton. Her triple expansion steam engine consumed 30/32 tonnes of coal per day at sea and although her appearance suggested speed, the 4,583 ton vessel had a service speed of only 10 knots. She made her maiden voyage to Australia and did not visit New Zealand until the second half of 1891. A. W. M. Clarke, who served in the Tyser Line office in London, recalls the saloon in *Hawkes Bay* had a long table, at the end of which the master of the ship presided. At meal times he carved the portions of meat which were passed on to the officers who sat at

The smart lines of the first Tyser Line steamer *Hawkes Bay* are shown in this photograph taken in Adelaide.

the table in order of seniority. The heating in the saloon consisted of an iron stove, with a chimney penetrating the decks above. Even so, he said, the saloon was very smoky at times.[9] *Hawkes Bay* could never be described as a lucky ship, as over her lifetime she had a whole series of incidents – machinery breakdowns, hitting dock walls, and the like.

In 1891 Tysers chartered the two-year old steamer *Indra* as a supplementary vessel for the carriage of wool and general cargo from Australia. Built by Thomas Royden & Sons, at their Liverpool shipyard, the vessel was managed by Macvicar, Marshall & Co Ltd and registered to the ownership of the Indra Steamship Co Ltd, a company owned by the Royden family. A few months later Tysers took a second Royden steamer on charter. This was the *Indramayo,* built in 1889 and she was fitted with refrigerating equipment and insulated holds in 1891. The Tyser association with the Royden family was to be an enduring one. The Royden family had a distinguished background in shipping. The founder, Thomas Royden was born in 1792 and through family connections had strong links with the shipbuilding industry in Liverpool. He commenced his own shipyard in 1818 in partnership with James Ward but six years later the arrangement was terminated and Royden remained on his own until his son, Thomas Bland Royden, came into partnership with him in 1859. Seven years later, a second son, Joseph, joined the business and it subsequently became known as T. B. Royden & Sons. By the 1860s iron was replacing wood in the shipyards and Thomas Royden told his sons, if the firm moved to iron he would leave. An order for two iron ships was accepted in 1863 and true to his word, the father retired from the business.

The shipyard lay close to the Brunswick Dock in Liverpool and between 1823 and 1893, until it was sold to the Mersey Docks and Harbour Board, it built a total of 262 ships, ranging in size from 84 tons to 4,500 tons. Some were built 'on spec' when no orders were available in order to keep the labour employed, as was the practice in that era. Members of the family also became shipowners and between 1854 and 1877

The *Indramayo*, built 1889 and equipped with refrigeration in 1891, came into the Tyser Line service in that year and remained under Tyser control until sold to Houlder Bros in 1901. WM. LIVERMORE

they launched 14 sailing ships in which they retained the principal interest. Originally building in oak, they moved with the times into iron, then steel and from sail to steam. Their clients included such well-known shipowners as T. H. Ismay, C. T. Bowring, R. Singlehurst, J. Bibby, Pacific Steam Navigation Co, Frederick Leyland, African Steam Ship Co, Rankin, Gilmour and Co and Macvicar Marshall and Co. The Royden ships had red funnels with black tops and black hulls and green boot-topping. Upperworks and masts were white and derricks painted light brown. The house flag was swallow-tailed with a pattern of two equal horizontal halves of blue and red with a white diamond in the centre.

The *Star of England, Star of Victoria, Celtic King, Maori King, Hawkes Bay,* and *Indramayo* maintained the refrigerated service in the early 1890s after the original charter ships had been replaced. When the two *King* steamers were withdrawn further new Royden and Corry vessels were ready to replace them. Tysers launched the second steamer built for the company on 11 March 1899. This was the bluff-bowed *Tomoana* and she was the first of a series of ships progressively built for the Tyser line. Apart from the use of the name *Hawkes Bay* for two Tyser vessels all the others were given New Zealand Maori names. *Tomoana* was initially registered to the ownership of the Tomoana Steam Ship Company – a company jointly owned by Tyser & Co and the Tyser Line Ltd. Tyser & Co wanted to order a further steamer but the Corry and Royden interests dissented on the grounds that this would only increase Tyser Line debt and their own ships could be employed. Tyser & Co went ahead and ordered a

It was eight years before the Tyser interests built their second steamer. This was the *Tomoana*, named after the site of Wm. Nelson's freezing works in Hawke's Bay. The photograph taken in Sydney in 1905 shows her still carrying yards so that she could supplement her steam power with sail, when wind conditions were favourable. WM. LIVERMORE

The third Tyser steamer was the *Mimiro*. She was built by Workman, Clark & Company in Belfast; all following ships came from this yard and had the distinctive straight stem and elliptical stern. The Maori name denotes a swirling current of water. WM. LIVERMORE

steamer on its own account, but the ownership of the *Mimiro,* was registered to the Mimiro Steam Ship Co with Tyser & Co and the Tyser Line each holding 50 per cent of the shares. In 1902 the two single ship companies were amalgamated into Tyser Line and there were no objections from Corry and Royden directors when a fourth ship, *Niwaru*, was launched for Tyser Line on 24 December 1901, with a fifth, *Marere*, delivered on 20 December 1902. To help finance *Niwaru* Sir William Corry advanced £20,000 which he secured by taking a new mortgage on *Hawkes Bay.* The increase in shipowning saw the company increase the capital of the line from £100,000 to £250,000 in December 1902.

The accounts for the Tyser Line in 1892 showed a debit balance of £58,000 and a £20,000 loss on completed voyages. The 1893 results showed little difference with voyage losses of £21,000 and an overall balance of £78,000 in debt. These were difficult years for the line and the company was unable to reduce the level of debt. No depreciation had been written off the value of *Hawkes Bay* for five years. Arrangements were made in September 1892 for Nelson Bros, James P. Corry & Co and T. B, Royden to take out debentures in order to dilute the debt load and strengthen the company. Nelson Bros took up £12,000 of five-year debentures with Corry and Royden taking £5,000 each over three years. Rival company, Shaw Savill & Albion also took up £3,000 of Tyser Line debentures. Following these moves, Sir Montague Nelson, Sir William Corry and Sir Thomas Royden joined the Tyser Line board of directors and their presence and support considerably enhanced the standing of the company. Sir Montague Nelson was also on the Shaw Savill & Albion board but he resigned in 1893. He remained a director of the Tyser Line, and later the Commonwealth and Dominion Line until his death in 1919.

The line continued to expand with the *Star of New Zealand* launched by Lady Corry on 24 January 1895, the *Indralema* of Roydens entering service in 1894, and *Indraghiri* early in 1896. The Sydney office of Tyser Line was also active as agents for ships loading wool. However it was not until 1899 that all the old debt was cleared and from October 1900 a maiden dividend of 6 per cent was paid. This rate was maintained until 1912 when a 2 per cent bonus was added and at the final Annual General Meeting of the Tyser Line in 1914 a 10 per cent dividend was paid. From April 1900 an agreement was made between Tyser, Corry and Royden that all freights on all vessels operating on the Tyser Line berths would be pooled.

New Zealand woolgrowers had grown increasingly unhappy at the rates of freight being charged for wool, and in 1897 they formed a Rates of Freight Reduction Committee in an endeavour to become a collective force to push for reduced charges. Although Shaw Savill & Albion, and the NZSCo made a token gesture and dropped the wool freight a farthing a pound, sheep farmers felt that they could do better and argued that the percentage of freight in their gross returns was 6.2 per cent for shipments from New Zealand and only 3.8 per cent from Australia. Initially employing

The *Star of New Zealand* was chartered by the Tyser Line on permanent running from when she was built in 1895. All the Corry steamers were built by Workman, Clark and Company of Belfast, the home city of the Corry family timber business. The photograph, taken at Adelaide, shows the sails furled on the yards.

a Dunedin agent, J. H. Stanley & Co, to charter ships, the Committee soon became disillusioned with this company's failure to provide ships to lift the seasonal volumes of wool being sent to ports for shipment. Eventually the secretary of the Rates of Freight Reduction Committee, George H. Scales, was asked to take charge of the shipping. Although the two British lines attempted to negotiate an agreement with Scales, their arrogance encouraged him to go it alone and he continued to charter sailing ships for several years, and then commenced chartering steamers from the 1908/09 season. Tyser & Company was never mentioned in the cut and thrust between Scales and the British Lines, its wool liftings being minor compared to the established lines. Scales formed a limited liability company in 1912, Geo. H. Scales Ltd. Only sheep farmers could become shareholders and despite difficulties from time to time finding suitable vessels, the company continued to charter a few steamers each season until the British government requisitioned the New Zealand wool clip during World War I.

During the summer of 1898/9 New Zealand farmers had a huge grain harvest and in order to allow them to export the surplus to London, the New Zealand government invited tenders from Shaw Savill & Albion, the New Zealand Shipping Co, Turnbull, Martin and Co and Tyser Line for a low rate of freight for shipping surplus grain in unused cargo spaces during the off-season from April to October. The first three companies tendered collectively at £1.12.6 per ton for wheat and £1.17.6 per ton for oats but Tysers offered £1.10.0 and £1.12.6 respectively and were awarded the business. Much of the surplus grain came from Canterbury and the *Lyttelton Times* criticised the government for being involved in a 'conspiracy with a foreign company to injure local undertakings of a similar kind' obviously referring to the NZSCo, which had been established in Christchurch in 1873.

In August 1898, Tysers announced, that in order to assist the trade, they proposed to commence a cargo service from New York to the ports of Melbourne, Sydney, Auckland, Wellington, Lyttelton and Dunedin. The first sailing was planned for 24 September and Funch Edye & Co was appointed agent in New York. For many years four United States merchant firms – R. W. Cameron & Co, Henry W. Peabody & Co, Arkell & Douglas and Mailer & Quereau – had been chartering sailing ships from New York to Australasia and they had also announced in August that it was their intention to charter steamers in future. The enthusiasm to provide a better service had been prompted by the actions of three British lines who in 1897 had decided to investigate developing a regular steamer service from New York to Australasia. Edward Lloyd of Bucknall Bros, Allan Hughes of the Federal Steam Navigation Co, and Frank Houlder of Houlder Bros had all gone to New York at much the same time for the same purpose. As a result the three decided to form a separate company and share the business. The American and Australian Line was established and the first steamer, the chartered *Ribston* (1894, 3,372) sailed from New York for Australia on 19 May 1898. The first New Zealand-bound charter for the A&A Line was the *Alnwick,* (1894, 3,019) which left New York on 18 September 1898. The NZSCo was appointed agent for the line in New Zealand.

The four U.S. merchant firms decided to pool their resources in a new company called the United States and Australasian Steamship Co and also dispatched their first steamer, *Queen Christina* (1896, 3,596) on 20 May. Adding a Tyser Line sailing in a service that hitherto had supplied a sailing a month was going to see some significant freight cutting. Tyser and Company chartered *Queen Margaret* (1890, 2,678) and she

The British tramp steamer *Queen Margaret* inaugurated the Tyser Line service from New York to Australia in 1898 and the photograph shows the vessel in Sydney harbour in the course of that voyage. WM. LIVERMORE

A new *Indralema* entered service in 1901 and was one of three Royden steamers which transferred to the Commonwealth & Dominion Line in 1914. Renamed *Port Alma*, she was sold out of the fleet in 1923.
WM. LIVERMORE

left New York on 25 September 1898.[10] Tysers influenced cargo through destination marketing by advertising their forward sailings in Australian and New Zealand newspapers, recommending that importers specify their service to their North American customers. The sailing ship freight of around 30 shillings a tonne, dropped to 10 shillings a tonne deadweight or 12 shillings and 6 pence per 40 cubic feet [c.a. one cubic metre] for measurement cargoes. On the second Tyser vessel, the *Tolosa* (1896, 3,269), a full lifting was obtained at rates ranging from 7/6 to 10/- a tonne, which the newspapers claimed would result in an 'enormous' loss for the voyage.[11] Tysers had been playing this game out of London for years and knew that sooner or later the parties would come to terms with each other and it was noticeable that the proposed monthly sailings by the three groups stretched out to longer gaps. The United States & Australasian Steamship Co had won contracts for the delivery of railway equipment to New Zealand and they programmed some of their steamers direct to New Zealand. A New York report of 18 August had commented – "This entire effort of English shipowners in their anxiety to be the first in the field to force the entire colonial trade into steam, is sure to be a failure", the article being based on the reality that steamer freights had to be 50 to 100 per cent higher than sailing ship rates for a viable charter.

After the first few sailings with chartered tonnage, Tyser & Co was able to

The *Star of Australia* was the first of three slightly larger Corry steamers. Shown here in Wellington Harbour, she ran in the New Zealand and Australia trade for 25 years, the last eight as the *Port Stephens*. The Tyser Line house flag can be clearly seen on the foremast and the Corry Line on the main. J. DICKIE, ALEXANDER TURNBULL LIBRARY

introduce its own ships and in 1902 had 12 vessels of the group in service on its routes, with *Hawkes Bay*, and *Star of England*, temporarily in the River Plate trade. With the outward sailings from London to Australia and New Zealand now operating within the Davis Conference, Tysers sometimes required to charter a vessel to fill the company's berth commitment. On several occasions between 1898 and 1903 the company chartered vessels from Shaw Savill & Albion and the NZSCo for the outward passage. Ships coming off-hire from the southbound New York/Australasian service were available for northbound loadings of all three lines. Many of the ships commenced their service for Tysers on the New York berth. They included *Tomoana, Indralema* (1894), *Mimiro, Indradevi, Indraghiri, Indralema* (1901), *Star of New Zealand, Star of Ireland,* and *Star of Australia.* Even if the vessels showed a loss on the New York–Australasian leg they had to be positioned to New Zealand or Australia for the homeward commitments, so the New York service enabled the additional ships required for the homeward services to sail out with cargo, rather than in ballast. A New York report in 1899 had stated that the fleets of Tyser, Royden and Corry had united and would sail interchangeably.[12] However, it was clear that the Tyser brothers were very much in control as the services were only described as Tyser Line, with Royden and Corry supplying their ships on a commission basis. Although the Corry and Royden Line vessels submerged their owner's identities on the Tyser Line berths, the ships invariably flew the Tyser Line house flag at the fore, and their own company's flag on the mainmast.

The American & Australian Line also moved to replace chartered ships with vessels owned by one of the three lines so that it would aid the placement of their vessels then loading back to London through Australian ports. In February 1901 the *Star of Australia* arrived in Melbourne with the largest cargo of manufactured goods ever to leave New York.

The four British Lines were also critical of the service operated by the New York merchants, as being suppliers and exporters of the cargoes carried by their chartered vessels they had the advantage of adding to the costs of the product and charging a lower freight rate. Raising their product prices did not go down well in Australia and a number of importers turned to Tysers and the A&A Line for their shipments. Tysers countered the merchant's practice by offering a Loyalty Rebate to regular customers and this was an important factor in retaining a supportive clientele. It was not always possible to find suitable steamers to charter and sailing ships continued to be employed. Between 1898 and 1899 Tysers dispatched 11 steamers from New York, in 1900 it was nine steamers and eight sailing ships, in 1901 seven steamers and seven sailing ships and thereafter sailings became more rationalised with the other groups. Tysers averaged only six sailings a year between 1902 and 1906. Freights had started to edge upward but even in 1905 they were generally 15/- to 20/- a tonne. Sailing ships continued to be used as they were so cheap to charter. If cargo was scarce at times, steamers tended to take on extra coal bunkers to avoid having to make coaling calls en route. In 1906 the three groups in the New York Australasian service came to an agreement on a pooling arrangement and thereafter freight rates started to move upwards.

The Tyser Line New York agent, Funch Edye & Co, was a prominent shipbroker established as early as 1847 as Funch & Meinke. The partnership became Funch, Edye and Co in 1869 and in 1872 the company had the agency for the Belgian White Cross Line which employed vessels transporting migrants from Antwerp to New York. The senior partner of the firm was Danish-born Christian F. Funch. He initially had another Danish partner Andreas F. Meinke but subsequently Henry W. O. Edye of Scottish extraction was admitted to partnership. Both partners had ships named after them, albeit briefly, as the 1,501 ton steamer *C F Funch* lasted a little over three years before she was wrecked in the Netherlands in 1870. *Henry Edye,* a 2,417 ton steamer was completed in 1879 and disappeared without trace in the Atlantic in 1881. In 1888 a German accountant, Paul Gottheil became a partner and remained so until 1915. His presence was influential in Funch Edye gaining the agency for two German shipping lines in 1907. The company was very good at soliciting cargo for the Tyser service and shortly after it was established, was appointed agent for a new service by Royden's Indra Line running between New York and the Far East.

Another identical Tyser Line ship of the Workman, Clark series, the *Whakarua* is shown on trials off Belfast in 1907. One of the Maori meanings for the name is the north-east sea breeze. PORT LINE ARCHIVES, UNIVERSITY OF LIVERPOOL

With the Corry and Royden Line ships now on a commission basis with Tysers, instead of separate charters, Tysers commenced building a fleet of new vessels. The ships were all built by Workman, Clark at Belfast and averaged around 6,400 tons. The first of the series, *Mimiro* completed in 1900, was followed by *Niwaru* and *Marere* completed in 1902. Sisters *Whakarua* and *Nerehana* were delivered in 1907 and the slightly larger *Muritai* in 1910.

The passage distance from New York to Melbourne via the Cape of Good Hope was about 400 miles longer than that from London to Melbourne and the long ocean voyage was, in the early years of the service, interspersed with coaling calls. However, as new ships were built, they had the ability to carry sufficient coal to reach Melbourne direct from New York. The average passage time from New York to Melbourne in 1907 was a little over 55 days. As with the Cape Horn route, masters on the haul from the Cape of Good Hope to Melbourne tended to go as far as south as they felt justified to make the shortest passage, when weighed against the likely weather conditions. There were occasionally other obstacles, such as icebergs, and in 1904 *Indradevi* struck a huge whale on the passage south.

In 1900 the New Zealand government called tenders for a six-weekly service from New Zealand to South Africa for a period of six years. Shaw Savill & Albion, NZSCo and Tyser Line responded with a service that would allow the ships to continue on to London. Sailings were commenced in 1901 with *Indramayo* leaving New Zealand 13

June for Fremantle, Durban, Algoa Bay, Cape Town and London. There was little cargo offering for South Africa and by the time the second Tyser Line vessel, *Indradevi,* was due to load in October she was withdrawn, due to lack of support. The New Zealand government called for further tenders in January 1902 for a three year contract providing a monthly sailing with a subsidy of £30,000 per annum. H. C. Sleigh of Melbourne won the tender but failed to produce any ships and the government issued new tender documents. This time the New Zealand & African Steam Shipping Company was awarded the contract. This company was registered in London on 11 October 1902. There were five shareholders – K. S. Anderson of Orient-Pacific Lines, Chas. Bethell of Bethell, Gwyn & Co, F. Houlder of Houlder Bros, Allan Hughes of Federal Steam Navigation Co and Wm. Milburn of Wm. Milburn and Co. The company was dominated by Federal and Houlder tonnage and the first sailing from New Zealand was the *Devon* on 31 December 1902. In the first year of the new service, in order to secure as much cargo as possible, the ships had to load at 67 ports, compared to the 48 port calls specified in the contract. By 1904 the limited quantities of cargo available for South Africa saw the ships extending to west coast United Kingdom ports. The line thus became linked to the Federal-Houlder-Shire main line service.

[1] *Otago Daily Times,* 21 Oct 1885.
[2] Len Anderson, *Throughout the East Coast Bays,* Pictorial Publications, Hastings, 1974, p. 34.
[3] *ibid,* p. 35.
[4] J.M. Ritchie to Shaw Savill & Albion, 29 Mar 1888, J.M. Ritchie papers, Hocken Collections.
[5] Ibid, to John Leslie 19 Oct 1888.
[6] ibid, 9 Jan 1892.
[7] *Otago Daily Times,* 16 Aug 1890.
[8] *ibid,* 12 Mar 1894.
[9] *GWCZ Calling,* No 8, Feb 1960.
[10] *Otago Daily Times,* 24 Sep 1898
[11] *ibid,* 13 Dec 1898.
[12] *Ibid,* 1 Jul 1899.

CHAPTER 2

From outsider to full conference member

By 1900 Shaw Savill & Albion and the New Zealand Shipping Company, commonly called 'the Liners', had reluctantly accepted the presence of Tyser & Company in the New Zealand trade. Even so, they remained wary of the 'outsider'. Writing to the Shaw Savill head office in London, J. M. Ritchie, its senior agent in New Zealand, commented that Isaac Gibbs of the NZSCo agreed with him on 'the danger which threatens us from Tyser, and does not see any more than I do clearly how it will be possible for us to curtail successfully their operations by anything like an attack on Nelsons as their chief supporter'.[1] The Liners also carried a share of Nelson Bros. frozen meat and were reluctant to upset this important shipper by getting in a fight for cargo with Tyser. They were surprised a month later when A. H. Turnbull of Christchurch, who purchased much of the frozen meat from the Westfield works in Auckland, indicated that he preferred Tyser over the NZSCo. Investigations by the Liners showed that Tyser vessels had made 17 calls at Auckland in the nine months to 30 June 1900, compared to ten by NZSCo and seven by Shaw Savill steamers. On some voyages Tyser was loading frozen meat after discharge and then returning later in the voyage to top off with more meat. When Turnbull awarded his Auckland business to Tyser and to Shaw Savill, Isaac Gibbs was extremely angry that the latter did not refuse the contract and insist on his company also being involved. Ritchie advised that shippers were supporting Tyser in protest against the monopoly of the Liners.[2] Despite the attitude of the Liners against Tyser, Ritchie commented that "we still find Captain Todd (Tyser's Colonial Superintendent) a most excellent man to have in his position and there was no evidence whatsoever of any points of possible friction in connection with the working of the business.[3]

The Liners were not above 'buying' their cargoes through purchasing frozen meat directly from the works and selling it in London, and they also gave financial support to new freezing works to become established, such as providing £100,000 debentures to the Christchurch Meat Co, £24,000 to the N.Z. Refrigerating Co and £10,000 to the Gisborne Freezing Co. In 1907 the NZSCo provided £30,000 towards the establishment of the Tokomaru Freezing Co. In 1893 it and Turnbull Martin and Company (Shire Line) took 4,000 shares in the Southland Frozen Meat Co, and the NZSCo did not sell its shares until 1934. The shipping companies were also asked to guarantee Southland Frozen Meat's overdraft of £10,000 but the London head offices would not agree to that. Shaw Savill & Albion also took shares in the Wairau Freezing Co.

Up to the turn of the century, virtually all the trade with Australia and New Zealand was handled through London. The growth of manufacturing on the West Coast of the UK saw merchants and others continually seeking direct loadings at Glasgow and Liverpool. Apart from the 1891 grand plans of McIver Bros, mentioned in the previous chapter, Liverpool brokers James Dowie & Co and Gracie Beazley & Co announced they wanted to build steamers for a direct West Coast service to Australia and New Zealand. Turnbull Martin & Co also announced a new monthly service from UK ports in March 1893. In 1894 a Manchester firm pressed for direct sailings. From 1891 Tysers had already offered New Zealand and Australian exporters through rates to Liverpool and Manchester in their London sailings but the merchants wanted direct calls. It was clear that the NZSCo/Shaw Savill partnership would have to extend beyond London if it was to retain its monopoly over the bulk of the New Zealand trade. At the end of 1903, therefore, Shaw Savill's *Kumara* was programmed to load on the Clyde and Liverpool for New Zealand as a counter to the Federal Steam Navigation Co. Federal had been making considerable purchases of meat in New Zealand in 1902 and 1903, and was starting to send its own ships to lift the cargo. In January 1904, Tysers announced that it would provide sailings from Glasgow and Liverpool to Melbourne, Sydney, Auckland, Wellington, Lyttelton and Port Chalmers, with the *Indralema* taking the first sailing out of Liverpool on 4 February 1904.

The New Zealand government, a major importer of goods from the UK, wanted to support a direct West of England service, and on 23 December 1903 called tenders for one. Shortly after they closed on 7 January 1904 it announced that the Federal, Houlder Bros and Turnbull Martin's Scottish Shire Line, trading as the Federal-Houlder-Shire Line, had secured a three-year West Coast contract, commencing in June 1904. The Liners were very bitter about the government calling tenders in the middle of the Christmas/New Year holiday season, but could do little but watch when the Federal steamer *Essex* (1902, 7,016) sailed from Liverpool on 8 May. The consortium also announced a direct return service from New Zealand ports to Liverpool, Manchester and Glasgow in September and the *Devon* (1897, 5,489) sailed Wellington on 20 December 1905. Early in 1906 Federal-Houlder-Shire decided that due to lower support than expected, and as allowed under the contract, the company would also work through London on their West Coast service. This decision was also taken because NZSCo/Shaw Savill were attempting to 'jockey' Federal-Houlder-Shire out of the trade.[4] This annoyed the other two lines who in June announced that they, too, would commence a direct West Coast service; the Shaw Savill steamer *Waiwera* (1899, 6,237) sailed from Wellington on 13 July 1906 direct for Cardiff. Both groups reduced freights and passenger fares to secure support. The general manager of New Zealand Shipping said the position was quite clear. 'These people have been pinpricking us for sometime; now they are attacking us'. Matters had been further inflamed when the Federal steamer *Dorset* (1903, 6,990) was dispatched from London on 2 May 1906 direct for New Zealand. As early as March 1904, Ritchie was writing to his Shaw Savill masters in London suggesting 'it may be that for the sake of the future, perhaps also of bringing Tyser into line, the sacrifice must be made and this much may be said with confidence that both Hughes (Federal) and Tyser are more than likely proceeding at present on the firm persuasion that neither S.S.& A/N.Z.S. will fight. It might pay to show that they are wrong'.[5]

An interim agreement was proposed between the Liners and Federal in October 1904 which would have seen the Federal-Houlder-Shire lines remaining solely in the West Coast service and the Liners retaining the London trade. In addition Federal was guaranteed 30,000 bales of wool per annum, but there was no agreement on the freights, which remained very competitive. This arrangement was insufficient to satisfy Hughes, who was leading the group, and the Liners were weighing up whether Federal should be given some London sailings as well. Finally on 26 October 1906, London cabled that agreement had been reached giving the Federal consortium the West Coast service, with the exception of six sailings a year to S.S.&A/N.Z.S. In a final twist, Hughes had also extracted a guarantee of 50,000 bales of wool per annum from New Zealand, whether the line was able to actually ship it or not. The agreement was for seven years and homeward freights would be under a pooling agreement between the lines. Hughes also wanted Tyser excluded from any closer association with the three groups, and this was also agreed. Uniform rates of freight would be charged on all Federal services, including the New York trade. The whole settlement involved the New Zealand government, as it was anxious that stability should return to the trade. The death of the premier, Richard John Seddon, on 10 June 1906 had removed a strong opponent of 'the Liners' and their monopoly. His successor, businessman Sir Joseph Ward, was more conciliatory towards the concept of shipping lines pooling their resources to provide a regular and balanced service.

Throughout all the bitter fighting, Tysers continued its own sailings southbound from both London and the West Coast of the United Kingdom without disruption. Its name was never dragged into the newspaper stories and it was as though the Tyser Line did not exist in the eyes of the two warring factions. Following the settlement with Hughes, Ritchie wrote to Walter Savill in London stating, 'as for Tyser, I am afraid that his attitude always will be to leave S.S.& A/N.Z.S to pull the chestnuts out of the fire for them. I'm afraid it is impossible to force them to share any part of the sacrifice S.S.& A/N.Z.S. have made. However they were as eager as any out here to have the freights raised'.[6] Two months later Ritchie added: 'As to Tyser, I am hardly surprised at his attitude and policy. So long as there was no material advantage to him to joining and binding himself, it is pretty evident that he is none the worse, if not better, to keep himself free. I have little doubt he will adhere to the rates of freight'.[7]

Now reinforced with the Federal-Houlder-Shire connection, the Liners still exercised strong control over New Zealand refrigerated cargoes and could block the Tyser Line from securing any dairy produce.

In 1904 the Associated Australia Brokers approved an increase in Tyser Line outward sailings from London from 12 to 14 and in 1907, thanks to increasing trade volumes, to 16 sailings. The Tyser New Zealand homeward service was by now firmly established with increasing volumes of frozen meat, wool and general cargoes and the New York/ Australasia run was settling down, although competition between the three groups in that trade was still keen. Whilst the Tyser vessels loading homewards from Australia secured the regular frozen meat shipments from Rockhampton and the wool shipments from Ostemeyer, Dewez and von Rompaey and other buyers, there was huge potential for the company to increase its liftings of wool, particularly from New South Wales, the largest producing area. Tysers had initially employed Balchin, Johnston and Co as their agents in Sydney but the company opened its own office at 51 Pitt Street, Sydney in 1899, later shifting to 12-14 Loftus Street. Tyser & Co had been chartering wool ships for some years and on 17 December 1891, the steamer *Arroyo* (1890, 3,564) sailed with 14,750 bales of wool, which was believed to be the largest consignment of wool to be shipped from Sydney in the one bottom. There were other charters in later years and in 1899 they dispatched three steamers *Amana* (1895, 3,412), *Ayr* (1894, 3,050) and *Tiger* (1895, 3,273). The potential to expand wool shipments seemed unlimited. The company could also see that the shippers would no longer accept sailing ships and the trade was looking to better frequency of sailings, reliability and improved speed that only steamers could provide.

Whilst Tyser and Co had the ships to mount a monthly sailing out of Australia for London and a continental port, weekly sailings were essential during the six-seven month wool season if the company was going to build the same relationships with the wool exporters that the larger companies enjoyed. Norddeutscher Lloyd of Bremen, Deutsch-Australische Dampfschiffs-Gesellschaft of Hamburg and the principal British Lines had the capacity to provide the tonnage to meet the seasonal demands. Tyser conceived the idea of forming a new line, which could draw ships from several of the smaller shipping companies and the collective strength of such a group would be very competitive against the larger wool carriers, as well as providing a sailing frequency which would attract greater support from the wool trade.

One of the principal liner agencies in Australia was the firm of Gibbs, Bright and Co and it handled the agency for William Milburn's Anglo-Australasian Steam Navigation Co of London and R. P. Houston and Co of Liverpool. The Liverpool-based Bright Bros had first established an office in Melbourne in July 1853, acting as merchant bankers and shipping agents, financing many early business ventures in Australia and New Zealand. Bright Bros. had supplied the initial mortgage finance to the Union Steam Ship Company of New Zealand Ltd, which was founded in Dunedin

Liverpool ship owner, R.P. Houston and Company, provided steamers for the Australian Union Line such as the *Hortensius*, shown in Sydney Harbour in 1905. She was the first Houston sailing for the Australian Union Line, finalling from Adelaide on 17 October 1905 for London and Antwerp. WM. LIVERMORE

in 1875, and which subsequently became the largest shipping company in the Southern Hemisphere. In 1881 Bright Brothers were acquired by Antony Gibbs and Co of London and became Gibbs, Bright and Co, with branches being established in Melbourne, Sydney and Brisbane. A branch was established at Adelaide in 1883 and Newcastle in 1885. Harry Benson of Tyser & Co in Sydney could see the potential to strengthen the Tyser base in Australia through an association with Gibbs, Bright. In July 1904, Tyser and Co entered into discussions with Gibbs, Bright and Co with a view to forming a regular line of steamers homeward from Australia. It was not until May the following year that a firm proposal was in place and the Australian Union Line was first advertised. No company was formed. The Australian Union Line was essentially a marketing name but Tyser and Company was confident the frequency of sailings, and the quality of the carrying vessels, would attract the attention of the wool trade. The joint agents for the Australian Union Line were Gibbs, Bright and Co, Tyser and Co and W. & A. McArthur Ltd. The latter company had for some years been agents for Ritson Branch Line steamers and Tysers had been regular users of space in Ritson vessels. On one occasion there had been five of their vessels listed on the one Tyser Line charter party.

The *Star of Victoria* took the first AUL sailing from Melbourne on 29 June 1905 for Durban, East London and Cape Town and the following vessel, *Indraghiri,* left Melbourne on 2 July for London. The line was seeking all classes of cargo, not just wool. Thereafter sailings were integrated primarily for the wool trade. Even though Corry and Royden steamers were involved, they were always described as Tyser Line vessels in the advertisements. R. P. Houston steamers, such as the *Hortensius* (1899, 3,472), *Hylas* (1899, 4,233), *Halizones* (1902, 5,093), *Hesperides* (1899, 3,393),

Hellenes (1900, 3,332), *Hostilius* (1900, 3,325) and *Hyanthes* (1899, 5,756) came under the AUL sailing roster in the following three years. Ships of the Anglo-Australasian Steam Navigation Co, handled by Gibbs, Bright and Company, all had names beginning with *Port*. The first Anglo-Australasian vessel to sail on the AUL berth was the *Port Albert* from Sydney to London and Dunkirk on 6 November 1905 and *Port Caroline* followed from Melbourne on 7 November. The Melbourne agents for the new line were Joseph Gill & Co and Gibbs, Bright and Co. When there were insufficient ships from the three lines to meet the trading needs, Tyser and Co continued to charter 'outside' vessels and within a few years AUL was a major wool carrier from Australia. From the advent of the Australian Union Line the long name of Anglo-Australasian Steam Navigation Co was dropped by Wm. Milburn and the ships in the service were referred to as 'Port Line' or Milburn Line vessels. By 1908 W. & A. McArthur had withdrawn as one of the joint agents for the line and a year later R. P. Houston and Co no longer actively participated in the sailings.

The *Daily Commercial News and Shipping Guide* in 1909 described the AUL as one of the most important cargo lines running between Australia, England and the Continent. The collective efforts of Tyser and Gibbs, Bright saw AUL shipping 146,705 bales of wool from New South Wales alone in the 12 months to 30 June 1907, compared to the German Australia Line's 144,754 bales and Norddeutscher Lloyd's 133,000 bales. Gibbs, Bright by 1912 was handling 16 per cent of the wool exports from the main wool producing states (New South Wales, Queensland, Victoria and South Australia). Much of the credit for the success of the AUL must go to Harry Benson, the Tyser representative in Sydney who was made a partner of Tyser and Company in July 1906. The Australian Union Line worked closely with the Federal Company and for a time the two companies had a pooling agreement.

The creation of AUL strengthened the Wm Milburn service, as in earlier years the line had difficulty finding sufficient northbound cargoes and was forced to load charter parcels of coal at Newcastle for eastern destinations. At other times they could only secure parcels of wheat or low-paying mineral cargoes. The 'Port' vessels invariably went to Port Pirie after discharge of their southbound cargo, to load 2/3,000 tonne parcels of lead concentrates to provide bottom weight, which with a lighter wool cargo on top, provided a better trim for a speedier homeward passage. The main discharging ports were Dunkirk, Hull, London and Antwerp, with the company being the first line in the Australian trade to introduce direct calls at Hull with wool for Yorkshire from December 1905.

William Milburn and Co's Anglo-Australasian Steam Navigation Co Ltd of London had been operating a service to and from Australia since 1883. The founder of the line, William Milburn, was born at Ashington, Northumberland in 1826 and although he became a butcher by trade, he purchased a quarter share in his first ship in 1849. He held the 16 shares in the brig *John Twizell* (1849, 149) until 1854. In

Harry Benson, the Tyser Line Australian manager, who played such an important role in the development of the Australian business in the early 1900s. He was made a partner of Tyser and Company in 1906 and was a director of the Commonwealth & Dominion Line from 1915-1924. PORT LINE ARCHIVES, UNIVERSITY OF LIVERPOOL

1851 he purchased 43 shares in the snow *Pero* (1850, 212) and within five years he was running seven small sailing ships. His financial stability had been strengthened in 1850 when he married Mary Davison, whose family had extensive shipping and grain interests at Blyth. The Milburn ships sailed to many parts of the world in general trading and in the 1860s several were employed in the China tea trade. Family records tell the tale of one of his vessels that went out to South America. Nothing was heard of the ship for over a year and then one day a remittance came through a London bank for an amount larger than Milburn had paid for the vessel. She had been trading on the west coast of South America and the master had been unable to get to a city from where he could remit the accumulated freights. Amongst the last composite clippers built for Milburn for the China trade were the *Taunton* (1868, 705) and *Lutterworth* (1868, 883). The latter vessel was subsequently acquired in 1879 by Shaw Savill and made 23 voyages to New Zealand with migrants, before ending her days there as a coal hulk.

In 1857 Milburn joined forces with another Newcastle ship owner, Edmund Hannay Watts, to form Watts, Milburn and Co. Both Watts and Milburn quickly realised the potential of the steamship and became one of the first shipping companies to commence a trade to the Black Sea with steamers. The *Chu Kiang* (1869, 1,008) was the first Watts, Milburn steamer, and also one of the early steamers to pass through the Suez Canal. Watts Milburn introduced four steamers into the China tea trade from 1869 and as a result of their successful voyages, three larger steamers were built

– *Hankow* (1873, 3,594), *Whampoa* (1873, 3,834) and *St. Osyth* (1874, 3,541). Watts, Milburn also had a contract with Siemssen and Company of Hamburg, for aggregating feeder cargoes around the China coast ports of Hong Kong, Canton, Swatow and Amoy, in the five small coasters operated by the German company.

The China tea trade was essentially a seasonal one-way service and Watts and Milburn were anxious to increase profitability by filling their larger vessels both out and home. The outward trade to China was over-tonnaged and very competitive. The partners saw potential in Australia. In the early 1870s there was plenty of outward cargo to Australia, as well as migrants, but little export cargo was available from that country. By loading out to Australia, then taking a cargo of coal, or ballasting to the East, a profitable triangular trade could be developed.

The *St. Osyth* sailed from London on 31 October 1874 for Melbourne, via Cape Town, under charter to Anderson, Green and Co, the forerunners of the Orient Steam Navigation Co. She was the first full-powered steamship to run between London and Australia, via the Cape, and by completing the passage in 42 days, she beat the regular P&O service via Suez. Other Milburn steamers, *Whampoa, Huntingdon,* (1881, 2,224), *Fenstanton* (1882, 2,405) and *Normanton* (1882, 2,367) made voyages to Melbourne and Sydney under John Flint's Colonial Line of Australian Packets. Watts, Milburn was involved in several other liner services as well as in the carriage of coal. The partners also became involved in a short-lived venture with Hamburg ship owner August Bolten in forming the Hamburg-Brasilianische Dampfschiffahrts-Gesellschaft (Hamburg-Brazil Steam Navigation Co). Their first steamer in this service was the *Criterion* (1868, 965) and she was later joined by other steamers running from Hamburg and Lisbon to Bahia, Rio de Janeiro and Santos. They included the Watts, Milburn steamers *Brazilian* (1869, 1,359), *Santos* (1869, 1,016) and *Rio* (1870, 1,494). The venture was not a great success and in November 1871 Bolten formed the Hamburg-Sudamerikanische Dampfschiffahrts-Gesellschaft (Hamburg-South American Steam Packet Co), with a share capital of 5,000 shares of 250 talers. A German bank took 3,260 shares, Bolten interests 840 and Watts, Milburn and C. Mitchell took 250 each. German interests bought out the English shareholders later in 1871 and the Hamburg-Sud eventually became the principal German company in the South American trade. Today (2006) the line remains the second largest German liner company.

In 1873 Watts, Milburn developed a concept for a six-ship passenger service from London to Melbourne with backing from the Victorian government, and was also looking for support from New Zealand interests who were promised an extension of the service. The Anglo-Australian Steam Navigation Co was floated with a capital of £1,250,000 but the badly-needed Australian and New Zealand support did not materialise. The Watts, Milburn partnership was amicably dissolved in 1879 and the parties thereafter developed their individual shipping interests. By this time Milburn could see the importance of London as the centre for liner shipping and opened an office there. William Milburn and his son John remained in Newcastle while two other sons, William Jnr and Charles, controlled the London office.

Milburn persisted in trying to establish a regular line to Australia and on 30 April 1883, the Anglo-Australasian Steam Navigation Co Ltd was registered in London. A monthly service from London to Adelaide, Melbourne and Sydney was proposed and the first sailing was taken by the Milburn steamer *Chollerton* which sailed from London on 7 May 1883. Unfortunately she lost her propeller in the Indian Ocean and had to make course for Bombay under sail where her spare propeller was fitted – a distance of 2,100 miles from where she was disabled. As a result, the following vessel *Teddington*, which left London on 9 June, arrived at Adelaide first on 12 August. The *Chollerton* sailed from Bombay on 4 August and arrived at Adelaide on 30 August. They were followed by other Milburn steamers – *Coniston*, *Normanton* and *Tiverton* before the first 'Port'-named steamer, the *Port Jackson,* sailed from Plymouth on 12 November 1883. The ships ordered for the new company were all given the name of an Australian port, prefixed with the word *Port.* Several of the early vessels had fine lines with clipper bows. The ships had a black funnel and black hull with a thin white line just below the bulwarks. The colours flown were a combination of two pennants – the top one with W.M. and Co in red on a white background and the lower with a red ground and white letters showing A.A.S.N.Co. In later years the two pennants were reduced to a standard flag which horizontally contained the letters portrayed on

The first vessel built for Wm. Milburn's Anglo Australasian Steam Navigation Company with a 'Port' name was the *Port Jackson*, built in 1883. She sailed from Plymouth on her maiden voyage to Australia on 12 November with 211 steerage passengers. The photograph shows her anchored at Gravesend. F.C. GOULD & SON the pennants. A mixture of Milburn vessels and 'Ports' maintained the service, but from 1891 all the ships had 'Port' names apart from the *Bothwell Castle* (1881, 2,542) on charter for several voyages, and the Milburn steamer *Hankow*. In addition to cargo and a few saloon passengers, the ships carried between 25 and 200 migrants. In September 1886 the *Port Darwin* brought out 219 Royal Navy marines and ratings for the Australian squadron. *Tiverton* was the first sailing at the end of 1883 to proceed via the Cape of Good Hope and thereafter vessels traveled via Suez or the Cape and called occasionally at Hobart en route to Australia. Between 1883 and 1914 33 '*Port*' ships were completed. The company had a unique relationship with Newcastle shipbuilder, R. & W. Hawthorn, Leslie and Company (formerly A. Leslie and Company) and 20 of the 33 vessels were built in this company's shipyard. In addition nine ships were laid down as 'Port' vessels, but for varying reasons were sold, with seven going to other companies in the Australian or New Zealand trades. Wm. Milburn and Co also had links with Allan Hughes of the Federal Steam Navigation Company, and William Milburn, Jnr. was on the board of directors of the Federal Line from 1895 until his death in 1903. Six steamers laid down by R. & W. Hawthorn, Leslie and Company, on behalf of Wm. Milburn and Co, were taken over on completion by the Federal Steam Navigation Co.

The *Port Augusta* in 1911 was one of the first vessels on a long distance service to be fitted with a Johnston's superheated steam installation. The degree of super-heat in the vessel averaged 550 degrees Fahrenheit at the engine stop-valve and it was estimated this would reduce daily coal consumption by 15 per cent. Some other vessels in the company were similarly fitted.

A second *Port Augusta* came into service in 1906. Transferred to the Commonwealth & Dominion Line in 1914 she remained in the fleet until 1925. WM. LIVERMORE

The Anglo-Australasian Steam Navigation Co suffered a number of total losses. The one-year old *Port Douglas* struck rocks off Cape Verde Islands on 24 May 1892. She was on passage from London to Melbourne and was making for Dakar to take on coal bunkers. She quickly became a total loss. The *Port Melbourne* went missing in 1899 between New York and London while on charter to the National Line of Liverpool. Last reported on 27 January 1899, she was never seen again. The third ship to be lost was the *Port Stephens* of 1894 which had been chartered to the Union Steam Ship Company for cargoes of coal from Newcastle, New South Wales to New Zealand. After discharge of her second cargo, the *Port Stephens* left Oamaru on 1 October 1906 for Newcastle, making her course south of New Zealand. Her tail shaft broke on the 3rd in position 45.50S, 164.04E, and the ship drifted south in gale force conditions. By 8 October she had drifted 229 miles south to latitude 49.20S. There was no way of controlling the movements of the ship, and when the sailing ship *Ravenscourt* (1892, 1,353), on passage from Newcastle to Callao, spotted it on 8 October the crew were taken off and brought to the Otago Heads a week later. Although the Union Company freighter *Rakanoa* (1896, 2,246) searched for *Port Stephens,* she was not located and her final fate was never established. Incredibly, the marine inquiry censured the master of *Port Stephens* for not staying with his ship, and ordered him to pay the costs of the inquiry. Several experienced ship masters felt he was unjustly treated and presented him with a purse of sovereigns.

One other 'Port' vessel had a very lucky escape from disaster. The clipper-bowed *Port Chalmers* of 1891, on passage from London to Sydney, had just rounded the Cape of Good Hope on 27 July 1895 when she ran into a massive iceberg. Her bowsprit,

A sister ship to the *Port Elliot*, the *Port Stephens* was chartered out by Milburn Line to undertake voyages from Newcastle, Australia to New Zealand with coal. On the second of these in 1906 she broke her tail shaft and was abandoned by the crew, drifting south towards Antarctica, and was never seen again. WM. LIVERMORE cutwater and figurehead were all torn away, the bow plating was badly damaged and the lifeboats were staved in. An estimated 100 tonnes of ice crashed onto the starboard side of the ship and she almost capsized. Fortunately her collision bulkheads held and she was able to continue her voyage to Adelaide, her pumps working throughout the remainder of her passage. Permanent repairs, carried out in Mort's Dock, Sydney, involved stripping 32 plates, taking out 12 frames and reverse frames from keel to top-gallant forecastle deck, as well as replacement of considerable other steelwork, a new figurehead and bowsprit. Her namesake, built in 1905, also experienced an unusual occurrence after rounding the Cape. On 24 April 1910 a tidal wave hit the ship with great force, placing her in peril. The seas were already rough and the turbulence from the tidal wave remained for sometime. The *Port Chalmers* released oil on the waters and hove to for 14 hours while minor damage was repaired. One of the officers commented on arrival in Adelaide that 'we blame the comet for our experience and we will be heartily glad when it has disappeared'. He was referring to Halley's Comet which was visible at that time.

Early in 1907 Funch Edye of New York was approached by the Deutsche Dampfschiffahrts-Gesellschaft 'Hansa' of Bremen (Hansa Line) and the Deutsch-Australische Dampfschiffs-Gesellschaft of Hamburg (German Australia Line) to act as agents for a new six-weekly service from New York to Australia and New Zealand. Funch Edye initially declined the appointment because of the commitment to Tyser Line, but as a result of discussions between Tyser and the German companies, it was agreed to mount a joint service under the name of United Tyser Line with Tyser having a 50 per cent share of the line. Sailings every three weeks would be provided between New York and Melbourne, six weekly between New York, Adelaide and Brisbane and a direct service every six weeks to New Zealand. Otto Harms, the founder and chairman of the German Australia Line wrote in his history of the company that 'the co-operation with Tyser and Company was good and friendly'. Tyser's *Hawkes Bay* took the first sailing of the United Tyser Line to Australia and New Zealand, sailing New York on 20 April 1907 for Fremantle and the usual range of eastern Australian and New Zealand ports. The first German Australia Line steamer to load for United Tyser Line was the *Itzehoe* (1899, 5,134) which sailed New York on 1 June 1907. Tyser Line strengthened its presence in the New York trade by leasing Pier 10 in Brooklyn in June 1907 as its permanent berth.

There were fears of another freight war developing and although the A.&A. Line and the United States and Australasia Line scheduled a fortnightly service between them from New York to Australia and a monthly service to New Zealand, United Tyser Line held to the previous freighting structure and that provided stability to the rates of freight. The vessels of the Hansa Line invariably left Australia or New Zealand after discharge to load on the company's berth from India or the Dutch East Indies, while the German Australia Line vessels loaded back in Australia for Europe on that

George Walter Tyser was the eldest son of the founder, G.D. Tyser. He and his brother William ran the Tyser business from 1886 until William's death in 1908. George was then head of the family business until 1914 when he retired in favour of his son, Walter. TYSER FAMILY

company's service commenced in 1886. All three groups in the New York service maintained close links and a pooling arrangement was in place. To better utilise available ships for southbound loadings it was common for ships of one consortium to be chartered for the scheduled sailing of another group. By 1910 the New York freights had worked their way up to around 55/- a ton for high value cargo, 47/6 for general cargo and between 37/6 and 40/- shillings for case oil. In fact, the firming-up of the rates saw the larger oil companies, like the Vacuum Oil Company, chartering their own ships, even though they also extensively used the liner sailings. From 1910 the Hansa Line provided the chartered tonnage for the United States and Australasia Line but the German Australia Line continued to load ships on the joint Tyser berth until just before the outbreak of World War I.

William H. Tyser, the second son of the founder, died on 30 June 1908 aged 63, leaving his brother George in charge of the business, assisted by his son Walter Parkyns Tyser and W. H. Tyser's son, Harry. An imposing man, nearly 6 foot 4 inches in height, Walter Tyser increasingly assumed responsibility for the shipping interests and most of the initiatives leading to the formation of the Commonwealth & Dominion Line some five years later were taken by him. Walter Tyser made his first visit to Australasia in 1903 and from that time had overseen this section of the company business. He had become a partner in Tyser & Company in 1893 and a director of Tyser Line Limited in August 1896. His cousin, Henry (Harry) Erskine Tyser, was elected a director of the Tyser Line in 1903.

Niwaru, shown here in Sydney harbour, was the Maori name for James J. Niven, who had built an engineering business at Napier. WM. LIVERMORE

With the experience gained on the long ocean hauls in the Southern Ocean, either coming from United Kingdom or New York to Melbourne, or travelling home via Cape Horn from New Zealand or the Cape of Good Hope for Australian departures, masters of vessels carefully watched the weather and went as far south as practical. In December 1907 *Hawkes Bay* encountered huge icebergs in 57/58 degrees south and a year later the same vessel, on passage from Melbourne to Hull sailed 600 miles further south than normal in order to get her wool cargo to Hull faster than any other ship. In 1910 *Niwaru* sailed along the 60th parallel to make a fast passage to catch the London wool sale but found ice all around and for three days the ship could not see water for ice. As it was daylight throughout 24 hours there was no danger from night navigation, but the vessel had to slow down to prevent damage. Without radio, ships depended entirely on the reliability of their machinery. Even in modern times with satellite navigation and radar, vessels do not generally go beyond 50 degrees south. One can only admire the tenacity and skill of these shipmasters over a century ago.

As new ships were introduced, passage times improved. In 1904 *Marere* made a non-stop passage from London to Melbourne in 39 days 16 hours, a record for the company and one of the fastest by a cargo liner of that era. Next year *Niwaru* on a similar voyage covered the distance in 40 days 6 hours and went down to 52 south and encountered a number of icebergs. In 1909 the *Star of Canada*, on her maiden voyage, covered the distance from London to Melbourne in 37 days 20 hours. The vessels loading in New Zealand or Australia invariably sailed full and where there was

The *Indrabarah* ashore north of Wanganui in May 1913. She was ashore for 58 days but was successfully refloated, and the repairs at Port Chalmers, were amongst the largest ever undertaken in New Zealand at that time. EDWARDS

going to be a shortfall of wool or general cargo in Australia, the spaces could usually be filled with metals. A typical cargo by *Marere*, from Wellington to London in 1910 comprised 100,037 carcasses of mutton and lamb, 4655 quarters of beef, 32,965 legs and pieces of mutton, 527 bags of kidneys and 7000 bales of wool and general cargo.

A further development took place in March 1910 when New Zealand Shipping Company gained a Canadian government contract, with a $24,000 subsidy, for a monthly sailing from Montreal (from St John, New Brunswick during the three winter months) to Melbourne, Sydney, Auckland, Wellington, Lyttelton and Dunedin. The *Rakaia* (1895, 5,628) sailed from Montreal with the first sailing on 21 May. In October the company announced that the service had exceeded initial expectations and in line with the co-operation dating back over 25 years before, it would share the trade with Shaw Savill & Albion. Alternative sailings were taken by vessels of the two lines although for the customers, the Shaw Savill vessels were always described as being chartered to New Zealand Shipping and the latter handled the agency for the service in New Zealand. Thus all the lines in the New Zealand trade now had service connections with the East Coast of North America.

Although there were instances of ships losing their propellers, collisions at sea, fires in port or otherwise disabled, the Tyser Line was fortunate that between 1887 and 1914 there was only one total loss. The *Indrabarah* came close when she stranded five miles north of the mouth of the Rangitikei River on 9 May 1913 and was not refloated until 6 July. She had arrived off Wanganui from Gisborne to load in the

Blown ashore in a heavy gale while anchored in the Gisborne roadstead in 1912, the *Star of Canada* is shown with the ocean swell pouring over her forward holds. She later broke her back and became a total loss. The bridge deck and her master's cabin are now preserved in the Tairawhiti Museum, Gisborne. TAIRAWHITI MUSEUM, GISBORNE

roadstead but there was a very strong gale blowing from the south east and the master decided to stand off due to the tremendous seas. In poor visibility she drifted onto a sandy base at 0330 hours on the 10th and with the force of the wind was pushed further up the beach. The Union Company's tug *Terawhiti* (1907, 260) was sent from Wellington and over the next fortnight various attempts were made to haul the freighter clear. Mushroom anchors were laid out to prevent her moving any closer inshore and the cargo of tallow, flax and wool was jettisoned – although some delays were experienced with this, as the waterside workers demanded more money. It was not until 6 July that a combination of a very high tide, a favourable wind and the use of the vessel's damaged propellers saw *Indrabarah* slip back into deep water. Quite a number of shore-side 'experts' had long given up hope the vessel would ever leave the beach and the announcement that the ship had been saved surprised more than a few. *Indrabarah* was initially taken to Wellington and then down to Port Chalmers for docking. She remained in the dock from 29 July until 10 September and the repairs undertaken over this period were widely praised by Lloyd's Register and the vessel's owners. They were amongst the largest undertaken in New Zealand to that time. Apart from bottom damage, both propeller shafts had to be re-aligned, propellers replaced and a new rudder fabricated and fitted. Coming off the beach at Rangitikei, both propellers had been broken to half their normal length. That she survived the prolonged pounding on the beach reflected great credit on her builders – Swan Hunter & Wigham Richardson.

The total loss occurred when the *Star of Canada* was at anchor in the Gisborne roadstead on 23 June 1912. She was blown ashore in a severe southerly squall in some of the worst weather experienced for many years. Her anchors would not hold and she was forced into shallow water. By daylight the following morning, there were 5.2 metres of water in her three forward holds. Heavy swells battered *Star of Canada* and on 3 July she broke her back. The bridge deck and captain's cabin were salvaged and became part of a house at 274 Childers Road, Gisborne between 1927 and 1985 and from 1985 it has become the main feature of a maritime museum attached to the Tairawhiti Museum at Gisborne.

Whilst the outward trade from London to Australia was still very much controlled by the Associated Brokers group in the Davis conference, attempts to tighten up on the homeward service were all fraught with problems. With so many ships loading homeward cargoes, it was difficult for the major lines to achieve any rationalisation or order in the trade. Although the sailing ships had largely disappeared from 1907, and the slow speed tramps received little support in the liner services, it was not until 1913 that a formal homeward conference for general cargoes was established.

Ships with refrigerated capacity were invariably converted or built for the trade and it was thought that a homeward conference of the refrigerated carriers was going to be in place from 1 January 1894. However, various lines were nibbling at the carryings of the larger lines in the trade and the largest carrier, P&O, was not anxious to give too much away. Likewise, newcomers such as Allan Hughes' Federal Steam Navigation Company and Tyser Line were not keen to lock in a fixed allocation before they had increased their shares through competition. Between 1909 and 1913 there were further attempts to achieve agreement and the Australian Refrigerated Tonnage Committee was finally formed in 1913. World War I then intervened and the Tonnage Committee was re-activated in stronger form as the Australian Tonnage Committee in 1925 and effectively controlled the movement of refrigerated cargoes from Australia to the UK for almost the next half century.

Shippers had been objecting to the practice of shipping lines forming conferences since the first Calcutta Conference in 1875 and the tightening up of the Australian trade in 1913 gave rise to much criticism. Shippers were always seeking a 'special deal' to steal a march on their competitors so that when the lines closed ranks to rationalise sailings to meet trade demands, and to agree on standard freight rates for all, there was always dissension. Despite the dissatisfaction of the conference control and the deferred rebate system to ensure shipping loyalty, the shipping lines always seemed to be successful in arguing their case that the conference system was best for all parties. Sir Montague Nelson, in giving evidence before the Royal Commission on Shipping Rings in 1907, strongly supported the conference principles.[8] He said his opinion 'with regard to combination and deferred rebates was that the system was calculated to ensure steady and uniform rates of freight and an excellent and rapid service to

Australasia, which was beneficial alike to importers and exporters'. Both classes, he said, were strong enough to safeguard their own interests and he thought that all that was necessary was to let the trades alone. He would not approve of any government interference which would regulate the rates of freight. His companies had not suffered from any dictation of terms on the part of the ship owners. In the final report of The Royal Commission of Shipping Rings, released in 1909, shipping groups were able to uphold the concept that standard freight rates and co-ordinated sailings provided a better deal for shippers than the uncertainty of irregularity of sailings and the ups and downs of unstable freight structures. The Australian government endorsed this philosophy in later years when all the aspects of shipping services to and from the country were discussed.

In 1911 Allan Hughes of the Federal Steam Navigation Co was negotiating a three-year agreement with the Victorian government for the carriage of migrants from London to Melbourne at £13 per head. Tyser and Co decided to enlist the assistance of Wm. Milburn & Co, and the P&O Branch Service to mount a counter bid at £12 a head. They were successful and on 23 January 1912 an agreement was signed between the three lines and the Agent General for Victoria to carry 24,000 migrants over three years. In the last series of large cargo carriers built prior to World War I, Tyser & Company took advantage of this migrant contract to provide temporary accommodation in the shelter decks for up to 1,000 migrants a voyage. Well-lit cabins and dormitories, fitted with iron beds and washbasins, were provided in the vessels with a dining room for 500 people, along with smoking and sitting rooms and additional lavatories. Once the passengers were landed in Melbourne, the upper deck dormitories and cabins vacated by the migrants were quickly taken down and stored on board for the next voyage. All four shipowners, Tyser, Milburn, Royden and Corry, built or converted ships for this migrant contract. The ships all carried additional lifeboats and other life saving equipment for everyone aboard.

The first of the migrant sailings was the Tyser Line *Makarini* which sailed from Plymouth on 12 June 1912 with cargo and 900 migrants for Melbourne via Cape Town. She berthed in Melbourne on 22 July. The following vessel was the *Indrapura*. Built in 1911, as a sistership to the *Indrabarah*, she was subsequently converted to carry migrants after her maiden voyage to Australia. She sailed from London on 2 October 1912 with 1000 assisted immigrants, 300 men and 700 women and children. *Hawkes Bay*, an exact sister of *Makarini*, was launched 9 December 1912. The Milburn sailings were also integrated with Tysers and of the Milburn ships, *Port Lincoln* was launched on 3 April 1912 and the *Port Macquarie* three months later. At 7,200 tons, they were larger than any previous Milburn vessels, which had generally averaged less than 5,000 tons. They had service speeds of 13 knots. For the Corry family interests, the *Star of Victoria* ran trials 14 January 1914 and left London on 3 February. The final vessel, the *Star of England,* sailed from London for Melbourne on 14 May 1914

In 1912 the Tyser Line built two larger ships with temporary accommodation in the shelter decks to carry up to 1000 migrants from London to Melbourne. The first steamer was the *Makarini*, shown here on trials. *Makarini* was the Maori name for Sir Donald McLean, the third Superintendent of Hawke's Bay. PORT LINE ARCHIVES, UNIVERSITY OF LIVERPOOL

The second migrant carrier and the last steamer built for the Tyser Line revived the name *Hawkes Bay*. Built in 1912, she became the *Port Napier* in 1916 and had a 24- year career in the New Zealand trade. J. DICKIE, ALEXANDER TURNBULL LIBRARY

The *Star of Victoria* was the first Corry Line contribution to the migrant contract and was building when the Commonwealth & Dominion Line was formed in January 1914. She became the *Port Melbourne* in 1916, and was intended to be scrapped in 1939, but was retained in service throughout the war and was finally broken up in 1948.

and made the passage in 36 days 14 hours at an average speed of 13.32 knots.

Although the Tyser-owned vessels and those of Corry and Royden, invariably had accommodation for up to 12 passengers, Tysers had little experience of handling migrant traffic and asked their friends in the Aberdeen White Star Line, just around the corner in Billiter Street, to transfer them an experienced staff member who could help organise the handling of up to 1,000 migrants per sailing. Aberdeen White Star Line sent Tysers a young 21 year old Aberdonian named William Donald. It was a significant appointment, as in later years Bill Donald headed the management of the Commonwealth & Dominion Line and ultimately became chairman of Port Line.

In later life, as he travelled in luxurious comfort as surgeon on the *Port Auckland* in 1954, Sir Bernard Dawson, recalled his experience as a young ship's surgeon fresh from medical school on a voyage from London to Melbourne in the *Port Lincoln* in 1912. On that voyage he had to look after the crew and 700 migrants, including 150 children, who were accommodated in cramped eight and sixteen-berth dormitories, hedged with flimsy walls and lined with wooden bunks scarcely softened by straw mattresses and pillows. The start to the voyage was inauspicious but when *Port Lincoln* entered the English Channel and sailed south she encountered a rain-bearing westerly gale. The passengers hastily retired to their bunks 'to suffer those agonies which on the first day made them think they were going to die, and on the second made them afraid that they would not. Seven hundred people were promptly and incontinently sick, and the shelter deck was awash with a grumous mixture of seawater and the vomit of sad people thinking regretfully of grimy rooms in the Wandsworth Road or a hillside cottage in Cumberland'.

The ship's surgeon, who was also greeting green seas for the first time, was far from happy with recurring waves of nausea, but something had to be done to relieve the distressed migrants. This was long before the beneficial anti-histamine drugs such as Dramamine, Avomine and such; indeed no one had then even heard of histamine, let alone its antagonists. However with a jorum of strong potassium bromide, laced with tincture of ginger, he waded round from bunk to bunk to ensure that all – some even beyond caring – swallowed their doses. It seemed to do good, at least the passengers said so, and when kindlier latitudes were reached, hope revived and cheerfulness returned after the shelter deck had been hosed and cleansed.

So much for the passengers, who were a fair cross-section of decent working class, batches of lads and girls to fill the urban labour market for better wages and social conditions, a skilled Dutch gardener sure of a good job in the gardens of Toorak or Mosman, a giant Cumberland farm hand accepting with dumb kindness the responsibilities of a wife and six children while nursing a nebulous ambition for land of his own – all of them a nebula which consolidated within five years.

And what of the ship's company on the *Port Lincoln*? The captain alone had accommodation of space and comfort on the boat deck, with that seclusion which is

Wm.Milburn & Company contributed two new steamers to the Victorian migrant contract, both much larger than previous vessels. The first, the *Port Lincoln*, was completed in July 1912, and is seen here in the Adelaide River. E. FLUCK

the need, privilege and penalty of authority. His mates, chief and three others, had each a cabin in a starboard alleyway, opening on to the after well deck and balanced by a parallel group for the engineers on the port side. Between them were the doctor's cabin and dispensary, also facing aft.

Fresh water was cherished and sparingly issued to the tanks which supplied the folding washbasin of the old-fashioned compactum, which subtended, too, the purpose of chest of drawers and writing shelf. There was one bathroom supplied with salt water and a steam jet to warm it, a capricious affair which played tricks, filling the room with steam and sometimes sending the occupant out like a scalded cat. The two alleyways were cut off forward by the galley, which for some strange reason lay athwart the ship, shutting off the ventilation to the cabins while getting little of its own. The cabins were well furnished and comfortable except in warm latitudes, where lack of through ventilation made them intolerably hot. There were neither fans nor blowers.

The captain and the officers shared a small saloon for meals of good plain food; dinner being equivalent to the farmers' 'ordinary' in any market town hotel. The crew, ordinary seamen, A.B.s, stokers, trimmers, deckhands still lived in the very congested forecastle, hot, overcrowded with tiers of rough bunks, with poor facilities for personal hygiene; living, sleeping and eating in space so limited that only patient tolerance and forbearance made life just possible without brawls. The crew was, by and large, a good natured crowd of rough men, many illiterate since their youth antedated free and compulsory education; often life's failures without hope, and recurrent victims when on shore leave of alcoholic binges.

Although the forecastle of the *Port Lincoln* was a step ahead of its time – the food better and congestion less – it was a survival of the bad days of hard tack, hard living and low pay, where men, tolerant, through usage, of their lot and grateful for small amenities, lived under conditions which offered little or no hope of advancement, human decency or human dignity."[9]

In the six years prior to the outbreak of World War I there were significant changes to the ownership of British shipping lines in the Australian and New Zealand trades. In 1908 wealthy shipping financier, Sir John Ellerman purchased Bucknall Bros & Co, one of the three partners in the American & Australian Line, then in 1910 Ellerman secured a controlling interest in Shaw Savill & Albion. Allan Hughes of Federal had his own ideas of expansion and consolidation and had made overtures to buy Houlder Bros. in 1910 but was rebuffed by the Houlder family who sold the company to Furness Withy. However two years later the NZSCo was able to purchase the Houlder Bros Australian business. Hughes was running out of options and he wanted to merge his Federal Line with the NZSCo and this took on some urgency when Sir John Ellerman started picking up parcels of NZSCo shares as they came on the market. The merger of the two interests was achieved through an allotment of 27,818 un-issued shares in NZSCo valued at £20 in exchange for 43,116 shares valued of £10 each in the Federal Line.[10] Hughes, who had done so much to bring about the amalgamation joined the board of the NZSCo. The seven year pooling agreement between Federal and SS&A/NZSCo in the New Zealand trade was due to terminate in 1913 so this was another important benefit of the takeover as it gave the Federal/NZSCo grouping the largest pool share and strength in negotiating a new agreement. It also provided improved access for NZSCo in the Australian service through the larger share Federal held in that trade. For trade pool purposes the four Houlder vessels acquired were sold to the Union Steam Ship Company and retained in the same service between the UK, Australia and New Zealand. Hughes also became a director of the Union Company's London board.

Following these consolidations, the NZSCo/Federal and Shaw Savill & Albion finally signed an agreement with Tyser Line in April 1913 giving it status as a full member of the conference. After all the battles since 1887, and being on the 'outside' of the decision-making since then, Tyser Line, in signing the agreement had decided that the company had achieved as much as it could outside the consortium. The trade had huge potential for growth and Tysers would proportionately share that growth with the other lines.

These moves may well have convinced Tysers to also consolidate the ships and businesses of the other three companies with whom they had contractual associations. It would probably have been relatively easy to convince the wealthy aristocrats of the

Corry and Royden families to amalgamate their interests into a separate company, in which the larger fleet of vessels would spread the risks and hopefully increase the profits. Likewise the Milburn family, controlling the Anglo-Australasian Steam Navigation Co, would also gain benefits by strengthening that company's base with a larger company, which also had valuable trade shares for both refrigerated and general cargoes in the New Zealand trade, then tightly controlled by the three British lines. Considerable economies would be achieved in the management of the fleet and the combined strength of the new company would be an important factor in combating future competition.

Walter Tyser, with his father, G.W. Tyser as chairman, was obviously leading the move to merge the various interests. At the meeting of the board of Tyser Line Limited in November 1913, there was evidence of a split between the younger generations of the two families. Before opening the business, the chairman stated that he had just received a letter from H. E. (Harry) Tyser which he proposed to read to the meeting.

> Dear Uncle George,
> In view of the fact it is impossible for me to take any part in the proposed new undertaking which has to be explained at today's board meeting in order to obtain approval of the Board, I have come to the conclusion that it is better for me not to attend the Board meeting. The moot-idea involved in the proposed closer combination of the Tyser Line Limited, with the various interests already working in friendly relations with it (and in this category I include Messrs Wm. Milburn and Company and the steamers they own or manage) – the moot idea seemed to present undeniable advantages for the interests concerned provided only that they all enter into it willingly and I am informed that they do that. The formulation of the detailed arrangements necessary to make the idea a reality is best able to be carried out by the persons about to be engaged in performing the work of whom I am not able to be one. I have written this letter only that the Board may know my view as one of the Managing Directors in regard to The Tyser Line's policy.
>
> Yours very truly – Harry Tyser

After some discussion it was unanimously decided that the chairman should thank Harry Tyser for his approval of the amalgamation scheme and regretting the causes which led him to refuse to take part in its working. The company solicitor would draft the letter. As result, Harry resigned from the Tyser Line board and almost immediately sold all his shares in the company. He also resigned from the partnership, and had no further involvement with the Tyser family business, either shipping or insurance. He joined the army on the outbreak of war and rose to the rank of lieutenant until he was killed in action in Arras, France on 9 April 1917.

The amalgamation of the four interests in proportion to their financial contribution was unanimously approved at a special meeting held on 31 December

1913. It took effect from 1 July 1913 with interest at 5 per cent on the capital employed from 1 July to 31 December. Existing steamers had been valued at cost less depreciation at 5 per cent per annum and the value of those still building had been apportioned. Vessels built for the Anglo-Australasian Steam Navigation had limited refrigerated space compared to the Tyser Line vessels, but the *Port Albany,* laid down for Wm. Milburn in early 1913, had 6,509 cubic metres of refrigerated space. The *Port Kembla* was also equipped in 1914 with insulated space of 3,655 cubic metres in order to provide compatibility with the refrigerated ships of the new company.

All eight Tyser vessels and the three Corry steamers (plus two further vessels under construction) went into the new company, along with the three Indra vessels working in the Australasian services. Milburns contributed eight of their 'Port' line fleet (along with *Port Albany* under construction) making a fleet of 25 vessels. Although discussions had been taking place between the four lines on and off over several years, news of the proposed amalgamation and the formation of the new company to be called the Commonwealth & Dominion Line Ltd first broke in December 1913. All Tyser, Corry and Milburn London office staff and personnel in the Tyser Sydney office transferred to the new company but only one person came from the Royden office, J.R. Rooper. The Belfast shipbuilder, Workman, Clark & Co, had a shareholding in Tyser Line Ltd, but did not become a shareholder in the Commonwealth & Dominion Line.

Although the Tyser name was submerged in the new company, the insurance broking and underwriting agents remained a separate entity and retained much of the hull insurance work for the C&D Line. It was not until 4 March 1914 that the advertisements for the Australian Union Line were replaced by the Commonwealth & Dominion Line name in the Sydney shipping newspapers. Once the amalgamation was fully operational a liquidator was appointed on 20 January 1915 to wind up Tyser Line Ltd.

1 J.M. Ritchie to Shaw Savill & Albion, 28 Jun 1900, J.M. Ritchie papers, Hocken Collections.
2 ibid, 29 Nov 1901.
3 ibid, 19 Oct 1903.
4 *Otago Daily Times,* 11 Apr 1906.
5 J.M. Ritchie to Shaw Savill & Albion, 10 Mar 1904.
6 ibid, 17 Nov1906.
7 ibid, 15 Jan.1907.
8 *The Times*, London, 12 Dec.1907.
9 *Otago Daily Times,* 16 Jun 1954.
10 *ibid,* 5 Jan 1912.

CHAPTER 3

The amalgamation

On 23 January 1914 the Commonwealth and Dominion Line Limited was registered in London, where its eight directors met for the first time five days later. Walter P. Tyser, Sir E. Montague Nelson and Paris K.F. Foot represented the Tyser interests, while Sir William Corry and his son Robert came from the Corry family. Charles T. Milburn and W.H. Moore were the nominees for the Anglo-Australasian Steam Navigation interests of Milburns, and the youngest member of the new board was 43-year-old Thos. Royden, the sole representative of the Royden interests. In 1912-13 he had been attending some Tyser Line board meetings in place of his father and was a close friend of Walter Tyser. He was also a member of the Cunard Steam-Ship board and had been appointed a director there at the age of 34 in 1905. Walter Tyser was nominated as chairman but in view of the dominant Tyser involvement with the new company he tactfully agreed to serve as acting chairman and retained this title for some months until May 1914 when he and Charles Milburn were elected chairman and deputy chairman respectively.

Walter P. Tyser became a partner in the family firm of Tyser & Company in 1893 and was a director of the Tyser Line from 1896 to 1915. He was the first chairman of the C&D Line in 1914 and remained in this position until 1939, retiring as president of the company in 1940. He played a leading role in the affairs of the company. TYSER FAMILY

The final Corry Line steamer was the *Star of England*, which entered service in May 1914. She, too, followed the career path of her sister *Star of Victoria* as the *Port Sydney* and remained in service until 1948. Both ships were lucky ships during World War II and each completed 34 years service. PORT LINE ARCHIVES, UNIVERSITY OF LIVERPOOL.

The head office of the Commonwealth and Dominion Line was at 9-11 Fenchurch Avenue , in offices previously occupied by Tyser & Co and James P. Corry. For many years Tyser & Co had its office at 3 Crosby Square but shifted to 16 Fenchurch Avenue in the late 1890s and then to 9-11 Fenchurch in 1911. During the period Tyser & Co was loading broker for the New Zealand Shipping Co from 1888-90, the company occupied the Shipping Company premises at 138 Leadenhall Street.

The 25 ships had all been valued, as well as the properties, stevedoring equipment and other interests being transferred to the new company. They amounted to £2,600,000, but in order to have a lower capital than the market value, the nominal capital was reduced to £2,000,000 made up of £750,000 in 6 per cent preference shares and £1,250,000 in ordinary shares. The paid-up capital on commencement totalled £1,991,536 with Tyser family interests holding 48 per cent, Milburn 27 per cent, Corry 13 per cent and Royden 12 per cent. When the total number of shares were added to debentures and cash, the contributing percentages for the eight entities representing the family interests were The Tyser Line Ltd (31), Tyser & Co (17), The Anglo-Australasian Steam Navigation Co Ltd (11), Wm. Milburn & Co (15), The Star Line Ltd (14), James P. Corry & Co (1), The Indra Line Ltd (10) and T. B. Royden (1). Shares were later allocated to senior executives, with the work of Captain Richard Todd and secretary Julius Sandtmann in New Zealand being recognised with a grants of 5,000 and 1,000 shares respectively.

The C&D fleet comprised all the existing Tyser Line steamers – *Mimiro, Niwaru, Marere, Whakarua, Nerehana, Muritai, Makarini* and *Hawkes Bay.* The full James P.

The *Port Albany* was ordered in March 1913 but was not completed until May 1914, some months after the Commonwealth & Dominion Line was formed. As it was known that she would be going to this company, she was equipped with 6,509 cubic metres of refrigerated space. Something of an oddity in the fleet, she was sold to the Blue Star Line in 1929. E. FLUCK

Corry 'Star' Line fleet of five steamers – *Star of Australia, Star of Scotland, Star of India, Star of Victoria* and *Star of England* were included, although the *Star of Victoria* and *Star of England* were still under construction and did not enter service for the C&D Line until February and May 1914 respectively. Only the three ships of Royden's 'Indra' Line then working on Tyser Line berths were brought into the new company, the *Indralema, Indrabarah* and *Indrapura.* The other seven 'Indra' steamers were engaged in a service from New York to the Far East and they, and the rights held by the line in the New York-China Conference, were sold to Alfred Holt's Blue Funnel Line in August 1915. The remaining nine ships of the C&D Line were 'Port' steamers from Wm. Milburn & Co or that company's Anglo-Australasian Steam Navigation Co Ltd. Eight were in service and the new building *Port Albany* ran trials on 26 May 1914. The fleet was reduced to 24 after the sale of the *Port Pirie* in April 1915.

One of the first decisions of the board was a colour scheme for the new line. It decided to adopt the Tyser Line colours of grey hull, white upperworks and a buff black topped funnel. The Tyser houseflag – a red St Georges and a blue St Andrews cross on a white ground (the widths of the crosses being equivalent to one fifth of the flag width) – also became the company house flag. The existing names of the ships were retained. It eventually proved difficult to maintain uniformity with the Tyser Line lavender grey and the company adopted in later years a Pacific grey colour, common to Royal Navy warships on duty in Pacific waters. The funnel was originally red, but after World War II a more orange-red was developed, almost comparable in shade to what was commonly known as 'red lead' undercoat.

On commencement, the company had three sailings a month to Australia and a slightly better than a monthly sailing to and from New Zealand with not less than a monthly dispatch from New York to Australia and New Zealand. (The story of the East Coast North American service and the formation of the Montreal Australia & New Zealand Line is contained in Appendix 1). The seven large, recently completed, ships (*Makarini, Port Lincoln, Indrapura, Port Macquarie, Hawkes Bay, Star of Victoria* and *Star of England*) also carried up to 1,000 migrants to Victoria in specially fitted accommodation in the tween decks. The company quickly moved to order new tonnage to replace older ships which were now becoming too costly to operate. In October 1914 Workman Clark gained orders for two new vessels and three months later a third ship was ordered. A fourth new contract was added in March 1915. Hawthorn Leslie was also asked to submit bids for two further ships and a third vessel was later added. In May 1914 the new company had also decided to increase the modest 159 cubic metres of refrigerated space in the newly completed *Port Lincoln* and *Port Macquarie* to 6,560 cubic metres, but as a result of the war this additional capacity was not installed.

The new board also saw the benefit of having senior managers from London permanently based in Sydney, New Zealand and New York. Harry Benson from Tysers remained in Sydney. In May 1915 ill health forced him to retire from his position and he came to London, being replaced in Sydney by Herbert Corry. Captain Richard Todd, had for many years been the senior Tyser line representative in New Zealand, and he continued in this role, but on his sudden death on 30 May 1916, his assistant Julius Sandtmann, was appointed manager. The company was concerned with its image on this change as Sandtmann was of German nationality. He was initially asked to revert to his former position of secretary but London felt he would have to be replaced, even though he had already served Tyser & Co in New Zealand for 30 years. Sandtmann understood the situation and voluntarily resigned on 31 December 1917. London-based John Royden Rooper (pronounced Roper), a grandson of Sir Thomas Royden, and a nephew of C&D/Cunard director Thos. Royden, who had been sent out to New Zealand in 1916, replaced him. Jack Rooper (known to his colleagues as Jack and to his family as Jos) could trace his ancestry back to Norman days. Although rising to the rank of captain and adjutant in the territorials in the Denbighshire Hussars Yeomanry, the family affliction of deafness eventually saw him invalided out of the army. He had commenced his business career in the Royden shipbuilding business in Liverpool and through that company operating steamers on the Tyser Line berth, he moved to London. When the Tyser interests formed the C&D Line he became, at the age of 24, a key figure in the management of the new company. In New Zealand Jack Rooper soon decided that the New Zealand-wide business of the new company necessitated moving the head office from Napier to Wellington, which was done in 1916. He also arranged for an office building (the Maritime Building) in Wellington

Jack Rooper was a key figure in the management of the C&D Line and Port Line. He headed the New Zealand management from 1916 to 1921, and then returned to London, becoming London manager and a director of the company from 1926 to 1957, and for much of this time in a managing role. MRS SHIRLEY RICHARDSON

to be jointly built for the C&D Line and the New Zealand Shipping Company, as both firms had purchased adjoining lots. The contract was signed 9 May 1917 and although Port Line vacated it when container services were introduced, it remained until 2004, when it was demolished hurriedly and despite public outcry, the New Zealand office for P&O Nedlloyd – P&O being the parent of the NZSCo from 1916 and became P&O Nedlloyd in 1997. T. Ashley Sparkes went to the New York office. These managers maintained a good rapport with the London management and the close 'family style' adopted worked well for the company.

Shortly after the establishment of the C&D Line, it signed an agreement on 12 March 1915 with Gibbs Bright & Co Ltd, Sydney, to act as agents for the ships at nearly all the ports on the Australian mainland. Gibbs Bright had been the agent for Wm. Milburn's Anglo-Australasian Steam Navigation Co service since shortly after its ships first came to Australia and had subsequently worked closely with Tyser and Co in the promotion of the Australian Union Line. The agency contract was reviewed in 1924 and a long-term agreement was signed. Gibbs, Bright and Co, which became Gibbs, Bright & Co Pty Ltd, in 1963, remained the agents for Port Line until December 1967. The agency was conducted with the utmost trust and C & D/Port Line later became partners with associated companies of Gibbs Bright involved in stevedoring and wool dumping.

In New Zealand most of the agency appointments remained the Tyser Line agencies although a number of changes took place during World War I or shortly after. In Auckland the merchant firm of Heather, Roberton & Co was superseded by

Farmers Co-op Auctioneering Co, stock and station agents. On the East Coast, Williams & Kettle shared the agency work in Napier with the Hawke's Bay Farmers Co-op Association, another stock and station agency able to influence wool cargo to the line. Williams and Kettle relinquished the agency in Gisborne to the Gisborne Sheep Farmers Frozen Meat Co. Merchants W. M. Bannatyne & Co were the agents in Wellington, but were replaced in 1916 when the C&D Line opened its own office there. The principal partner in Bannatyne & Co was Harold Beauchamp and a subsidiary company, Smith Beauchamp & Co obtained the C&D Line business in Wanganui and New Plymouth. In the South Island, Kinsey, Barns & Co, (later Kinsey & Co) at Christchurch and D. C. Turnbull & Co Ltd, Timaru were agents at the ports of Lyttelton and Timaru. J. W. Swift & Co, Bradford woolbuyers with a Dunedin office, initially looked after the agency work at Port Chalmers and Dunedin but later shared this work with H.L. Tapley & Co, who also stevedored the C&D ships; (Swift & Tapley merged in 1949 to become Tapley Swift Shipping Agencies). The first agent at Invercargill was D.W. Henderson & Co, but stock and station agency J. E. Watson & Co soon took over and remained the agents through the history of C & D/Port Line. With further changes over the years and with the company becoming involved in branch offices in the late twentieth century, D.C. Turnbull & Company in Timaru and Tapley Swift Shipping Agencies in Dunedin are the only original Port Line agents still in business under their existing names as shipping agents (2006). Until 2005 Williams & Kettle Limited remained a prominent independent rural servicing company on the East Coast of the North Island but was no longer a shipping agent.

Fortunately the strenuous efforts of the Tyser Line in breaking into the Australian and New Zealand trades from the 1880s and Milburn's Anglo Australasian Steam Navigation Company from 1883 to Australia, saw the Commonwealth and Dominion Line commence business with comfortable pool shares within the consortium of other British lines in the same trades. Had it not been for the outbreak of World War I in early August 1914, the excellent operating profit of £227,799 for the first nine months might have been higher.

As soon as war was declared with Germany, the British government requisitioned *Muritai*, which joined the Battle Cruiser Squadron as a storeship. The New Zealand government took *Hawkes Bay* and the *Star of India* for conversion to troopships. The Australian government made similar requisitions of the *Star of England, Star of Victoria, Port Lincoln, Port Macquarie* and *Marere.* The *Star of England* had only been delivered on May 1914 and was fitted out in Australia to carry 29 officers, 499 troops and 476 horses. The *Star of Victoria* was equipped to carry 30 officers, 511 troops and 537 horses, *Port Lincoln* 25 officers, 370 troops and 371 horses, *Port Macquarie* 25 officers, 371 troops and 456 horses and the smaller and older *Marere* 10 officers, 100 troops and 475 horses. All these vessels, with the exception of *Port Macquarie,* and including the two New Zealand requisitions, carried the first Australian and New Zealand troops to war. The huge convoy of thirty-eight transports assembled in King George's Sound, Western Australia and sailed on 1 November 1914, escorted by four cruisers. On the way to Alexandria, where the troops and horses disembarked, HMAS *Sydney* broke away from the convoy in the Indian Ocean and effectively destroyed the German cruiser *Emden. Port Macquarie* was employed to transport members of the Royal Australian Naval Reserve from Melbourne to Suvla Bay during June to August 1915. Shortly after she had been renamed in 1916, *Niwaru* as *Port Lyttelton,* carried C Company, 20th Reinforcements from Wellington (sailed 8 December 1916) and arrived Plymouth, England on 18 February 1917.

Other vessels in the fleet were diverted on British government service as their voyages terminated. Eventually all vessels were under imperial government requisition but in virtually every case were still managed by the company under the direction of the Shipping Controller. It was not until 11 September 1919 that all steamers were released from requisition. When it came for the first Australian troops to return home, *Port Hacking* sailed Devonport on 3 December 1918 with 673 personnel and the following year *Port Napier* was the last transport when she left England on 23 December 1919.

The first wartime casualty was the former Tyser Line steamer *Marere,* sunk by gunfire from the submarine *U-35* 36 miles east of Malta in January 1916. The submarine was on the surface and the *Marere* decided to fight with her three-pounder Hotchkiss gun, but the shells all fell well short. Although Captain P. E. Mello was urged by radio not to surrender, the bolts holding the gun mounting were beginning to give way and not one shot had got anywhere near the submarine, so when German shells started to hit, he gave the order to abandon ship. The submarine fired two torpedoes which both missed and she had to sink the *Marere* by gunfire. The crew was picked up by the hospital ship *Neuralia* (1912, 9,082) and taken to Alexandria.

In March 1916 the C&D Line board decided, for the sake of uniformity, to name all the ships in the fleet after Australian or New Zealand ports and the *Marere* was the only ship in the fleet that was never given a 'Port' name. When it came to selecting new names, not all the company's wishes were granted. It was intended to call *Mimiro* the *Port Douglas, Nerehana,* the *Port Nelson* and the *Star of England*, the *Port Jackson*, but the Board of Trade declined these names and the vessels became the *Port Hacking, Port Hardy* and *Port Sydney* respectively.

The second vessel lost was the *Port Nicholson* in January 1917. She had carried 1,000 troops from Sydney and after they had disembarked at Devonport, she was ordered to Dunkirk to discharge frozen meat. She struck two mines eight miles from Dunkirk, both exploding simultaneously, one near the forepart of number five hold and the other in the after part of the engine room. An attempt was made to tow her into shallow water but she gradually settled down, capsized and sank in 11 metres of water.

Three weeks later the *Port Adelaide* was torpedoed without warning at 4 pm

Troops line the decks and rigging as the *Port Nicholson*, formerly the *Makarini,* sails from Sydney on 8 November 1916 with 1000 troops for Plymouth. No sooner had she landed the troops and crossed to Dunkirk to discharge her frozen cargo than she was mined and sunk in January 1917. A. DUFTY

and again at 5 pm and sank 180 miles south west of Fastnet Rock, Ireland on 3 February 1917. The master was taken aboard the submarine and became a prisoner of war but the 96 passengers and crew were safely picked up by the Dutch freighter *Samarinda* (1912, 6,825) and landed at Vigo. The company gave £100 to the master and crew of *Samarinda* for taking care of the crew.

The *Port Curtis* was also caught by a submarine and shelled. She fought back for four hours but exhausted all her ammunition and eventually had to be abandoned. The submarine sunk *Port Curtis* with time bombs. Captain William Mason, who was badly wounded in the engagement, was awarded the DSC for his ship's gallant fight.

When an underwater explosion sank the *Port Kembla* so close to New Zealand, off Cape Farewell in September 1917, it was widely thought that a bomb had been planted by a saboteur. It was eventually accepted that the ship had hit a mine laid by the German commerce raider *Wolf.*

Although *Port Victor* was torpedoed on 26 September 1917 about 30 miles south of St. Catherines Point in the English Channel, she was able to limp into Southampton the same day.

The remaining two losses by enemy action saw the *Port Campbell* torpedoed and sunk 115 miles WSW of Bishop Rock in April 1918 and the *Port Hardy* was lost

A sister ship to the *Port Curtis*, the *Port Kembla*, followed two months later in 1910. She was sunk in 1917 by a mysterious explosion, thought to be a bomb, but subsequently confirmed as a mine laid by the German commerce raider *Wolf.*

The Tyser Line steamer *Muritai* was renamed *Port Victor* in 1916. Shown here in Adelaide River, she remained in the fleet until 1935. E. FLUCK

Between 1919 and 1920 the Commonwealth & Dominion Line managed the surrendered German cargo and passenger ship *Valencia*, seen here at Sydney. WM. LIVERMORE

on passage from Buenos Aires to Genoa with a full cargo of foodstuffs for the Italian government. Although the ship sighted a torpedo track, she was unable to change course before it struck. The explosion wrecked the engine room and probably blew in the bulkheads. The *Port Hardy* sank stern-first in 20 minutes with the loss of seven lives.

While on passage in a Transatlantic convoy from New York, the *Port Stephens* collided with the *North Cambria* (1907, 4,635) off Ushant on 2 August 1918. Both ships were running without lights and the *Port Stephens* struck *North Cambria* at right angles. She sank within three minutes and all 26 members of her crew were drowned.

In October 1918, *Port Phillip* collided with the U.S. Navy collier *Proteus* (1913, 10,653) in Ambrose Channel, New York and sank in shallow water in Gravesend Bay. The company received £137,017 in compensation for the *Port Phillip/Proteus* collision. Less than a month later, the *Port Hunter* collided with the tug *Covington* (1899, 401) off Vineyard Haven as she steamed out of Boston bound for St Nazaire. She was badly damaged by the smaller vessel and was beached at Hedgefence, Vineyard Shed, Nantucket. By January, all hope of salvage was abandoned and she was considered a total loss.

In 1919 the C&D Line was asked to manage the former Hamburg America Line steamer *Valencia* (1913, 5,232) for the Shipping Controller until she was sold to new owners. During 1918 C&D had also been asked take over management of *War Hecuba* (1919, 7,920) then under construction with delivery early in 1919, but she

Sir Alfred Booth, (left) was chairman of the Cunard Steam-Ship Company in 1916 when it acquired the Commonwealth & Dominion Line. With Sir Alfred is Herbert Corry, who was vice-chairman of the Commonwealth & Dominion Line from 1926 to 1939 and chairman 1939 to 1947. He was also a director of the Cunard Line and was deputy-chairman of that company for several years. M. REEVE

was sold to Blue Star Line prior to delivery and completed as the *Albionstar*.

The most significant event for the Commonwealth and Dominion Line during the war was the amalgamation with the Cunard Steam-Ship Company of Liverpool. Orchestrated by Thomas Royden, who sat on both boards, Cunard acquired all the shares in the C&D Line in exchange for 561,811 new ordinary Cunard shares, £365,000 5 per cent preference shares, £1,000,000 6 per cent 2nd preference shares as well as some war loans and cash. On the share prices at the time the value of the transaction was just on £5,000,000, almost double the value of the company set on the establishment of the C&D Line just over two years previously. The price also recognised the value of the goodwill of the extensive trade pool shares held by the company. The arrangement was finalised on 25 May 1916 and signed 8 June 1916 but was kept very much 'in house'. The chairman of Cunard, Sir Alfred Booth, explained the reason for the purchase by pointing out that the basic Cunard business centred exclusively on the passenger and cargo service between Liverpool and the United States and this single trade was subject to wide variations in earnings. By widening the business coverage, firstly to Canada and India, and now to a line trading to Australia and New Zealand 'a sound balance has been secured, which would enable the company to face with confidence, the difficulties, and the fluctuations in trade after the war.' The acquisition had to be approved by a special meeting of Cunard shareholders. In a remarkable speech, the chairman, Sir Alfred Booth, never went into any detail of the financial figures involved, and essentially asked shareholders to trust the directors and approve the deal.

> I cannot give the exact price to be paid for the Commonwealth and Dominion Line shares, or, as I should prefer to put it, the exact terms of the conversion because it is

not in your interest that such details should be published. In any case such figures would be misleading, unless accompanied by a searching analysis of balance sheets of the two companies drawn up on the same date and a careful estimate of the immediate prospects of each company with regard to profits. I am sure you will agree that it would be foolish to make public such intimate details... 'Your real justification for supporting the resolution which I am submitting to you is that you have confidence in your directors. If you have not that confidence you should vote against the resolution in spite of the most plausible figures. The point I want to impress upon you then is this: We are not buying a great business at the inflated prices of today, but entering into partnership with it in such a way that our new shareholders on the one hand, and our old shareholders on the other hand will each take their fair share of whatever opportunities of profit the future may bring. In coming to terms it was, therefore, possible to eliminate on both sides, war values and war profits, except in so far as it was necessary to make certain adjustments in cash or fixed interest-bearing securities. I should not have been willing, and it would not have been financially possible, to have carried through the transaction on any other basis, and it was because the Commonwealth and Dominion Line directors also made it a condition that their shareholders should retain in full their interest in the future profits of the combined undertaking that it has been possible to arrive at an agreement at all. The attitude of the Commonwealth and Dominion Line directors throughout the negotiations is the best augury for the future success of the enlarged Cunard Company. They, with their fellow shareholders in the Commonwealth and Dominion Line Ltd., of today, will become large shareholders of Cunard ordinary shares, and they believe, as I do, that the future earning capacity of these shares is not necessarily measured by a Stock Exchange quotation based very largely on immediate dividend prospects. When the agreement is carried into effect the interests of these new ordinary shareholders will be identical with yours. The partnership will prove advantageous both to the new shareholders and the old, because it will give increased strength and greater power of development in every section of the combined business."[1]

Thomas Royden, Cunard deputy chairman, seconded the motion and it was carried unanimously. Nowadays, the approval of a transaction of this size, would require the production of full sets of financial analysis, projections and explanations, all bound in a prospectus of a 100 pages or more! Ironically those C&D shareholders who retained their new Cunard shares found that by 1936, after all the Depression years, the £1 shares were valued at five shillings and the 6 per cent dividends on the 2nd preference shares were five years in arrears!

W.P. Tyser and C.T. Milburn, chairman and deputy chairman of the C&D Line, were appointed to the Cunard board while the Cunard chairman, Sir Alfred Booth and Sir Percy Bates joined the C&D board. Walter P. Tyser became the largest individual shareholder in Cunard with members of the Milburn, Royden and Corry families also having sizeable holdings. Considering the humble beginnings of the Tyser brothers

The first steamer built for the C&D Line was the *Port Darwin*. Initially ordered in 1914, she was delayed due to wartime conditions and did not enter service until early 1918. A very lucky and successful ship, she served for 30 years. E. FLUCK

and the battles they had to secure pool shares in the various trades they had entered, it must have been somewhat satisfying for Walter Tyser to achieve the largest shareholding of any family in one of the major British shipping companies.

Having the Cunard Line as a parent proved a significant factor in later years as without the Cunard guarantee it was clear that the C&D Line could not have maintained the levels of new buildings at the pace that they were ordering new ships. In 1921 payments for ships under construction were expected to total £2,500,000 over the next two years and this level of expenditure could not have been handled without Cunard backing. Writing to his New York director in 1916, Walter Tyser said the amalgamation with Cunard had enormously strengthened the C&D Line.

In February 1917 it was decided to use the name Cunard Line Australasian Service Commonwealth and Dominion Line Limited and this name was to be placed on all doors and stationery. Some confusion arose outside the United Kingdom on the prominence of the Cunard Line name and it was emphasized that this appendage was secondary to Commonwealth and Dominion Line. The only other significant change occurred after the war in 1919 when the fleet was returning to peace-time colours. It was agreed that all the ships would paint the funnel in Cunard Line colours, red with black top and two thin equally spaced black bands on the red.

Cunard seldom interfered in C&D business and the minute books record that there was more discussion between the companies about charitable donations and occasionally Cunard would suggest the one amount be given, but from both companies. In 1919 Cunard also purchased a controlling interest in Thos. & Jno. Brocklebank

The *Port Bowen*, shown outward-bound from Adelaide, her final Australian port on the run to Europe, ended her career just prior to the outbreak of war by stranding off the port of Wanganui in July 1939; she was eventually scrapped on the beach. E. FLUCK

An oddity compared to all the other ships built for the C&D Line fleet after World War I, the *Port Curtis* had been intended as a standard single screw G class steamer, a class designed to replace many of the refrigerated ships lost in the war. E. FLUCK

Limited, a Liverpool shipping company dating from 1770, which had services from United Kingdom and Continental ports to Ceylon and India and from those countries to United States eastern seaboard ports. Cunard allowed Brocklebanks to operate on a similar 'arms length' basis as it had with the C&D Line. In 1929 the chairman of Brocklebanks, Colonel Denis Bates, joined the board of Port Line and Herbert Corry, deputy chairman of Port Line, was invited to join the board of T. & J. Brocklebank Ltd.

By the end of 1917 the C&D Line was anxiously waiting to receive new buildings to replace the vessels lost. The first new ship, and the first to be specifically built for the line, the *Port Darwin,* was to be delivered in November 1915, but was not able to undergo trials until 18 December 1917 due to wartime delays in the shipyard. The four other ships from Workman Clark were delivered 30 April 1918 (*Port Denison*), 20 May 1919 (*Port Bowen*), 11 November 1919 (*Port Caroline*) and 15 May 1920 (*Port Curtis*). The *Port Curtis* had been laid down as a standard G class war-built standard type. Twenty-nine were ordered but only one had been completed when hostilities ended. The *Port Curtis* was therefore fitted out to the company's requirements. She was the only single screw ship amongst the vessels built for the company until the late 1930s. The three Hawthorn Leslie buildings were the *Port Nicholson* delivered 13 May 1919, *Port Adelaide* on 23 December 1919 and *Port Kembla* on 20 July 1920. Before these vessels were all delivered the company ordered a further four more steamers from Workman Clark and two more from Hawthorn Leslie.

In 1920 the *Port Stephens* came upon the disabled American steamer *Tashmoo* (1919, 3,283), 1,200 miles west of Ireland and towed her to safety in Queenstown, Ireland. The fully-laden *Port Stephens* was on passage from Melbourne to Hull, via Norfolk, Virginia when she encountered *Tashmoo,* which was carrying general cargo from New York to Cork, on 26 April 1920. The American ship had burnt-out boilers and over five days *Port Stephens* towed her to Queenstown throughout heavy sea conditions and a strong easterly gale. The C&D Line gained a £10,000 salvage award, and a further £3,200 was distributed between the master and the crew.

Between 1914 and 1920 the company had few concerns about securing sufficient cargoes to fill the ships as the imperial government in 1914 had undertaken to buy all the New Zealand exports and they had concluded a similar arrangement with Australia for meat, wool, wheat and other commodities. As a result, the British lines with pool shares in the respective trades co-ordinated the tonnage available to meet requirements and for the first time Lines' committees were set up to handle the shipping. When the war was coming to conclusion there was a degree of apprehension about what would happen in peacetime, but this came more from the meat producers in New Zealand than any one other sector. In 1914 the C&D Line had confirmed new contracts with the principal Tyser line customers, Hawke's Bay Farmers Meat Company (Nelson Bros), Southland Frozen Meat Company and Otaihape Farmers Meat & Produce Company, Wanganui.

From 1918 W. Douglas Lysnar, a former mayor of Gisborne and Chairman of the Poverty Bay Farmers Meat Company, began writing regularly to the New Zealand government warning it of the consequences when the British commandeer of New Zealand meat ended. He predicted powerful overseas trading interests would dominate the production and sale of New Zealand meat and these companies and the British shipping lines would have a total monopoly over the trade. Meetings of farmers around

The spartan British tramp ship *Admiral Codrington*, which was purchased by the Poverty Bay Farmers Meat Company in 1920, made three loss-making voyages to London with Gisborne meat. She is shown at anchor in Sydney harbour. WM. LIVERMORE

the country echoed his thoughts, and although the government later moved in 1920 to develop a Control Board for the meat industry, it did not move fast enough for Lysnar, who decided to protect his company's interests by acquiring a ship to carry Gisborne meat to Britain.

Arriving in Auckland in January 1920, the 6,629 ton steamer *Admiral Codrington* (1918, 6,629) had been purchased by the Poverty Bay Farmers Meat Company at Port Said, complete with crew. In Auckland several of her holds were insulated and refrigerating machinery was installed, to give a total frozen capacity of 9,447 cubic metres. From Auckland she sailed to Gisborne to load her first cargo of 105,000 carcasses of mutton, sailing from Wellington on 3 May for London via Wallaroo where she was fixed to load 64,000 sacks of wheat. Apart from 700 carcasses of mutton and 800 cases of offal which were condemned on arrival in London, all her remaining meat cargo was well frozen, but somewhat stale. However the ship was not responsible for this condition as in order to build up sufficient carcasses in Gisborne to fill the insulated spaces, storage of cargo had to start many months in advance of the arrival of the ship. Almost immediately from this first voyage Lysnar found it was difficult to provide a premium service for Gisborne meat exporters with only the one ship. Over the next three years she made two further voyages with Gisborne meat, closely watched by C&D and the other lines in the trade. Shortly after she arrived in Liverpool on her third voyage it was revealed that the Poverty Bay company was close to bankruptcy as there was insufficient livestock in the area to supply three meat-processing plants. The company was sold to Vestey Bros, but the *Admiral Codrington,* which had accumulated losses of £6,000, was excluded from the Vestey purchase.

While the *Admiral Codrington* was pioneering a 'do it yourself' shipping service by a New Zealand company, the pressure was coming on the government to establish a shipping line owned by the meat producers and the government, with the capital coming from a levy on exports. The government would commit no funds to the concept, but in association with the farming interests, legislation was passed in 1922 establishing the New Zealand Meat Producers Board. A similar move was made for the dairy industry through the creation of the New Zealand Dairy Board in 1924. The boards had very wide powers and full authority to negotiate all the contracts for the shipment of meat and dairy cargoes.

The three British groups, Shaw Savill & Albion, NZSCo/Federal and the C&D Line had in 1920 signed an agreement 'in order to facilitate the continuance of the co-operation between the Lines' and thus promote the efficiency and the economy of the services'. Effective from 1 January 1921, the agreement became known as the Benmacow Agreement (named after H.C. Benson of the C&D Line, John MacMillan of Shaw Savill & Albion Line and C.J. Cowan of the NZS/Federal.) Historically the C&D interests on formation of the line had been more concerned with the carriage of frozen meat so the company only had a 10 per cent pool share of dairy cargoes but as all ships would be nominated to load in sequence under the new arrangements the C&D line share of dairy cargoes was increased to 17.5 per cent. Overall the split between the lines in the 1920 agreement was Shaw Savill & Albion 35 per cent, NZS/Federal 42.5 per cent and C&D Line 22.5 per cent. Any Union Steam Ship Company share was accommodated within the NZS/Federal allocation. A similar agreement between the same lines was signed 24 December 1920 to regulate the outward schedules from the United Kingdom to Australia and New Zealand.

Ironically, the 'leader' of the three British shipping groups at this time was Allan Hughes, the former head of the Federal Steam Navigation Company and the youngest participant in the exclusive club. Hughes had battled to secure a share of the New Zealand trade, finally achieving a foothold at the end of 1906. Although his company was technically taken over by New Zealand Shipping Company in 1912, Hughes was invited to join the board of that company. In 1919 he became the chairman and was therefore in effective control of the NZSCo's 42.5 per cent of the trade. For the next eight years, Hughes dominated conference affairs and ensured the Lines consolidated their grip on the trades. Jack Rooper commented that 'as Herbert Corry reminds me, old Hughes once said any fool can carry 100% of the trade at cut rates'.[2] Whilst the Tyser Bros, and later Hughes, had fought the established two lines in the 1880s/1890s, they became the strongest supporters of the conference once inside it. Hughes's strong leadership also benefited the C&D Line, although in another aside, Corry commented that 'Hughes was clearly a wily old man, with few decisions being taken in his absence'.[3] On another occasion, Jack Rooper, writing to a colleague said 'Allan Hughes has been down on the Riviera and not one of his minions here will lift a little finger to make a decision while he is away'.[4] Corry quietly worked hard in succeeding years to unite the Lines with more collective decision-making.

When the New Zealand Meat Producers Board concluded its freighting requirements with the British lines in September 1922, the *Admiral Codrington* was excluded and she was eventually sold in 1926 by the Glasgow consortium which held the £60,000 mortgage on the vessel. The costly losses built up on her voyages, as well as a dramatic decline in ship values between 1920 and 1926, were a salutary lesson to any other parties who might be ambitious enough to run their own shipping line.

With the clean-up of the British Government stocks of meat after the war, the surplus, mainly beef, held in cold stores in England, Australia and New Zealand was sold to Vestey Bros, owners of the Blue Star Line. Over eight months from October 1920, this company sent its own steamers *Albionstar* (1919, 7,920) (2 voyages), *Stuartstar* (1899, 5,715), *Vikingstar* (1919 6,445), *Normanstar* (1919, 6,817) and *Royalstar* (1919, 7,900) to lift the New Zealand portion, and apart from the *Admiral Codrington* shipments, these were the first and only occasions that significant quantities of New Zealand meat were shipped to Britain, outside the control of the Conference Lines.

The three British lines had enjoyed the benefits of dealing with the one party during wartime requisition and welcomed the new arrangements. Staff from the companies set up conference committees to manage the trade and to apply uniformity of freighting methods, while other committees dealt with scheduling the fleets to meet the producer boards' requirements. The companies were also able to better rationalise their outward sailings from the UK to Australasian ports. The service frequencies were all centred around the requirements for the meat and dairy cargoes, but the coverage was more than adequate for wool and general cargo shipments. Some companies had links with the Australian trade and with that country taking more import cargo than New Zealand, many of the lines' ships loaded out to Australia and then crossed to New Zealand to load back. The combination of the two countries provided better space utilisation over the whole of the 24,000 mile round voyage.

On 26 November 1920 the British lines in the Australian trade signed a pooling agreement to cover the homeward trade shares and this arrangement became effective from 31 March 1921. Herbert Corry had been a leading negotiator in finalising the agreement. The signatories were P&O, British India Steam Navigation Company, Orient Line, Commonwealth & Dominion Line, Alfred Holt, P&O Branch service (the former Wm Lund's Blue Anchor line service), Oceanic White Star Line, Geo. Thompson's Aberdeen Line, Federal Steam Navigation Company, Trinder Anderson's Australind Shipping Company and Ellerman & Bucknall Lines. The pool required over-carriers to reimburse under-carriers within it, so the arrangements provided an incentive for lines to plan their sailings so they only achieved their pool entitlement. Outside of the traditional liner cargoes, the C&D vessels also carried parcels of asphalt, chalk, cement, wheat, metal concentrates, sugar, potash, and timber all under separate charter party contracts. Most of these bulk cargoes were considered 'non-pool' cargoes and were excluded from the agreed trade shares. There were also shipments of both domestic and wild animals and this was a common practice throughout the history of

The C&D Line carried more steel for the Sydney Harbour Bridge than any other shipping line, and the photograph shows *Port Auckland* leading a group of cargo ships as they sailed under the bridge at its opening on 19 March 1932. PORT LINE ARCHIVES, UNIVERSITY OF LIVERPOOL

the company. Some shipments were quite large and included 25 polo ponies from Sydney to Hull, 15-quarter horses from London to Australia, 10 polled Hereford beasts from Australia to Liverpool. Mrs. Jessie Tyser, the wife of Walter P. Tyser, had a keen interest in birds (as well as Australian and New Zealand postage stamps) and for many years C&D Line masters were asked to carry various Australian exotic and colourful birds home to Britain. In quite a number of cases, masters had to report that the birds had died on the voyage. The London office accumulated a considerable file of correspondence dealing with the shipment requests from the chairman's wife over a long period of years, and even after his retirement.[5]

One important contract in 1922 was from Dorman Long to transport all the steel for the Sydney Harbour Bridge. The ships loaded it at Middlesbrough and discharged it at a special temporary berth close to the north tower of the bridge. In order to meet the regularity required for each shipment, C&D Line elected to share the contract with the Aberdeen Line and the P&O Branch Service. The bridge took a total of 53,650 tonnes of steel and, of this tonnage, the C&D Line carried 19,300 tonnes. When it was opened on 19 March 1932, the *Port Auckland* led the flotilla of cargo ships passing under the structure.

In later years, another modest, but historically important cargo, was the shipment of Captain James Cook's cottage from Great Ayton in North Yorkshire to Melbourne. Purchased by the government of Victoria it was dismantled, brick by brick, and shipped to Melbourne in *Port Dunedin* in February 1934.The shipment was made up of 300 cases with each stone and brick carefully recorded so that the cottage, dating from 1769, could be re-built in Fitzroy Gardens, Melbourne to coincide with the 1934 centenary celebrations of the State of Victoria.

The C&D Line, in conjunction with the Aberdeen White Star Line, introduced a direct fortnightly service from Hamburg to Australia, with the *Port Curtis* taking the first sailing on her departure from Hamburg 8 June 1922.

The line's services out of Australia from 1914 related solely to the Australian mainland, exclusive of Tasmania. That island had been well served in the years prior to the opening of the Panama Canal in 1914, as Tasmania was conveniently placed on the great circle route and as a coaling destination for the early steam services of ships mainly en route to New Zealand. The ships of Shaw Savill & Albion and the NZSCo had regularly called at Hobart but with the opening of the Panama Canal, the companies notified the Tasmanian government in 1919 that they would have to discontinue direct calls. The two shipping brokers in the Tasmanian trade, Anderson, Green & Company and Staley, Radford & Company, made arrangements for the C&D Line to provide monthly calls at Hobart. The *Port Nicholson* made the first on 19 April 1920 and thereafter vessels of the line became frequent visitors to Hobart and other Tasmanian ports. The *Port Hobart* visited her name port for the first time in March 1927.

From 1922 another way-port to be regularly serviced by the New Zealand lines was Suva in Fiji. A vessel of SS&A/NZS or C&D Line was programmed to call at Suva every six weeks, diverting from the usual passage direct from Panama to Auckland. In 1925 the C&D Line inaugurated direct calls at South Island, New Zealand ports on vessels coming from London to Fiji. Instead of the Fiji sailings proceeding to Auckland they were loaded in London with South Island cargo to give a faster direct service to Port Chalmers and Lyttelton. The *Port Dunedin* inaugurated the direct South Island service on her maiden voyage in 1925. The service was maintained until the container services took over, with Blue Star vessels taking their turn in the scheduling from 1958.

The second group of new buildings entered service between 1922-24 with the *Port Campbell* delivered 27 June 1922, *Port Auckland* 3 August 1922, *Port Brisbane* 4 December 1923, and *Port Wellington* 22 February 1924, all from Workman Clark. The company initially decided to name the second vessel *Port Douglas,* but when this was not approved *Port Auckland* was nominated with *Port Clinton* as a second choice. Port Clinton was the original name for Port Bowen in Queensland, and it was also the name of an obscure port in the Gulf of St Vincent, on the western side north of

The first *Port Auckland* in the fleet was originally intended to be named *Port Douglas*, but the British Board of Trade would not approve this name. She was a victim of the submarine war in the North Atlantic in 1943. E. FLUCK

Ardrossan and almost opposite Port Wakefield. It is not known which Port Clinton the company had in mind, but the name was never again proposed or used for any later ship. The two Hawthorn Leslie vessels were *Port Hunter* delivered 30 September 1922 and *Port Hardy* on 6 February 1923.

During the war several ships had their passenger accommodation temporarily increased and in 1919 the board agreed to look at the carriage of third class passengers in the tween decks if demand arose. All the main line trade ships built for the line from 1918 were fitted with accommodation for 12 passengers. Apart from use of the accommodation by management and staff travelling to the company's trading areas, the berths also had a marketing value in that they were keenly sought after by a number of the line's customers. A quiet pleasant voyage and being well looked after by the ship's company from the captain down was welcomed by those who did not want to spend six weeks or more having a high social life on a regular passenger ship.

The C&D Line directors had decided in 1922 to send two junior staff members from the London office on an educational tour of Australia and New Zealand each year and they also travelled in the company ships. The practice continued throughout the life of the company and many firm friendships evolved between head office staff and company and agency staff in Australasia.

With the British lines being asked to carry more refrigerated cargoes, other than meat and dairy shipments, the British Department of Scientific and Industrial Research sent some specialists to Australia in 1923 to investigate the reasons behind the heavy losses incurred with the carriage of Tasmanian applies. The apples were being affected by 'brown heart', which they found was caused by an accumulation of carbon dioxide, which the fruit itself produced. There was also an excessive depletion of oxygen which was consumed by the fruit. By controlling the ventilation in the

The *Indrabarah*, which spent 58 days ashore off Wanganui in 1913, was not so lucky in 1924, when, as the *Port Elliot*, she ran onto a reef in heavy weather off Horoera Point, north of Gisborne. Much of her cargo was salved, but she gradually broke up over several years. V.H. YOUNG & L.A. SAWYER

cargo spaces, safe carriage of the apples was assured and vessels were fitted with fans in the tween decks and trunking in the lower holds. A further delegation in 1928 studied the problem of achieving uniform temperatures over the deep hold stowages, as the apples generated heat as well as carbon dioxide. In later years the staff of the Low Temperature Research Laboratory at Cambridge was employed to assist the lines with technical matters of this nature.

In 1920 the State Industrial Commission gave approval for the C&D Line to be a self-insurer and this was renewed in 1926 with the company buying investments in lieu of premiums. As the company expanded it was not prudent to assume too large a role in this field and the insurance broking interests of Tyser and Company handled more and more of the company's hull insurances. There were several important claims between 1924 and 1926. Running against a heavy set inshore and in thick weather, the *Port Elliot* drove into a reef off Horoera Point, 80 miles north of Gisborne on passage from Auckland to Wellington just before midnight on 12 January 1924. The ship remained upright with her forward holds flooded. A considerable amount of cargo was later salvaged but the ship never moved from her position on the rocks and was a familiar site for several years before she was finally broken up by the seas, When

The *Port Nicholson* was the first of the steam turbine vessels built for the company after World War I. Because of turbine troubles with a number of vessels, later ships of the series were altered in 1922 from four steam turbines to six. E. FLUCK

The *Port Kembla* was wrecked in the West Indies less than six years after completion. She had bunkered at Norfolk in Virginia, USA, due to a coal shortage in England, and was not travelling on the usual course from the United Kingdom to Panama. E. FLUCK

leaving Launceston for Hobart on the evening of 24 January 1924, the *Port Lyttelton* ran aground on the middle bar, at the mouth of the Tamar River, outside Low Head, and suffered bottom damage. She was refloated on 26 January and re-berthed at Launceston where part of her cargo was transferred to the *Port Hunter* and *Port Lincoln.* She then went to Sydney, arriving there 15 February 1924 where the balance of her cargo was transferred to other vessels. Temporary repairs were effected and it was intended the ship would be sent to Batavia (Jakarta) for permanent repairs. The *Port Lyttelton* was later declared 'black' because of the decision to take her out of Australia for repairs, and she was not able to leave for Batavia until 18 July. She arrived at Batavia on 5 August and after dry-docking it was decided that her age (23), and her damaged condition, as well as the economic situation at the time, did not justify permanent repairs and she then steamed to Genoa for demolition. A fire broke out on the vessel at Genoa on 12 December 1925 and all her timberwork was destroyed.

Another significant insurance incident occurred when the *Port Nicholson* was badly damaged when she struck rocks off Isleta, Las Palmas, on 23/24 October 1924. She was not refloated until 3 November but grounded again at the entrance to the inner harbour. She was eventually taken alongside a wharf on 5 November and after temporary repairs, the Dutch tug *Roode Zee* (1908, 573) towed her to the Tyne for permanent repairs. The company suffered its second marine total loss when the *Port Kembla,* on passage from London to Lyttelton, via Norfolk, Virginia, was wrecked at San Salvador, Watling Island (Bahamas) on 8 July 1926. She was abandoned on 27 August and the master and second officer left the employ of the company. Ironically there was a coal strike in the UK and the vessel had to proceed to Norfolk, Va., to take sufficient bunkers for the passage to New Zealand. As a result she was not on the direct company passage from London to Panama.

On 5 August 1919 a pension scheme for office staff was established (some had been with the company since 1890). The scheme was later enhanced to provide allowances for widows and children of members and in 1956 women office staff could be admitted as contributors. Further refinements were added in 1961 to bring the scheme more in line with modern funds and to guard against inflation. Finally from 31 December 1974 the Cunard and Port Line pension funds were administered as one fund.

After World War I, Jack Rooper returned to London from New Zealand in 1921 and became London manager. Warwick Gregory was placed in charge of New Zealand from 1927 to 1939. Herbert Corry returned to London in 1923, being replaced in Australia, initially by S.J. Coggins and then by W.G. de Gruchy, who controlled the Australian interests of the company from 1927 to 1946. C&D Line established a separate local board of directors in Sydney from 1927 to oversee Australasian trade matters with de Gruchy, and F.G. Murdoch from Gibbs, Bright and Company, being the first two appointments. Bill Donald, who had come into the company from Tysers on its formation in 1914, became London manager in 1927 and retained this role until 1945. He was a director from 1938 and became Chairman 1947 to 1960, President from 1961 to 1965. Herbert Corry was also on the London Board 1923-49 with Jack Rooper 1927-57. T. Ashley Sparkes in New York was also appointed a director in 1917 and remained so until 1952. Messrs Tyser, Benson, Corry, Rooper, Sparkes and Donald were the key players in the affairs and leadership of the

Nursed by the tug Otago, the *Port Dunedin* in her twilight years arrives at her name port of Dunedin.

Port Alma lies at anchor at Hobart 7 October 1962 REX-PRIEST

The *Port Wyndham* anchored in Wellington harbour in August 1965, 30 years after she was built. V.H. YOUNG & L.A. SAWYER

A stalwart of the MANZ Line service, the *Port Saint John* has just completed discharge of her American cargo at Dunedin, and is shown sailing for northern ports on her return voyage.

The *Port Quebec* enters Otago Harbour. The last specialist MANZ Line building for the 1930s, she was requisitioned for war service, before entering commercial service for Port Line at the end of 1947.

Still with her wartime "stump" masts, the *Port Phillip* sails through the Otago Heads in the 1960s.

company, and its success and growth in its first 40 years can be largely attributed to them. Harry Benson, who had done so much to promote the Tyser Line Australasian business in the period from the 1890s up to 1914, retired as managing director of the C&D Line in April 1924 and died in December 1935.

Some years after the acquisition of the C&D Line by Cunard, it was decided that it would be appropriate for both companies to have their own premises in London. It took many months to find a suitable site but eventually Cunard House in 88 Leadenhall Street was completed and was occupied from 26 September 1932. The C&D line managed the building for both companies.

A nasty situation developed in 1925 when the Seamen's Union allowed the employers to take £1 a month from the seamen's wages, an amount which had been given to them the year before. Shipowners were having a lean time financially and induced the union to take this step. Industrial trouble took place mainly in Britain, Australia and New Zealand and at least six C&D Line vessels were held up in Australian ports where several militant union leaders promoted strikes. Trouble started from 19 August and carried on until 30 November but was spasmodic in Britain and New Zealand. The *Port Dunedin* crew refused work at New Plymouth and they were summoned to appear in court where all 28 men were imprisoned for one month and lost six days pay. The vessel was detained at New Plymouth for five weeks before leaving for Wellington where the gaoled crew re-joined the ship once they had agreed to resume work. By the end of October, Australian farmers were preparing to march onto the wharves and take action against the seamen and Queensland ports were the worst effected. The *Port Curtis* had arrived Cairns on 1 September to load a few tonnes of meat. However she got caught in the strike and after ten weeks the police finally removed the striking crew. Prior to this the engineers had been quietly raising steam in order to slip away. This she did at 1.00 am in the morning with a skeleton crew of 15 men, which saw the pilot on the bridge handling the navigation, the chief engineer alone in the engine room and the master trimming coal in the bunkers. Virtually all the rest of the crew were employed as firemen or coal trimmers. She made a rendezvous with the *Port Hardy* to secure water and coal and then proceeded to Brisbane.

In another incident the crew on the *Port Victor* at Brisbane had returned to work and a gang of strikers from the Australian steamer *Barrabool* and deserters from the *Ports' Sydney* and *Auckland* raided the *Port Victor* on 9 November to attack the crew. They carried iron bars, knocked down the quartermaster and proceeded to give the crew in the forecastle a serious beating, as the men could only defend themselves with their bare fists. The chief officer drew his revolver, and the strikers quickly fled over the side of the ship. However, another fight had broken out at the gangway and two more shots were fired with two of the strikers being injured. By this time the police had arrived. The second radio officer was subsequently charged with grievous bodily harm, but after two deferments the charge was dropped. The seamen gained

Sir William Corry, who played a significant role as a financier of the early Tyser Line services. He was a director of the Tyser Line Limited from 1892 to 1915 and the C&D Line from 1914 until his death in 1926. He was also a director of the Cunard Steam-Ship Company 1916-1926. CORRY FAMILY RECORDS

nothing, and lost all their wages while on strike, with most of the disruptions being generated by shore based troublemakers with Communist leanings.

When the C&D line was formed in 1914, Alexander McDonald was appointed superintendent engineer and H. Glover Dearden, assistant superintendent engineer. McDonald was highly respected for his skill as an engineer and also of his knowledge of refrigeration methods. He came into Tysers from being a chief engineer on Corry Line ships. He had received an award in 1894 from a firm of underwriters for having saved a cargo of meat being carried on the *Star of England.* H. Glover Dearden succeeded him as superintendent engineer on his retirement in 1923 and played a leading role in the switch from steam to motor propulsion a few years later. When Alexander Galbraith, the Cunard Line superintendent engineer retired in 1918, the C&D Line engineering team was asked to take over specialist engineering requirements for Cunard Line as well.

The steaming performance of a number of the new ships had not met expectations, and from 1927, seven steamers (*Port Darwin, Port Denison, Port Campbell, Port Auckland, Port Hardy, Port Brisbane* and *Port Wellington*) were equipped with Bauer-Wach turbines. This modification was a low pressure turbine which utilised the remaining energy in the steam exhausted from the reciprocating steam engines and was coupled to the main drive shafts by double reduction gearing through a hydraulic clutch (identical in design to the automatic clutches used in motor vehicles). Swan Hunter & Wigham Richardson had guaranteed an increase of 0.75 knot in loaded condition without any increase in fuel consumption. This was an important benefit over the 12,000 mile passages the ships were operating and the *Port Sydney* and *Port Melbourne*, built in 1914, were also fitted with Bauer-Wach turbines. Of the

During the 1930s and 1940s, many Port Line coal burners were converted to oil fuel, but the 1922-built *Port Campbell*, pictured at Wellington, remained a coal burner all her life until broken up in 1953. V.H. YOUNG & L.A. SAWYER

vessels completed with double expansion steam turbines, only the *Port Nicholson* was left with her original units, while the *Port Bowen, Port Caroline, Port Adelaide* and *Port Kembla,* which were originally built with double expansion steam turbines, were refitted with triple expansion steam turbines, double reduction geared to the two shafts. The *Port Hunter* was built with the triple expansion steam turbines. The single screw *Port Curtis* was fitted with a Star Contra propeller as the supplier had guaranteed an 8 per cent improvement in performance. Up to 1925, 120 Star Contra propellers had been fitted and the manufacturer's expectations had generally been achieved.

In later years some of the coal-burning vessels were switched to oil fuel although the *Port Campbell,* was still burning coal when she went to the breakers in 1953. It was agreed in 1924 that directional wireless would be installed in all vessels. Echo sounding equipment and gyro compasses were progressively added to vessels in the fleet, but some not until the late 1930s. R. & H. Green & Silley Weir Limited of London won a contract to undertake any repairs required on company vessels and in consequence of this, Robert Corry was appointed a director of the repair company.

Both Jack Rooper and Herbert Corry had closely watched the development of the motor ship by Scandinavian companies in the Australian trade, and were enthusiastic about introducing motor ships. In December 1923 Robert Corry was authorised to secure tenders for one vessel propelled by internal combustion engines.

Tenders were received from Messrs John Brown, Swan Hunter & Wigham Richardson, Vickers, Workman Clark and Hawthorn Leslie and considered at the March 1924 Board meeting. There was clearly some apprehension over the proposed change, as the minutes recorded that 'the question of the type of engine to be adopted was discussed and extreme caution was recommended'. Next month the board threw caution to the wind and accepted a tender from Workman Clark for £262,500. At the May meeting directors awarded Swan Hunter & Wigham Richardson a £270,000 contract for a second motor ship. They were delivered as the *Port Dunedin* on 27 May 1925 and the *Port Hobart* on 2 July 1925. Each had two four-cylinder Doxford diesel engines. Previously Doxford engines had been fitted only to single screw vessels, so the *Port Dunedin* and *Port Hobart* were the first twin screw ships with Doxfords. On her maiden voyage the *Port Dunedin* averaged 14.12 knots on a total daily consumption of 20.3 tonnes of oil and the new machinery worked exceptionally well. The *Port Dunedin* and *Port Hobart* both had tall steamer-like funnels when they came into service, but after experience showed that fume problems were limited in motor ships, they were shortened. Some of the Scandinavian motor ships had no funnel at all, and when Jack Rooper was asked why the C&D Line retained traditional funnels he said the company was proud to carry its distinctive colours, and the funnel also acted as a ventilator to the engine room and served as a receptacle for the silencers.

The excellent maiden voyage performances of both ships encouraged the board in January 1927 to order a further motor ship from Workman Clark and two more from Swan Hunter, provided it could match the Workman Clark price. In October, Swan Hunter obtained contracts for two more ships to be driven by Doxford diesels. The five ships were delivered as the *Port Fremantle* 6 April 1927, *Port Huon* 7 June 1927, *Port Gisborne* 4 August 1927, *Port Fairy* 19 October 1928 and *Port Alma* on 3 December 1928. The company had specified that one Swan Hunter vessel was to have Sulzer engines, and *Port Huon* was so fitted.

When the *Port Gisborne* was launched by Iris Rooper, the wife of Jack Rooper on 30 April 1927, it made history by being the first time a launching had been broadcast over the BBC. The breaking of the champagne bottle was heard all over the country. Listeners also heard workers knocking out the launching chocks to the accompaniment of sea shanties, and the ship sliding into the water to the cheers of the guests and shipyard workers.

They were the first motorships built by any of the British lines in the Australasian trades. The *Port Fremantle* was designed for a service speed of 14.5 knots fully laden, but achieved 15.51 knots light over the measured mile and worked up to 18.1 knots on overload. It was estimated that the *Port Fremantle* class would operate in loaded condition on 27.4 tonnes of oil fuel per day; a steamer of similar capacity would consume 66 tonnes of oil or 96.5 tonnes of coal. In 1927 the *Port Fremantle* made the passage from Dover to Melbourne in 33 days 22 hours, a new record for the company.

In May 1925, the C&D Line took delivery of its first motorship, and also the first twin screw motorship powered by Doxford diesels. She was also the first motorship in New Zealand's overseas trade. Named *Port Dunedin*, she is shown arriving at her name port of Dunedin on her maiden voyage in August 1925. Initially she had a tall funnel like the steamers.

A second motorship quickly followed the *Port Dunedin*. The career of the *Port Hobart* was cut short when she was intercepted and sunk by the German heavy cruiser *Admiral Scheer* in November 1940. She is shown painted in the darker shade of grey used at the time of her building. E. FLUCK

The first of a new class of motorship, the *Port Fremantle*, shown here arriving at Melbourne, entered service in 1927 and had a successful 33-year career with the company. E. FLUCK

In November 1927 *The Motor Ship* reported that up to October, *Port Dunedin* and *Port Hobart* had each completed five round voyages to Australasia, covering approximately 170,000 miles. On none of these voyages did either ship make a lower average speed per round trip than 13.4 knots, while the maximum figure was 13.9 knots, so the vessels were running since completion without varying more than half a knot. At the same time it was reported that the *Port Fremantle* had averaged 14 knots over the whole of her 30,682 mile maiden voyage. Seven new motorships were delivered to the C&D Line between 1925 and 1928, and in May 1930, Sir Thomas Royden, Chairman of Cunard, and a director of C&D Line, said that they had proved eminently satisfactory.

By this time the company had developed close links with all three shipbuilders and there was a high level of trust and understanding between the senior personnel in dealing with the day-to-day aspects of each contract. Agreements with the builders often specified that in recognition of the high costs of labour and materials, the C&D Line would accept a fixed sum for profit, instead of profit at 10 per cent of cost as was provided in most other shipbuilding contracts.

With all the new tonnage built after the war coming into service, the company progressively disposed of the older vessels from the early 1900s, and following completion of the seven new motorships, the *Port(s) Hacking, Lincoln, Macquarie* and *Albany* were all sold between 1927-29.

Although no further tonnage was ordered for several years the company became

Another of the second series of motorships, the *Port Gisborne* is shown in Adelaide river. She was torpedoed and sunk in October 1940. E. FLUCK

The Commonwealth and Dominion Line had a 22.5 per cent interest in the former Scottish Shire Line steamer *Argyllshire* between 1929 and 1932, when the three New Zealand Conference Line ship owners agreed to purchase and operate the ship as part of a settlement in a pooling dispute dating back to pre-World War I days. E. FLUCK

involved in the ownership of the Scottish Shire Line steamer *Argyllshire*. Disagreement over a pooling agreement in 1912 saw the Scottish Shire Line Ltd sue the NZSCo and the Union Steam Ship Company, and in a separate related action, Federal. The issues were complex as during the course of the pooling agreements at issue, Houlder Bros had sold its share of the Australian trade in 1912 and a few months after this, the NZSCo amalgamated with Federal. In addition, as ships declared in the 1912 pool were lost during the war, they were replaced by others. After a fortnight before a judge in 1927, the parties decided to settle out of court. One of the ramifications of the agreement reached between James Caird of the Scottish Shire Line and Allan Hughes, chairman of New Zealand Shipping, resulted in the New Zealand Conference Line members agreeing to buy and operate the vessel, which was purchased in December 1929. Appropriately, the Federal Steam Navigation Company became the registered owners and operators, as the *Argyllshire* was identical to the former Federal vessels *Shropshire* and *Wiltshire.* Shaw Savill & Albion and the C&D Line contributed 57.5 per cent of the purchase cost. When the ship was sold again in December 1932, C&D received its 22.5 per cent from the proceeds.

For some years the British lines in the Australian trade had been endeavouring to get a pooling agreement with the Continental lines for the carriage of wool. All the pre-war carriers, including the two German lines, had now returned to the trade. An arrangement was finally reached in 1929. This saw the British Lines holding 64 per cent, with the German lines (German Australian Steamship Company and North German Lloyd) securing 17 per cent. The Holland Australia Line had 5 per cent, Wilh. Wilhelmsen of Norway 10 per cent and Transatlantic Steam Ship Company, Gothenburg had a 4 per cent pool share. Other lines, East Asiatic Company of Copenhagen, the two Italian Lines (Lloyd Sabaudo and Navigazione Generale Italiana), and Messageries Maritimes of Paris also had ships on the berth for wool but the liftings were insufficient to justify a separate trade share. C&D Line had a 15.83 per cent pool share for the carriage of wool, representing about 249,000 tonnes. There was a lively rivalry each year for the ship carrying the first of the new season's wool from Sydney to Dunkirk. The Norwegian Wilhelmsen Line saw the race as an important marketing event and faster 16 knot motor ships entered the Australian trade from the 1930s. Wilhelmsen's *Tricolor* (1933, 6,850) was first home in 1933 and *Taronga* (1934, 7,964) made a record passage of 30 days and 6 hours in 1934 but she met her match the following year when the *Port Wyndham* beat her by one hour!

Australia had started to follow the New Zealand model, and various industry boards were also established. A Dairy Produce Control Board and a Control Board for Dried Fruits were established in 1924, a Canned Fruits Board in 1926, Wine Oversea Marketing Board in 1929 and a Meat Board in 1936. However none had the extesive powers which the meat and dairy boards enjoyed in New Zealand to control the shipment of the product. The Australian government convened an Overseas Shipping Conference in Sydney in April 1929. The outcome of the conference made little criticism of the shipping lines and stated that 'during the last three years, the regular British cargo lines have suffered heavy losses in the Australian trade'. A previous

A wet, early morning scene showing the C&D line steamers *Ports Darwin, Adelaide* and *Melbourne* alongside the company's wharves at Pyrmont, Sydney on 14 November 1932. PORT LINE ARCHIVES, UNIVERSITY OF LIVERPOOL

Australian Industries Preservation Act had outlawed trade agreements which involved the payments of rebates, primage, discounts and the like. A 1930 amendment to the Act authorised agreements made between shippers and shipowners which were approved by the Australian Oversea Transport Association (AOTA), and which allowed for periodical sailings by the shipowners, to carry freight at agreed rates, and for shippers to agree to ship exclusively by the shipowners. The amendment was a major victory for the shipowners as the government was clearly condoning the various shipping conference trade monopolies. The amendment also specifically allowed discrimination against shippers who declined to enter an AOTA agreement. The prohibition of rebates was also lifted by allowing for loyalty rebates, which were not deferred, but paid on shipment. One of the functions of the AOTA was to secure economies in shipping by rationalising the tonnage employed. All these changes were of significant benefit to the C&D Line and virtually gave a government stamp of approval to the pool share the company held in the Australian northbound conference to the United Kingdom and Europe.

New contracts were agreed with the New Zealand producer boards in 1932 which resulted in a 2.5 per cent freight reduction. The C&D share of the pool moved from 22.5 per cent to 25 per cent in what was intended to be an eight-year term. The three British lines remained in total control of the New Zealand export trade to the United Kingdom and Europe, with the exception of an annual allocation to the Scales Line of Wellington, of 55,000 bales of wool and 1,500 tonnes of general cargo. Scales Line had resumed chartering in 1921 and the Lines decided to reduce freights to chase them out of the trade. However, the strong farmer support given to Scales convinced the Lines they were unlikely to achieve their goal and the fixed annual allocation was agreed. The Scales agreement with the Conference was kept strictly confidential, and for over 50 years, wool shippers booking cargo with Scales thought they were supporting an independent shipping line in competition with the British lines, and were unaware that Scales was operating with the blessing of the conference on a fixed cargo allocation.

Of the lines in the New Zealand trade, the NZSCo and the associated Federal Steam Navigation Company were acquired by P&O in 1916 while the Commonwealth & Dominion Line had been purchased by Cunard in 1916, but Shaw Savill & Albion Company was not acquired by one of the larger shipping groups until the 1930s. The White Star Line of Liverpool had initially supplied ships to supplement the Shaw Savill & Albion service under a joint service arrangement from 1884 but it was not until some years later that the White Star Line purchased a 40 per cent share in the company. From 1910 the principal shareholder in the company was Sir John Ellerman holding 55 per cent of the ordinary shares. In 1927 control of Shaw Savill & Albion was acquired by Lord Kylsant's Royal Mail Group, and although it remained profitable throughout the ramifications of the collapse of the Royal Mail Line, a series of financial transactions between 1933-5 saw the company being sold to the major British group of Furness Withy and Company.

Virtually all the Commonwealth and Dominion Line vessels built in the decade between 1918 and 1928 had their insulated capacity increased to cater for the increasing demand for refrigerated cargoes. Since 1894 there had been a number of experiments with shipping chilled meat. The first attempt was made with a shipment of 1000 quarters of beef from Sydney in the *Port Pirie* on 2 August 1894 but it eventually had to be frozen down on the passage. The *Muritai* shipped 70 quarters of chilled beef from New Zealand in 1911 under the Nelson-Dicks-Tyser process and it was delivered successfully, but the process was too expensive to make regular shipments viable. From the mid 1920s there were several more experimental shipments of chilled beef, but with the long transit times, the shipments invariably had to be frozen down on the voyage. A shipment of chilled beef from Melbourne to London in 1925 was delivered in a satisfactory condition after a protracted voyage of 63 days. It was not until 1932 that beef lockers were made airtight and CO2 gas introduced and maintained at a concentration of 10 per cent to stem any onset of mould. Prior to hanging the quarter beef in the lockers everything was sterilized and the beef cooled right down to the carriage temperature of minus one Celsius. Great care was required to ensure a firm but not too tight stow. The *Port Fairy* in 1932 was the first vessel to carry chilled beef from Australia using this method. She made the passage from Sydney to Dunkirk in 32 days, 10 hours at an average speed of 15.187 knots on a consumption of 29.7 tons of oil per day. In the following year she also became the first vessel to undertake a similar voyage with chilled beef parcels from New Zealand. In 1935 the chilled beef capacity was increased in 12 vessels in the fleet.

The world depression started to bite from the early 1930s and after Cunard Line had reduced staff wages by 10 per cent, the C&D Line was asked to follow suit. This became effective from 1 May 1931 and remained in place until February 1936. With a number of ships laid up there was a surplus of junior officers and when the *Port Gisborne* sailed from London for New Zealand in July 1931 she was entirely manned on deck by 18 unemployed fourth officers and certificated ex-apprentices, most of whom had their second mate's certificate. There were hundreds of merchant vessels laid up around Britain at this time and many budding officers were unable to find any employment at sea. Some of the deck crew remained with the *Port Gisborne* for 18 months before starting their careers with the company as junior officers.

There were signs of the depression easing and at the Imperial Economic Conference held in Ottawa in July 1932, Britain agreed to buy more produce from her British Empire constituents and thus reduce foreign imports. It was a decision which greatly pleased the British Lines but their tranquility was shattered when they found that the Blue Star Line, owned by the British meat giant, Vestey Bros, was planning to enter the New Zealand and Australian trades. Vesteys had extensive interests in South America and could see the Ottawa Agreement reducing the large volumes of refrigerated cargo that their ships had been shipping from Argentine to Britain. At the time Vesteys controlled 50 per cent of Argentine beef shipments.

Vesteys already owned three freezing works in New Zealand (Tomoana, Hawke's Bay, Kaiti, Gisborne and Westfield in Auckland) and the meat marketing company, W. & R. Fletcher Ltd, was a significant buyer of New Zealand meat from several freezing works throughout New Zealand for W. Weddel & Co of London, one of the principal importers of meat from New Zealand and another Vestey subsidiary. A similar situation existed in Australia where Vesteys had extensive interests, particularly in the major beef production state of Queensland. The Blue Star Line was not interested in just carrying meat on its parent company's account, it wanted to share in the sailing frequencies of the other British Conference Lines in the Australian and New Zealand trades.

The lines were always poised to fight any competition which would erode their protected pool shares but it was a lot more difficult to resist the overtures of a well-

The Blue Star Line incursion into the New Zealand, Australian and South African trades in the 1930s upset the existing British Lines. The first ship to New Zealand was the *Tuscan Star*, which arrived Auckland 17 November 1933. The photograph shows her on trials in 1930. W. PARRY & SON LTD

established British company. Blue Star Line sought a 10 per cent pool share and made approaches to the New Zealand Farmers' Union for support, which was readily forthcoming. The company took large advertisements in the main daily newspapers and the claims for support there were challenged with advertisements inserted by the three British lines. The Lines argued that in their contracts with the producer boards there was a clause which prohibited the shipping companies in the trade from being involved in the purchase of sheep, lambs and cattle but Vesteys promptly reminded them of the C&D Line shareholding in the N.Z. Refrigerating Company and the NZSCo shareholding in the Southland Frozen Meat Company.

By the time the first Blue Star ship, the *Tuscan Star* (1930, 11,449), had sailed from London for New Zealand on 13 October 1933, the Lines had capitulated and signed an agreement for the New Zealand trade, confirming a 10 per cent pool share for three years. This also protected the Scales Line agreement and secured an undertaking from Blue Star that it would not enter the Australian trade for one year from 30 September 1933. Overall, New Zealand freight charges dropped by 7.05 per cent.

The decision of the Lines to keep Blue Star out of the Australian trade until late in 1934 was a judgment that cost them dearly. As with New Zealand, the Australian farming interests and exporters were delighted to welcome and offer support to another line specialising in the carriage of refrigerated cargoes. Australian freights were approximately 53 per cent higher than pre-war levels and there had been no reductions in tariffs since 1927, despite all the economies made with new motor ships. The prospect of a new line proposing a freight reduction was a big factor in shipper enthusiasm. In January 1934 P&O chairman Alexander Shaw made a tongue-in-cheek comment that 'Vesteys would be assured of a fair deal and a hearty welcome' if they decided to enter the Australian trade.

Blue Star Line initially sought 5 per cent of the wool and 7.5 per cent of the outward refrigerated cargoes from Australia but the Australian Conference countered with a modest 2.5 per cent and 5 per cent respectively and discussions dragged on for months, with offer and counter-offer being made. The delay was such that, as a result of the promised shipper support, Vesteys indicated it would need a significant 17.5 per cent of the northbound Australian liftings, as the ships it was ordering were designed to carry at least 285,000 tonnes annually. It only wanted 20 sailings out of 212 conference voyages and felt the increased volumes of cargo moving to Britain would easily absorb its liftings. Whilst Shaw Savill & Albion chief Basil Sanderson exhorted his other colleagues to stand firm and resist Blue Star, no contract was initially signed and in the first year of operation Blue Star carried 20 per cent of Australian cargoes northbound. The first ship, the *Albion Star* (1919, 7,920), sailed from Sydney 30 July 1934 and the *Royal Star* (1919, 7,900) followed from Melbourne on 5 September. The *Stuart Star* (1926, 10,646) sailed from Fremantle on 19 October with the largest cargo (500 tonnes) of chilled meat ever to leave Australia. After that first year the other Lines quickly moved to reach an agreement with Blue Star. The Lines' pool shares in the Australian trade after the admittance of Blue Star Line were P&O 27.39 per cent, White Star 16.60 per cent, Port Line 16.02 per cent, Alfred Holt 9.36 per cent, Clan Line 7.32 per cent, Ellerman & Bucknall 6.31 per cent and Blue Star 17.00 per cent. Because of the surprising success of Blue Star's liftings in the company's first year in the Australian trade, the British Lines' negotiators had convinced the Continental lines to also reduce their pool shares to make provision for the newcomer. By October 1938 the Blue Star Line pool share had increased to 18 per cent.

A lot of bitterness had been generated and Blue Star was always regarded with suspicion by the other British lines, being treated as the 'outsider' of the group for many years. It was not until 1958, for example, that the New Zealand Conference allowed it to load export cargoes from the UK to New Zealand on its own account, instead of having to charter one of its ships to one of the other conference members for the southbound passage. Blue Star continued aggressively to 'over-carry' within the New Zealand conference pool and by 1949 its share had risen from 10 per cent to 15 per cent; by 1954 it was up to 18 per cent. The other lines seemed content to reluctantly grant increased pool shares in case Blue Star got frustrated and left the conference to operate independently. Even in the 1950s, and later, in New Zealand, it was an established instruction to the secretary of the Overseas Shipowners Committee

With six holds instead of five, the *Port Chalmers* was laid down during the Depression years and was a larger edition of earlier motorships. Electric welding was used extensively in the hull construction, more so than any other ship built to date. Coming through two of the famous Malta convoys with little damage, she was extraordinarily lucky. She is shown in Otago Harbour on her way to her name port of Port Chalmers. E.A. PHILLIPS

that on matters effecting the Lines, he was to approach each in order of seniority; Blue Star was always the last to be consulted.

Blue Star Line also extended calls at South African ports and in a conversation between Jack Rooper and Leonard Dewey, Blue Star's London manager, in September 1935, the latter commented that he was amazed at the weakness of the South African Conference in giving the company what it asked for, as it had absolutely no 'entitlements' in South Africa and no trade connections, unlike their position in Australia and New Zealand. Robertson Gibb, chairman of the Union Castle Line, the premier line in the South African trade, was so annoyed at the Blue Star incursion that he wrote to Belfast shipbuilder Harland & Wolff, warning it that Union Castle would be reluctant to give it more orders if it continued to build new ships for Blue Star.[6] The Vestey family entry into the New Zealand, Australian and South African trades was certainly not welcomed by the other British shipping companies.

Despite the erosion of the C&D line trade pool share by Blue Star, more ships were ordered. In December 1932 it privately asked Swan Hunter to commence a new improved *Port Fremantle* class motorship to C&D specifications, offering if the order did not proceed, to reimburse the shipbuilder for the costs incurred to date. That did not happen and the *Port Chalmers* was delivered on 28 December 1933. At her completion, Herbert Corry commented that between 1923 and 1933, exports of frozen cargoes from New Zealand to the UK had significantly increased. Butter had doubled

The final vessel in the series of six-hatch motorships, was the *Port Townsville*. All three vessels had trials with cold air systems which provided more efficient refrigeration of the holds compared to the solely brine systems of earlier years. The *Port Townsville* was bombed and sunk in March 1941. E. FLUCK

in the period, cheese exports had increased by 70 per cent and the number of carcasses of mutton and lamb exported had climbed from 6,400,000 in 1923 to over 11,000,000 in 1933. At the time of her building many shipyard workers had been laid off through lack of orders, with the result that *Port Chalmers* was almost lovingly put together by managers, foremen, charge hands and permanent staff.

Further tenders went to John Brown, Wm. Hamilton, Harland & Wolff, Hawthorn Leslie, Swan Hunter & Wigham Richardson and Workman Clark for another vessel of the same type. John Brown won the order and Swan Hunter secured a third contract with the *Port Wyndham* being delivered 24 January 1935 and *Port Townsville* on 24 August that year. With *Port Townsville* it was decided to install Sulzer engines, instead of Doxfords, solely for the purpose of evaluating the performance of both types. All three had increased capacity for the carriage of chilled beef and after experiments with the *Port Wyndham* a forced air cooling system was developed. Superintendent Engineer H. Glover Dearden, J.D. Farmer of J. & E. Hall Limited, and Dr A.J.M. Smith of the Low Temperature Research Station at Cambridge were responsible for the changes from the system of cooling by means of cold brine circulating through grids arranged on the ceiling and sides of the holds to one of cold air circulation by electrically driven fans drawing the air from the refrigerated spaces and pushing it through a battery of brine cooled pipes, then returning it through specially designed trunkings and ducts. The following new building, *Port Jackson,* was the first Port Line vessel to be fully fitted with this system.

The *Port Jackson* of 1937 was the first of a larger class of motorship with an increased refrigerated capacity, and the first ship to fully incorporate more efficient cold air systems of refrigeration throughout. For some years she was plagued with vibration problems which it was thought stemmed from her two four cylinder engines. Later ships in the series had two five cylinder engines. E. FLUCK

On her outward maiden voyage *Port Wyndham* averaged 15.56 knots on oil consumption of 23.5 tonnes per day for the voyage to Melbourne and homeward from Sydney to Dunkirk she averaged 16.747 knots on 29.34 tonnes per day.

The success of these three motorships saw the company order a slightly larger vessel, the *Port Jackson*, launched on 26 November 1936 by Lady Adeline Hankey (the wife of Colonel Sir Maurice Hankey) and delivered 20 January 1937. She was the forerunner of a series of similar vessels built between 1940 and 1946. Another tranche of older vessels was progressively disposed of, the *Port Pirie, Port Victor, Port Curtis* in 1935 and *Port Napier* in 1936. Swan Hunter was invited to submit a tender for another *Port Jackson* class vessel in September 1938 but acceptance was delayed until February 1939. The *Port Jackson* had experienced a troublesome vibration in service and cracks had developed in the transverse beam of the main engine. The company wanted to establish the cause before ordering a new vessel. Instead of the two 4-cylinder Doxford engines fitted in the *Port Jackson*, the new vessel had two 5-cylinder Doxford diesels, which it was hoped would obviate any further trouble with vibration. Although the *Port Jackson* may have experienced vibration problems, this did not seem to interfere with her performance, as on her return maiden voyage from Wellington to London she made a passage time of just under 29 days, the fastest ever by a Port Line ship. She made over 16 knots for much of the passage.

From the advent of the rounded stem on *Port Jackson* in 1937, most ships in the fleet carried a bow plaque of the house flag, encircled by a gold cable, placed at the

Outward bound direct for London with all her derricks stowed for the long ocean passage via Panama Canal, the *Port Brisbane* looks like a yacht.

Sailing deep-sea, the *Port Macquarie* moves down Otago harbour, with a large Port Line house flag flying from her signal mast.

With her paintwork immaculate the *Port Victor* arrives at Hobart on 20 September 1958. REX-PRIEST

With her distinctive goalpost mast, the *Port Adelaide* moves down Otago Harbour on passage for the United Kingdom via Mediterranean ports.

Fully dressed, the *Port Montreal* lies alongside at Kobe, on one of her early Crusader Line charters. Her identity in the service was portrayed with her large Crusader crest welded to her bow.

A broadside view of the *Port Melbourne* at Nelson in April 1967.

top of the prow, almost a reminder of the figureheads of the early Phoenicians, Greek and Roman navigators.

At the Board meeting in December 1935 the directors decided that for popular usage the company should in future be known as the 'Port Line'. Throughout the Continent, wool shippers had for years referred to the company as 'zee Port Line', and it was common throughout Australia and New Zealand to call it the Port Line. There was also some confusion of the name between the Commonwealth and Dominion Line and the Aberdeen and Commonwealth Line. The original name was clearly too long for convenient, every day use. At the February Board meeting, managers revealed that the new name had proved very popular. It was not until 11 November 1937 that the company legally changed its name to Port Line Ltd and the Board of Trade gave its approval on 18 November.

Both ships with names associated with Otago had collisions during 1937. *Port Chalmers* collided with the *City of Oran* (1915, 7,323) in dense fog off Portugal on 2 September, and the resultant damage, buckled plates and a large hole in her bow forced a return to Falmouth for repairs. On 7 December *Australia Star* (1935, 11,122) struck *Port Dunedin* during poor visibility in the Thames off Gravesend. She suffered extensive damage above the water line. In both cases the other vessel was deemed to be at fault.

Between 1925 and the start of World War II, the three British lines built 40 new ships for the Australasian trades, all driven with oil-powered diesel engines. Of these 40, the C&D Line and NZSCo/Federal built 11 each, Shaw Savill & Albion ten, and newcomer Blue Star Line, eight large motor ships between 1934 and 1939.

Through 1938 and into 1939 there was continuing talk of war and in July 1938 the German, Dutch and Italian lines gave notice of their intention to withdraw from the Australian pool. In April 1939 Port Line started looking for a large house in the country, like a golf club, where the company could carry on business in the advent of a war. A country home, *Oaklawn,* situated between Oxshott and Leatherhead in Surrey, was purchased on 12 June 1939 and the evacuation there from 88 Leadenhall Street commenced on 1 September 1939.

As the company prepared for war, news came from New Zealand that the *Port Bowen* had run aground at 1.00 am on 19 July 1939 on Castlecliff Beach, Wanganui as she was preparing to anchor in the roadstead, where 20,000 carcasses of meat were to be lightered out. Several attempts were made to pull the vessel into deeper water but the sand held her fast. Despite the removal of all her coal bunkers and cargo, the *Port Bowen* was abandoned to the underwriters in October 1939, and at the inquiry in November, the court found that Captain F.W. Bailey had made an error of judgment in coming in too fast, and in not paying sufficient attention to the echo sounder, nor stopping the ship when a sounding of over 24 metres was recorded. The court did not suspend his certificate as the assessors felt the errors were caused by a lack of local

This pre-1939 photograph of the *Port Fairy* discharging frozen carcasses of mutton in the London docks emphasises the primitive handling methods. SPORT & GENERAL

knowledge, rather than by any culpable act. The company, however, demoted him to chief officer.

Port Line was served with a notice to remove the vessel within six months! Finally this formidable task was helped along by the war-time conditions and the jump in the price of metals. The New Zealand government engaged a contractor, Wm Cable and Sons of Wellington, to completely remove the ship using all salvageable material for the war effort. A lot of fittings were used in the construction of New Zealand-built minesweepers. Pumps and mechanical equipment were installed in the Wellington Public Hospital and the refrigerating machinery was acquired by the Kakariki freezing works near Wanganui. Just under 6,000 tonnes of metal was taken ashore over a special rail track along the beach. The salvage was not completed until August 1943. In consideration of the government assuming responsibility for removing the vessel from the beach, the C&D Line insurers, Tyser & Co, made an 'ex gratia' reimbursement to the Wanganui Harbour Board for all its costs associated with the stranding.[8]

MOVE ON, PLEASE

Cartoonist Minhinnick in October 1939 aptly portrays the Wanganui Harbour Board order to Port Line to remove the wreck of the *Port Bowen*, firmly settled on the beach at Wanganui, within six months! NEW ZEALAND HERALD

Waterfront conditions in New Zealand had started to deteriorate from the mid 1930s and shipowners were faced with steadily rising costs and lower productivity. Jack Rooper went to Australia on a fact-finding tour and then spent two and a half months in New Zealand at the end of 1937/early 1938 studying waterfront conditions and practices at virtually all the ports. In February 1938 he gave an extensive interview to the press in which he bluntly said that the position was little short of tragic, having regard to the fact that New Zealand was so dependent on its overseas trades. He went on to say: 'The New Zealand waterside worker, whose physique and living conditions give him superiority over any on earth, is, in fact, as many of themselves acknowledge, giving a worse performance than a half-starved native, and he and his employer are held up to derision all over the world'. He was a firm believer that waterside workers should receive incentive payments, based on individual performance, but the union was resolute that any bonus payments would be paid into a pool and distributed equally to all the waterside workers on each port register.

As a result of the poor situation on the waterfront, the lines' negotiations with the producer boards in 1939 sought a 15 per cent freight increase, with the lines' reminding their clients that since the 1922 agreement freights had been reduced by 21.5 per cent. They also stressed that the lines had continually met the needs of the boards and also continued to build modern ships for the trade, incorporating increased refrigerated capacity. At the time the ships in the Blue Star Line and Port Line fleets each averaged only 12 years old, NZSCo/Federal 15 years and Shaw Savill 16 years. This time the shipowners were firm in their demand for a 15 per cent increase and an impasse remained between the parties by the time war was declared on 3 September 1939. Shortly after, the lines unilaterally increased rates by 10 per cent. As in World War I, the British government again undertook to take all the New Zealand produce so no further discussions took place on the freight rates other than between the Lines and the British government. In 1939 the Port Line fleet comprised 28 vessels of 225,864 gross tons.

In the first 25 years of C&D/Port Line it had performed very well, paying Cunard a 15 per cent dividend each year until 1933, when the capital of the company was increased from £2,000,000 to £2,600,000, after which the dividend became 10 per cent. When the Port Line directors decided to reduce it to 5 per cent for the 1941 financial year, Sir Percy Bates, chairman of Cunard wrote to Herbert Corry, Port Line chairman, that he was 'obliged to press for the 10 per cent dividend'.[7] The request was honoured.

1 *Shipping News,* 16 Aug 1916.
2 J.R. Rooper letter, PL9/6-9.
3 ibid, PL9, 21 Sep 1922.
4 ibid, PL9, 8 Apr 1925.
5 Port Line archives, PL3/61/22-12-13.
6 Letter G.G. Duggan (Northern Ireland Govt.) to E.J. Foley (Board of Trade), 11.7.1935, PRO file T190/241
7 Port Line Directors Meeting 25.3.1942
8 See Ian Farquhar, "Port Bowen" – the Ship That Never Left', *New Zealand Marine News*, Vol. 54, No.2, 2006, pp. 58-68

CHAPTER 4

World War II

A week before the declaration of war on 3 September 1939, the British government gave the Admiralty complete power over all merchant ships – their loading, discharging and routing. In order to meet the Admiralty requirements, senior managers from leading shipping companies were seconded to set up departments in the Ministry of Shipping. Port Line manager Bill Donald would spend almost the next six years there, for much of this time chairing the Diversion Room in Ports and Transport Control at the Ministry of Transport. With Donald away, Jack Rooper handled company affairs from *Oaklawn* in Surrey.

The *Port Napier,* very similar to *Port Jackson,* but with more powerful engines, was well advanced in construction on 27 December 1939 when the shipbuilder advised that an Admiralty team had fully inspected her, since it was looking for a ship of this type. On 28 January 1940 the Admiralty telegraphed that the *Port Napier* was being requisitioned effective from 30 January. All protests were in vain. She was launched by Mrs B.P. Arrowsmith, the wife of the superintendent engineer, on 23 April 1940. The reality of war had hit home and until hostilities ceased it was going to be a very difficult and demanding time for the company. Thirteen ships were lost by enemy action and one managed vessel blew up in Bombay harbour. One hundred and sixty seven sea staff were lost and management was further disrupted as staff went into the services or were seconded to government agencies or special duties. In addition over 220 officers and crew became prisoners of war, including some passengers. Three prisoners of war died in captivity. The last outward sailing to Australasia was the *Port Hobart* in January 1940. The first cargo ship requisitioned was *Port Adelaide* on 4 February 1940. From 1941, all shelter decks in the vessels were closed to allow them to load deeper.

As the head office moved to the country, some staff enlisted or were mobilised if they were already involved with the territorial forces. Ships were armed and supplied with gunners. The first to fire a shot in anger was the *Port Auckland.* She was passing through the locks of the King George V dock in London on 15 September 1940 when her gunners opened fire with the 12-pounder stern gun and the bridge machine gun on a Junkers Ju-88 bomber. They were subsequently credited with shooting it down. On 20 December 1940, the *Port Alma* lying alongside in Liverpool, was badly shaken and developed a leak when two bombs exploded close by. The *Port Fremantle* suffered minor damage at Liverpool the following day.

On 2 December 1939 the German heavy cruiser *Admiral Graf Spee* shelled Blue Star Line's *Doric Star* (1929, 10,441) in the South Atlantic as she was proceeding to the United Kingdom with a full refrigerated and general cargo. She was instructed to stop and to cease use of her wireless, as the ship had sent the special RRR (enemy warship) message signifying that she was under attack. The warship sent a boarding party and the *Doric Star* was scuttled by time bombs in position 19.15S, 05.05E. The radio operator of the *Port Chalmers*, also in the vicinity steaming homewards, heard the distress call. When it ceased, Captain W.G. Higgs instructed his wireless officer to repeat the message and sign it with the signal letters EADG, the *Port Chalmers'* call sign. The message was repeated for sometime until it was acknowledged by South African shore stations. The warship sank the Shaw Savill & Albion freighter *Tairoa* (1920, 7,983) next day and again *Port Chalmers* repeated the signal from the *Tairoa.* The signals received from *Port Chalmers* convinced the Admiralty to send a cruiser force after the *Admiral Graf Spee.* The alertness and initiative of the *Port Chalmers* enabled British naval forces to search the South Atlantic for the raider, which was destroyed in the Battle of the River Plate a fortnight later.

While travelling in convoy, *Port Fairy* collided with the Glasgow-registered freighter *Loch Dee* (1937, 5,252) in March 1940, suffering damage. The *Port Darwin* was proceeding from Newcastle to Auckland, running without lights under wartime conditions, when she was in collision in the North Sea (55.25N, 1.22W) at 10.30 p.m. on 28 August 1940, with the Dutch steamer *Driebergen* (1923, 5,231). The Dutch freighter quickly sank and her crew was rescued by the trawler *Kopanes* (1915, 351) and taken to London. The *Port Darwin* returned to the Tyne with extensive bow damage, and the repairs delayed her outward passage by three weeks.

The relocated company office was not immune from attack and on 28 October 1940 the shock from a bomb explosion in the grounds dislodged a few tiles, and on 12 November a small high explosive bomb hit *Oaklawn,* but the only damage was some broken panes of glass in the glasshouse, kitchen and pantry. Throughout the war, Jack Rooper lived at *Oaklawn* during the week, returning to his home at Reel Hall, Surrey at weekends, which he often threw open to Port Line managers and senior sea-staff. Very conscious of the strain imposed on masters who had lost ships, he urged them to spend time in the country to recover.

The reality of war was again reinforced when the *Port Denison* (Captain J.B. Bradley), which sailed from Methil, Scotland, as flagship of a 44-ship convoy bound for New Zealand, was bombed and sunk north-east of Peterhead. At 7.50 p.m. on 26 September 1940 a German aircraft came in over the convoy flying low, attacking the lead vessel and dropping two bombs. One missed but the other landed on the boat deck and travelled down into the lower tweendeck, where it exploded, blowing a large hole in the ship's side. Fire immediately broke out and the ship listed badly. Within a short time the order to abandon ship was given and the crew escaped in the only serviceable lifeboat and liferafts. All were safely picked up but 16 had died in the explosion and fires. The *Port Denison* sank next day, six miles north east of Peterhead. (British Admiralty reports state that *Port Denison* was torpedoed but it seems clear from the company records of the 1940 attack that she was bombed).

At 9.50 p.m. on 11 October, 350 miles west of Ireland, the *Port Gisborne* was torpedoed without warning and immediately started to go down by the head. The crew abandoned the vessel in gale force winds and one boat capsized in the heavy seas and 27 lives were lost. The ship was sunk by *U-48* in position 56.38N, 16.40W. The weather abated somewhat on the following day but it was not until 13 days later, that the boat containing the master (T. Kippins), the chief officer (H. McGregor Post), and the majority of the remaining crew were picked up by the steamer *Alpera* (1920, 1,777). The other lifeboat kept close to another boat from the French steamer *Saint-Malo* (1917, 5,779) and the two were rescued on their 11th day by the naval tug *Salvonia* (1939, 579). The survivors had a harrowing time in the two boats and several spent time in hospital suffering from exposure following their return to safety.

The *Port Fairy* was involved in a tragic mishap on 22 October 1940, while travelling in a small fast convoy, about to rendezvous with the main body of a larger convoy en route to Halifax. The escorting destroyer, HMCS *Margaree,* made a sudden, inexplicable turn to port, and was sliced in two by the *Port Fairy,* which was unable to avoid the impact. After the collision *Port Fairy* held her stern alongside the after part of the destroyer to enable ratings to clamber aboard. The forward section of HMCS *Margaree* sank within minutes. The captain, four officers and 136 ratings from the destroyer were lost; many had come from HMCS *Fraser*, which had been cut in two by HMS *Calcutta* in June. The stern section of HMCS *Margaree* remained afloat, despite the *Port Fairy* using up virtually all her ammunition trying to sink it. It sank the following day. No blame was attached to *Port Fairy* and no reason for the destroyer's sudden turn was ever determined.

The company then lost two ships within three days of each other in November 1940. The *Port Brisbane,* fully laden, on passage across the south Indian Ocean from Adelaide, was attacked at 9.45 p.m. 21 November in position 29.22S, 95.36E, without warning by the German commerce raider H.K.33, known as the *Pinguin.* The captain of the raider, Ernst-Felix Kruder, had decided that a fast ship traveling alone without any lights must be another auxiliary cruiser. *Pinguin* initially fired one shot but when the *Port Brisbane* radioed she was under attack, the fire was directed at the bridge and the radio room. This disabled the communications and bathed the *Port Brisbane* with the lights from two powerful searchlights. A fire started in the bridge area and began to spread. One of the radio operators and an apprentice were killed in the action. The engines were stopped and all passengers and crew, with the exception of key personnel were instructed to abandon ship. The raider sent a boarding party and took the master (H. Steele) and the remaining crew, in two of the ship's boats, back on board the

Built in 1923, the *Port Brisbane* was captured and sunk by the German commerce raider *Pinguin* in the Indian Ocean in November 1940. Most of the crew were interned in Germany but one life boat, containing 27 men escaped and was picked up by HMAS *Canberra* the following day. E. FLUCK

Pinguin. The bombs set to scuttle *Port Brisbane* failed to do the job completely and at 0100 on the 22nd, the raider fired a torpedo to finish the task. The *Port Brisbane* went down by the head about an hour later. The third boat endeavoured to get away from the area close to the raider, showing no lights and with those on board keeping a low profile in the darkness. The raider soon gave up searching and sailed away. This boat was in the care of second officer Edward W. Dingle, who was resolute he would sail the boat back to Australia, rather than take an enforced 'holiday' in Germany. Dingle's boat found two of the ship's lifeboats and he put four men in each to reduce the overcrowding of 27 crew in his own boat. A third damaged boat was also boarded and several cans of raisins and some mailbags were taken off it. The mailbags contained parcels of food for service personnel and anything edible was retained. In the morning sail was set on the three boats, and emphasizing the need to conserve water and food, Dingle set a course for Mauritius. Fortunately at 6.30 p.m. the same day the three lifeboats were sighted by HMAS *Canberra* which had come searching for the *Pinguin* and the men were eventually taken to Fremantle. No trace of the raider was found despite extensive searching by the *Canberra*'s aircraft. Dingle (in later years in command he was affectionately known as 'Steady Eddie') won the MBE for his initiative and bravery, although Captain Steele always contended Dingle had actually abandoned ship before the final order was given and the two men were at loggerheads until they died.

On 24 November 1940 the German heavy cruiser *Admiral Scheer* encountered the *Port Hobart* south-east of Bermuda as she was heading for the Sombrero Passage into the Caribbean. The *Port Hobart* had sailed in convoy from Liverpool on 3 November but broke off after a few days at 25 degrees west to proceed independently to Panama and then on to New Zealand. Once spotted it was easy for the *Admiral Scheer* to overtake her and although the RRR enemy raider signal and the ship's position (*Port Hobart* gave 24.44N, 58.21W while German records state 24.30N, 58.30W) was broadcast, the warship did not open fire until about a mile off and then only with a shot ahead. Captain G.S. Hall on *Port Hobart* ordered the engines stopped and calmly waited in his cabin for the boarding party to come aboard. The *Port Hobart* had a crew of 60 and eight passengers, seven of them women. The boarding party was busy searching the ship when there was a sudden order to abandon ship. The demolition squad had automatically set charges to scuttle the ship without being aware of the leisurely search. Some charges had exploded before the boarding party left but the *Port Hobart* was reluctant to sink and the *Admiral Scheer* fired shells which screamed over the heads of the survivors as the ship's lifeboats hauled to the warship. The women passengers were transferred in the boarding party's launch. Captain Krancke had apparently decided to leave the area after sinking *Port Hobart* and that was the reason he allowed the ship to broadcast that she was being attacked by an enemy raider. The Germans had boarded *Port Hobart* shortly after 1.00 p.m. and by 3.30 p.m. it was all over and *Admiral Scheer* headed east at full speed. The women were accommodated in a small cabin aft and the men were confined in the forecastle. On 18 December they were all transferred to the German naval tanker and supply ship *Nordmark*. Disguised as the American ship *Dixie*, she reached Bordeaux on 2 March 1941.

On 27 November 1940 the company lost the *Port Napier*, requisitioned on 30 January 1940 while nearing completion and converted into a fast minelayer. Although a Royal Navy vessel, all her engineers were Port Line men, transferred to the Royal Naval Reserve. The chief engineer was Commander Hamish. N. Weir. She had 600 mines on board ready to leave the Kyle of Lochalsh in northwest Scotland with her squadron, when a severe squall blew up. The *Port Napier* dragged her anchor which snagged the cable of a nearby collier and the two ships were blown across Loch Alsh into shallow water. Next morning the crew began clearing the fouled propellers and a barge commenced bunkering. Owing to an alteration in the location of the fueling pipe, as a result of an Admiralty requirement, it passed through the engine room close by the oil fired boiler. Pumping should have been stopped when the double bottom tank was 95 per cent full, but it was not, and the pressure on the hose caused it to burst, sending a jet of oil across the engine room. A fire quickly engulfed the engine room and after 20 minutes it was seen that it could not be got under control. As the ship was moored less than 100 metres from the shore, it was an easy matter for the 240 crew on board to swim ashore or clamber on to drifts, tugs or Carley floats. The people in the houses in the area were quickly evacuated. The ship continued to burn fiercely throughout the day and as the expected explosion had not occurred, volunteers boarded the ship and found the engine-room still burning and the mine decks searing hot. They set out discharging mines through the stern until smoke, flames and fumes forced them to leave the ship. No sooner had they left than two explosions occurred, followed by a third massive blast. The vessel seemed to lift bodily out of the water and then settle down in shallow water on her side in some 21 metres of water. Shipbreakers later salvaged as much steel as they could but the presence of unexploded mines made the job extremely hazardous and portions of the ship still remain. The final chapter of Port Line's involvement with *Port Napier* took place at a special board meeting in London on 29 April 1952 to authorise the abandonment of the wreck to the Admiralty. The remains of the *Port Napier* are now a popular wreck-dive where divers have the opportunity to explore the vessel, with some of the armaments still intact, as is the mine-laying railway system, while piles of mine anchors litter the seabed. The wreck lies in 16 metres of water on its starboard side with the port side just projecting clear of the surface at all times other than high water.[1]

The fourth vessel to be sunk during November 1940 was the *Port Wellington.* She was steaming across the South Indian Ocean on passage from Adelaide to a United Kingdom port when she became the second victim of the *Pinguin.* It was a very dark night and the *Pinguin* got to within half a mile of *Port Wellington* when she opened fire without warning at 11.50 p.m. The first salvo hit the bridge and wireless room, seriously wounding Captain E.O. Thomas and killing A.F. Haslam, the radio officer. The master later died on board the *Pinguin.* The ship caught fire and was burning from funnel to right aft when she was abandoned shortly after midnight. A boarding party from the raider set time bombs and scuttled *Port Wellington,* which sank at 1.31 a.m. on 1 December. Apparently the crow's nest on the foremast of *Port Wellington* had been painted, and as the paint was still wet, there was no lookout, which might have spotted the raider in advance of the shelling. The officers and crew (with chief officer F.W. Bailey senior officer) joined the crew of *Port Brisbane* in the raider's forecastle. They were eventually taken to Bordeaux by a German navy supply ship on 1 February 1941 and spent the next four years in either the Marlag or Milag Nord prison camps in Germany. As with *Port Hobart* the sinking position recorded by the Admiralty of 29.22S, 95.36E differs slightly from the German records, which gave 29.29E, 95.35E.

Captain Kippins, who commanded the *Port Gisborne* when she was torpedoed and sunk off the west coast of Ireland on 11 October 1940, had the misfortune to be in command of the *Port Townsville* when she was bombed and sunk in the Bristol Channel on 3 March 1941 when travelling independently to Melbourne. At around 1.40 pm two German aircraft approached the *Port Townsville* at low altitude, strafing her with machinegun fire. They made a second run dropping bombs, one of which struck No 3 hatch and exploded in the hold below, blowing a hole in the ship's side.

Sister ship to the *Port Brisbane*, the *Port Wellington* also fell victim to the German raider *Pinguin*, in the Indian Ocean nine days after she had captured and sunk the *Port Brisbane*. The photograph shows the *Port Wellington* coming in to berth at Lyttelton. D. JONES

Fire broke out and the main engines were put out of action. Return fire from the *Port Townsville* was disadvantaged by the fact that the ship's smoke floats had caught fire, covering her in a dense pall of smoke. The order was given to abandon ship and the survivors were picked up by the French escort vessel *La Moqueuse* (1939, 630) and taken to Milford Haven. Two passengers were killed in the attack and two more were injured. The *Port Townsville* finally sank on 4 March in position 52.05N, 05.24W.

In December 1941 Port Line's Captain William Gilling was seconded to the Ministry of War Transport, along with five other British shipmasters, to be sent to Gothenburg, to bring back to Britain six Norwegian cargo vessels which had been held in Sweden since the German invasion of Norway in April 1940. Captain Gilling got the motor tanker *Rigmor* (1931, 6,305) and on 31 March 1942 the small convoy sailed for Britain. They were attacked by German aircraft with bombs and torpedoes, and although the vessels responded with the modest defensive weapons they had, *Rigmor* was torpedoed and sunk on 2 April 1942 in position 57.27N, 03.21E. Captain Gilling was injured in the attacks and was subsequently awarded the OBE, as well as the St Olav medal with Oak Leaves from Norway. Another Port Line master, Captain A.A. Cooper, was not so lucky. He was on secondment to the Ministry of War Transport and was travelling to Canada to take up the appointment when the ship carrying him – the Federal Line's *Nottingham* (1941, 8,592) – was torpedoed and sunk on 7 November 1941, 550 miles south east from Cape Farewell (53.24N, 31.51W), on her maiden voyage with the loss of all 62 aboard. Other Port Line officers who had been in the Royal Naval Reserve before the war were called up for naval service and several were killed in action on Royal Navy ships or on special missions.

When another of the *Port Napier* class, the *Port Phillip,* was delivered on 20 March 1942, the shipyard rushed her delivery, leaving no time to cover the steel decks with timber. They had to wait until after the war for a proper covering, matai planking loaded in New Zealand which was laid on her return to Britain, making her the only ship in the New Zealand trade to be decked in New Zealand timber. She had some accidents. In September 1942 she was damaged in a collision with *Seatrain Texas* (1940, 8,108) at Port Tewfik in Egypt, and a fortnight later, while on passage from Aden to Bombay, the stern gun blew up during a practice session killing the 3rd Officer and a DEMS gunner, and injuring seven other DEMS ratings. The *Port Phillip* retained a 'wartime' look throughout her 28 years with the company, by retaining her 'stump' masts.

In addition to the *Port Phillip*, the company had placed orders for three *Port Napier* class vessels – two with Swan Hunter & Wigham Richardson and one with John Brown and Company. The Clyde-built ship was laid down at the end of 1941 as the *Port Pirie* but the shipbuilder made little progress on her because the yard was swamped with naval work. In May 1942 it advised that it could not complete the contract and the material was sold as a 'chattel' to the Admiralty as she was not far enough advanced to be described as a 'ship'. She was completed as the escort aircraft carrier HMS *Nairana.* The Admiralty also took over one of the Swan Hunter orders, which became the escort carrier HMS *Vindex*. The remaining *Port Napier* class vessel was launched 27 June 1942 and delivered as the *Port Victor* on 12 October 1942. She averaged 16.73 knots on trials. The only other ship completed for the Port Line during the war was the single-screw *Port Macquarie*, also built by Swan Hunter. She was launched 19 August 1943 by Shirley Rooper, the daughter of Jack Rooper, and delivered 22 February 1944. The company received a licence to build a sister ship to this vessel and the keel for *Port Lincoln* was laid on 21 September 1944.

The former Italian vessel *Leme*, which had been detained in the United States from June 1940 was laid up until placed under U.S. Government control in July 1941. She was transferred to Britain under Lend Lease in December 1941 and allocated to Port Line to manage. The 8,059 ton steamer, which had been built in 1925, was owned by the 'Italia' Societa Anon.di Nav., Genoa. Under the British flag she was renamed *Lowlander.* She had a Chinese crew and an officer from the Blue Funnel Line experienced in working with Chinese seafarers was transferred to the ship.

Getting supplies to the fortress island of Malta was one of the more important tasks of the war. The isolated British island was surrounded by enemy territory. Convoys of fast merchantmen, heavily protected by naval ships, were sent to Malta and the *Port Chalmers,* under the command of Gordon Higgs, was in the July 1941 convoy. The fast modern refrigerated ships in the United Kingdom-Australasian trades were

Photographed in the Cape Cod canal in 1941, the *Port Halifax* has her A frame on the bow for lowering in the water to hold the paravane wires designed for cutting the wires of moored mines. Machine gun nests on the wings of the bridge and a gun on the stern also emphasize her wartime role. W. A. SCHELL COLLECTION

the best suited for the hazardous journey and other New Zealand Conference Line vessels *Durham, Melbourne Star* and *Sydney Star* as well as the Blue Funnel Line *Deucalion* and Ellerman's *City of Pretoria* sailed with *Port Chalmers.* As the convoy approached the central Mediterranean and in range of enemy aircraft, Vice Admiral Sir James Somerville, sent the following message to all ships:

> For over twelve months Malta has resisted all attacks of the enemy. The gallantry displayed by the garrison and people of Malta has aroused admiration throughout the world. To enable this defence to be continued, it is essential that your ships, with their valuable cargoes, should arrive safely in the Grand Harbour. The Royal Navy will escort and assist you in this great mission, but you, on your part, can assist the Royal Navy, by giving strict attention to the following points.
>
> Don't make smoke. Don't show any lights at night – a torch can be seen for miles. If you have to signal by day or night, use the lowest possible power light. Keep good station and don't straggle. If your ship is damaged keep her going at the best possible speed.
>
> Provided every officer and man realises it is up to him to do his duty to the very best of his ability, then I feel sure we shall succeed, because we of the Royal Navy have

the greatest confidence in you, our brother seamen of the Royal Merchant Navy.

Remember, everyone, that the watchword is:-

THE CONVOY MUST GO THROUGH

HMS *Renown* 20/7/1941.

Captain Higgs had copies of the message posted throughout the *Port Chalmers.* Although there were some warnings of enemy aircraft, the first attack came at 9.35 a.m. on Wednesday 23 July and hereafter follows Captain Higg's graphic report:

> This was the real thing at last. The whole convoy, the escort, and Admiral Somerville's force away on our port beam opened fire with all the anti-aircraft weapons, and it was as though all hell had been let loose. The air vibrated with thunderous crashes, the sky was filled with bursting shells and white puffs of smoke showed vividly against the blue. Bombs were dropping and exploding amongst the ships, but none were hit. I looked over to *Ark Royal,* a couple of miles away to port. Bombs seemed to be falling close to her and at one moment she was almost hidden by the geysers of water and spray thrown up by the explosions. She was blazing away with all she had, but was quite untouched, and in a minute or two we could see the fighters taking off from her flight deck to engage the Italians. The main enemy formation was now right overhead, and our guns, pointing vertically upwards shook the bridge and deafened us, for we were standing not more than four feet from their muzzles when they had maximum elevation.
>
> At 9.37 a.m. when every gun in every ship was pointed to the zenith, two torpedo bombers came in at low level from ahead right down the middle of the convoy. It took several seconds to depress the guns and these grim planes were coming on at speed. One attacked *Durham* and dropped bombs and a torpedo. Then she came straight at us, at a height of not more than 24 metres above the water. Every gun that could bear was now firing at her, but she came on with sinister determination. It is an unpleasant sight to see your enemy, bent on your destruction, coming at you with tremendous speed. 4th Officer Thompson, with great presence of mind, fired our port P.A.C. (Parachute and Cable) rocket, and I think this disconcerted the attacker, for he swerved away slightly and passed down our port side. Machine gun bullets seemed to be pouring into him. Our over-zealous gunner, was so keen that he almost severed the port fore-top-gallant backstay with his fire. The din was indescribable. Every ship had her own particular problems, and I fear that each was fully occupied defending herself and quite oblivious of what was happening to others. In a few seconds the low-level attackers disappeared astern, and one seemed to be losing height. In the silence that followed I had time to look around and saw that the destroyer *Fearless,* was on fire aft and sinking. The cruiser *Manchester* had been torpedoed and she left the convoy and turned back to Gibraltar. Out to starboard, a mile or so away, was a damaged plane which at first

> looked like one of ours, its tail sticking up out of the water; but we soon saw the unmistakable Italian markings.
> Everything had happened so quickly. At one moment we are travelling peacefully over a quiet sunlit sea beneath a cloudless sky – the next we are in an inferno of crashing sound with spouts of water caused by bombs all around us... I think that the enemy were taken aback by the fire power of the convoy and the escorts.[2]

Captain Higgs reported that further attacks were sustained throughout the day, and in the early hours of 24 July a determined attack was made by E-Boats. As he writes:

> The air was filled with the high-pitched hum of E-Boat engines – they seemed to be all around us. Suddenly *Edinburgh*'s searchlights swung round to port, we had a glimpse of a small object in their glare, and the cruiser let go what must have been a complete broadside – a shattering blast of sound. The spray leaped up from a score of places and when it subsided there was no sign of the small object. Cruisers and destroyers were using searchlights and guns all around the convoy. The merchant ships, not having searchlights, could see nothing to fire at, and our guns were of necessity silent... This E-Boat attack was the most hair-raising episode yet. It was the darkness that made it so much worse than our previous experiences. [2]

One vessel was damaged by a torpedo in this attack but made Malta safely under her own power. Further air attacks followed during the forenoon but all were beaten off and the convoy arrived safely off Malta at 2.45 p.m. 24 July. Thousands of cheering inhabitants of the island crowded every bastion to welcome the ships. Once her cargo was discharged the *Port Chalmers* sailed from Malta unescorted in September 1941 and was attacked by an E-Boat the same evening. By constant manoeuvring and skilful use of her 4-inch gun, the *Port Chalmers* drove off the Italian vessel. Next day, while flying the French flag to confuse the enemy she was twice followed by enemy bombers but the Italian aircraft took no action. She reached Gibraltar on the third day and safely returned to Britain – a very lucky ship.

She was again selected to join the Malta convoy in August 1942 and of the 15 merchant ships which left United Kingdom ports for Malta only five reached Valletta. Vice-Admiral Sir Neville Syfret commanded the convoy, known as Operation Pedestal, and the escorts included the battleships *Rodney* and *Nelson,* the aircraft carriers *Victorious, Furious, Eagle* and *Indomitable* as well as a number of cruisers and destroyers. The convoy steamed into the Mediterranean on 11 August and attacks thereafter were almost continuous. Throughout it all, *Port Chalmers,* this time commanded by Captain H.G.B. Pinkney, led a charmed life and reached Malta undamaged – the only vessel not to have suffered damage or casualties. During the height of the actions, it was noticed that the starboard paravane was behaving strangely. Paravanes are submerged floats towed from the bows of a ship by wires which stream out at an angle

On her second Malta Convoy, the *Port Chalmers* found her starboard paravane was acting strangely and when the line was hauled in, a 21-inch torpedo was entangled at the end of it. The ship slowly went astern as far as she could on the line and cut it clear, leaving the torpedo to sink to the bottom where it exploded, giving the *Port Chalmers* a considerable shaking. PORT LINE ARCHIVES, UNIVERSITY OF LIVERPOOL

and protect the ship's sides from mines. The ship was slowed down and when the crew had almost wound in the paravane wire, they found an unexploded 21-inch torpedo entangled by its propellers. The vessel was stopped and then as she slowly went astern the paravane was let out as far as its wire would take it and then cut adrift. The paravane and torpedo sank to the bottom of the sea where it exploded and gave the *Port Chalmers* a tremendous shaking. The *Port Chalmers,* the Blue Star liners *Melbourne Star* (1936, 11,076) and *Brisbane Star* (1936, 11,076), Union Castle Line's *Rochester Castle* (1937, 7,795) and the tanker *Ohio* (1940, 7,795) were the only ships to reach Malta, the *Ohio* being so badly damaged that she was declared a constructive total loss and was scuttled off Malta on 19 September 1946. In his report on Operation Pedestal, Admiral Syfret praised the merchant ships involved and said: 'The steadfast way in which these ships pressed on their way to Malta, through all attacks, answering every manoeuvring order like a well-trained fleet unit, was a most inspiring sight... The memory of their conduct will remain an inspiration to all who were privileged to serve with them'.

As a result of these two remarkable voyages to Malta and return, 18 medals and commendations were awarded the men of the *Port Chalmers*, as well as four Lloyd's Silver Medals for Meritorious Service. Captain Gordon Higgs got the OBE, and Captain Pinkney, the DSO, (having already been awarded an MBE as chief officer on the first voyage). Chief Engineer S.G.L. Bentley and Second Officer Richard Bettess were both awarded the DSC.

Eighteen years after she was completed in 1923, the *Port Hardy* was torpedoed and sunk northwest of Ireland in 1941. Her bridge deck house, being made of wood, floated and was subsequently spotted by a trawler. The ship's bell was recovered and presented to the Wolverhampton High School for Girls, who had 'adopted' the *Port Hardy* through the British Ship Adoption Society. E. FLUCK

Between 1941 and 1943 four Port Line ships were torpedoed in the North Atlantic at the height of the U-Boat menace with packs of submarines attacking British convoys on the vital seaway between Britain and America. *Port Hardy*, under the command of Captain J.G. Lewis, was one of them. She had left Halifax, Nova Scotia on 16 April 1941 to join a 48-ship convoy. On 28 April the convoy was attacked north-west of Ireland and at 6.00 p.m. *Port Hardy* was hit on the port side abreast the mainmast with a torpedo fired by *U-96*. The ship was quickly abandoned and all crew were picked up safely by the escort *Zaafaran* (1921, 1,559), with the exception of a crewmember killed in the explosion. She sank in position 60.14N, 15.20W, less than two hours later. Some time later an American trawler came across her wheelhouse, which being made of wood, had remained afloat. The ship's bell was recovered and returned to Captain Lewis. The Wolverhampton School for Girls had adopted *Port Hardy* under the British Ship Adoption Society programme and Captain Lewis presented the bell to the school on 25 September 1942.

In early 1942 the company started taking over several ships on management from the Ministry of War Transport. Most were standard built 'Fort' ships built in Canada or 'Liberty' ships built in the United States. *Fort Chambly* was completed in mid April 1942 and taken over, with *Fort Stikine* coming under Port Line control next month, commissioning in July. Four Liberty ships were delivered in the United States as follows – *Sampler* 21 July 1943, *Samblade* 8 August 1943, *Samleven* 14 February 1944 and *Sameden* on 14 March 1944. In addition to these vessels Port Line also managed a standard British-built ship. This was the *Empire Treasure* built by Lithgows Limited at Port Glasgow. She was launched 28 December 1942 and handed

Many United States-built Liberty ships were placed on bare-boat charter with the Ministry of Transport and allocated to British shipping companies to manage. They were all given the pre-fix SAM. The Port Line managed the *Samblade* from 1943 to 1947. She is shown in Wellington Harbour in October 1943. ROYAL NEW ZEALAND AIR FORCE

over to Port Line management on 9 March 1943. A second vessel, *Empire Moulmein,* was launched 8 June 1944 but was only under Port Line management for a few months before she was delivered to the French Republic in June 1945.

Two days after leaving Halifax for New York on 16 June 1942, off Portland, Maine, USA, the *Port Nicholson* was struck by a torpedo from *U-87* near the engine room on the starboard side and a second torpedo hit further aft a few seconds later. Communication systems within the ship were cut off and within a short space of time the order to abandon ship was given. Two men in the engine room were killed. Fourth Engineer Dibley was trapped in the stokehold and was rescued by fireman Blundell at great personal risk. He was subsequently awarded a British Empire Medal and Lloyd's War Medal for his bravery. A Canadian escort vessel picked up all officers and crew. The *Port Nicholson* was still afloat and the escort vessel stood by all night. At about 7 a.m. the following morning, Captain H.C. Jeffrey, Chief Officer Munday and the first lieutenant and five ratings from the escort went on board *Port Nicholson* to ascertain her condition. About 7.45 a.m. her stern was settling rapidly and although the eight men got into their cutter, they were unable to get clear and were dragged down by *Port Nicholson* which quickly adopted a vertical position with her bow in the air. She disappeared within 30 seconds. Four men were picked up but Captain Jeffrey, the chief officer and two men from the escort were lost. The vessel sank in position 42.11N, 69.25W.[3]

On 7 June 1942 the Harrison Line steamer *Historian* collided with the *Port Auckland,* which had to put into Falmouth for repairs. The *Historian*'s owners accepted liability for the incident.

A wartime view of the *Port Darwin* in New York harbour in 1943. With a gun on the stern, anti-aircraft guns above the after part of the bridge deck and Carley life rafts from the masts, her wartime role is clearly portrayed. U.S. COAST GUARD, E. JOHNSON COLLECTION

In May 1942 the *Port Montreal* (Captain J.G. Lewis) sailed from Halifax for Australia via the Panama Canal. Early on 8 June the convoy dispersed and the *Port Montreal* proceeded south alone. Later that day she sighted two lifeboats and picked up 43 survivors of the Honduran freighter *Tela* (1927, 3,901) which had been torpedoed earlier that day N.E. of Belize in British Honduras. Two days later at 5.05 a.m. on 10 June, north of Colon, a torpedo struck the vessel on the port side. She immediately began to sink and was quickly abandoned. The two lifeboats and two dinghies were lashed in line ahead. Sails were set and at 2.30 p.m. on 13 June, the survivors were picked up by the Columbian auxiliary schooner *Hilda*; two men from *Tela* had died in the boats. They were all taken to Cristobal on 16 June. The *Port Montreal* had been sunk in position 12.17N, 80.20W by *U-68*.[4]

The sinking of the *Port Hunter* (Captain J.B. Bradley) on 11 July 1942 in approximately 31.N, 24W, has never been fully explained. She had travelled in convoy from Liverpool and when about 100 miles north west of Sierra Leone, she left the convoy to proceed independently in accordance with orders. She was carrying general cargo, including ammunition and there were 72 officers and crew, 14 Royal Navy gunners and five passengers on board. At 11.45 p.m. that same night the convoy saw a brilliant flash far to the west and when the investigating sloop turned back next morning, it found three survivors clinging to debris and a patch of oil in the water. The survivors had been sleeping in aft upper-deck cabins. Woken up by a tremendous explosion and a blinding flash, they rushed on deck and leapt into the water. By the time they surfaced the ship had disappeared – just a pall of black smoke and debris falling from the sky. It is assumed she fell victim to a submarine which followed her

The *Port Hunter,* completed in 1922 was the most tragic loss of World War II; only three crew members of the 91 passengers and crew onboard survived the July 1942 sinking. E. FLUCK

when she broke away from the convoy. Eighty-eight died – the greatest loss of life from any wartime Port Line casualty. German sources say she was torpedoed by *U-582.*

On 1 March 1943 the *Port Wyndham* (Captain L.H. Swan) was attacked by a German Focke-Wulf bomber 400 miles west of Finisterre on passage United Kingdom to New York. The aircraft was flying low and initially it was thought to be an Allied machine but as the *Port Wyndham* was circled it was identified as German. The ship radioed that she was being attacked and opened fire. The enemy aircraft gained height and made a run over the ship at about 1,700-metres, dropping five bombs, the nearest striking the sea 34 metres away. Fire was maintained from the *Port Wyndham* and although no hit was claimed, the aircraft shortly after flew back to its base with black smoke coming from its fuselage. The aircraft also strafed the ship with machine gun fire and two gunners were wounded.

The *Port Jackson* (Captain G.L. Hazlewood) was more fortunate on 26 August 1942 when at 11.42 p.m. on a moonlit night a submarine (*U 516*) was sighted on the surface about half a mile away. She was 506 miles west of Ireland, travelling at full speed on passage from Buenos Aires to Liverpool. She immediately swung round to present her stern to the submarine and developed maximum speed of 17 knots. The enemy was briefly lost from sight but at midnight was seen in the ship's wake gaining fast. At 12.15 it moved to a more stable firing position and opened fire. The *Port Jackson* responded at a range of 500 metres and her third round exploded in a shower of sparks which indicated it had hit its target. Two of the 12 shells fired from the submarine hit the *Port Jackson* but caused only minor damage. At 00.28 a.m. the

A sister to the *Port Chalmers*, but built in a different shipyard, the *Port Wyndham* also survived World War II, although she had a narrow escape from becoming a total loss after being torpedoed in the dying stages of the war in April 1945 and spent 15 months under repair.

submarine broke off the attack and was not seen again. The following day the *Port Jackson* picked up a boat containing 27 survivors from the British tramp ship *Sylvia de Larrinaga* (1925, 5,218) and subsequently all arrived safely in Liverpool.

Another North Atlantic casualty in 1943 was the *Port Auckland* (Captain A.E. Fishwick) which was torpedoed by *U-305* when homeward bound in convoy on 17 March 1943 in position 52.25N, 30.15W south-east of Cape Farewell, Greenland.

Carrying several large cases as deck cargo, the *Port Auckland* passes through Cook Strait in 1942. ROYAL NEW ZEALAND AIR FORCE

The torpedo struck at 10.17 p.m. on the starboard side in the engine room and it was flooded in a few seconds. The fourth engineer and seven crew were not seen after the explosion. The *Port Auckland* may have been unlucky. She had been ordered back from a faster convoy HX228 to travel in a slow convoy SC122. This convoy of 38 ships and five escorts was traveling in close proximity to the faster 50 ship convoy HX229. Thirty-one U-boats were shadowing what they thought was one convoy and assembled their forces to attack at night. *U-305*, under the command of 26-year old Rudolph Bahr fired a fan of four torpedoes and in his report he stated that he thought he had hit two 8,000 ton ships of the *Port Adelaide* class (the other vessel was the tramp ship *Zouave* (1930, 4,256). When one of the torpedoes struck *Port Auckland*, the terror generated cannot easily be contemplated as everyone made a dash for the ladder in a scene that saw the sea pouring in and everything else in complete darkness. One of the lifeboats was destroyed by the explosion but the remaining three boats were lowered and scrambling nets were set overside. Ten RAAF pilots travelling as passengers joined the crew in abandoning ship. Within a short time 100 men had escaped in the lifeboats but as one boat's crew was being rescued, another torpedo from *U-305* tore into the *Port Auckland* making a terrific noise. The buffer of the ship saved the lives of all in the lifeboat, as the U-boat sought to hasten the sinking.

Twenty-two ships, carrying over 162,500 tonnes of cargo, were sunk from convoys HX229 and SC122, costing the lives of 360 crew and 12 passengers. This was the height of the U-boat war in the North Atlantic. The U-boats never again achieved similar successes as more escorts were available, escort carriers were introduced and more comprehensive air cover was provided as aircraft were equipped to operate over a greater area and were able to bridge the gap in the middle of the Atlantic that was out of reach of air support in the early part of the war. Escort carriers enabled the Allies to attack U-boats night and day.

The last Port Line owned ship to be sunk was the *Port Victor* (Captain W.G. Higgs). Following trials, at which she had reached 16.73 knots, she was delivered to the company on 12 October 1942. The *Port Victor* had made her maiden voyage to Australia and was returning from Buenos Aires to Britain on her second voyage with a full cargo and 65 passengers, half of whom were women and children. On 30 April 1943, 600 miles South West of Ireland, and travelling independently, she was torpedoed in the engine room at 8.34 p.m. All lights went out but the engines continued to turn over the propellers until the chief engineer cut off the fuel injection. Two of the eight boats were destroyed in the first explosion and seven minutes after, a second torpedo struck the ship, blowing up No 2 boat, killing four persons, including two women and injuring several others. Ten minutes later a third torpedo struck. It blew up No 8 boat killing 11 men. The submarine (*U-107*) surfaced and whilst the German officer expressed his pleasure at sinking a cargo of foodstuffs, he showed concern for the women passengers and apologised for not having any room in the submarine. Although

The *Port Victor*, a further improved *Port Jackson* class vessel, was completed in October 1942, seven months after the *Port Phillip*. The photograph shows her in New York Harbour a month after entering service. Just five months later she was torpedoed and sunk in the north Atlantic with the loss of 17 passengers and crew. U.S. COAST GUARD

the *Port Victor* was settling fast, the submarine fired a fourth torpedo and the ship sank shortly afterwards in position 47.49N, 22.02W. A Liberator aircraft which had been dispatched in response to the *Port Victor*'s distress message spotted the five lifeboats and three rafts the following morning, strung out in line ahead. The aircraft guided HMS *Wren* to the flotilla of craft and by 5.00 p.m. the following day 149 survivors were safely aboard the warship. Loss of life totaled 17 – three passengers, ten officers and crew, two Royal Navy gunners and two DBS (distressed British seamen), and it was clear that 16 of these deaths were caused by the submarine not allowing sufficient time to abandon ship.[5]

After the war Captain Higgs made contact with *U-107's* commander, Captain Harald Gelhaus. He told Higgs he had spotted the *Port Victor* at about 6.00 p.m. (German Summer Time) and later surfaced to keep in front of her. Because of *Port Victor*'s high speed he decided he could not attack during the day below the surface, so he kept ahead of her in order to attack on the surface at night. He watched the British ship's zigzag pattern and when he was preparing to fire a fan of three torpedoes, the *Port Victor* carried on 10 degrees further than anticipated so he then fired a stern double fan, with one of the torpedoes striking amidships. Captain Gelhaus fired the two further torpedoes to sink the *Port Victor* as quickly as possible so that he could leave the area. The fourth torpedo broke her back and she then sank fairly quickly. He said he had already sunk 19 vessels and without this experience he could not have sunk *Port Victor* because of her high speed.[6]

The *Port Fairy* (Captain J.G. Lewis) was in a convoy on passage from Glasgow to Buenos Aires when near Gibraltar she was attacked by German Focke-Wulf aircraft

One of the managed Canadian-built 'FORT' ships, the *Fort Stikine* was discharging cargo in Bombay in April 1944, when cotton caught fire, spread to explosives, and the ship blew up with such devastating force that much of the port area was destroyed and some 750 people were killed and more than 2,400 were injured. U.S. COAST GUARD, BAIN-WRIGHT COLLECTION

over a two-day period. She was directed to proceed to Casablanca but on 12 July 1943 when in position 37.18N, 14.37W, she was again attacked by an enemy aircraft. She was struck by a bomb which pierced the main deck and exploded in the upper tween deck, creating a large hole and setting the ship on fire. Her steering gear was also damaged. Part of her cargo of high explosives was dumped overboard but it proved difficult to extinguish the fire. Chief Officer A.J. Knell was lowered overside to direct a hose at the seat of the blaze. Others relieved him and HMS *Swale* came alongside and also directed her hoses and, after about four hours, the fire was extinguished. *Port Fairy* then made course for Casablanca, using her twin screws to steer. Repairs took six weeks. A.J. Knell had already received a DSC as a master in the Sea Rescue Service earlier in the war and was awarded the MBE for his brave work on *Port Fairy.* A total of six Lloyd's War Medals for Bravery at Sea were awarded members of the crew of *Port Fairy.* In another incident about the same time, *Port Alma* was damaged by an air attack in the Mediterranean.

In February 1944, the managed freighter *Empire Treasure* (Captain A.R. Martin) lost all her propeller blades in an Atlantic gale and the ship was left wallowing helplessly. It was an anxious time for everyone as she was a sitting target for a submarine and for this reason it was not possible to use the radio to advise her position and seek help. She lay for 12 hours before she could send a short-wave message. Three further days passed until the Admiralty tug *Bustler* (1941, 1,104) arrived to take her in tow. The weather was still very rough and the tug had to exercise great care to ensure the towline was not broken. On many occasions neither the *Empire Treasure* nor the tug could see each other due to the sea conditions. The *Empire Treasure* was towed 1,091 miles and the two vessels safely arrived at Newport, Monmouthshire, six days after the mid Atlantic link-up.

Another of the managed ships had a tragic end when the *Fort Stikine* (Captain A.J.

One of 15 standard British-built Y class Empire steamers, the *Empire Treasure* was managed by the Port Line from 1943 to 1946. On one voyage in January 1944 she lost her propeller blades in the Atlantic and had an anxious wait for a tug to tow her to safety.

Naismith) blew up in Bombay Harbour on 14 April 1944. She was discharging a cargo of cotton and had 1,417 tonnes of explosives in the lower holds, including shells, torpedoes, mines, signal rockets, magnesium flares and incendiary bombs, when fire broke out amongst the cotton bales. It got out of control. Everyone had left the ship and were standing on the wharf when there was a first explosion and flames shot up 12-15 metres in the air. Captain A.J. Naismith and Chief Officer W.D. Henderson went back on board to ensure no one else was left on board. They, and A. Jopp, the cook, were never seen again and an urgent effort was made to move as many people as possible away from the area. Thirty-four minutes later a huge explosion rocked the port and part of the city, spreading debris and blazing cotton skyward. A tidal wave saw the ship *Jalapadma* (1929, 3,935), moored close to the stern of the *Fort Stikine,* being lifted bodily into the air with the stern coming down on the roof of a cargo shed with her bows floating on the water. There was a huge loss of life – 231 port or related workers killed and 476 injured while it was estimated that over 500 civilians had been killed and 2,400 injured. Twelve ships were sunk or were constructive total losses, and several more were damaged. There was massive devastation within the port area and fires raged. Buildings had to be demolished to create fire-breaks and prevent the fires sweeping through the city. Wartime conditions meant that the magnitude of the disaster was never published to the world to the extent it would have been in peacetime.

In the dying stages of the war the *Port Wyndham* (Captain E.J. Syvret), on passage from London for the United States, was severely damaged by a torpedo from a German midget submarine *U-5070* which exploded abreast of Numbers 2 and 3 hatches. She

The 24 year old veteran *Port Caroline* in New York harbour in September 1943. U.S. COAST GUARD, E. JOHNSON COLLECTION

was travelling independently, with a destroyer escort, HMS *Vesper*, when the explosion occurred at 7.14 a.m. on 11 April 1945, as the vessel was five miles off Dungeness Light in the English Channel. The submarine was subjected to depth charge attacks over the next few hours but escaped. The *Port Wyndham* stopped her engines and the vessel was headed towards shallow water. She began to list heavily to port and take in water. Several small craft came to stand by the stricken vessel and opportunity was taken to disembark the 22 passengers while the ship took steps to correct the list. Pumping temporarily stopped when the vessel started listing to starboard and she appeared in a very tender state. Tugs had been called for and at 9.25 p.m. the tug *Lady Brassey* (1913, 362) arrived and an hour later the salvage vessel *Dapper* (1915, 419) was made fast alongside. The salvage people wanted to shift the vessel to a safer position closer to shore where she could be inspected by a Lloyd's Surveyor. Captain Syvret was not happy with the proposal and some arguments ensued. The master won the day and *Lady Brassey* took *Port Wyndham* in tow while the crew were discharging sand ballast from No 1 hold to lighten the vessel. Another tug, *Lady Duncannon* (1914, 181), was made fast aft to assist with the towage. At 5.15 p.m. both tugs were cast off and returned to Dover and the *Port Wyndham* anchored in 10 fathoms of water. By 8.00 p.m. it was seen the water was gaining and an urgent call went out for more pumps to be brought to the vessel. The Port Line marine superintendent ashore arranged for pumps from a local fire station to be taken out to the ship, and these, along with pumps from the Salvage Authorities, controlled the inflow of water into No 1 hold. Next morning the tugs *Lady Brassey* and *Saucey* (1942, 597), with salvage vessels in attendance, towed *Port Wyndham* stern first to Southampton where she safely arrived at 4.41 p.m. on 15 April. Repairs took 15 months to be completed.[7] On her first voyage after repairs, the chief engineer reported that he felt the ship was slightly out of alignment because she had been on blocks in the dry dock for so long, but he was confident she would settle down – and so she did for another 21 years of service.

Although the European war ended in May 1945, the conflict with Japan continued until 14 August 1945 and Port Line ships remained engaged on Ministry of Transport service. Refrigerated ships were in demand by the Allied forces and it was a Port Line vessel (*Port Macquarie*) that took the first full cargo of refrigerated foodstuffs and other stores to American troops serving in the front line islands of the Pacific as they pushed the Japanese back. Almost all the larger motor ships were involved and their cargoes included frozen turkeys, chickens, fruit and vegetables and the Port Line personnel on board the ships were impressed with the excellence and variety of the food supplied to the American forces. The ships discharged at isolated places in the Pacific where the Americans had constructed ports and refrigerated storage facilities such as Pearl Harbour, Guam, Manus (Admiralty Islands), Finschafen, (New Guinea) and Leyte in the Philippines.

In the latter stages of the war the *Port Sydney, Port Melbourne* and the captured Italian cargo liner *Lowlander* were mainly employed on a North Atlantic service. The dry cargo war-built ships were on general trading, unrelated to traditional Port Line services. For a time the *Samblade* ran a shuttle service between the Thames and Antwerp carrying stores and foodstuffs for the BLA (British Liberation Army) and the people of Belgium and Holland. The *Samleven* was as far afield as Los Angeles loading for India and loading back from Calcutta to Santos in Brazil. The *Sampler* carried coal from Philadelphia to Carentec, France.

Senior company masters and engineers who were seconded as advisers and technical specialists in a wide range of tasks were also committed for considerable time after hostilities ceased. Captain P.S. Ball was 'loaned' by Port Line to the Control Commission for Germany and from 1945 to 1947 served as marine superintendent for the Port of Lubeck while Captain F.W. Bailey performed a similar role at Flensburg. It also took many months for former staff to be released from the Armed Forces and prisoners of war in Germany to be repatriated. It was not until 2 March 1946 that the Liner Requisition Scheme ended and vessels could once more operate to the direction of their owners. Slowly, but surely, Port Line was able to return to a peacetime mode.

1 Port Line archives PL4/15 20/2/77.
2 ibid.
3 ibid.
4 ibid.
5 *GWCZ Calling*, No 20, Feb 1962.
6 Port Line archives PL4/15 20/2/77.
7 ibid.

An outstanding figure in the affairs of the Port Line, Bill Donald became London manager of the company in 1927, a director from 1938, and company chairman in the great growth period 1947 to 1960. PORT LINE ARCHIVES, UNIVERSITY OF LIVERPOOL

CHAPTER 5

Postwar Port Line

Although the war was over it took several years for Port Line to rebuild its management structure and fleet. Walter Tyser remained chairman until 1939 and had a year as president before retiring in 1940. He died in 1944. The company's tribute included the comment that 'with his charm of manner, determination, self confidence, and imposing presence he found it possible to employ a direct manner of speech which might have caused offence if used by those who lacked his gifts'.[1] Tyser made a major contribution to the success of the company in its first quarter century and worked very ably with directors and managers. Herbert Corry, vice-chairman since 1927, succeeded him as chairman from 1939 to 1947. A cautious man who rigorously considered every proposal before making a decision, he helped improve the climate of trust and frankness between Port Line and the other British lines. In strongly protecting and fighting for the interests of the company, his peers said that his weapons were friendliness, fairness, good humour and moderation.

For most of the war Bill Donald chaired the Diversion Committee at the Ministry of War Transport, work that led to him being made a CBE. He had been handpicked by Basil Sanderson, then with Shaw Savill & Albion, who in his autobiography *Ships and Sealing Wax*, outlined Donald's qualities: 'In pre-war days he (Donald) had been manager of the Port Line and had the widest knowledge of ships in every particular, including structure, engines, cargo working and refrigeration. He was a man of great mental ability, with an infinite capacity for hard work, gifted with an instinct and perspicuity possessed by but few, and above everything else of the most patent and transparent honesty'.[2] He became managing director of Port Line in May 1945, a month after also being appointed to the parent company Cunard board. He became Port Line chairman in 1947 and was a key figure in re-moulding its fortunes in the postwar era. R.H. Senior, who was assistant manager in 1939, and who ended the war as a brigadier, having won the DSO and Bar for distinguished service at La Bassee Canal and in the Western Desert, also joined the board in September 1946.

In New York, Port Line's resident director, Sir T. Ashley Sparks (he received the KCMG in 1941 in addition to the KBE awarded in 1919), continued the role he had undertaken in World War I as director-general of the British Ministry of Shipping in the USA in 1918-19, by being appointed the United States representative of the British Ministry of Shipping 1939-41 and then the representative of the Ministry of War Transport 1941-45.

The *Port Lincoln*, a sister ship of the *Port Macquarie*, was laid down in September 1944 but was not delivered until January 1946. The photograph shows her in Otago Harbour. BAIN-WRIGHT COLLECTION

Port Line staff, 127 of them sea staff, won 140 awards during the war. Several senior managers and masters were seconded to the war effort and also served ably as advisers to Allied forces and other organisations. The war had affected not only the UK personnel but also Port Line staff and agents in Australia and New Zealand, and the return to a peacetime lifestyle took sometime to accomplish. Head office moved back to 88 Leadenhall Street and *Oaklawn* was sold in November 1945. The wartime management of the company had been led by Jack Rooper, assisted by Warwick Gregory who had come over from New Zealand.

All the lines needed to rebuild their fleets. Shaw Savill & Albion had lost 12 ships, New Zealand Shipping/Federal 19 and Blue Star Line 29. Like them Port Line, (14 ships lost), had to move promptly to order new tonnage for its trade shares to Australia, New Zealand and the east coast of North America, from British shipyards whose order books were filling fast.

The single-screw *Port Lincoln,* laid down on 21 September 1944, was launched by Mrs Martin, wife of the marine superintendent Captain A.R. Martin, on 23 August 1945 and delivered 24 January 1946. She was the first postwar cargo ship to be completed on the Tyne. Next came a sixth modified *Port Jackson* class ship, similar to the *Port Napier*. Ordered from John Brown & Company, the *Port Wellington* was launched on 4 February 1946 by Lady Freyberg, the wife of Sir Bernard Freyberg, governor-general designate of New Zealand. The company needed large capacity refrigerated ships quicker than the shipyards could build them, so the *Empire Wessex*

In order to rebuild the fleet quickly, the Port Line purchased the twin-screw refrigerated ship *Empire Wessex* in 1946 and renamed her *Port Hobart.* She was similar to the Shaw Savill & Albion 'W' class and had 13,948 cubic metres of refrigerated space. She initially had accommodation for 128 passengers, but when post-war demand eased this was reduced to 12. V.H. YOUNG & L.A. SAWYER

was purchased for £603,000 and converted to its requirements. As the *Port Hobart,* she was delivered on 29 August 1946. Her accommodation for 128 passengers, in big demand immediately after the war, was left in place until 1950 when the ship was reduced to the usual 12-passenger capacity.

Swan, Hunter & Wigham Richardson had been given an order for a further standard twin-screw vessel and she was launched as *Port Pirie* in May 1946 by Lady Hurcomb, the wife of Sir Cyril Hurcomb, director general of the Ministry of War Transport. She was delivered on 30 January 1947. A further single-screw vessel, an update on the *Port Macquarie* and *Port Lincoln,* was launched by Mrs de Gruchy, the wife of the former local director of the company in Australia, in September 1946 and delivered by Swan, Hunter on 24 March 1947 as the *Port Lyttelton.* Although the company's emphasis had been directed at replacing vessels lost in the war with the larger twin-screw ships, the three single-screw vessels were useful in providing service frequency and flexibility, and for most of their lives they were employed on the main line trade. They each gave around 25 years of reliable service.

The Liberty ship *Sampler,* which had been managed since 1943, was purchased outright on 18 April 1947 and renamed *Port Albany.* Slow (maximum service speed of 10.5 knots) and with only general cargo capacity, she was a stopgap, and after mainly MANZ Line service, was sold in 1951. During 1947 the other war-managed vessels such as *Sameden, Samblade,* and *Samleven* were all released for sale or returned to the

As a temporary vessel for the MANZ Line service, the Port Line purchased the Liberty ship *Sampler* in April 1947, renaming her *Port Albany*. She was sold in 1951. I.J. FARQUHAR

The Port Line also managed two Canadian-built 'FORT' type steamers and the illustration shows the *Fort Chambly* at Cape Town. She was under Port Line control from 1942 until 1947. V.H. YOUNG & L.A. SAWYER

United States. The *Fort Chambly* had been purchased from Canada by the US government under the Hyde Park Agreement of April 1941 and was one of 90 Fort-type vessels lend-leased to Britain. She was returned to the USA early in 1948 and laid up in the reserve fleet and scrapped in 1959. The years from 1942 to 1947 under Port Line management were the only times she carried cargo. Port Line managed the *Lowlander* from October 1941 until 4 September 1947 when she was re-delivered to the United States Maritime Commission in New York for return to her Italian owners.

During the war the Royal Navy took over two more incomplete *Port Napier* class ships for conversion to escort carriers. After the war the company purchased the ships for £50,000 each and rebuilt them as refrigerated cargo ships. In deference to the distinguished wartime service of HMS *Vindex*, the first was named *Port Vindex*, the only Port Line vessel not to be named after a port. B. FIELDEN

The remaining wartime managed ship, the *Empire Treasure,* left Port Line control when she was sold to the Donaldson Line and became the *Gracia* in 1946. For a time both *Lowlander* and *Empire Treasure* had Chinese crews, which must have been a challenge for their Port Line masters used to British crews.

The company also reclaimed the two vessels similar to the *Port Napier* taken over by the Admiralty very early in their construction and converted to escort aircraft carriers. It offered £50,000 each for HMS *Vindex* and HMS *Nairana*, a price that reflected the fact that it would cost at least £500,000 each to convert them to modern refrigerated cargo liners. The ships were delivered to shipyards to begin the long conversion process. Although not the name of a port, the former HMS *Vindex* was delivered as *Port Vindex* on 1 June 1949, to recognise the ship's distinguished wartime record. She was the only ship built for the company not named after a port or location in Australia, Canada or New Zealand. The second vessel, named *Port Victor* after the earlier ship in the class lost in 1943, was delivered on 16 September 1949.

These two ships had interesting wartime histories. HMS *Vindex* was commissioned on 15 November 1943 and initially protected convoys under the Western Approaches Command. She became the first dedicated night anti-submarine carrier, operating with elderly Swordfish aircraft, described as 'Stringbags', and Sea Hurricanes. The aircraft were used to attack U-boats on the surface, particularly at night. She later transferred for escort duty on the convoys from northern Scotland to Murmansk. Her planes were credited with sinking three submarines and damaging several others. On her second Russian convoy, she was joined by HMS *Nairana* which had also been operating in the Atlantic. HMS *Vindex* escorted four convoys to and from Loch Ewe in Scotland to Kota Inlet where the ships reached the safety of Murmansk and HMS *Nairana* made three round voyages in a similar role. During her service as an escort carrier, HMS *Nairana* carried between 20 and 24 aircraft and a complement of 558 personnel.

When the European war ended in May 1945, HMS *Vindex* was transferred to the British Pacific Fleet, but the war finished shortly after she arrived in Sydney. She made two voyages to Hong Kong and other eastern ports, operating in a humanitarian role and repatriating prisoners of war. She returned to Rosyth at the end of 1946 and was decommissioned. HMS *Nairana* was transferred to the Royal Dutch Navy on 20 March 1946 and renamed *Karel Doorman*. She 'showed the flag' around the world, particularly in South Africa and the Dutch East Indies, before being handed back to the Royal Navy on 28 May 1948.

The *Port Quebec*, which had been requisitioned by the Royal Navy for employment as a minelayer in 1939, finally entered the fleet as a cargo liner on 20 December 1947. Between her entry into service as HMS *Port Quebec* in 1940 as a minelayer, and by the time she completed this role in October 1943, she had laid 33,494 mines. She had been working in concert with HMS *Port Napier*, laid down as *Port Napier*, and subsequently requisitioned by the Admiralty in January 1940. After her minelaying experiences she was sent to John Brown's shipyard on the Clyde for conversion to the first-ever aircraft repair ship and she re-entered naval service as HMS *Deer Sound* in early 1945. For this work she was given a complete machinery refit with a measure of steel protection on the sides of the hull and the top deck, while her buoyancy was improved with the addition of a large number of empty drums. She was placed with the Pacific Fleet during the closing stages of the war and stayed with it during the gradual re-occupation of Japanese-held territories. She returned to Britain in May 1946 and was laid up in the Forth for some time before being sent to the Tyne for conversion to a cargo ship. This was a huge task as all the armour plating had to be removed, necessitating filling-in the 4,000 rivet holes which had been holding it in place. Her crew accommodation was almost completely rebuilt, as postwar all accommodation was amidships.

All these vessels were largely designs of the late 1930s adapted quickly to meet the immediate need for new tonnage, as the shipyards did not have the staff or time to cope with new designs. In 1947, however, Britain undertook to buy all the New Zealand meat for a period of seven years, creating demand for ships larger than the prewar *Port Jackson/Port Napier* class ships. The company had placed orders for three 17-knot vessels with up to 16,992 cubic metres of insulated space. Two came from Swan, Hunter & Wigham Richardson and the other from Hawthorn Leslie. The first of the series, the *Port Napier*, was launched by Mrs J.E. Beasley, the wife of the Australian high commissioner on 12 November 1946. She was delivered 1 September 1947 and immediately took line honours for several years as the largest refrigerated cargo ship

The *Port Quebec* was built for the MANZ Line service and although launched on 17 August 1939, she was requisitioned and did not assume a commercial role until December 1947. As a minelayer she laid 33,494 mines between 1940 and 1943. She was later converted to an aircraft repair ship as HMS *Deer Sound*, and is shown in this role in Sydney Harbour, fitted with extra steel plating along the sides of the hull and around the stern. NATIONAL LIBRARY OF AUSTRALIA

in the world with insulated space of 16,508 cubic metres – a capacity that could accommodate the equivalent of 180,000 carcasses of lamb, 12,000 crates of cheese, 60,000 boxes of butter, as well as 750 casks of tallow and the equivalent of 8,000 bales of wool in the general cargo spaces.

She and her companions enabled the company to pay off overage tonnage. The veterans *Port Melbourne* and *Port Sydney* were sold to British shipbreakers in 1948. In her 34 years of service, the *Port Sydney* had steamed 1,671,000 miles, and had been commanded by 18 masters. The three pre-1920 steamers (*Ports Darwin, Caroline and Adelaide*) that had survived the war were sold to breakers in 1949-50. The *Port Caroline* had a brief reprieve by being used as a floating meat storage vessel at London from 31 October 1949 until 5 February 1950.

The large refrigerated ships invariably had to spend up to ten days to a fortnight on the New Zealand coast being cleaned and battened out after discharge prior to loading frozen produce. This involved the removal of all the outward dunnage used for tomming up the cargo to prevent movement on passage and between ports, then clean and wash the holds before laying clean pine timber at spaced intervals to allow for cold air circulation throughout each insulated space. The wooden spar ceilings in the general cargo spaces, and the wooden sheathing in the refrigerated compartments also required extensive painting to maintain the high standard of cleanliness required and the insulation was often damaged as the outward cargo was discharged. Port Line employed specialist carpenters from a Wellington company who travelled to the ports to assist local carpenters and waterside shipwrights to prepare the holds. It was a long and costly process. With the *Port Napier* a trial was undertaken with special Birmabright

A painting by Oswald Birley of Thomas, Lord Royden of Frankby. Thomas Royden was a C&D Line director when it was formed in 1914 and remained on the board until 1950. He was also on the board of the Cunard Steam-Ship Company from 1905 until his death on 6 November 1950. ROYDEN FAMILY

(permanent aluminium alloy panels) replacing the wooden sheathing and ceilings of the holds and this new concept reduced re-painting, but was still expensive to repair.

The two other vessels were more distinctive than the traditional style of the new *Port Napier.* Both had streamlined bridge fronts and sweptback funnels. The *Port Brisbane* was launched by Mrs Bill Donald on 6 July 1948 and the *Port Auckland* by Mrs Jack Rooper on 4 October 1948. Both vessels attracted worldwide attention for their revolutionary design. Each cost £1,500,000 – the two ships costing more than the value of the 25 ships that made up the Commonwealth and Dominion Line fleet in 1914! The *Port Brisbane* even attracted the interest of the royal family. On 3 March 1949, Queen Elizabeth and Princess Margaret visited her in the London docks, prior to her maiden voyage. They were shown all over the vessel, even going into the tween deck where a mock-up of a refrigerated hold showed how the cargo was stowed. The visit was a red-letter day for Port Line which invited its crews around the world to 'splice the main brace' in honour of the visit. It was the first time since the reign of Queen Elizabeth the First (1558-1603) that a reigning Queen had inspected a cargo vessel in the London docks.

On her maiden voyage to New Zealand the *Port Brisbane* carried over 14,000 freight tons of cargo including 5000 tons of motor vehicles, 1200 tons of drapery, 750 tons of newsprint, 350 tons of carpets, 350 tons of tractors and bulldozers, 250 tons of cigarettes, 75 tons of beer and 50 tons each of pianos and millinery as well as a host of other manufactured items. She extended the use of Birmabright, with all her insulated spaces sheathed with aluminium alloy, representing in itself, a saving of 260 tons in weight. The ship also had a 3-ton deck crane positioned between numbers four and five hatches so that it could be used to supplement the single set of cargo derricks at those hatches. It was the first time in the post-war period a deck crane had

Built by Hawthorn, Leslie, the *Port Auckland*, sister to the *Port Brisbane*, also attracted much interest – 30,000 Aucklanders inspected her on her maiden voyage in July 1949. Both the *Port Auckland* and the *Port Brisbane* had a 3-ton deck crane between hatches 4 & 5 – the first to be fitted to a British ship in the Australian/New Zealand trade. The photograph shows her dressed for her first visit to Port Chalmers on 13 January 1950. E.A. PHILLIPS

been installed in a British ship in the Australasian trades. Instead of the top hatch openings made up of steel beams and large wooden insulated plugs, electrically driven steel roller hatch covers were installed on the weather decks.

The *Port Brisbane* was delivered 28 February 1949 with the *Port Auckland* following from Hawthorn Leslie's yard on 26 April. The *Port Auckland* had a more rounded funnel top than the *Port Brisbane* and created much interest in her name city where over 30,000 Aucklanders inspected her during an open day. The two sisters arranged a brief rendezvous off Rangitoto Beacon, Auckland on 9 July 1949. In 1951 the *Port Auckland* sailed from London for New Zealand with a record outward cargo of 15,813 freight tons. By 1950 Port Line had 25 vessels with a gross tonnage of 224,559, still slightly short of pre-war capacity.

A number of British shipping companies had made a practice of appointing their senior master commodore of the fleet. In 1948 the Port Line appointed distinguished master mariner W. Gordon Higgs as the first commodore of the line. Apart from his wartime record, Commodore Higgs had joined the Tyser Line in 1907, obtaining his first command in 1919 and had commanded more than a dozen Port Line vessels prior to *Port Brisbane.* He first went to sea in 1902 and went around Cape Horn in the sailing ship *Celtic Monarch* (1884, 2,119) in 1905. The practice continued over a period of 21 years with commodore chief engineers being appointed from

In 1951 the Port Line commissioned three single-screw ships, from different shipyards, for the MANZ Line or the main line berth to and from Australia and New Zealand to the United Kingdom/Europe. The first was the *Port Adelaide* from the Hawthorn, Leslie yard in May 1951. She initially had a single pole mast forward, but it vibrated so much, particularly when going astern, that it had to be replaced after the maiden voyage. The photograph shows her at Adelaide at the end of the first leg of her maiden voyage. A.D. EDWARDES

The *Port Adelaide* at Wellington with the new goalpost mast structure used for the remaining 20 years of her Port Line service. R.A. PRIEST

In February 1954 the Port Line took delivery of a 16.25 knot single-screw motorship named *Port Montreal* for the MANZ Line service. However, with her refrigerated cargo space enhanced from 2,494 cubic metres to 7,702 cubic metres in 1959, she was more often employed on the Crusader Line services until her sale in 1972. R.A. PRIEST

1954. The appointments were not automatic and not all senior masters or chief engineers became commodore. The board made the appointments and there were gaps between 1948 and 1969 when no commodore was in place. The practice faded away on the advent of the Blue Star Port Lines Management Company.

Three smaller single-screw ships followed the larger trio. They were 15.5 knot, 14,159 cubic metre capacity vessels, designed for the flexibility of either the main line run or the East Coast North America service. They also had streamlined bridge fronts, but each varied slightly as they came from different shipyards. The *Port Adelaide* was launched on 8 December 1950 by Mrs B.P. Arrowsmith, wife of the former engineering superintendent and a director of the company, and entered service 30 May 1951. Lady Corry, wife of Sir James Corry, launched the second, the *Port Nelson,* on 19 June 1951. She was appropriately built at Belfast, the home city of the Corry family with Sir James being a great grandson of the founder of the Corry timber business. The final vessel was launched as the *Port Townsville* by Mrs Geoffrey Gibbs on 21 June 1951 and delivered on 22 October that year. Mrs Gibbs was the wife of Hon. Geoffrey Gibbs, (later Sir Geoffrey) a director of Antony Gibbs & Company, the owners of Gibbs, Bright & Co, the Port Line Australian agents, as well as being chairman of the Australia & New Zealand Bank. He was subsequently appointed to the Port Line board in 1966.

Three years later the company built a smaller 16.25-knot motor ship specially for the American trade MANZ Line service. This was the *Port Montreal,* launched on 22 September 1953 by Mrs H.E.T. Ross, the wife of the London manager and a director of Port Line. She was delivered 4 February 1954, but in her 18 years in the fleet, she was mainly employed in the service of associated companies like Crusader Shipping

Looking immaculate, sister ships *Port Sydney* and *Port Melbourne* berthed at Adelaide in the late 1950s. Port Line instructions to masters directed that vessels should arrive on the Australian or New Zealand coast in a newly painted condition, rather than on the home coast. FREEMAN-PRIEST

Company, Compass Line or Atlas Line. Prior to entering Crusader Line service in 1960, her refrigerated capacity was increased from 2,494 cubic metres to 7,702 cubic metres, which also included 1,099 cubic metres for carrying chilled meat.

The enhancement of the refrigerated capacity in *Port Montreal* marked the use of a new refrigerant in place of the traditional CO2. It had been developed by Du Pont in America in the mid to late 1930s, but World War II delayed its adoption. A refinement of methyl chloride, its technical name was dichlorofluoromethane, but it was marketed as Freon 12. Almost harmless, it had no taste or odour, and did not attack ferrous metals. Initially costly, it did not start to replace CO2 in larger British refrigerated ship installations until 1959. Freon 12 was introduced in the refrigerated enhancement of the *Port Quebec* in 1960 and then all new buildings from the *Port New Plymouth*. In the 1959 refit of the *Port Montreal*, opportunity was also taken to fully air-condition the vessel for the more tropical voyages of Crusader Line. She was the first Port Line ship so equipped, and air-conditioning was incorporated into all new-built vessels from the *Port Alfred* in 1961. In May 1962 the company began installing it in the earlier postwar vessels. From the mid 1960s, Freon 22 superseded Freon 12 for air-conditioning and main marine refrigeration installations. While it was a perfect refrigerant for the carriage of fruit it was not as satisfactory for cargoes of fish, carried at much lower temperatures.

Two 17.75 knot, twin-screw motor ships with 16,990 cubic metres of cargo space, built specially for the Australian trade, went into commission as the *Port Sydney* on 3 March 1955 and the *Port Melbourne* on 7 July 1955. They were launched by the wives of the deputy chairman and the chairman of the company, with the Hon. Mrs Ronald Senior launching the *Port Sydney* on 29 October 1954 and Mrs Bill Donald the *Port Melbourne* on 10 March 1955. They were smart-looking vessels and served the trades for 17 years before being superseded by container ships. The pair subsequently achieved

The southernmost port in the world that Port Line vessels regularly called was Bluff, at the bottom of the South Island in New Zealand. It was an important export port for frozen meat and wool. The photograph shows the *Port Phillip*, *Port Wellington* and *Port Chalmers* lined up at the old wharves on 9 April 1952. HAZELDINES STUDIO LTD

greater longevity through being converted to cruise liners and have survived several extensive refits. They remain in service today (2006) over 50 years since entering service, with their original hulls, twin B&W engines, and some of the engine room equipment.

Sudden changes in government policies in Australia and New Zealand which increased import cargoes, often required the time-chartering of dry-cargo vessels. These vessels were mainly British-registered tramp ships, in many cases owned by subsidiary companies of the P&O, Furness Withy or Cunard shipping groups, which would be fixed on the open charter market. Because of supply and demand within the world charter market, hire rates in the period 1949 to 1970 for a 10,000 ton deadweight vessel varied between £223 per day to over £1,000 a day, although shippers would only be aware of the normal Conference freight rate. In addition to these 'one-way' charters, Port Line from 1954 time-chartered several dry cargo vessels to supplement ships to the main line trades. In most cases they could be classed as 'liner tramps'. They were left in their owner's colours except that the funnel was painted in Port Line colours. They were also given Port Line names for the duration of the charters.

On 1 June 1950 the company purchased a site at 50 Young Street in Sydney for an office block and a contract for construction was signed in 1954. The 12-storey, fully air-conditioned building, was opened in February 1958. It also had a mezzanine floor and basement garage. Its front was marked 'PORT LINE' in large white enamel and bronze letters, flanked on either side with the Cunard and Port Line crests. It was by far a more significant identity for the company than the buildings in London, New York or Wellington. It was sold in June 1969 as part of the Cunard Line drive to dispose of surplus properties. The 50 per cent share in the 51-year old Wellington office building, jointly owned by Port Line and N.Z. Shipping Company, was sold to New Zealand Shipping in September 1969 and remained the head office of P&O, later P&O Nedlloyd, in New Zealand until 2004.

The practice of having local directors in Australia, New Zealand and New York continued after the war. Warwick Gregory had left New Zealand in 1939 and remained in the UK during the war, but briefly returned to New Zealand in 1945 before proceeding to Sydney as Australian director from 1946 to 1951. There he replaced W.G. de Gruchy who had been resident director in Sydney from 1927 to 1946. Both men had been significant figures in the Australasian business of the company with De Gruchy being appointed a director in 1938 and Gregory joining him in 1940. Derek Hollebone, who was demobilised as a major in the army, went out to New Zealand to manage the Christchurch agency, Kinsey & Company, and became a local director in 1950. He then moved to Sydney in 1951, and was appointed a director of the company in 1954, returning permanently to London in 1958. Norman Binnie had been appointed New Zealand director in 1946 and retained this role until retiring in 1954. John Cook, who had joined the company in London in 1920, and had spent the years from 1932 to 1954 in Sydney office, replaced him in Wellington. Cook was appointed New Zealand manager in 1954 and became the local director in 1956. When Hollebone returned to London in 1958, Pat Fuller and John Cook assumed total responsibility for the company's affairs in Australia and New Zealand respectively. They both joined the main board of directors in 1963. The final appointments as local directors were made when George Archer became the local director in Australia in 1966, and in 1968 David Binnie (a son of Norman Binnie), who had joined the Wellington office in 1940, became the local director in New Zealand. Sir T. Ashley Sparkes, in New York, retired in 1952 and his successor was Brigadier J.H. Hardy, CBE, MC from 1952 until 1961. Brigadier Hardy was literally a 'huge' man with a height of 6 foot 7 inches. Whenever he travelled on Cunard or Port Line vessels the bunk in his cabin was extended.

In London, descendents of the Corry and Royden families continued to be represented on the directorate. Sir James Corry, who had been secretary of the company from 1924 to 1955, was a director from 1941 to 1955. He was a son of Sir William Corry, a founding director. John Corry, a son of former chairman, Herbert Corry, joined Port Line in 1932 and was made an assistant manager in 1948. He was a director from 1957 until he retired through ill health ten years later. Thomas Jerome Royden, a nephew of Lord Royden, went to Canada in 1946 and served as president of the Cunard division there until 1950, then transferred to New York where he was

President of Funch Edye from 1950 to 1968.

Jack Rooper retired in 1957 after 41 years with the company. A grandson of Sir Thomas Royden, he initially spent a year in the Chas. Connell shipyard at Whiteinch, Scotland before he joined T.B. Royden and Son in 1909. He also worked in the Far East with Jardine Matheson, the Royden Line agents, before returning to London in 1913 and joining the C&D Line on its establishment. There is little doubt that his business ability and style were significant factors in the growth of the company pre World War II; with others managers away on war service, the burden of running the company had fallen largely on his shoulders. His compassion endeared him to senior sea staff who had lost their ships and shipmates. Despite being hampered by deafness throughout his business life, he always had a positive outlook, and was one of the most dedicated and loyal leaders of the company. Few could match his enthusiasm or his pride in Port Line. He was also a director of the Cunard Steam-Ship Company and Cunard White Star Line from 1941 until May 1953.

Jack Rooper's son, David Royden Rooper, was briefly at Oxford prior to embarking on an army career. He served in the North African campaigns and reached the rank of major until an illness saw him demobilised in 1944. He joined Port Line in 1946 and was appointed a director in 1957. When he left in 1968 it marked the end of the founding families' involvement with the company.

By 1955 the fleet had been restored with new tonnage that was innovative in terms of both ships and cargo handling equipment. As in the first three decades of the C&D Line, much of its success in this area can be attributed to the excellence of their superintendent engineers. Between 1947 and 1969, B.P. Arrowsmith, R.W. Cromarty and Captain W.S.C. Jenks served on the board of the company as well as in their executive roles. Some British companies may have occasionally appointed their senior marine superintendent to their boards, but Port Line was one of the few companies to acknowledge its superintending engineers in this way. It was also significant that all ships designed and built for it came from British shipyards skilled in the building of refrigerated vessels.

Despite this engineering excellence, the design and hold layout of some of the post-war ships made life difficult for stevedores. The very large No 3 hold and upper decks, with the hatchway off-centre, in the *Port Napier* class occupied over 27 per cent of the total insulated cargo spaces in the ships and always created an imbalance with the vessel turnaround, particularly with the limited hours that could be worked on the New Zealand waterfront. The proliferation of superstructure cargo spaces on ships built from 1949 were not as efficient to work and stow, compared to the majority of the other Conference Line ships, which, by and large were flush deck vessels.

Marine and cargo superintendents were chosen from sea-going personnel who had master mariner qualifications and in most cases had been in command before coming ashore. The only marine superintendent to sit at the board table was Captain

A. G. Russell. Joining the company as an apprentice in 1927, Gordon Russell gained his first command during the war and was appointed the company's youngest marine superintendent in 1950, taking up his post in Sydney in 1951 before returning to London in 1960. He remained as marine superintendent from 1960 until 1966 when he was appointed to the board, and there he stayed until retiring in 1973. He was also appointed to the Cunard Line board responsible for personnel. He was a man of boundless energy and drive and was active in the affairs of the British Sailors' Society as a director for 36 years. He was also a member of the Honourable Company of Master Mariners and wrote the book *Port Line*, which was published in 1985.

Port Line and its forbears had indentured apprentices to train as deck officers and the practice continued throughout the life of the company. Most of the engineering officers came by way of British shipbuilding yards, but in 1952 the Port Line took in the first group of engineering apprentices.

The mid 1950s was the heyday of the Port Line, with the fleet completely rebuilt. But the first sign of an eroding business base came in 1958 when the Blue Star Line was allowed to load out from the UK on its own account, at the expense of some of the Port Line's entitlements. Britain was moving closer to Europe and free access for Australian and New Zealand produce was going to be subject to quotas which would further reduce cargo volumes to the UK. Then in the late 1960s would come the steady wind-down of conventional tonnage in favour of container ships.

The pattern of sailings in the 1950s from London to Australia saw almost three sailings a month to either Adelaide, Melbourne, Sydney and Brisbane or Adelaide, Melbourne, Sydney and Hobart. Occasionally vessels loaded at Middlesbrough or Grangemouth while in Australia the ports of Burnie, Newcastle and Geelong were spasmodically called direct. The Port Line had only eight ships a year from London to Auckland, Wellington, Lyttelton and Port Chalmers or Dunedin with outport calls on demand to Napier, New Plymouth, Nelson, Timaru and Bluff. The West Coast of the UK had long been the domain of the former Federal Company, now part of the New Zealand Shipping Company, and with the Conference agreements, the Port Line had only six sailings per year from Glasgow and Liverpool to New Zealand and none at all to Australia. Direct sailings had been maintained from the main Continental ports to Australia since 1922 but after 1963 when the New Zealand European Shipping Association was formed, the Port Line also had a direct sailing from the main Continental ports (Hamburg, Bremen, Antwerp, Rotterdam, Le Havre, Lisbon and Genoa) to New Zealand every two months. Where any loadings were undertaken on another Conference Line's entitlement a berth commission of 7.5 per cent was payable to the other line, but this was always preferable to a 12,000-mile ballast voyage.

From 1947 and up to 1969 Port Line and the Norwegian company, Wilh Wilhelmsen, provided a three-monthly direct call at Takoradi in West Africa to load cocoa beans, (and small consignments of mahogany timber) for discharge at Hobart in Tasmania and Dunedin in New Zealand, places where Cadburys had chocolate factories.

Homeward from Australia, the vessels loaded at Brisbane, Sydney, Melbourne, Adelaide and Fremantle, with direct calls at Townsville, Bowen and Port Alma, and very rarely Wyndham in northwest Western Australia, during the beef season. Vessels also loaded at Port Pirie, and occasionally Risdon in Tasmania, with concentrates for bottom weight. Australian fruit was an important commodity in the season with vessels loading at Hobart, Beauty Point (Launceston) and Port Huon in Tasmania as well as the principal southern mainland ports. Discharge ports for fruit in Europe extended to Oslo, Gothenburg and Stockholm in Scandinavia. New Zealand had two or three sailings a month for the UK/Continent range with the ships all being allocated to specific loading ports in New Zealand in accordance with the producer boards' requirements and the sharing arrangements between Shaw Savill, New Zealand Shipping and Blue Star. The range of four or five ports was selected from Auckland, New Plymouth, Napier, Wellington, Lyttelton, Dunedin or Port Chalmers, Timaru and Bluff and some years after World War II, loadings were extended to Opua, Gisborne, Whangarei, and Nelson. Other vessels were utilised on the Port and Associated Lines, and the MANZ Line services, operating to and from the east coast of North America and by this time the smaller vessels in the fleet were being chartered for the Crusader Line Pacific services.

One minor diversion for the ships travelling across the Pacific was a call at Pitcairn Island. The island, settled by descendants of the HMS *Bounty* mutineers, was under British jurisdiction and designated vessels of the four British lines regularly made calls of a few hours duration off the island, while Pitcairners came out in their long boats to take off supplies, exchange mails, and barter locally-made goods. The ships also used to throw surplus dunnage overboard, which was collected by the islanders. Some ships not carrying supplies for the island, called anyway, as the visit provided interest for passengers on the long ocean passage to or from the Panama Canal.

Wool cargoes from both Australia and New Zealand were delivered at Dunkirk, Antwerp, Bremen and Hamburg in Europe, and for the wool manufacturing area in Bradford, ships either delivered direct at Hull, or trans-shipped their cargoes at London for carriage to Goole by coaster.

To assist stability in some of the postwar tonnage, because of the large volumes of lightweight carcase mutton and lamb, most vessels commenced their northbound loadings at first or second port, by taking quantities of butter and cheese at Auckland or New Plymouth for bottom weight.

There was considerable flexibility in all scheduling and with the greater cubic volumes of refrigerated cargoes out of New Zealand, some ships were required in the December/May season to ballast to New Zealand from the UK and at times vessels made ballast trans-Tasman voyages either way to meet trade requirements. With the long ballast voyages from the UK, for many years the ships used to load up to 1500 tonnes of hard ballast (mainly sand) to aid stability but this requirement was steadily reduced as costs continued to rise. Occasionally, pending the commencement of the new meat season from New Zealand, Port Line vessels might 'lay up' at a local port for several weeks until cargo became available.

In addition to the regular services some Port Line ships made voyages to the Red Sea, Seychelles, East India or Chittagong on the Brocklebank services. Occasionally vessels would ballast to Jamaica to load citrus fruit for New Zealand or to Famagusta in Cyprus to load oranges for Australia.

Vessels operating through the Panama Canal invariably bunkered at Curacao, or very rarely Aruba, while Las Palmas was generally the bunkering port for vessels outward via the Cape of Good Hope and Aden was the main fueling port for vessels proceeding through the Suez Canal. Teams of lines' committees in the United Kingdom, Australia and New Zealand worked closely with the shipper groups to plan the forward needs of the various Conference groupings.

For many years the company had alternatively routed the vessels from the UK to Australian ports via either the Suez Canal or the Cape of Good Hope and there were regular calls at Cape Town and Durban. With the sailing of the *Port Sydney* from London on 22 October 1959, it introduced an express service to Melbourne, Sydney and Brisbane via Suez. The passage time from London to Melbourne was 28 days. Despite this faster service, monthly services were retained to South African ports as well as the usual fortnightly sailing to Australia via the Cape or the Suez Canal. In 1963 the service to Cape Town and Durban was finally abandoned and all Port Line sailings to Australia proceeded via the Suez Canal with the *Port Lincoln* making the last call at Durban in May.

Tyser and Company remained the leading hull and machinery insurance broker for the Port Line until the formation of Blue Star Port Lines Management in 1968 when Albion Insurance, owned by Vestey interests, offered significantly cheaper premiums. However, insurance cover for risks not covered under normal policies was handled through the various Protection and Indemnity Clubs. With Port Line, four P&I clubs were used – Standard, London, United Kingdom and the Liverpool and London Club. Likewise where ships were diverted from their normal voyage routing, or vessels were time-chartered and, for other reasons, additional cover was needed, these risks were taken by the P&I clubs. Originating almost two centuries ago, the clubs were not intended to compete with the regular insurance market, but to provide cover against risks outside a normal marine cover. The clubs were funded by 'calls' made from time to time on members at a rate per gross ton of the tonnage entered by each liner company in each club. Port Line ships were mainly entered with the United Kingdom or Standard P&I clubs but the company had long standing relationships with all four clubs, and because of the extensive experience of the club managers, claims arising within the ambit of a P&I Club seldom became the subject of court action.

The Port Line remained loyal to Doxford engines and the *Port Huon* of 1927 and *Port Townsville* of 1935 were the only Sulzer-powered motor ships until the *Port New Plymouth* in 1960. The *Port Hobart,* acquired as the *Empire Wessex,* had Burmeister & Wain engines made by the shipbuilder, Harland & Wolff, and all subsequent ships built by Harland & Wolff, Belfast or Govan had this machinery, which generally provided better speed and fuel efficiency. The last five ships built for the company between 1965 to 1968 all had Sulzer engines.

In 1950/51, the Port Line experienced a spate of major engine problems. When the electrical connections to her steering gear burnt out, the *Port Fremantle* had to sit in Wellington, fully laden, for 39 days before she could safely proceed to sea. The *Port Wellington* had main engine trouble and lay at Wellington from 26 May 1951 until 13 August under repair. For both these incidents, Assistant Superintendent Engineer L.A. Willoughby was flown out from London to expedite repairs. In 1954 Len Willoughby was appointed the first engineering superintendent for the Port Line in New Zealand. There were problems in Australia as well when one of the main engine scavenge pumps on the *Port Chalmers* failed, detaining her at Sydney from 26 May until 18 August 1951.

The early motor ships all burned diesel but from the late 1950s vessels were fitted with improved steam heating in the tanks to enable a mixture of diesel and heavier fuel to be pumped to the fuel purification system. Fuel heaters ensured that it was at the correct viscosity to allow the pumps and fuel valves to provide the correct ignition timing. This modification, effected on all the Doxford-engined vessels and the *Port Hobart,* brought considerable cost savings. Although most of the later new buildings from the 1960s were designed to use heavy fuel, Port Line vessels continued to burn the blended fuel, and while this was preferred by the engineers, it may not have been cost effective. Most other British lines were already using the cheaper heavier fuel.

Whilst the Port Line was building faster, and more efficient tonnage, much of the benefits were being lost by the ships spending longer times in ports in the United Kingdom, Australia or New Zealand. The waterfront labour had traditions of restrictive work practices, which they were reluctant to abandon. The largest individual employer of waterfront labour in New Zealand was the Union Steam Ship Company (New Zealand-registered but owned by the P&O group) but the collective operations of the British lines were not far behind and when adding in the influence the lines held over their stevedoring contractors in the various ports, British shipping interests were by far the major employers of waterside workers in the country. They were obviously keen for the work force to be 'straightened out', knowing that at the end of any

SEA FEVER

After World War II the New Zealand waterside workers became known around the world for their restrictive practices and special payments, and cartoonist Waite summarizes some of their demands with a parody on John Masefield's poem 'Sea Fever'. OTAGO DAILY TIMES

stoppage, a freight surcharge could be applied to recover their losses. A period of industrial unrest was heightened from a dispute with the *Mountpark* at Auckland in 1948. Watersiders refused to obey their leaders and the union was expelled from the New Zealand Federation of Labour in 1950.

Matters came to a head on the New Zealand waterfront in early 1951 when the port employers' 'locked out' the waterfront workers. The stoppage that ensued lasted three months. The government saw that the watersiders were relatively isolated from the rest of the union movement and declared a 'state of emergency' on the wharves. There was widespread public support for this action, as many people were fed up with the state of affairs on the wharves. There was, however, strong local support for the watersiders amongst the communities in the smaller ports. Servicemen were employed to load and discharge ships and this was an important factor in eventually encouraging a return to work. The Australian Waterside Workers' Union supported their New Zealand compatriots with money and placed a 'black ban' on ships coming into Australian ports which had been worked by military personnel in New Zealand. As a result, Australian servicemen had to work the *Port Halifax* in Melbourne and the *Port Wellington* at Bowen in Queensland.

During the period of the strike, the *Port Vindex* spent a record 157 days on the New Zealand coast, while the *Port Auckland* took 135 days to discharge and load instead of the average 60 days. The *Port Lyttelton* at Auckland, *Port Vindex* at Timaru and *Port Dunedin* at Bluff were some of the vessels loaded by servicemen with ship's crews of most vessels also being involved in cargo-handling. The Lines applied a strike surcharge of 50 per cent on freight (there had been a 7.5 per cent surcharge on freight to Auckland for sometime) from 7 May 1951 and this was continued until 31 July 1951 when it was announced that the Lines would recover 70 per cent of their additional costs from the surcharge, but would absorb the rest of their losses from the strike as a conciliatory gesture. Farming groups called on the government to purchase and operate at least two ships to reduce freights and break the British lines' monopoly.

The Lines, feeling that the port employers' management was not achieving a satisfactory industrial rapport with the Waterside Worker's Union, sent out 'one of their own' to head the New Zealand Port Employer's Association. The move was blessed by the Union Steam Ship Company, and Sir Basil Sanderson, head of Shaw Savill & Albion, arranged for Vivian P. Blakeley, then an assistant secretary of the British Shipowners Association to come to New Zealand. Arriving in Wellington in 1950, Blakeley took over as assistant general secretary and from 1956 became general secretary of the NZPEA. The Port Line's David Binnie took a prominent role in the affairs of the NZPEA and became something of a mentor for the new secretary. Blakeley was appointed chairman of the body in 1967, and until he retired in July 1974, was the principal negotiator for the Port Employers Association. When he first arrived in New Zealand waterfront stoppages occurred daily and shipowners could not predict how long their vessels would spend on the coast. In London, prior to his departure, Blakeley was told that if he could get the employers and the leaders of the workers to talk to each other constructively, without striking, it would be a major breakthrough. Viv Blakeley played a significant role in waterfront labour relations over nearly a quarter of a century, but was always conscious in dealing with disputes, that the industry was best served in keeping ships moving, rather than adopting a confrontational approach. For this reason some of his employer colleagues felt that at times he was too conciliatory towards the unions. Compromise and expediency largely prevailed and whilst an uneasy peace generally existed on the waterfront, overall conditions, and rates of work continued to decline, pushing up stevedoring costs.

As a result the Conference Lines continued to come under pressure from their producer board customers to reduce the ever-increasing demands for freight increases.

In addition to the Meat and Dairy Boards, a New Zealand Wool Board had been set up in 1944 and the New Zealand Apple and Pear Marketing Board was established in 1948. They also had the responsibility for arranging shipping space for wool and fruit. New ship designs needed to incorporate new ideas and systems to improve cargo-handling efficiencies but overall the protection afforded individual ship owners through their Conference Line pool shares was not conducive in encouraging the Lines to improve matters. Up to 1936 the Meat and Dairy Producer Boards' had always claimed the association with the four British Lines in the New Zealand trade had saved New Zealand millions of pounds. Wartime conditions had seen freight rates determined by the British government in consultation with the lines. However, after the war, an analysis of the rates charged from 1936 to 1955 showed the freight on lamb to Britain had increased by 200 per cent. Even though all costs rose dramatically after the war, the goodwill and trust which the Lines and the boards had enjoyed pre-war had eroded away, and the personalities on both sides had also changed.

New Zealand now demanded justification for freight increases. The impasse was finally overcome with the London Agreement of 1956. The lines undertook to provide information on their earnings and costs to an independent firm of London chartered accountants nominated by the producer boards (Thos. McLintock & Company). The producer boards employed another set of accountants (Peat Marwick) to check the Lines' costs. This cumbersome and costly solution helped to assuage matters, and in 1958 some Australian shipper groups pushed for, and gained, a similar checking system with the lines they were dealing with. Between 1955 and 1971 rises (there were no freight reductions) in the lamb freight from New Zealand to the United Kingdom increased by 85.45 per cent. The parties may have evolved a checking formula, but it did not tackle the reasons for the continuing spiral in the cargo handling costs. The exercise continued until the early 1980s when commonsense finally prevailed and the costly checking system was abandoned.

In the period from 1947 to 1972, it seemed that the Port Line and the other lines were prepared to take the view that if New Zealand meat exporters wanted to ship their produce in such a complex way with individual freezing company marks and grades, small farmer parcels and the like, all separated individually in the holds, and sorted again on discharge, they would have to pay for it. The lines' negotiators were very experienced and knowledgeable on the finances and operation of their business, but it was doubtful if the producer board farmer members, who negotiated at the freight contract talks, had sufficient financial knowledge to understand the ramifications of the service being provided and all the costs they were incurring, when set against the relative benefits. One chairman of the Meat Board, Sir John Ormond, used to describe freight negotiations as a 'good old horse trade'.

The security offered by Conference membership over-ruled any incentive for individual lines to invest in pioneering improvements to the system. The Lines had always put an element of fear into the boards' by pointing out that New Zealand was only a small country, the remotest in the world from its markets, and unless they had guaranteed cargoes there would not be any incentive to build specialist ships and steam such great distances to pick up cargo, let alone service the seasonal peaks the trade created. There was a high cost in providing specialist ships, which would have difficulty finding employment anywhere else in the world. Conventional refrigerated ships were invariably fully refrigerated whereas the vessels built for the New Zealand and Australian service had a mixture of refrigerated and general cargo spaces designed for the ratios of the cargoes handled. If New Zealand did not want to use this specialist fleet of around 110/120 vessels, where would it find other shipping companies with the same level of capacity to fill its needs? This threat was always in the background at every freight negotiation. In the late 1950s/early 'sixties the New Zealand Overseas Shipping Lines published three series of half- and quarter-page advertisements in the main newspapers promoting the services provided by the Conference. They also produced an 8 mm promotional film.

Apart from providing the ships, most of the Lines, including the Port Line and their agents, also owned or controlled stevedoring companies employed to load and discharge the cargoes in the main ports in Britain, Australia and New Zealand. In Australia and New Zealand some shipping companies also owned or part-owned ancillary interests like wool dumping companies and the carpentry contractors used for dunnaging out the holds prior to loading.

Not even the post-strike conditions improved waterfront productivity. Costs continued to rise. In October 1962 the producer boards (meat, dairy, and fruit) and the lines agreed to examine ways to improve things. The comprehensive 255-page report which followed in 1964, generally known as the Streamlining Report, proposed a number of changes including rationalisation of port calls and stevedoring interests. Napier, Timaru and Bluff were designated the principal meat loading ports using the mechanical loaders installed at the two latter ports. (On 8 February 1967, *Port Pirie* was the first vessel to use the mechanical meat loaders at Timaru.) An Exports and Shipping Council was to be set up with membership from the lines and the producer boards, with all the parties to examine ways to become more efficient and reduce costs. The report also noted that at that time it was estimated that the lines were handling 80 per cent of all the cargoes in control of the producer boards and 75 per cent of the wool and general cargo shipments.

As a further recommendation of the Streamlining Report, the lines also agreed to amalgamate their stevedoring interests in New Zealand in the belief that this would provide a better and more even utilisation of resources in staff and cargo handling equipment. The New Zealand Stevedoring Company was formed, but it did not achieve the anticipated improvements in productivity because of the entrenched attitudes of the labour force and restricted hours of wharf work.

The Streamlining report also indicated that the financial results of the four lines in the service between United Kingdom and New Zealand in the period 1959 to 1962 had shown a deficit of £2,898,000 in 1959 and by 1962 this deficit had almost doubled to £5,485,000. The report also came to the conclusion that 'containers are unsuitable for the New Zealand trade at present, or in the foreseeable future'!

It also proposed greater simplification of handling meat cargoes by moving away from the multitude of different marks and parcels by loading common grades of meat in bulk, irrespective of different shirt brands. As an example of the time, it was reported that a ship carrying 100,000 carcasses had these spread over 217 bills of lading parcels for delivery purposes and 915 different marks and numbers. In 1921 the Lines' quoted an example of the *Matatua* shipping 116,000 carcasses of meat, which were covered on 181 separate bills of lading and 701 different marks. One can only imagine the time and cost of labour required to stow and mark off all the carcass meat between the two examples so it could be discharged and delivered correctly to parcel at the discharge port.

Likewise, in the 43 intervening years between the two examples there had been little change in stevedoring practices. Carcass meat was still loaded out from the freezing works into insulated railway wagons for transport to the port. There the carcasses were landed onto rope and canvas slings, individually made up on the wharf, and again, each carcass was individually stowed in the hold. Since 1936 the government-owned New Zealand Railways had protection for the carriage of all cargo transported over 50 kms. In 1977 the limit was raised to 120 kms and it was not abolished until 1983. In many instances road transport could have handled the product more economically and with greater flexibility. Each gang of watersiders loading refrigerated cargo totalled around 24 men.

The same labour intensive process was repeated for the discharge in London. Trucks at the discharge port incurred long delays as they waited for shop orders of various grades of meat under a particular bill of lading to be discharged and sorted. Discharge in London was very primitive with some carts still pulled by horses not uncommon. Chief officers who had taken such good care of their frozen cargoes on the passage were often horrified at horses relieving themselves amid stacks of meat carcasses on the wharf awaiting removal. One of the lines estimated it was costing 50 shillings a ton to sort meat cargoes on the wharf and, in addition, the Port of London Authority was making a charge to consignees of 28 shillings and sixpence for the same service. Meat in carcass form was still preferred by English butchers who liked to cut up the carcasses in their shops to customer requirements. During World War II, the carcasses were telescoped together to save space but this ceased in 1946. Despite all the rhetoric on simplifying and reducing the number of separate parcels, it was not until the end of 1971, less than a year before a container service with the UK was established, that the lines introduced a 'Small Parcels Additional' charge so that shippers

Two further single-screw 'general purpose' cargo liners of an improved *Port Adelaide* class were ordered in 1955. The first was delivered in March 1957 as the *Port Launceston.* This photograph shows her passing Port Chalmers on her way up to Dunedin. BAIN-WRIGHT COLLECTION

consigning small parcels of meat finally paid a premium to cover a portion of the additional sorting costs in UK ports.

Better scheduling of vessels and loading larger cargoes at fewer ports did achieve some cost savings, but overall costs kept rising, adding to New Zealand scepticism that the Conference Lines were not giving the country the most cost effective service. With no competition there was no way of knowing whether freight costs were realistic or not. A group of influential farmers and politicians felt that New Zealand should participate in the shipping of her produce overseas and that the government should establish a national shipping line.

Between 1953 and 1967 all the remaining Port Line prewar vessels were disposed of, nine of the 11 going direct to ship breakers and two being sold for further trading. As export production increased in Australia and New Zealand, further ships were ordered to enable the company to lift its pool shares. Two improved vessels of the *Port Adelaide* design were ordered from Harland & Wolff, Belfast. Mrs Phoebe Hollebone sponsored the first vessel, the *Port Launceston,* which was launched on 21 November 1956 and delivered 12 March 1957. A riveters' strike in the shipyard delayed the launching by a month. As the industrial situation continued to decline in British shipyards, few of the new ships built over the next 12 years were delivered on schedule.

The *Port Launceston* was followed by a sister ship, the *Port Invercargill.* She was launched on 22 November 1957 by Mrs Doug Middleton, wife of the Sydney director of Port Line in Australia, who sent a radio impulse from the Hotel Australia 12,000 miles away, activating the launching triggers in the Belfast shipyard. Mrs. Middleton

As the remaining motorships from the 1920s came up for replacement, the Port Line took delivery of another large refrigerated ship in October 1960. She was the first ship in the fleet to be named after New Plymouth, an important meat and dairy cargo port on the west coast of New Zealand's North Island. The *Port New Plymouth* served only 19 years with the company, forced out of the trade by containerisation.

had previously travelled to the Harland & Wolff shipyard in Belfast for the launching but delays in construction prevented that taking place on the scheduled date. The *Port Invercargill* was delivered on 26 March 1958.

In October 1960 the Port Line took delivery of its largest refrigerated motor ship yet, the *Port New Plymouth*, the first vessel to be named after the New Zealand port of New Plymouth, and with 16,309 cubic metres of insulated cargo space, the fifth largest refrigerated ship in the world. At her launch on 29 March 1960 by Lady Brocklebank, Sir John Brocklebank, a director of Cunard Line and Port Line, said she could carry 160,000 carcasses of lamb and almost 2000 tonnes of butter, equivalent to a half pound pat per head for the entire nine million population of London.

Two further single-screw vessels, slightly larger and faster (17 knots) than the *Port Launceston* and *Port Invercargill* entered service in 1961. Both came from Harland & Wolff, Belfast and the first, the *Port Alfred,* was delivered on 1 March 1961 and the second, the *Port St. Lawrence,* on 20 October 1961. The *Port Alfred* was launched by Mrs Theresa Corry (wife of director John Corry) on 8 September 1960, 100 years since Mrs James P. Corry had launched the *Jane Porter,* the first iron ship built for the Corry Line. The 963 ton iron sailing ship was also built by the same Belfast shipbuilder. The *Port St. Lawrence* was launched by Mrs David Rooper, and the two ships were the last Port Line vessels to be launched by descendants of the Corry and Royden families.

Harland & Wolff, also built the 14,972 ton *Port Nicholson.* She was delivered the following year on 9 November 1962, as a slightly larger *Port New Plymouth* class vessel. With 17,098 cubic metres of refrigerated space, she was the largest cargo liner then built for the company. Designed for the New Zealand trade, it was fitting that Mrs. Thomas McDonald, wife of the New Zealand High Commissioner in London, launched her on 4 May 1962.

Two slightly larger versions of the *Port Launceston* class were built by Harland & Wolff in 1961. The *Port Alfred* entered service in March 1961. Although given a Canadian name, she was employed on all Port Line services, and when displaced by container ships, was transferred to the Port Line parent company, Cunard, in 1975. Renamed *Masirah* in 1978, she was sold to Greek owners in 1982. PORT LINE

One of the new navigational aids installed in the *Port Nicholson* was the first Marconi Argus 'true motion' radar set installed in a merchant ship. 'True motion' radar was the idea of Philip Beecham of the Port Line Marine Superintendent's Department. He promoted the idea to various radar manufacturers and Marconi took it up. The radar provided a screen where the ship's head could be placed at the bottom of the screen and adjusted back as the image moved up the display and all objects around remained at their relative bearing to the ship, exactly as anyone looking ahead would see them. The *Port Nicholson* also had a service speed of 18.5 knots and her two 17,000-horse power diesel engines achieved 20.9 knots on trials.

All the larger postwar ships continued the practice of providing first class passenger accommodation for 12 passengers (the larger single-screw ships accommodating up to ten). Compared to the temporary wooden and canvas swimming pools of earlier ships, some of the new ships (beginning with the *Port New Plymouth* in 1960) had permanent tiled swimming pools. There was also accommodation for a doctor, as the company found it reassuring to have a medical practitioner on board, rather than relying on the *Ship's Captain's Medical Guide*. Doctors enjoyed the status and comforts of passengers, but were signed on the Articles of Agreement for the voyage, and were paid one shilling a month for their services.

Although passenger accommodation was continually improved, so was accommodation for crew. The forecastle was abandoned for crew accommodation in the *Port Townsville* in 1935. From 1937, with the *Port Jackson*, only the poop was

A larger twin screw refrigerated ship than the *Port New Plymouth* was completed in November 1962 as the *Port Nicholson*. She was the largest ship then built for the company with a record 17,098 cubic metres of insulated space. She is photographed at Rotterdam in June 1976. V.H. YOUNG & L.A. SAWYER

used for crew and this practice continued for later war-built ships, including the 1940 *Port Napier* class. From the *Port Lincoln*, built in 1946, all accommodation for crew was amidships. Single-berth cabins, with the exception of two-berth cabins for apprentices, and four-berth cabins for galley and deck boys, prevailed from the *Port Brisbane* of 1949. The first occasion that director Jack Rooper was taken around the crew accommodation on *Port Auckland* he proudly commented, 'we will never be able to better this'. With the *Port Nicholson* built in 1962, the crew's recreation facilities included a crew hobbies room, which contained electric lathes and power drills for sailors to productively utilise their spare time. These improvements and the high standards of maintenance practiced by the company ensured it attracted crew who were proud of their work and their ship.

The Port Line may have had more of their seagoing staff on company contracts than some other liner companies. Generally all the deck and engineering officers, purser/catering officers (and occasionally second stewards), petty officers, quartermasters, bosuns, lamptrimmers, carpenters, engineroom storekeepers and donkeymen were on company contracts. Other sea staff were recruited from the pool. Some very long standing relationships developed between the company and able seamen, quartermasters and bosuns.

One such long time employee was Quartermaster L.J. (George) Godfrey who spent 28 years on the *Port Wyndham*, apart from one voyage when he was sick. He joined the vessel on her second voyage in 1935, having already been at sea with the Port Line for five years and prior to that had been in the Royal Navy. He was awarded the

British Empire Medal (BEM) for his war service with the ship, including when she was severely damaged by an explosion in 1945. He retired from the *Port Wyndham* in 1963 aged 70. Four other quartermasters, J. Evans, S.R. Lane, G. Law, and J.G. Urquhart, were all awarded the BEM for meritorious service in World War II and A.H. Dadson received the Distinguished Service Medal while serving in *Port Chalmers.* Quartermaster Thomas Dunne was awarded the BEM in 1966 and the following year the same award was made to Quartermaster Robert Grey. Magnus Anderson and Donald Campbell from Stornaway were two more well-known quartermasters, with the former often better dressed than the master of the ship when he went ashore. All had tremendous loyalty to the company and were remarkable workers. Many Port Line apprentices gained considerable seamanship skills from the quartermasters.

Crew recreational facilities were also enlarged and improved on most new ships. In May 1940 the board agreed to experiment with the sale of beer to members of the ship's crews at sea. Generally two cans of beer a day at sea was the allocation, but by the 1960s there was a push throughout the fleet to establish bars, many of them quite elaborate and set up to imitate an English pub atmosphere. Each also had a distinctive name. Usually there were three bars on the larger ships – officers (deck and engineer), petty officers, and crew (sailors, greasers and stewards). There was a high degree of pride generated in the care and control of each bar. Because of local regulations the stocks of British beers on board were put under seal by the Customs on arrival in either Australia or New Zealand, so local beers were then purchased for use in the bars as the ships travelled coastwise around either country. On both coasts the local police invariably turned a blind eye to the hours ship's bars were operating on the premise, that as long as the ship's personnel (and the friends they had invited on board) were on their own vessel, they would not be getting into trouble ashore.

From 1947 the Port Line ran a film exchange with the British company, Cecil Cattermoul Ltd, and the set of films supplied in the UK was generally exchanged at least once on the voyage in Australia or New Zealand. The *Port Pirie* in January 1947 was the first to use the facility. Ships endeavoured to show films twice a week and the service was appreciated by passengers and crew.

One of the features of every Port Line ship was a suggestion box which sought ideas for practical improvements from anyone on board, from the captain to the galley boys. Shore staff could also put forward suggestions. The suggestion box was opened at the end of each voyage by a director or marine superintendent. Suggestions which were adopted often attracted a small payment – generally ranging from between £1.10. and £10.00, but all were acknowledged. Whether it was a circular saw to cut dunnage, a roof over the crow's nest or permanent lighting on deck, ideas kept coming and their acknowledgement helped staff feel wanted. Back in 1932 a young man in London office had suggested the staff should be paid by the bank as it would save money. When costed out, the saving was not significant and the idea was not proceeded with, but three years later the company made the change for other reasons. Manager Bill Donald then wrote to the staff member who had suggested the original idea, and who had since transferred to Sydney office, to tell him the company had implemented his suggestion and again thanked him. Actions like this helped build up staff loyalty.

In order to keep all the staff, both ashore and afloat, in the UK and overseas, informed on company and staff matters, a series of stenciled monthly notes were produced between 1940 and 1958. A printed magazine entitled *GWCZ CALLING* (GWCZ was the general radio call sign for all Port Line vessels) then superseded the *Monthly Notes* and it contained all manner of personnel information, news of new tonnage, incidents and functions on voyages, reports on retired personnel and the inevitable obituaries. As with the later issues of *Monthly Notes* it also contained a list of senior personnel on each ship as the vessel commenced her outward voyage from the United Kingdom. Fifty four issues of *GWCZ CALLING* were published until 1968. After the establishment of the Blue Star Line and Port Line Management Company in 1968, there was no company magazine, although between 1970 and 1972 there were ten issues of a glossy publication entitled *BLUEPORT.* Then from 1973 Port Line news was published in the *Cunarder*, the house journal of the Cunard Shipping Group. From monies generated from bar takings while the company was run during the war from *Oaklawn,* a fund was built up and after the war donations from it were made to the various company social groups such as cricket, snooker, rifle, tennis and table tennis to buy or replace equipment. In 1970 the *Oaklawn* trustees commenced a series of annual parties for pensioners which became known as Vintage Port.

The pride in the ships and the loyalties to the company saw quite a number of family connections develop as brothers joined each other at sea and other personnel joined the Port Line because others from the same area in Britain had preceded them. Amongst the sea-going brothers who were master mariners in the company were Captains J.B. and D.G.H. Bradley, W.G. Higgs and H.E. Higgs, H.W. Hazlewood and G.L. Hazlewood, C.F. Post and H.M. Post, David & John Hart, and David Sinclair and his younger brother, Norman.

There were three Stannard brothers associated with Port Line. Captain John Stannard was a master with the Port Line before coming ashore as relieving master for the company in New Zealand. His brother, Knowles Stannard, was an assistant superintendent engineer with the company. Another Stannard brother served his time with the Commonwealth & Dominion Line from 1908 to 1929. This was Captain Richard Stannard who subsequently joined the Orient Line and was awarded several decorations during Royal Navy service in World War II, including the Victoria Cross and the Distinguished Service Order. Their father was Captain G.D. Stannard of Blyth who was lost at sea in 1911, leaving the three boys as orphans.

Joe Datson, the son of a brother of Captain Hugh Datson, Port Line Marine

Superintendent 1953-60, served his time with the Port Line and was Assistant Marine Supereintendent in London in 1956, before settling in Australia. Joe's daughter Liz also chose a sea career and created history by becoming the first woman deck officer to be employed in Australia, later obtaining her master's certificate in 1989 and her first command in 1990.

Chief Engineer Hamish N. Weir's grandfather had commenced with Tyser Line in 1886 and later his father spent 42 years with the Tyser Line and the C&D Line. The son of Alexander McDonald, the first superintendent engineer, was for a time an assistant superintendent engineer with Port Line. C&D Line Marine Superintendent Captain T.B. Linklater had sons Captain R.B. Linklater and Chief Engineer T.C. Linklater in Port Line. Captain J.W. Jinman had a long career with Wm. Milburn & Company, retiring in 1910 as master of *Port Pirie*. His son George went to sea as a C&D Line cadet in 1911 and after gaining his master's certificate he subsequently came ashore in Auckland as a supervisor with the Auckland Stevedoring Company, spending 32 years in this role until his retirement in December 1968. Another father and son connection saw both the father, Captain J.A. Fairbairn and his son, Captain T.A. Fairbairn, masters in Port Line together at the same time 1960-61.

Captain William Gilling, who had been at sea with the C&D Line and Port Line for many years, and who became marine superintendent in 1942, had a brother, Edward, who was also a master mariner in Tyser and Milburn Line steamers. Edward's sons, Graham and Richard, did their sea time with the Port Line and subsequently went into service as pilots with Trinity House in the 1950s. Their father had been the Port Line's choice pilot for 18 years for the Thames Estuary and the North Sea.

A number of masters came from the West Country and Captains F.R. Gorman and R.C. Matthews may not have joined the Port Line, had it not been for the Hazlewood brothers and they were later joined in the company by their nephews, Captains R.H. Finch and J.R. Dolton. A grandson of Captain H.B. Conby, master of the Tyser steamer *Tomoana* in the early 1900s, was also a Captain H.B. Conby with the Port Line in the 1950s and 60s. For a brief time, Captain P.R. Lewis, a son of Captain J.G. Lewis also served with the Port Line. Captain Bill Bailey's sister married Chief Officer Harry Steele, and later on, as Captain Steele, their daughter maintained a further Port Line connection by marrying Port Line chief officer, Mike Mitchell. Captain William Craven, and his son Captain Richard Craven, who retired in 1930 after 48 years at sea, both spent most of their time at sea on Royden ships until they transferred to the Commonwealth and Dominion Line in 1914.

A former assistant marine superintendent, Captain A.J Braund, writes that in the 1930s, the C&D superintendent, Captain Lea, shared an office with Captain Manly of Cunard Line. Tony Braund grew up in the old fishing port of Brixham and there were many families living around and within the port, with relatives serving in both the Royal and merchant navies. The Manly family hailed from Brixham and understandably, Captain Manly's nephews, Harry and John Raymont, and later their cousin Geoffrey Manly, all joined the Port Line. Later still the Raymont's younger sister married Phillip, son of Captain J.G. Lewis referred to above. Tony Braund and John Peek were neighbours to both the Manly's and the Raymont's and they joined the Port Line to be with their friends. These examples only record some of the close-knit family associations within the company. There were also many shore based family links, apart from descendents of the Corry and Royden families.

It has long been a custom that British merchant ship masters who hold a commission in the Royal Naval Reserve are entitled to fly the Blue Ensign on the merchant ship under their command, subject to also having a number of RNR ratings in their crew. The first Port Line master to have this privilege was Captain W.J. Enright, OBE, RNR. His father and grandfather had both been at sea and after serving on the training ship *Conway* in 1904 he spent several years in sail before joining Royden's Indra Line steamers. A *Conway* prize had won him an appointment as a midshipman in the Royal Naval Reserve and he continued his role in the Reserve, holding the rank of Commander at the end of World War I. He retired from the RNR in 1937 with the rank of captain. He took command of *Port Pirie* in 1947, and with the requisite number of former naval ratings amongst the crew, the ship flew the Blue Ensign. Captain Enright became the fifth master of a British merchant ship, after World War II, to be granted this privilege, but as the other vessels were passenger ships, his was the first cargo ship approval. Other RNR masters in Port Line to also have this entitlement were Captain A.D. Braithwaite OBE, RD, RNR., and Captain M.H.C. Twomey RD, RNR.

Some other seagoing personnel distinguished themselves in other fields after doing most of their sea time with Port Line. Captain's D.J. Cloke and D.J. Orr, became Elder Brothers of Trinity House. Richard Tallboys, CMG, OBE, formerly Her Britannic Majesty's Ambassador to Vietnam and who had, prior to this appointment, held several senior Australian government appointments, was an apprentice with Port Line before he left the sea finally to pursue a diplomatic career. Ronald Warwick, a first trip apprentice on *Port Fairy* in 1958 undertook most of his early training with Port Line before joining Cunard Line. He subsequently succeeded his father, Bil Warwick, CBE, RD, RNR as master of the *Queen Elizabeth 2* (1968, 70,327) and at the end of 2003 became the first master of *Queen Mary 2* (2004, 148,528) – the largest passenger liner in the world as well as being commodore of the Cunard Line passenger fleet in the footsteps of his father who was also commodore of the Cunard Line. He was awarded the OBE in 2005. A few other officers came ashore and took up a teaching role, like Captain Chris Hunter, who was training manager in Cunard and then serving as Principal of the National Sea Training College at Gravesend, and later in the same role at the Glasgow College of Nautical Studies.

Another former Port Line apprentice was Michael Grey, who became a leading writer for the daily shipping journal *Lloyd's List*. He has done much to further public interest in the shipping industry and with his sea experience in Port Line always in the background, his writings have shown a deep understanding of conditions at sea today, as well as recording the decline of the British merchant service.

The majority of Port Line masters were voluntary observers for the Meteorological Office in the UK, and occasionally for the Australian or New Zealand authorities. Quite a number of vessels received awards for excellence and from 1948 the British Meteorological Office introduced a special award to recognise outstanding service over a long period of voluntary marine observing with a presentation of an engraved barograph. The first recipient in 1948 was Captain Gordon Higgs who had started observing in 1910 and over succeeding years his work was classed as "Excellent" on 42 occasions. No other master of any company over the history of presenting the barographs could match this record. Other Port Line masters awarded barographs were Captains' J.G. Lewis, E.T.N. Lawrey, E.E. Roswell, G.G. Langford, C.R. Townshend, J.S. Moate, C.A. Hodson, L.J. Skailes, L.W. Cady and V.A. Hunt. When taking into account Port Line's antecedents, the company had the longest connection of any shipping company with the Meteorological Office as the first observing ship was the James P. Corry full-rigged ship *United Kingdom* in 1854. In 1982, on his retirement as a senior master in the Port Line, Captain M.L.M. Coombs joined the Met. Office and spent ten years as the officer responsible for the Port Meteorological Officers in the various ports, as well as the assessment of the logbooks sent in from the various vessels.

Some of the senior masters were also recognised by the Panama Canal Authority, as with most of the ships proceeding to and from New Zealand via the Canal many transits were achieved, and the Canal Authority occasionally presented senior masters, generally shortly before their retirement, or to those who had made a considerable number of transits, with an Honorary Panama Canal Pilot License in recognition of the manner and efficiency their ships were handled through the Canal.

At the end of 1961 the exclusive pool shares enjoyed by the Port Line and the other lines in the New Zealand trade, were attacked by two Dutch shipping lines, Netherlands Steam Ship Company of Amsterdam and Royal Rotterdam Lloyd of Rotterdam, when they commenced a monthly joint general cargo service from New Zealand to Europe, mainly targeting wool cargoes. Both lines had been pushed out of the former Dutch East Indies trade in 1960 by the new Indonesian government and were seeking new trading links. Traditionally, wool bookings were taken from the buyers in New Zealand after a wool sale, but the Dutch lines had directed their efforts to the principal importers of wool in Europe. As a result of this destination marketing and an attractive freight rate, virtually all the wool for Europe, with the exception of purchases by one small French buyer, who remained loyal to the lines, was switched to the new Dutch service.

Whilst the lines could see the potential of a growing trade to Europe, they were also aware of the trend for importing countries to claim the right for their flag vessels to carry a portion of their country's cargoes. This level was often assessed at 40 per cent for each of the flag states involved and the remaining 20 per cent for cross traders. Since 1948 three Scandinavian lines had been mounting a monthly sailing to New Zealand, mainly carrying cargo from Scandinavia and then ballasting to Australia to load. The French line, Messageries Maritimes, was also anxious to re-enter the New Zealand trade so the British Lines, in making an accommodation over the Dutch incursion, would also have to take into account the needs of the French and the Scandinavian companies.

Agreement was finally reached with the two Dutch lines in September 1963 and the New Zealand European Shipping Association (NZESA) was formed with the British Lines, Wilh. Wilhelmsen of Oslo, Transatlantic Shipping Company of Gothenburg, East Asiatic Company of Copenhagen, Messageries Maritimes of Paris and the two Dutch lines all becoming members. Trade shares and sailing schedules in this new conference grouping were agreed, with the British Lines retaining the major proportion of the more remunerative refrigerated cargoes. Two German companies, Hamburg-Amerika Linie and Norddeutscher Lloyd joined NZESA services in 1969 (and resigned in 1984), while the Italian Line, Lloyd Triestino was admitted in 1974. For a brief period between 1986 and 1990 the Spanish Marasia Line was also a member. The Port Line had to relinquish some of its European pool share but rights to UK cargoes were unchanged.

The setting up of a separate Conference grouping in New Zealand highlighted the growing trade with Europe and at the same time protected the four British Lines with their exclusive coverage of the UK traffic. In announcing the formation of the NZESA, the lines emphasised that:

> The two years of uneconomic use of too many ships competing for the same volume of trade has created a situation in which ships have sailed with cargo spaces unfilled, and in which at times the port capacity in New Zealand has been unnecessarily strained. A disorganised trade must in the long run reflect adversely on the New Zealand economy as a whole and the new Association plans to achieve orderly sailings and properly rationalised use of port facilities. The point has been reached where it is accepted all round that the shipping services will have to be restored to an economic basis, not only in the reasonable interests of the Lines', but also of the New Zealand producers. Basic rates of freight for the coming season remain unaltered but there will be a reduction of 7% in the special rebates" (rebates granted since the entry of the Dutch Lines two years before).[3]

The increasing presence of the European Lines in the New Zealand trade saw them attempt to improve cargo handling by loading wool in 12-bale units – six double

Port Line chairman Ronnie Senior (left) and director Sir Basil Smallpeice (right) with former directors Sir James Corry and Jack Rooper photographed at the Port Line annual meeting 9 June 1966.
PORT LINE ARCHIVES, UNIVERSITY OF LIVERPOOL

dumps lashed together with steel strapping. There was a dramatic improvement in loading rates, compared to lifting of two double dumps (about 320 kg) with union purchase gear, which was all the watersiders would allow per heave on the grounds of safety. The Dutch lines actually built specialised ships with deck heights designed to fit the units and holds were also squared to provide a better stow. The Dutch and Scandinavian lines worked hard at gaining maximum benefit from handling unitised wool and to a lesser extent the French and Yugoslav companies followed suit. Although the British lines shipped quantities of wool in the tween decks of their vessels, the spaces were not squared to give the best stowage for units, and with smaller hatch covers, forklifts would always be required to fill the wings of each cargo space. The Port Line undertook only token experiments with unitised wool, although on one occasion all the 5,000 bale deck cargo of wool for the *Port Caroline* was unitised. In a number of cases with Port Line vessels, dumps of wool had to be manually rolled down alleyways or engine room casings and extensive use of forklifts would be needed until the hatch square was reached if all the wool was strapped in units. In addition lesser quantities of wool were being shipped to the UK with the bulk of the product from both New Zealand and Australia being discharged at Continental ports.

From the late 1950s the financial position of the Port Line steadily deteriorated. The protection afforded by Conference Line pool shares was insufficient to combat rising costs, and poor waterfront productivity. The larger ships were only averaging a little over two round voyages a year. It was also becoming harder to obtain increases in freight rates to restore profit margins. With the retirements of Jack Rooper in 1957 and Bill Donald in 1960, the company lacked decisive leadership and whilst there were competent managers, there was no visionary leadership, and with the declining returns, the Port Line also came under pressure from its parent, Cunard. A triumvirate of Ronald Senior as chairman, and directors Ted Ross and Derek Hollebone, had led the company into the 1960s, until Ross retired in 1966 and Senior a year later. Derek Hollebone remained a director until 1978 and was an important 'image' for the Port Line and the lines, as one of the chief freight negotiators (along with Alan Bott of P&O), with the producer boards. Correspondence between London and the regional directors was no longer the friendly, constructive style of the 1930s. It was becoming more confrontational with management in Australia and New Zealand being increasingly defensive in trying to explain to London, the ever-increasing problems of higher costs and poor productivity in cargo handling.

Sir Basil Smallpeice, formerly managing-director of British Airways, had been appointed to the board of the Cunard Steam-Ship Company in April 1964. Next year he joined the Port Line board and became chairman of the company in 1968. He quickly assessed the declining financial position of the company. In his biography *Of Comets and Queens*, he wrote that 'Port Line employed £20,000,000 of capital on written down values, but had succeeded only twice in the past ten years in making profits of £1,300,000, not even 7 per cent on capital. Over the years the profits made by Port Line (before tax) averaged less than 5 per cent. 'No business could survive indefinitely on that. What worried me was that its management seemed satisfied with things as they were'. In 1966 Port Line recorded the first loss since its formation in 1914. The company seemed to have lost its way.

It appeared that the board and management relied on trust, and the confidence of the friendly, comfortable associations with shipbuilders and the many long-term contractors, employed by the company. Throughout much of the life of Port Line, Gregson and Company was employed to repair and install all the insulation within the refrigerated compartments in the port of London and east coast ports. There was never any tendering for this work, just a telephone call to Gregsons to fix it. Some attempt was made in the 1960s to tighten up on Gregsons' operations but little was achieved considering the close relationships between the personnel involved.

The skills on the board may not have been sufficient to direct management to rigorously attack increasing costs, whose control offered the best means of improving profitability. Port Line was largely achieving set incomes, based on the pool shares it possessed in the various trades. This was protected with standard freight rates for all lines, so improved efficiencies in fleet construction, management and overall control of costs were paramount to restoring increasing earnings as well as improving and restoring good relations with Cunard. However there were few people with professional accounting skills on the board, or amongst the top management, and the culture of half a century would require strong hands to change. It would be a bold manager who would query the demands of engineer or marine superintendents without support at board level. The company operated more on a 'cost plus' basis and it was not until the early 1960s that formal budgeting was introduced at head office.

Sir Basil Smallpiece commissioned a management report from consulting firm Urwick, Orr in 1967. This found 'that authority and responsibility is not well defined, and for practical purposes, the executive management of the company is conducted by the Chairman and Managing Director. The lack of delegation of authority has resulted in some executives concerning themselves almost exclusively with administration. They have little knowledge of the majority of revenues and costs over which they are nominally required to exercise control'.[4] This situation was highlighted when Port Line and Blue Star merged their managements in 1968 and it was evident (and embarrassing for Port Line managers) that Blue Star Line management and superintendents had better leadership skills and used their initiative to properly oversee their levels of responsibility. At the time of the Urwick, Orr report, Port Line had 267 male and 96 female staff ashore and 1,065 men at sea.

The policy of building all new ships in the industrially-troubled British shipyards suggested that the company was reluctant to move out of its comfort zone. The other lines in the New Zealand trade all moved to build some of their ships elsewhere to take advantage of better prices and delivery guarantees. Shaw Savill & Albion built four ships in Germany between 1957-60 for a price 15 per cent lower than the best British offer, and with the German yard agreeing to restrict the escalation of cost to no more than 3.5 per cent over the tender price. Blue Star Line built five single-screw motor vessels at the Bremer Vulkan, Vegesack yard in Germany in 1956-8, and in 1967 took delivery of two large, 21 knot, refrigerated ships from the same shipyard. These were built at considerable cost reductions on vessels of equivalent size, and speed, from UK shipyards. When it came to providing two 21-knot ships, with 15,467 cubic metres of refrigerated space, and only slightly smaller than the *Ports Chalmers* and *Caroline*, the New Zealand Shipping Company had them built in 1968 at the Mitsui works at Tamano in Japan.

With pressure mounting to reduce overheads, management passed over the need for a drastic overhaul of company traditions, policies and practices, targeting crew reductions instead. When the *Port Sydney* and *Port Melbourne* came into service in 1955 they had crews of 85. By 1965 this had reduced to 79 and three years later just 60. Similar reductions were made throughout the fleet. Even the smallest vessel, the *Port Montreal,* which had a crew of 65 when built in 1954 was down to 50 by 1968.

Automation at sea and efforts by ship owners to reduce crew numbers saw the National Union of Seamen (NUS) start a vigorous campaign to raise wage levels, based on the long hours seafarers worked when vessels were at sea. Pay improvements to the equivalent of 13 per cent had been achieved in 1965 but in 1966 the NUS sought pay recognition for hours at sea worked in excess of 40 hours. Acceptance of this claim would have seen an average pay increase of 16 per cent and the employers stood firm. On 16 May 1966 all British ships went on strike when the ships reached a British or near Continental port. The British government finally declared a state of emergency, the first since 1955, and when the Court of Inquiry finding was rejected by the NUS, the Trade Union Council ostracised the NUS. Fortunately most Port Line ships were on the other side of the world and the parent company Cunard suffered the most. The strike ended on midnight 1 July.

Sir Basil Smallpeice said that whilst the strike had cost Cunard over £2,000,000 in actual costs, the disruption to schedules and loss of cash would add £250,000 a year in additional interest costs. The straightened cash position of the Cunard group, as a result of the strike, saw the company sell its 30 per cent holding in airline BOAC-Cunard, a few months later. The seamen's strike of 1966 may have caused the first domino in the set to fall, as the group was on a downward financial path from then on until the takeover by Trafalgar House Investments a few years later.

In 1962 two single-screw 19 knot, almost fully refrigerated ships, were ordered from the Caledon Shipbuilding and Engineering Company of Dundee, for delivery in October 1964 and January 1965. They were intended to make two high-speed voyages with fruit from Australasia each season (ballasting southbound to achieve the second voyage) and would be available for other trades requiring ships with fully-insulated space for the rest of the year. They were the first Port Line ships to have data-loggers for measuring and recording hold temperatures, although these were still manually controlled. They were also equipped with a 70-ton heavy lift derrick and three bulk tallow tanks. The vessels had no passenger accommodation and the decks were all steel and not covered by teak decking. The design and equipment of the vessels was almost identical to the recommendations made to the company by Captain Ian North, who had spent much time as master of the *Port Saint John* and *Port Quebec* on the MANZ Line service between 1959 and 1963. He had closely analysed the cargo flows and designed a ship to meet the trade needs, as well as for use as a fast refrigerated ship on other company services. The Port Line board had high expectations for the ships and subsequently ordered a third similar vessel from Barclay Curle & Company at Whiteinch, another shipyard not previously used by the company.

Shipyard delays kept the first vessel, *Port Huon*, there until 30 March 1965 and her sister *Port Albany* until 6 October 1965. Both were registered at Liverpool to the ownership of Cunard Steam-Ship Company and placed on bare-boat charter with Port Line – presumably because of Port Line's weakened financial state at the time of construction. The third vessel came into service on 12 January 1966 as *Port Burnie.* The ships had eight 5-ton capacity cranes replacing conventional union purchase derricks and all hatch covers were hydraulically operated. The *Port Burnie* was the first Port Line vessel to have bridge control of the main machinery. The system had

The last five ships built for Port Line departed somewhat from the standard classes of the past. All had Sulzer engines and were built in shipyards not previously used by the company. The first three were fast single-screw, almost fully refrigerated motorships, designed for service with the MANZ Line or the main line trade with fruit. Incorporating many automated features, the first was the *Port Huon*, delivered in March 1965. They were very tender ships and their service speed of 19 knots had to be dropped back in moderately rough seas. A former officer suggested they would roll on wet grass! The *Port Huon* made her maiden voyage to Port Huon, arriving 26 April 1965. FREEMAN-PRIEST

been developed from the Brocklebank vessel *Mahout* and enabled single lever control of the main engine from the bridge. Her first master was Captain Ian North.

Whilst the ships were fast, they were 'wet' on the foredeck, and so fine-lined they had to be handled carefully as they had a tendency to roll heavily. Under certain sea conditions speed had to be significantly reduced to avoid rolling which could quickly cause cargo to shift. Even on trials of the *Port Albany*, her master, David Sinclair, said that at the end of the measured mile, the helm was put hard to starboard. It was in the middle of the afternoon tea for the guests in the saloon. The *Port Albany* heeled over like a destroyer and the crockery slid off the tables into the laps of the guests. In service over a year later on a passage from Halifax to New York, some 40 miles west of Nantucket Lightship, she encountered heavy weather and rolled dangerously. With an alarming rumbling noise, three large road graders stowed in No 3 tween deck broke their lashings and slid across the deck. Large tyres protected the portside shell plating but the graders bulged out the hull plating on the starboard side and repairs took ten days in the Todd Shipyard in New York. On another occasion in rough weather off the Australian coast the violent rolling caused both radars to strip their gears. Captain North's designs were based on the optimum concept from the seagoing perspective but it was clear that there was little shore-based analysis undertaken of the cost benefits, or otherwise, of all the sophisticated equipment and specialist gear

The *Port Huon's* sister ship was delivered as the *Port Albany* in October 1965. They were designed as the 'optimum' vessel for the MANZ Line service but it appeared the company did not fully cost the economic benefits of all their features and equipment. As container services were steadily introduced from 1969 onwards, they were not profitable vessels for Port Line over their seven years with the company. FREEMAN-PRIEST

The last of the trio, the *Port Burnie*, incorporated further automation with bridge control of the engine room. The ships, surplus to the Port Line after all the trades were either wholly or partially containerised by 1972, were sold to a Greek owner who employed them on a service from South America to Eastern Mediterranean ports for the next 20 years. A. DUNCAN

installed to ascertain whether the ships could pay their way over their expected lifetime. They were never profitable over the short time they were in the fleet.

Another single screw ship entered service as the *Port Invercargill* in March 1958. Nine years later on 5 June 1967, she was trapped, along with 14 other vessels, in the Great Bitter Lake, during a Suez Canal transit, when the Six-Day War broke out between Egypt and Israel. She remained there until May 1975, but the Port Line had abandoned her to the underwriters in 1969. The illustration shows her passing Port Chalmers on her maiden voyage on 22 May 1958. BAIN-WRIGHT COLLECTION

The *Port Burnie* was launched by Mrs John Cook, the wife of the New Zealand director of the company. With few exceptions, apart from the wives of some governors-general and high commissioners, virtually all the ships launched for the C&D Line/ Port Line were sponsored by daughters or wives of directors or managers within the company. This tends to emphasise the 'cosy' protection afforded the line by holding specific pool shares in the various services. Nowadays, shipping companies invariably invite the wives of major shippers to launch their vessels as an important marketing exercise.

In June 1967 Port Line 'lost' one of its ships in most unusual circumstances. The *Port Invercargill,* with a crew of 67 and ten passengers, was passing through the Suez Canal from Australia with a cargo of apples, pears and grapes and general cargo, when the six-day war between Egypt and Israel erupted. She had dropped anchor at noon on 5 June 1967 in the Great Bitter Lake, to allow a southbound convoy to pass. The company radioed Captain H.B. Conby to proceed south out of the canal and travel to Britain by the Cape of Good Hope but he replied that navigation in the canal had been suspended and that the *Port Invercargill* was trapped with 14 other vessels. The passengers and most of the crew were repatriated and over the following months skeleton crews were maintained to keep systems working. Fruit from the *Port Invercargill* was distributed to other ships and they in turn supplied the Port Line ship with other foodstuffs.

On 7 October 1967 the ships' crews formed a Great Bitter Lakes Association. They designed a GBLA tie and postage stamps; there was a Bitter Lakes Swimming Club, a GBLA shooting club and a yachting club. They had to use considerable ingenuity to keep the ships and their equipment in order and there were forever exchanges of equipment, technology and food between them. Port Line crews generally spent three months on this relieving duty. There were four British ships (*Scottish Star* (1950, 9,996), *Melampus* (1960, 8,509), *Agapenor* (1947, 8,322) and *Port Invercargill*), two German, two Swedish, two Polish, and one each from the United States, France, Bulgaria and Czechoslovakia.

Port Line claimed for the loss of the vessel, which was declared a constructive total loss on 19 February 1969, although the P&I club settlement was not made until 15 October when the ship's ownership passed to the club. The various P&I clubs involved with the 14 ships subsequently rationalised the personnel looking after the small fleet but it was not until 30 May 1975 that the *Port Invercargill* was finally released. Extensively overhauled by her new Greek owners for further trading carrying general cargo, and under the name of *Kavo Kolones,* she lasted only a further four years in service before being scrapped.

1 *The Syren & Shipping,* 17 May 1944.
2 Basil Sanderson, *Ships and Sealing Wax: The Memoirs of Lord Sanderson of Ayot,* Heinemann, London, 1967, p. 166.
3 *Fairplay Shipping Journal,* 19 Sep 1963.
4 Port Line archives, PL13/4.

CHAPTER 6

Containerisation and Nationalism

From the early 1960s British liner companies had been taking a keen interest in developments in the United States where freight forwarders and shipping companies were experimenting in the carriage of cargo in containers. Like everywhere else in the Western world, cargo handling costs were rocketing, and experiments were being undertaken, particularly on the high-volume trades between the United States and Puerto Rico and from San Francisco to Hawaii. Containers and unit loading had been trialled for many years, but were usually restricted because of the inadequacy of the ship's handling equipment to lift larger units.

The international container concept was first tested in earnest when freight forwarder Malcolm McLean, who founded McLean Industries in 1955, shipped 58 loaded trailer units on the deck of a converted World War II tanker, the *Ideal X* (1945, 10,572), on 27 April 1956 from Newark, New Jersey to Houston. In August 1958 Matson Navigation Company in San Francisco loaded 20 containers on the deck of the freighter *Hawaiian Merchant* (1945, 8,300) for the passage from San Francisco to Honolulu. McLean quickly grasped the potential of the savings that could be made if volume could be created and he pushed ahead with further experiments, mainly using trailer systems. In 1960 he formed Sea-Land Service Inc and at the end of 1965 the company had more than 12,500 containers in service. One year later Sea-Land commenced weekly sailings from the United States to Europe.

British shipowners watched these developments closely, sensing that unless they took action to protect their significant trade shares in all major trades out of the UK, their break bulk handling systems could soon be superseded. They were clearly reluctant to spend huge capital sums to change their handling methods and in most cases they were operating reasonably modern fleets, steadily upgraded after the war. Several lines set up study teams to examine containerisation for their own services and those lines with close historical links started to undertake studies jointly as it was clear that none of the companies could afford to suddenly change systems and go it alone. The Port Line was probably on the fringe of all these studies and also envisaged being able to operate existing systems for some years to come.

However four companies which controlled more than 60 per cent of the liner trades to and from the UK announced on 27 August 1965, without warning, that they had formed a company called Overseas Containers Limited (OCL) to investigate and develop container handling services. The four companies were the P&O Steam

Navigation Company, Ocean Transport and Trading Limited, British and Commonwealth Shipping Company, and Furness Withy and Company. Ocean Transport had taken the early initiative and was well advanced in its planning. Each company initially held 25 per cent of the shares in OCL but the percentages were adjusted as each trade was developed, to reflect the Conference Line trade shares held. When it was decided to containerise the Australian trade the shareholdings became P&O 36 per cent, British and Commonwealth 15.24 per cent, Ocean Transport 19.45 per cent and Furness Withy 28.34 per cent. By the time the container services were introduced to the Far East the shareholding percentages became 36.9, 7.62, 49.0 and 13.4 per cent respectively.

This move threw the remaining British lines into disarray, as in most cases they were smaller family-owned concerns with little hope of raising the capital to convert their fleets to container ships. They were in fact companies like Port Line, who were comfortably operating within conferences under the collective protection of fellow conference members. The Port Line was somewhat more protected than some others, as the company was still under the umbrella of Cunard, a British 'listed' company of some stature. As P&O controlled the largest trade share in the United Kingdom-Australian trade, Ronald Senior and Sir Basil Smallpeice made overtures to see if Port Line could join OCL. P&O was already aware of the Cunard financial situation because of talks then current for a possible merger with Ocean Steam or P&O, and it politely rebuffed the approach. Blue Star Line also suggested to P&O that all lines in each trade should work together, but this also fell on deaf ears. In his erudite style, Sir Donald Anderson, chairman of P&O, explained to shareholders at the 1966 annual meeting why OCL had only four members. 'OCL has only four partners because they all recognise the natural law that the more you are together, the happier you may be, but the less you will actually do, and the longer you will take to do it. And in this case, when each extra partner would of necessity bring in several extra problems, they thought that enough was enough'.

Before they had the opportunity to read this, the other lines, described on one occasion by Sir Andrew Crichton, the first chairman of OCL, as the 'odds and sods' of British shipping, quickly came together to evaluate their own circumstances in the light of the creation of OCL. The companies involved were The Ben Line Steamers of Wm. Thomson and Company of Edinburgh, Blue Star Line, controlled by the Vestey family, The Charente Steam-Ship Company, managed by T. & J. Harrison Ltd, Cunard Steam-Ship Company for the Port Line and T. & J. Brocklebank, privately owned Ellerman Lines, and Bank Line Limited, managed by Andrew Weir and Company.

With trade shares in diverse services to the Far East, Australia, New Zealand, North America and South Africa, Ellerman Lines had the most to lose and was a strong influence in the collective discussions which resulted in the formation on 11 January 1966 of Associated Container Transportation Limited (ACT). Philip Bates and Derek

Hollebone were the Cunard directors appointed to the ACT board. Bank Line clearly felt its mixture of break bulk and liquid cargoes, often loaded at remote islands in the Pacific, would unlikely be containerised for many years and did not join the new consortium. It was a decision that it would later regret as the company, some years on, spent a lot of money trying to break into a trans-Atlantic container trade and failed. Compared to OCL where the four partners agreed to submerge their identities and create the one capital structure, ACT was set up on a different basis. It was really a 'holding' company that would 'share matters of mutual interest and evaluate the feasibility and viability of container services on trade routes in which they are interested'. For ACT, as each trade was containerised, the lines in the trade would make their individual capital contributions essentially based on the trade shares held and provide ships registered to the ownership of the individual companies. Personnel for each service both on shore and on the vessels would be drawn from the ACT partners involved.

Both British groups began intensive studies on how best to move forward. Staff was recruited from the partners in the consortia but there was also a move to secure 'free and lateral thinkers' untainted by years of traditional shipping company practices, to cut away any negative thinking within the respective teams. Whilst OCL and ACT did co-operate on matters of collective interest, regulatory controls, and to keep an eye on Continental lines already operating in existing trades with British companies, everything else was kept closely competitive and each group developed its own operational organisation, container control systems and marketing strategies.

When OCL announced that the first trade the company planned to containerise would be the Australian trade, ACT moved to follow suit and formed a subsidiary company in August 1967 – Associated Container Transportation (Australia) Limited (ACT(A) with Port Line and Blue Star Line each holding 42.5 per cent of the capital and the remaining 15 per cent being held by Ellermans. Sir Basil Smallpeice, mindful of the straightened cash position of the Cunard group, had gone to Australia in February 1967 to influence the Australian government to buy a substantial interest in the Port Line. This would provide Australia with the opportunity to share in the container shipping services to and from that country and give a significant cash injection to Cunard. The Australians were not in a hurry to move, but in August 1968, Cunard was advised that it was not possible to take a share in the Port Line, as under Australian law any Australian ships must fly the Australian flag and be crewed by Australian nationals. The government did, however, agree to take over one of the new ACT(A) container ships, and operate it within the consortium under the Australian flag. This arrangement was welcomed by Cunard as it strengthened the ACT(A) partnership, and Australia, as a national flag carrier, could claim a respectable trade share from all the conference member lines and not just ACT(A). The Australian agreement with ACT(A) was signed on 22 April 1969.

The subsequent history of ACT(A)/ANL is told in Appendix 1. Whilst all the discussions on container shipping were under way with the two British consortia, New Zealand was not included. Although the Port Line and Blue Star Line were working directly with ACT(A) in the Australian trade, the companies continued to talk independently with the other New Zealand trade lines and with the New Zealand producer boards, as well as being members of the Exports and Shipping Council. However the four British lines in the New Zealand trade did set up a special Container and Cargo Handling Committee to examine how New Zealand cargoes could be handled in the future. It quickly became known as the Molyneux Committee, after its chairman, William Molyneux, a chartered accountant who had been secretary of the Streamlining Committee of 1964. Each line contributed one member of the committee and the Port Line representative was Captain Ken Allen, the only master mariner within the group.

Its report was published in a 196-page book in May 1967. The Molyneux Report proposed a partial container service for New Zealand using four large container ships, operating on a 16-day frequency. These vessels would be supplemented by 32 conventional vessels. It was estimated that the four container ships would carry 80 per cent of New Zealand import cargo from the UK and Europe and ship back 50 per cent of the exports. The lines were clearly reluctant to proceed without the support of the producer boards, as apart from the cost of the ships, New Zealand would be required to finance and build terminals and improve the internal transport infrastructure to handle containers. Rail tunnels would also have to be enlarged to accept standard ISO containers. The government decided that the estimated cost required it to undertake its own survey, conducted by the Metra Consulting group of London. This was almost identical to Molyneux's, proposing four container ships, which would lift 66 per cent of the export cargoes and 81 per cent of the imports, with 31 conventional ships handling the balance of the trade.

The government and the producer boards were convinced, and the lines ordered four container ships from Swan, Hunter & Wigham Richardson Ltd in December 1969, with the first vessel to be delivered in October 1973 and the fourth by March 1974. The decision to build the ships in the UK, over Germany, was because there would be no exchange losses due to the strengthening of the German mark, and also, the consortium's spokesman, Bill Dawes, said 'we were also fortunate in having obtained a tender, based on a fixed price.' This proved far from the truth, as the shipyard was unable to contain the escalating costs and could never have continued the construction without a revision of the contract price. The vessels were to have a capacity for 1800 TEUs (twenty foot equivalent units) and would be built to maximum Panama Canal beam. Each ship was to be 42,000 tons gross and have a service speed of 21 knots. They were to be powered by twin screws being driven by 24,330 shaft horsepower steam engines.

At the time of the order, each vessel was to cost around £11 million but by 1971, the costs had dramatically escalated to over £20 million a vessel, and two of the lines, Shaw Savill & Albion and Port Line, could not afford to proceed with the orders. Both parent companies – the Furness Withy group for Shaw Savill & Albion and Cunard for Port Line – were already over-committed for expenditure for container ships in other trades, while Cunard also had heavy capital commitments for its passenger fleet. In addition, Cunard had also increased its involvement in container shipping by containerising its trans-Atlantic cargo business through buying into the Swedish-controlled Atlantic Container Line at the end of 1966. This investment required considerable capital for the provision of two large roll-on, roll-off container ships, the containers, and related equipment for the service. With two of the partners reneging on the agreement, the other two lines could not continue on their own, and in May 1971, without any warning to the New Zealand government, or their customers, the lines abruptly told the producer boards that they could not afford to proceed with the container service.

Derek Hollebone, chairman of the New Zealand Tonnage Committee of the Lines, and a Port Line director, commented in a press statement that 'despite the cost escalation of £30,000,000 for the construction of the four ships, a container ship service, plus the relevant shore equipment would be cheaper to build than a conventional fleet of equivalent carrying capacity. But in an inflationary age neither form of service can survive, let alone reward the investment made, unless rates of freight are raised more rapidly and by a substantially greater amount than New Zealand shippers have ever been willing to concede in the past.'[1] Hollebone also argued that one other reason that had caused the lines to cancel the four ship contract was New Zealand's failure to find funds to finance the cost of the terminals there. The reference to the need for a significant rise in freight rates for cargoes from New Zealand further inflamed attitudes there, as the Australian shippers had faced no such exorbitant demands with their newly-introduced container services.

The relationships between the Lines and New Zealand had been steadily deteriorating, but the arrogance of the decision, without any prior discussions, clearly angered the New Zealanders. It created a rift, which never healed, and was the final catalyst for New Zealand developing its own national shipping line. The country's minister of finance, Robert Muldoon, labeled the Lines' decision 'one of the most dismally inept displays of poor public relations in recent times.' It could, he warned, be the beginning of the end of British dominance of shipping to and from New Zealand, adding that 'the lesson which the ship owners must learn is that you cannot retain a monopoly if you insist on loading all the costs of your inefficiency and poor British industrial relations on the New Zealand producer.'[2] Hollebone hit back by drawing attention to the 12-day delay in working the *ACT 3* in Wellington earlier in the year, and 'of other expensive shipping problems arising from falling productivity in New Zealand ports, neither Mr Muldoon nor anyone else in New Zealand is in a position to point to poor British industrial relations as a main cost to the New Zealand producer. It needs to be said from time to time just what the British lines have done for New Zealand. In the early days ...it was the British lines who bore the brunt and losses in assisting New Zealand to develop new markets. In the US trade and the UK trade we have been supporting New Zealand for years and at well below an adequate return.'[3] While other mainline trades, including Australia, were being containerised, New Zealand shippers felt they were going to be left in the wilderness with labour-intensive conventional shipping and the prospect of continually escalating shipping costs.

With the cancellation of the container ship orders, the Port Line was involved in protracted discussions with the shipyard, spreading over many months, on the costs of the steel ordered for its ship, but not used.

Also in 1971 the lines lost the business of the New Zealand Apple and Pear Marketing Board, which turned to chartering fully refrigerated conventional ships for carrying fruit cargoes – mainly apples and pears – to the board's major markets in the UK and Europe instead of shipping part-cargoes in Conference vessels carrying all classes of cargo. From 1969 the lines had been indicating to the Apple and Pear Board that the meat and dairy exporters were subsidising the freight on fruit. The Conference contended that the fruit contract was uneconomic as the product became available for shipment at the peak time for meat and dairy cargoes. The increasing volumes of apples meant more ships had to ballast out from the United Kingdom to meet the short seasonal demand. It was clear that this impasse on philosophies would arise again in the future and the board contracted with the Danish firm of J. Lauritzen to carry the 1971 crop. Whilst this represented a loss of cargo, the lines were relieved that they would not be required to ballast in additional tonnage to handle the fruit. The Lines had also signaled that with the advent of containers, they would have difficulty meeting the needs of growers over a short period of three or four months. The Apple & Pear Board continued with chartered tonnage and although it paid 16 per cent more for its freight costs in the 1972 season, this was less than the increase the Lines imposed on their meat and dairy contract shipments in the same period.

Despite all the criticism of the British Lines and the Conference system, the New Zealand government had appointed a commission of inquiry into New Zealand shipping in 1970 and when it reported back in 1971 it had not found any satisfactory alternative to the existing system of shipping between New Zealand, the UK and Europe. It stated that 'despite the pros and cons of the Conference system, no critic of it has yet suggested a workable alternative arrangement which can provide what a shipper from New Zealand needs most – high-class specialised ships, regular sailings to ports as scheduled, whether the ship is full or half full, and a stable freight rate.'

The new Exports and Shipping Council in New Zealand, set up as a recommendation of the Streamlining Report, held a forum in Wellington in December 1968 entitled 'Maritime Policy for New Zealand'. It was attended by over 260 shipping and port leaders, politicians and other interested parties. The key speakers were Sir Donald Anderson, chairman of P&O, and Sir John Williams, chairman of the Australian National Line. Sir Donald assured New Zealanders that if they wanted to enter the shipping business, the other lines would welcome the move provided the 'rules' were observed. By this he meant that the British Conference Lines served the trade as a whole:

> We carry easy and difficult cargo; we serve good ports and bad ports; we send ships out to New Zealand in ballast because the trade is imbalanced; we get cargo on our merits or lose it on our demerits; we have no patronage, no special privilege, no exclusive rights that we haven't earned. We claim the right to make a fair return on capital invested and we do not accept the right of any shipper to criticise us just because we expect a return commensurate with what he makes in his own business, even though we don't seem to get it. And these are the rules I speak of which we would expect any entrant to accept if we were to welcome him into this service, because service in a liner trade is not an idle name. We offer service, and this is quite different from skimming the cream and leaving the rest to others.

Sir John Williams outlined the circumstances of the Australian National Line and commented that there was no magic in government control of shipping. Efficient management was all-important regardless of who owned the business. He felt that the role of government was better used to aid, rather than compete with the private sector, and to encourage competition amongst carriers.

Many of the other speakers also referred to a national shipping line and the concept was left to simmer and be picked up by the New Zealand Labour Party. When Labour ousted National in November 1972, it moved quickly and introduced legislation to establish a shipping line in October 1973. In February 1974 the Shipping Corporation of New Zealand Limited was registered. A subsidiary company, New Zealand Line, was formed with Shaw Savill & Albion as a partner with a 24.9 per cent interest. This line operated a service from New Zealand to the United Kingdom/Europe with two former Shaw Savill vessels until the Corporation's 42,000 ton container ship *New Zealand Pacific,* was built in 1978.

On the establishment of the New Zealand Line in 1974, the British Lines in the United Kingdom service conceded a small trade share to the new company. Then, with the introduction of the larger container ships and complete coverage with containers in 1977, it gained 14 per cent per cent of the main line trade. This was at the expense of the four lines, which prior to the advent of the Shipping Corporation, held the following northbound pool shares – the New Zealand Shipping Company

32 per cent, Shaw Savill & Albion 27.75 per cent, Port Line 22.25 per cent and Blue Star Line 18.0 per cent. Although the Corporation owned only one vessel, it was entitled to charter container space in all the OCL and Continental lines' vessels so that it could provide the same service frequency as its other partners. While the Corporation was set up to protect New Zealand being exploited by overseas ship owners, it was therefore totally reliant on the involvement of the other lines to provide it with the ability to operate a regular service. The British Lines also left the Shipping Corporation to pick up the lower freighted government cargo from the UK. The New Zealand government failed to fully capitalise the Corporation, and with large borrowings, operating ships with horrendous crewing costs and managing a small trade share, it could do little to reduce freight increases and, in reality, needed them more than any other carrier in the group.

One casualty, which followed from the formation of the Shipping Corporation, was the Scales Line. Under the agreement with the Conference Lines, Scales had continued chartering ships for their wool cargoes all through World War II whenever the company could find suitable tonnage. High freights stifled the profits but in the 1960s the three sailings a season achieved record returns for the company. When the Shipping Corporation was established, the British Lines took the view that here was an approved 'New Zealand National Line' and as Scales had been given a share of the trade as a New Zealand-owned company, it should now obtain the annual wool quota from the Corporation, rather than them. Since the original contract with the lines in 1924, they had made new agreements in 1948, 1958, 1964 and 1974 and the Scales entitlement had dropped to 46,000 bales. The company no longer had sufficient wool volumes to charter several ships a season, so it had contracted with the Scandinavian lines, for whom it acted as New Zealand agents, to lift its entitlement. When the Corporation was going to obtain a 14 per cent trade share from October 1977, the Lines told Scales their arrangements were over. Scales attempted to seek recourse from the London principals of the Lines but in a 20-minute meeting in that city, the Scales chairman received no consideration, and the wool carriage, which had commenced 79 years earlier, came to an abrupt end. On the formation of the Corporation, Scales was considered as a possible partner, but in the eyes of the Corporation promoters, the company appeared too small an entity for the role they expected the Corporation would play in international shipping. In 1954 Port Line management had talked to Scales about buying the company, but Scales decided to remain independent.

Despite all the talk in London about the inevitable introduction of containers, the Port Line placed a £6,000,000 order with Alexander Stephen & Sons, Linthouse at the end of December 1965 for two twin-screw conventional refrigerated ships, the first for delivery in December 1967 and the second in June 1968. It was the highest value order ever received by the 215 year-old shipbuilder and the first contract the

With container services in the wings, the Port Line nevertheless decided to build two of the largest conventional refrigerated ships in the world. They entered service within a year of the Australian trade with the United Kingdom and Europe being containerised. Coming from the shipyard of Alexander Stephen, Linthouse, the *Port Chalmers* was launched in October 1967 and delivered in April 1968. FREEMAN-PRIEST

company had received from the Port Line. They were the largest and fastest (21.5 knot) ships ordered by the company, or any line in the New Zealand trade, and with each vessel having 17,186 cubic metres of insulated space they were also the largest conventional refrigerated ships in the world. In addition they had 6,032 cubic metres of space for general cargo. The vessels were also the first Port Line ships to have bulbous bows. They were fitted with a new type of permanent corrugated steel dunnage, designed to avoid the cost of wooden dunnage. Cranes were again prominent with three 5-tonne travelling cranes and two 5-tonne fixed deck cranes, as well as a 25-tonne Thompson crane for heavy lifts. At service speed the fuel consumption was 94 tonnes per day. They were designed to handle ISO containers and could carry 1420 tons (71 full containers) on deck.

Lady Porritt, wife of the New Zealand governor-general designate, launched *Port Chalmers*, on 9 October 1967, and the ship was delivered in April 1968. The second vessel was named *Port Caroline*, after the large bay alongside the port of Timaru in New Zealand, and not the port in Lacepede Bay, approximately 160 miles south east of Adelaide, after which the *Port Caroline* of 1919 had been named. Launched on 16 April 1968 by Mrs W.S.C. Jenks, the wife of the retired engineer superintendent and then a director of the company, the *Port Caroline* was delivered in October 1968. Both were initially employed on their designed trade between New Zealand and the

The second vessel, the *Port Caroline*, was delivered in October 1968. Between them, the two ships made only 35 round voyages between the United Kingdom and New Zealand on their designed service, and of these voyages there were 26 outward passages in ballast. Thereafter they were employed spasmodically with charter work, interspersed with periods laid up, and within 15 years they were sold to Greek owners. The illustration shows the *Port Caroline* sailing deepsea from Port Chalmers with 5000 bales of wool as deck cargo firmly lashed down on her hatches. BAIN-WRIGHT COLLECTION

UK, mainly utilising the meat loading ports of Napier, Timaru and Bluff. In 1970 the *Port Caroline* made a ballast passage from Liverpool to Timaru in 23 days one hour 30 minutes, inclusive of Panama Canal transit, and this was thought to be the fastest passage to New Zealand by a Port Line ship, and possibly the quickest by any ship of the New Zealand Conference. In their first ten years of service, they jointly made a total of thirty-five homeward loadings from New Zealand ports to the East Coast of North America or the UK in the service they were built for, but of these voyages, the vessels ballasted the 12,000-mile outward passage from the UK to New Zealand to load on 26 occasions!

The Port Line had always circulated the cold air over the top and around the sides of the cargo in the refrigerated holds but with the *Port Chalmers* and *Port Caroline*, the now more universal system of bottom air delivery, was adopted. Even so the lower holds of the two ships were so large, compared to previous vessels, that they sometimes had air flow problems and great care was necessary in laying out the bottom stows to ensure the air flow would effectively cover all the cargo spaces.

For many years it had been customary for ships to carry any overflow of wool bookings on deck and Port Line kept a stock of very large canvas covers at selected ports to cover the on-deck shipments of wool. With the *Port Chalmers* and *Port Caroline* the large hatch covers were ideal for the stowage of deck wool over dunnage, covered with tarpaulins and well lashed down. Regular large shipments were made and on 4 December 1970 the *Port Chalmers* sailed from Bluff with 7,000 bales of wool on deck, the largest deck cargo of wool ever to leave New Zealand. Ostensibly for reasons of economy she was routed to Britain via the Cape of Good Hope instead of the Panama Canal. Unfortunately very heavy waves encountered as the ship was close to East London, washed about 200 bales from the forward hatches over the side. Despite this, the vessels continued to carry extensive deck cargoes of wool whenever cargo offerings exceeded the under deck spaces.

With container services being introduced to Australia from 1969 and New Zealand in 1972 the two ships soon had difficulty finding suitable employment. For the liner trade the ships had carried a mixture of frozen and general cargoes, but to aid earnings when they were used for full shipments of refrigerated cargo their insulated capacity was enhanced to 18,779 m^3. Port Line also investigated the potential for converting them to cellular container ships or cruise liners. Nothing came of these proposals and they continued to only gain employment spasmodically in between periods of 'lay up'. Their large capacity was ideal for break-bulk liftings of meat to the Middle East and Russia, or fruit from South Africa, but they were not competitive against more pallet-friendly vessels running with crews of only half the size of those on the *Port Chalmers* and *Port Caroline,* which in 1973 each carried 53 officers and crew. The normal complement, when the ships were built in 1968, was 68.

They were magnificent cargo liners with excellent stability, but with containers starting to dominate cargo handling in the United States, and the major British liner companies undertaking studies to follow suit, one must wonder why such large and expensive ships were ordered. None of the other Conference lines in the Australian or New Zealand trades ordered ships of their quality, capacity and speed at that time. An inference might be drawn that the engineering influences at board level were dominating the decision making, without equal consideration being given to the suitability of the ships to secure full employment, or an adequate return on the capital invested over a life of at least 20 years, in a transport world that was rapidly moving away from costly break-bulk cargo handling to unit load and container systems. With the spasmodic nature of their employment, and over the few short years they were in service prior to being replaced by container ships, the vessels made few profits and the occasional satisfactory return from a single voyage was quickly offset by standing charges when they went back into lay-up.

As planning for containers was developing apace, the Port Line would soon be left with several conventional ships, solely required to provide supplementary capacity for the container services. As ACT(A) had its own administration, it was clear that much of the Port Line conventional staff, both on shore and at sea would become surplus as fleet numbers shrank. It was equally important to find a solution, which would also significantly improve Port Line profitability. Blue Star Line was in a similar position and on 1 January 1968 a separate company, Blue Star Port Lines Management Limited, was established to manage the 56 ships in the combined fleets. It became operationally effective from 15 March 1968. This also enabled the two companies to better plan the phase-out of conventional services as the various container ships came into service. The London joint management was extended to Australia with Joint Cargo Services being set up. This company also included the third partner in ACT(A), Ellerman Lines. On 1 January 1969 Blue Star Port Lines Management (N.Z.) Ltd commenced operations in New Zealand and in preparation for the introduction of the North American container service, the Ellerman Line agency was taken over from 1 October 1970. Blue Star Line conventional sailings were also integrated into the East Coast North American sailings. The rapid transition from conventional shipping to containers placed a considerable strain on the staff of the management companies. Port Line withdrew conventional tonnage from the United Kingdom-Australian trade in 1969, the East Coast of North American trade to both countries in 1971 and finally from the United Kingdom-New Zealand service in early 1979. In the run-up to the development of a container service between the UK and New Zealand, a series of trial container shipments were undertaken, and in March 1972 the *Port New Plymouth* carried the first two ISO containers for ACT(A) from Liverpool to New Zealand.

Whilst the concept of joint management should have been an efficient solution to the problems of managing a declining number of conventional ships, what could be described as the differing philosophies and cultures put the two companies on a collision course. In August 1968 the Port Line directors' minutes blandly stated that 'whilst areas of difference in policy between the two companies were identified, it was agreed that it might take sometime to achieve uniformity'. Port Line personnel could never understand the tremendous loyalty shown by the Blue Star people towards the Vestey family, especially since in many cases the Blue Star Line staff had poorer pay and conditions than Port Line personnel. Port Line officers often thought Blue Star superintendents were arrogant and brisk because they would not observe the niceties of a chat or a meal on board. There was certainly more dedication to the job shown by Blue Star personnel and there was also some bitterness amongst Port Line senior staff that Blue Star seemed to 'have the upper hand' in the management company. As a result of these widening rifts, the joint management arrangements ceased from 1 January 1972 and thereafter the remaining conventional vessels within their respective fleets were managed by the individual lines. At least the management company had started to get shippers used to dealing with the one company as a forerunner to the establishment of ACT(A) and the container services. It was clear that Blue Star Line regarded shipping as its long-term business, whereas Port Line was now under close scrutiny by its parent, Cunard, because of its poor financial performance. This situation had become more acute after the takeover of Cunard by Trafalgar House Investments in 1971. The influence of Cunard was clearly shown by the Port Line withdrawals from both the associated companies – Compass and Crusader Lines. The shore personnel in offices overseas handling the agency work and liner traffic of the companies continued working together for some years after 1972, particularly in New Zealand.

At least the formation of the management company and the tightening up of costs saw Port Line show profits before tax of £3.6 million in 1968 and £3.8 million the following year, but results for the 1970 year had dropped back to £1.0 million. In that year the jointly-owned Cunard House at 88 Leadenhall Street was sold to a property company for £8,250,000, netting a book profit of £6,000,000.

When it came to rationalising the rest of the Cunard group conventional shipping interests (the passenger ships were already separately managed), Sir Basil Smallpeice was clearly impressed with the management team running its other cargo ship subsidiary, T.& J. Brocklebank. In 1967 Cunard-Brocklebank Limited was set up to manage the residual cargo fleets, effective from 1 January 1968. Senior management in the new company largely came from Brocklebanks rather than Port Line, and the 'esprit des corps' that had characterised the Port Line loyalty and their pride in the fleet for half a century was even more eroded as a result of these moves. The redundancies and restructurings that subsequently took place through the steady transition from conventional to container shipping, the reduction of the retirement age, and the financial belt-tightening, also took its toll on morale. Port Line, as an entity, never survived the withdrawal from Blue Star Port Lines Management, as when the split came, Port Line personnel went directly into Cunard-Brocklebank Ltd and then later on in 1979, into Cunard Shipping Services Ltd. Cunard, through the subsidiary T. & J. Brocklebank Ltd, had purchased H.E. Moss and Company's Tankers Ltd, Liverpool in 1964 and some Port Line personnel were also employed on the three tankers run by this company. In 1972-3 Cunard ordered eight 15,500 ton bulk carriers from Astilleros Espanoles S.A. Seville, Spain and again some Port Line officers and engineers went to them. A small number also worked for Cunard's Off Shore Marine, on anchor handling and deep sea tugs serving oil rigs mainly in the North Sea.

In 1972 Port Line still had 18 conventional cargo ships but by 1975 this number had been halved and there were only five ships left in 1977. Interestingly the three fast single-screw refrigerated ships built in 1965 and 1966 were all sold in the early 1970s to the same Greek owner and spent almost the next 20 years employed in a semi-liner service between east coast South American ports and ports in western Mediterranean, but were operated at more economical speeds than they were originally designed for. Most of the other refrigerated ships were sold directly to ship breakers, although the *Port Auckland* was sold and converted for use as the live sheep carrier *Mashaallah* for three years prior to final scrapping. Cunard Line had a shareholding in the Kuwait company operating the vessel, which could carry 25,421 live sheep.

Apart from the five remaining ships, the *Port St. Lawrence* had already been transferred to a Cunard subsidiary in 1975 and renamed *Matangi.* Whilst *Matangi* sounded like a Brocklebank name, it was never one that company had used. It originated as a result of a directive from the managing-director who wanted an Australasian name beginning with *Ma*, which would blend in with Brocklebank nomenclature. Matangi is a small community seven miles from Hamilton, New Zealand. Of the other five, the *Port Launceston* was sold for further trading in 1977, *Port Alfred* was transferred to Cunard, under the management of Cunard-Brocklebank Bulkers Limited in 1975 and renamed with the Brocklebank name of *Masirah* in 1978. Both the *Matangi* and *Port Alfred* in 1977 were placed on a new Cunard Line refrigerated and general cargo service between South America and the Middle East (known as SAMEL) loading at such ports as Rio de Janiero, Santos, Monte Video and Buenos Aires for Khorramshar, Kuwait and then into the Red Sea ports of Jeddah and Aqaba. The vessels then returned to Brazil through the Mediterranean. On the passage to the Arabian Gulf calls were often made at Cape Town and Durban. They were withdrawn from the service in early 1982.

As the last of the five new container ships for the main line service from the UK and Continent to Australia and New Zealand, did not arrive in New Zealand until May 1979, the Conference Lines continued to provide sailings of conventional ships to meet the requirements of the producer boards. The last Port Line conventional ship to load direct for the UK on the main line trade which had commenced with the *Balmoral Castle* in 1887 was the *Port Caroline* which loaded at Napier, New Plymouth, Whangarei, and Mount Maunganui in 1978, sailing from Mt. Maunganui for Avonmouth and Liverpool on 25 November 1978. There was a further conventional Port line loading in March 1979 when *Port Nicholson* loaded on her last voyage at several New Zealand ports for Cyprus, Piraeus and Malta with the balance of her cargo for Avonmouth.

The *Port Nicholson* was sold for demolition in Taiwan in 1979 after a short career of 17 years. This left only the *Port Chalmers* and *Port Caroline* under their original names until 1981 when they were given the Brocklebank names of *Manaar* and *Matra* respectively. They were finally scrapped in Shanghai in 1985 after a mere 17 years, quite a proportion of this laid up. When they did get a cargo, it often involved a long ballast voyage. In 1976 Cunard purchased ten fully refrigerated ships from Maritimecor S.A. (Maritime Fruit Carriers) and in the nine years they were in Cunard ownership employed as fast fruit carriers, a number of Port Line sea staff had the opportunity of working on them.

At the time of the merger of the managements of Port Line and Blue Star, Cunard was going through a difficult period financially. There were signs of decay and the company was struggling to produce capital for a range of new projects (including £20,000,000 for one of the four container ships being built for the United Kingdom-New Zealand container service). Somewhat like Port Line, the Cunard Line board was heavily involved in the management of the group and efforts were belatedly being made to give greater responsibility to management. In addition the Cunard Line Transatlantic business was continuing to lose money, in the face of ever-growing competition from air travel. Cunard's other main cargo line, T. & J. Brocklebank, was also in trouble, not having made a profit since 1957. Sir Basil Smallpeice sought Board approval to bring in American consultants, McKinsey, to evaluate the prospects for the whole Cunard group. Time was not on the side of the company, and the fast-growing property and construction group, London based Trafalgar House Investments, made a takeover bid for Cunard in June 1971. In reality there was no white knight in the wings, and little the company could do to resist the bid. Approaches for a merger with Liverpool based Alfred Holt & Company and P&O in London were both rejected. Cunard directors held their last board meeting of the 93-year old company on 25 August 1971 before Trafalgar House Investments assumed control, acquiring assets with book values of £43,000,000 at a cost of £26 million. Trafalgar House, generating more profits than Cunard, was also able to gain full benefit of Cunard's accumulated free depreciation allowances which exceeded £50,000,000.

Port Line was on the fringe of the takeover drama but as we have seen, the company had already lost much of its independence, once its financial position had started to decline. As Trafalgar House progressively took control of the Cunard empire, it steadily sold off the minority interests the Port Line had in various stevedoring companies, shipbrokers, shipping agencies and wool dumpers, as well as any surplus properties. The Trafalgar House Investments board was bereft of a director with cargo shipping experience until W.B. Slater, head of Cunard-Brocklebank Limited, was appointed a director in December 1973. In 1984 he became managing director of Cunard Steam-Ship Company, responsible for the group's cargo shipping and its offshore marine division. On Slater's retirement in 1985 he was succeeded as managing director by Alexander Macintosh, who had joined ACT(A) in 1967 as commercial manager and had subsequently been appointed managing director of that company from 1974-1985.

With the disposal of all the conventional tonnage, the only significant remaining Port Line investment was the shareholding in ACT(A) and its associated concerns. In 1991 when P&O acquired these interests, Port Line Ltd just became a dormant subsidiary of P&O, then with P&O Nedlloyd from 1997 and was passed to A.P. Moller-Maersk when it acquired P&O Nedlloyd in 2005. Former staff of the company and associated personnel from agencies and subsidiaries around the world still continue to meet in London at an annual reception each year in May; in recent years it being held on board HQS *Wellington,* moored in the Thames. Some funds remained from the accumulation of bar collections from the *Oaklawn* days and these were used to finance the first few gatherings. Thereafter the reunions have been self-funded under the name of Vintage Port. Following each gathering a booklet is sent to all members of the group around the world, listing the names of those who attended and the comments of those who sent apologies. Much of the credit for the success of these gatherings must go to former superintendent, Captain A.D. Braithwaite, OBE as chairman, and Cyril Simmons, as secretary. On average the numbers attending total around 150 although everyone acknowledges that with the passage of time this figure will reduce. Smaller regional gatherings of former staff (including former ACT(A) personnel) take place on a regular basis in various cities in the United Kingdom, Australia and New Zealand as well as smaller groups getting together for a beer or two and a nostalgic chat.

In addition, a former member of the sea staff, Don Ramsey, living in Dubai, developed a 'Vintage Port' website from 5 June 2000 and this now has over 430 members communicating by email from around the world. In the time the closed website has been under way a considerable amount of historical information, photographs of ships and personnel, and individual records of sea staff have been placed on the site and as time passes, more and more former Port Line staff are becoming aware of the facility and are making contact with old friends they may not have seen or heard from for many years. It would seem that Port Line will be nostalgically remembered for many years to come.

Whilst the Port Line name may have disappeared, the Tyser name is still very much alive with Tyser & Company, being the oldest continuously-trading firm of Lloyd's brokers. The company operates an international business with a global client base and has a staff approaching 200. It also has a successful UK retail operation. Under the trading name of Tysers, it provides insurance and risk management solutions to a wide range of companies, with some of these associations extending back over many decades. There are no longer any members of the Tyser family involved with the firm.

1 *Fairplay International Shipping Journal,* 27 May 1971.
2 *Containerisation International,* 10 Oct 1971, p. 51.
3 *Lloyds Register 1973-74.*

APPENDIX 1

Port Line associated companies

THE AMERICAN SERVICE AND THE MANZ LINE

With the withdrawal of the Tyser Line joint venture partner, German Australia Line, just prior to war being declared in August 1914, the newly-formed Commonwealth & Dominion Line was left with a service at more than monthly intervals from New York to Australia and New Zealand ports. One of the partners in Funch, Edye, & Company, the Tyser Line agents in the United States, was a German national, and it was necessary for him to resign after war was declared and to terminate the agencies for the German lines. As a shortage of shipping developed, sailings on the New York service were often less than monthly until after the war. There was a strong demand from oil companies for the carriage of case oil, and from March 1914 to August 1915, 953,561 cases of oil or kerosene were shipped on C&D vessels. In 1916 the company secured a significant contract from Vacuum Oil to carry up to 75,000 cases of case oil per month.

From 1 January 1917, Funch Edye & Company was taken over by Cunard Line and the C&D Line North American representative, T. Ashley Sparkes, joined the board of Funch Edye in that year and remained a director until his retirement in 1952.

The American & Australian Line and the United States and Australasian Line also had limited sailings during the war. The New Zealand Shipping Company's acquisition of the Houlder Bros' Australian service in 1912, and then the integration with the Federal the same year, had given it 66 per cent of the American & Australian Line. The remaining partner in the line, Bucknall Steamship Lines, had been taken over by the interests of Sir John Ellerman in 1908, so the A&A Line was under completely new ownership, but effectively controlled by the NZSCo. That company continued with sailings from Canadian ports every two months throughout the war.

After the war the services changed significantly. The C&D Line and the A&A Line continued with a New York sailing every month, but the merchant-owned company, United States & Australasian Line, fell by the wayside completely in 1922. As a result A&A increased its sailings to three-weekly. Ellerman & Bucknall Steamship Company employed its own vessels while the NZSCo mainly chartered tonnage from other P&O affiliates including the Hain Steamship Co and Trinder, Anderson & Co, as well as vessels from J. Edgar & Co. The C&D Line improved its monthly departures to three sailings every two months.

From the end of 1921, the NZSCo ran into competition for Canadian cargo from a new monthly service from Canada to Australasia. During the war, the Canadian government had developed an extensive shipbuilding programme. Finding itself stuck with over 60 war-surplus ships, it decided to employ them in international trades to boost the Canadian economy. When this news reached London, C&D Line's Jack Rooper wrote to the Canadians. He pointed out the route to Australasia was already well covered, and quoted the Canadian government's declared policy of not butting into established trades, but to no avail.

The first few years of the Australian and New Zealand service were profitable but as British companies replaced war losses, overtonnaging complicated a world-wide slump in trading. In 1928 the NZSCo tried to rationalise sailings with the Canadian Government Merchant Marine (CGMM), as neither party could make a profit with two ships a month leaving for Australasia. The Canadian Line, as a national flag carrier, however, preferred to force out the NZSCo, even though it had been maintaining a service from Canada since 1910.

A freight war developed. The New Zealand Shipping Co dropped its rate from around £5 a ton to a £1 flat rate for all cargo. In August 1928 its chartered *Baron Inchcape* (1917, 7,005) sailed from Canada with a full cargo. The CGMM announced its next four sailings would also carry freight at £1 a ton. Peace was declared in October after eight vessels had been loaded. The Canadian Line refused to discontinue its monthly service, obliging the NZSCo to withdraw from Canada. By the end of 1928 freights had returned to previous levels, but between 1921 and 1934 the CGMM had lost $C11,064,725. High crewing costs alone ensured the line would never be profitable. The Canadian ships sailed to Australian and New Zealand ports from Montreal, or Halifax in winter, via Boston and New York, so were also competing with the A&A Line and the C&D service from U.S. ports.

In view of the continuing losses being made by the CGMM, the C&D Line, as early as 1932 made the first approaches to take it over. Whilst the Canadians were interested in receiving an offer, they were slow to provide financial information, so the offer lapsed. In 1934 Rooper travelled to Canada for follow-up talks, only to find representatives of Ellerman & Bucknall and the NZSCo already there for the same purpose. They decided to mount a collective bid and he returned to London. In April 1936 Rooper, Leonard Harris, managing-director of Ellerman and Bucknall Steamship Company, and Arnold Trinder, a director of the NZSCo, crossed on the *Aquitania* (1914, 45,647) and re-opened discussions with the Canadians. A heads of agreement was achieved but it was not until 8 June 1936 that a final agreement was signed. The Lines agreed to purchase ten CGMM vessels totaling 88,050 deadweight for £160,000 and to run approximately 24 sailings per annum to Australia and 12 to New Zealand for at least five years. All sailings were to be from Montreal, except for the three winter months, and if insufficient Canadian cargo was available, the ships could call at US ports. The Lines also undertook to form a new Canadian-registered company to operate the service and to take over CGMM sea and shore staff, stores and other supplies. An undertaking was also given that rates of freight would not exceed rates charged from US ports to Australia and New Zealand.

The preferred name of the new company was to be the Canada Australia New Zealand Line Ltd, but it was not approved by the company registrar, so the word Montreal replaced Canada. Throughout its 30-year lifetime, it was universally known as the MANZ Line. Its headquarters was Montreal, with separate MANZ Line companies in London, Sydney and Wellington to handle its business in each country. The resident Canadian board of directors comprised Messrs W.R. Eakin, I.H. Eakin, Eric Reford, G.D. Huband and E.W. Foulds. Eric Reford's company, Robert Reford and Co, was the agent in Canada for the Port Line and the Cunard White Star Line. Foulds handled all the NZSCo business in Canada. F.G. Wood, formerly

The most modern Canadian ship was the *Canadian Constructor*, built in 1922. She was not sold until 1939 and is photographed at Adelaide. The Canadian Line funnel colours were red, white band and blue top but under the MANZ Line the blue top was intended to be repainted black but it appears that this was not done. W. BURCH

in the management of the Canadian Government Line to Australia and New Zealand, was appointed general manager of the new company.

The *City of Batavia* (1907, 5,655) left Canada on 22 May 1936 for Auckland, Wellington, Sydney, Melbourne and Adelaide and inaugurated the first voyage of the MANZ Line prior to the final agreement being signed. She was followed at the end of May by the *City of Delhi* (1925, 7,443) bound for Brisbane, Sydney, Melbourne, Dunedin, Lyttelton and Wellington. At the time MANZ Line was formed, Port Line pooling entitlement with the other two lines gave it one sailing in four on a ten-day schedule to Australia and one sailing in three to New Zealand.

The partners decided to sell the Canadian ships, all prefixed by *Canadian,* (the *Britisher, Challenger, Conquerer, Constructor, Cruiser, Highlander, Leader, Planter, Scottish* and *Victor*), as soon as ships of their own became available. In fact the sale of five of the ships in the first financial year of the MANZ Line realised £103,250 and the directors of the new company were concerned that the capital profits realised on the sale of the vessels would attract the attention of the Inland Revenue Department, as the company seemed to be in the business of buying and selling ships rather than running a shipping line! The *Canadian Challenger, Canadian Conqueror* and *Canadian Constructor* continued in the trade under MANZ Line until May 1939.

On 23 September 1936 Port Line ordered three new single-screw, mainly general cargo carriers, from three different British shipyards. The NZSCo also ordered new tonnage, but Ellerman & Bucknall elected to employ existing vessels from its extensive fleet. All the Canadian ships were sold by mid 1939. While on MANZ Line service, they retained their Canadian livery, although it had been intended that the top of the red, white and blue funnel would be painted black instead of blue. The old Royden Line house flag was donated to the MANZ Line by Jack Rooper on behalf of Sir Thomas Royden, and a maple leaf set on the white diamond made it totally appropriate

Following the formation of the Montreal Australia and New Zealand Line, the Port Line ordered three, mainly general cargo economy motorships, for the new service from the east coast of Canada and United States to and from Australia and New Zealand. The first of the 13 knot ships was the *Port Montreal*, launched in August 1937. She was torpedoed in the Caribbean in 1942. E. FLUCK

for the new company. Amongst the CGMM 'assets' acquired by the Port Line was Captain R.P. Fuller, a native of Nova Scotia, whose friendly, competent style quickly endeared him to everyone.

The first new ship was the *Port Halifax,* launched on 7 July 1937 by Ellen (Nell) Corry at Swan Hunter & Wigham Richardson. The *Port Montreal* was launched by Evelyn Corry (another daughter of Robert Corry, a director of C&D Line from 1914-1941) at Wm. Doxford and Sons at Sunderland on 10 August 1937, and she was the first of the three to be delivered. On her maiden voyage to her home port, she averaged 12.32 knots on 12.22 tons of oil per day, and highlighted the cost-efficient nature of the new ships. When the Hon. Mrs R.H. Senior (a daughter of Lord Joicey, owner of the Albyn Line of Sunderland), launched the third ship, the *Port Saint John* (laid down as the *Port Quebec*) at the yard of Joseph L. Thompson, Sunderland on 9 August 1937, she could not have contemplated the misfortunes the vessel was going to experience on her maiden voyage.

Delivered on 3 January 1938, the *Port Saint John* grounded near Sydney, Nova Scotia 14 days later, her master being unaware that a buoy normally marking a reef had been removed because of winter ice conditions. The ship was refloated eight hours later and was found to have sustained extensive bottom damage. After repairs she sailed from Halifax on 2 March, but returned next day with a defective thrust block. Later in the same voyage as the *Port Saint John* was approaching the Queensland coast at full speed on a ballast passage from New Zealand, she ran onto a coral reef near Lady Elliot Island on 5 May 1938 and was not refloated until nine days later. Temporary repairs were undertaken in Sydney and the ship returned to Sunderland for permanent repairs to her bottom plating. The inquiry censured the master, Captain W.L. Lynd and the third officer, and Lynd left the company. Apart from these troubles, the *Port Saint John* was plagued with engine trouble for sometime. Port Line blamed this on poor workmanship and materials by Richardsons Westgarth and Company of West Hartlepool, which Jack Rooper ensured built no more engines for the company. All three ships had poor visibility over the bow due to the

The third ship of the MANZ Line series, the *Port Saint John*, delivered in January 1938, had an unlucky start by running ashore in Nova Scotia on her maiden voyage, then driving on to a coral reef in Queensland four months later. Repairs and a new master restored the situation, although all three MANZ Line ships had varying engine troubles. The photograph shows the vessel with the raised bridge. BAIN-WRIGHT COLLECTION

low bridge front and an extra 10 foot high deck was later added to the superstructure on the *Port Halifax* and *Port Saint John* in 1952/53 to improve the situation and provide more accommodation.

In December 1938 Port Line ordered a fourth vessel for the MANZ Line service. She was launched as the *Port Quebec* by Mrs Warwick Gregory, the wife of the Port Line local director in New Zealand, on 17 August 1939. She was almost two knots faster than the others and had a larger refrigerated capacity. Although registered in the name of the company on 24 May 1940, she had already been requisitioned for war service in November 1939. It was not until December

A fourth, slightly larger, and more powerful, motorship was ordered for the MANZ Line service, but she was requisitioned prior to completion in 1939 and entered service as the minelayer HMS *Port Quebec*, and was later converted to an aircraft repair ship. In deference to her war service the ship's bell was inscribed HMS *Port Quebec* 1939-1945 on one side and HMS *Deer Sound* 1945-46 on the other. V.H. YOUNG & L.A. SAWYER

The only ship owned by the MANZ Line after World War II was the standard Canadian-built *Mission Park*, completed in 1944. She was renamed *Ottawa Valley* on her acquisition by the company in 1947, and remained in the MANZ Line service until 1954. V.H. YOUNG & L.A. SAWYER

1947 that she was re-delivered to Port Line to commence her first commercial voyage.

From 1936 MANZ Line had some limited competition from Norddeutscher Lloyd of Bremen, which was programming vessels with cargo from Bremen and Hamburg coming to Australia and New Zealand via the eastern seaboard of the United States and Gulf of Mexico ports. On arrival in Australasia they loaded back for Europe on their owners' Australian/Europe berth. World War II ended the German competition but it also disrupted MANZ Line's operations. In June 1941 American Pioneer Lines offered to help out by providing ships but only two had sailed south before the USA's entry into the war in December 1941 prevented any further assistance. As in World War I, the Canadian government embarked on a major shipbuilding programme. In 1944 the Canadian government line, Park Steam Ship Co, asked MANZ Line to crew and manage the war-built ships *Rondeau Park* and *Runnymede Park*, which were delivered at Montreal on 27 April 1944 and 8 June 1944 respectively. A year later MANZ Line was asked to take two more ships, and *Fairmount Park* and *Highland Park* were delivered at Vancouver on 1 February 1945 and 9 June 1945. MANZ Line crewed and operated them, securing commercial cargo when space was not required for government or military equipment. It also operated the *Leaside Park* (1944, 7,160) and *Crystal Park* (1944, 7,100) on single time charter voyages in 1945 and 1946.

All the Canadian-built ships were returned to Park Steam Ship Co by 1946. In 1947 MANZ Line purchased a Canadian 'Victory' class steamer. Launched as *Fort Berens,* she was completed as *Mission Park.* MANZ Line took delivery of her at St. John, New Brunswick on 16 February 1947. As the *Ottawa Valley,* she became a familiar sight in Australian and New Zealand ports between 1947 and 1954, overly familiar on one voyage when she was declared 'black' during a Canadian seamen's strike, and remained idle at Auckland for 64 days in 1949. To prevent a repeat performance, she was transferred to London registry in 1950 and managed by Trinder, Anderson and Co, with Britons replacing Canadian seafarers.

In November 1945 the *Port Saint John* resumed MANZ Line Port Line sailings, and by 1947 the service was almost back to normal with 36 southbound sailings to Australia and 11 to New Zealand. No other ships were built specifically for the service, and most of the Port Line single-screw ships did spells on the MANZ Line run. Some of the smaller time-chartered dry cargo ships, such as *Ports' Campbell, Curtis, Denison* and *Wimbledon,* also sailed for the MANZ Line. Crews often spoke of their ship being 'shanghaied' in Australia and New Zealand for MANZ Line voyages when they expected to be working between the home country and Australasia. Other Port Line ships with Canadian names, like *Port Montreal, Port Alfred* and *Port St. Lawrence* were employed on services throughout the main line trades, and with associated companies like MANZ Line, Atlas Line and the Crusader Shipping Co.

The MANZ Line service did not supercede the traditional New York sailings of C&D/ Port Line and the A&A Line to Australia and New Zealand. Vessels operated out of New York on the Port and Associated Lines berth to Australasia with import cargoes but with the ever-increasing volumes of export cargoes, MANZ Line ships covered all the ports in East Coast of North America (ECNA) on their northbound voyages. Where demand exceeded capacity for refrigerated cargoes, vessels on the main line trade to Britain were diverted to discharge at one or two eastern US ports. In the last four years before containerisation, the larger *Port New Plymouth, Port Chalmers* and *Port Caroline* also made MANZ Line voyages. New Zealand Dairy Board shipments of cheese to ECNA were covered within the New Zealand/UK contracts and Conference Line main line trade vessels carried these to North America en route to Britain.

After World War II the main discharge ports were Philadelphia, New York, Boston, then Montreal, or Halifax/Saint John at ship's option in winter. However, because Saint John was on the Canadian mainland, Canadian importers preferred it and discharge was usually undertaken there. In 1964 the *Port Nelson* became the first Port Line ship to transit the St Lawrence Seaway, calling at Hamilton and Toronto to handle cargo. Northbound, Charleston was added as permanent call from 1954 and ten years later calls at Norfolk were introduced. Occasional visits were made to Galveston and Portland, Maine and MANZ Line vessels regularly served Balboa/Cristobal. Occasionally northbound calls were made to Matarani/Mollendo in Peru, Vera Cruz in Mexico, Hamilton in Bermuda and Kingston, Jamaica but from New Zealand these way-port calls were later covered by a direct New Zealand-West Indies service by vessels en-route to the UK. In 1961 this way-port service was replaced with a six-weekly round voyage to and from New Zealand. From 1983 direct calls were extended to New Orleans in the US Gulf.

Southbound, the ships loaded at Montreal, Trois Rivieres (Three Rivers) and Quebec, (occasionally Baie Comeau for aluminium) during summer months and at Saint John in winter. All-year-round calls were made at Cornerbrook for newsprint and because there was insufficient Canadian cargo to fill the ships, they also loaded at New York, Newport News and Savannah on the way south.

In February 1966 the NZSCo withdrew from the MANZ Line Australian service because of the 'tooth and nail' resistance by the Australian and United States governments to what it felt were justifiable freight increases. The other partners continued under their own names. MANZ Line Australia was wound up. The Port Line endeavoured to maintain eight annual northbound sailings from Australia using the *Port Albany, Port Huon* and *Port Alfred.* Four other Port Line vessels loaded southbound at US ports supplementing this service. In New Zealand, from 1965, Shaw Savill and Blue Star also berthed ships to ECNA. In the early days of the MANZ Line the main export cargoes from New Zealand seemed to be rabbit skins, wet salted pelts and wool from both Australia and New Zealand. After World War II the most valuable commodity shipped from New Zealand was deep frozen crayfish tails, but after 1958 the growth of frozen cartonned beef was significant and this became the main export cargo for the line from both countries. In that year there was a drought in Texas and additional tonnage was needed to cope with demand. Some of the older ships of the *Port Fremantle* class had to be employed, and in the North Queensland heat, they had difficulty keeping down the hold temperatures and loading had to stop at times. This delayed their arrival in the USA. David Gill, from Port Line London office, who was in the US at the time, recalled an irate meat importer describing the *Port Alma* as 'that damn bucket of bolts' and threatening to sue for late delivery.

With the establishment of ACT in 1966 and ACT(A) with the three American trade partners in 1967, the decision was made to containerise the total services to and from the East Coast of North America. ACT(A), operated the ECNA service under the marketing name of Pacific America Container Express Line (PACE) and assumed responsibility for the total trade and the operation of, and eventual phasing out of the conventional vessels. The *City of Canberra,* sailing from Auckland on 28 February 1972, was the last break-bulk sailing. The last conventional Port Line vessel to load for ECNA was the *Port New Plymouth,* which sailed from Auckland for Galveston on 24 July 1971. MANZ Line Limited was wound up on 26 April 1971.

ALBION & OVERSEAS SHIPPING AGENCY LIMITED

In December 1963 Port Line Ltd acquired all the shares in the Albion & Overseas Shipping Agency. The company had been established in 1952 as Continental Carriers Ltd and was renamed in 1956. It was a Baltic Exchange chartering broker and it was felt there would be considerable benefit having an 'in house' shipbroker handling the chartering for both Cunard and Port Lines. Funch Edye in New York also handled chartering business and the new company took over its requirements as well. In October 1964, Cunard Line purchased Liverpool-based H.E. Moss & Co's Tankers Ltd, which also included a London shipbroker, H.E. Moss & Company Ltd. The Albion & Overseas business was subsequently integrated into H.E. Moss, about 1966, although the company remained a dormant entity within the Cunard group. The business was successful and by 1974 it was reported that two thirds of the brokerage handled was chartering work outside the Trafalgar House group, a percentage that rose to 80 per cent by 1975. It was also in 1974 that H.E. Moss expanded into ship agency services and also offered ship management, technical superintendence and crew training. Trafalgar House sold the company to P&O Containers in 1991, and it was integrated into Anderson Hughes, a P&O subsidiary, effective from 1 July 1998. H.E. Moss was closed down in 2000. Albion and Overseas was revived as an oil broker in the 1980s buying futures options and swaps on behalf of Cunard passenger and cargo business. It continued in this role for Cunard and was not sold to P&O in 1991.

ATLAS LINE

When the rival British container consortia, Overseas Containers Ltd (OCL) and Associated Container Transportation Ltd (ACT), were set up in 1965 and 1966, ACT found that the trades their members served lacked any link between Australia and the Far East. The ACT partners felt this cross trade would help to better utilise containers within their worldwide network and might also assist with the supply of empty containers. ACT members having Australian links, Blue Star Line, Port Line and Ellermans, applied to the Australian Northbound Shipping Conference for a share of the trade. When the application was rejected they decided to mount their own service and established a new company called Atlas Line in August 1967. Initially the name Equatorial Line was chosen, but it was felt Atlas had more impact, and was more easily pronounced by Asians. No registered company was formed in the UK but Atlas Line (Australia) Pty Ltd, was registered as a South Australian company on 8 September 1967.

As both P&O and Ocean Steam, two major partners in OCL, were members of the Northbound Conference, the three lines kept their intentions strictly confidential until it was absolutely necessary to mount a marketing campaign for the new service. They realised that launching Atlas Line would harm relationships with the other British lines and when the service was announced, it could be said 'all hell broke loose'. An OCL director described the Atlas Line move as 'irresponsible and untimely opportunism, which threatens to upset the negotiations now going on between British liner shipping and our friends in other countries to introduce container services worldwide in an intelligent and sensible manner'. Atlas Line offered a 17 per cent rebate off the freight on northbound cargoes while the conference reduced southbound freights by 15 per cent.

The *Rockhampton Star* (1957, 9,847) was the first vessel sent north. She loaded at Adelaide, Melbourne, Sydney, Brisbane and a north Queensland port in September 1967 for Yokkaichi, Yokohama, Nagoya, Osaka/Kobe at ship's option, and Hong Kong. Next came the *Gladstone Star* (1957, 10,365) and the *Port Montreal.* Because of the secrecy involved, the *Port Montreal* had ballasted out to Australia without the crew knowing which service the ship would enter. She made two round voyages. The only other Port Line ship to be employed was the *Port St. Lawrence.* Both retained their Port Line hull colours but the funnel was painted with a blue base and black top with a thin white line dissecting the two colours. On the blue was a white circle with a horizontal red strip through the middle. A large black ATLAS LINE was painted on each side of the hull.

Cheaper freights won the Atlas Line exceptional support, forcing the Australian Northbound Conference to appeal to shipper loyalties by taking full-page advertisements in the newspapers. The conference stressed that the extensive conference coverage ensured that one of its ships was available in every major Australian port every day. 'Bring an intruding shipping partnership on the scene and you immediately upset the efficient and economic development of the trade' it warned. 'The ultimate of this destructive freight war is that total and predictable service will not be available to you. There will be no one with whom you, the shipper, can negotiate any long term planning as to how much tonnage can be placed at what ports and what times... It's your freight, mate. Experience counted in shipping and 'your business and Northbound Conference

The *Port Montreal* was the first Port Line vessel employed on the Atlas Line service from Australia to the Far East in 1967, and she is shown in Sydney with an Atlas Line funnel. With a blue base and black top with a thin white line dissecting the two colours, the white circle on the blue had a horizontal red strip. The painting of ATLAS LINE on the side of the hull further promoted the new company. FREEMAN-PRIEST

The third Atlas Line sailing was taken by the *Port St. Lawrence*, the only other Port Line ship to be employed on the service, which lasted little more than four months. FREEMAN-PRIEST

Lines have that experience. Their system of eleven co-ordinated, yet competitive shipping lines, supplies all the tonnage needed to handle your freight right now at the most economical rates possible. The Federal Government knows this and recognises Conferences in its Trade Practices Act'.

As the scramble for cargo took place, the Northbound Conference members told the British companies involved (P&O through the Eastern and Australian Steam Ship Company, and Ocean Steam, with its interest in the China Navigation Company) to sort out their invading countrymen. Just two months later on 29 November 1967, the five parties, Eastern & Australian Line, China Navigation, Blue Star Line, Port Line and Ellermans announced that 'arising out of discussions following the establishment of the competing Atlas Line in the trade from Australia and the Far East, it has been agreed that in return for the payment of an appropriate sum, Atlas Line members

The *Port Invercargill* only had nine years of service with Port Line before being trapped in the Suez Canal from 1967 to 1975. She is shown passing Harington Point in Otago Harbour.

Often considered one of the more attractive vessels of the fleet, the *Port New Plymouth* is shown outward bound from Bluff to London on 17 March 1971.

Immaculately painted, the *Port Alfred* lies berthed at Bluff's Island Harbour.

Inward bound from Lyttelton, the *Port Nicholson* enters Otago Harbour.

The *Port Huon* was one of three fast refrigerated vessels built in 1965-6. With the advent of container services, they were sold to Greek owners and spent the next 20 years running between South America and the Mediterranean. R.A. PRIEST

Dressed for the occasion, the *Port Caroline* arrives on her first visit to Port Chalmers on 30 January 1969.

may subscribe in due course for a minority interest in the capital required for any wholly-or-partly containerised or unitised services which may be developed out of the interest in the Australian Far East, now held by Eastern and Australian Line and China Navigation. As a result of this agreement the Atlas Line will withdraw its ships from the trade and will confer with the Conference so as to make suitable arrangements for the carriage of cargoes booked by the Atlas Line in order to protect the interests of shippers'. By now six sailings had been dispatched. The *Port Montreal* took the seventh and last northbound leg, clearing from Brisbane on 27 December 1966. Whilst the Atlas Line vessels carried refrigerated cargoes northbound, they also accepted parcels of bulk wheat. The southbound cargoes were tightly controlled by the conference but the ships secured large shipments of coiled steel (12-ton lifts) from Yawata to Geelong and picked up general cargo from Taiwan and Hong Kong.

Under the conference agreement, ACT(A) (the additional A denoting the three Australasian partners in ACT) had a financial interest in the Australia Japan Container Line, formed in 1968. The Port Line share of the expenditure was going to be £592,779 towards the cost of two containerships but the option to enter the Japanese trade was never exercised. In April 1971, when P&O was going to be a minority player in a new containerised trade from the East Coast of North America to Australia and New Zealand, the company agreed to withdraw its planned new container ship *Chesapeake Bay* from the service, subject to ACT(A) not exercising the 'rights' obtained as a result of the Atlas Line freight-war of 1967. P&O eventually had the last word, taking over ACT(A) in 1991 and the remaining Blue Star Line container services in 1998. In one minor retaliation against the Atlas Line partners, China Navigation Co took away the New Zealand agency for that company from Port Line and gave it to the NZSCo. Atlas Line (Australia) Pty Ltd was de-registered 13 June 1975.

COMPASS LINE

The *Port Townsville* had her funnel painted in Compass Line colours. The Compass Line service to and from South Africa to Australia lasted only 18 months between 1969-1971. R.E.J. VARNS

Port Line and Blue Star ships from the UK had regularly called into South African ports on the way to Australia to discharge cargo. Each had pool share rights, Port Line's dating from the nineteenth century and Blue Star from 1934. To find work for surplus conventional ships after the introduction of direct container services from the UK and Europe to Australia, Blue Star and Port Line decided to market a separate entity to develop trade between South Africa and Australia. Registered as Compass Line (Pty) Ltd, the first sailing was taken by *Port Melbourne* in October 1969. Initially Blue Star planned to transfer some of its own fleet to South African registry but this would have incurred an import duty. The ships retained their company colours but had a blue funnel with black top with a thin white band dissecting the two colours. On the blue was a white circle with the design of compass points in red on the white. Ships in the service also flew a blue swallow-tailed house flag with a white circle and the red compass design on the white. The ships were chartered to the line. However, they were really too large for the cargo offering and other lines, particularly the Dutch Royal Interocean Lines, with interconnecting services around Africa, could secure much bigger liftings. There was a greater flow of cargo from Australia to South Africa than in reverse. With the parent company Cunard under financial pressure in 1971, Port Line withdrew from Compass Line effective from the end of March 1971.

CRUSADER SHIPPING COMPANY

The bulk purchase of New Zealand meat by the British government prevailed from 1940 until 1954. In 1947 Britain had extended the agreement for free access for a further seven year period from October 1948 and in 1966 Britain gave an undertaking to accept New Zealand meat without restriction of quantity up to September 1972. Australia had a similar arrangement. However, by the time New Zealand signed for its contract extension, signs were pointing towards Britain getting closer to Europe. It seemed likely that the day was not far off when Britain might have to introduce quotas on refrigerated produce from Australasia, restricting the free access these countries had enjoyed for 70 years. The meat and dairy industries would have to diversify their markets and from the mid 1950s pressure was exerted by the producer boards on exporters to do just that. Any such diversification would have a significant effect on the British Lines. They knew that if they wanted to retain control of the cargoes, they would have to provide development services to assist the new marketing thrust.

From March 1953 the Lines, including the MANZ Line, had started advertising direct way-port calls on sailings from New Zealand to Aruba, Curacao, Trinidad, Barbados, Jamaica and Bermuda at regular intervals. Each designated vessel called at one or two ports en route to the UK or ECNA. After a trial period, Trinidad had a six-weekly service, Barbados, Jamaica and Bermuda approximately three-monthly and Curacao monthly. This latter call was convenient, as the ships invariably bunkered there, or Aruba, which also developed as a market for New Zealand produce. By 1956 trade with Jamaica also justified six-weekly calls. More specifically for dairy produce, a direct service from New Zealand to Mollendo or Callao in Peru was established by the Lines in 1958. Initially it was a two-monthly service.

In 1957 the Port Line contributed 25 per cent of the cost of the *Crusader*, the Crusader Shipping Company's first ship. Almost a brand-new vessel, she became a familiar sight in New Zealand ports until 1972. The thump of her 10-cyl Swedish engine could be heard from a great distance. A. DUNCAN

The Lines decided to form a subsidiary company to expand their services around the Pacific basin. Each took a 25 per cent share in the Crusader Shipping Company Limited, which was formed on 22 November 1957. Shaw Savill & Albion managed it. Crusader purchased a 17-knot, fully refrigerated ship being completed at Uddevalla for Swedish owners. Briefly named *Edith Thorden*, she became the *Crusader* and was delivered on 21 December 1957. She had a refrigerated capacity of 6,230 cubic metres and was intended to operate on a new service to Japan. It was hoped that her speed would ensure a round voyage every eight weeks. The *Crusader* loaded at four New Zealand ports and sailed for Yokohama and Kobe in February 1958. She remained on that run for several years, but small parcels of meat spread around New Zealand freezing works to make up the one larger shipment often increased the New Zealand port calls to seven or eight, and the discharge ports in Japan to five or six out of Nagoya, Yokkaichi, Osaka, Kobe, Yokohama and away up north to Otaru in Hokkaido. The combination of a small, high-powered ship, small parcels of cargo, and a multitude of port calls, cost the line dearly. On one southbound voyage from Japan in 1962, *Crusader* carried only 27.5 freight tons.

On 1 September 1958 the company took delivery of an almost identical sister ship, the *Saracen,* although she was specially fitted to carry deep frozen cargoes. She loaded in New Zealand ports in October 1958 for a pioneering new service direct to Honolulu, Los Angeles, San Francisco, Seattle and Vancouver. Both ships had been intended as fast fruit carriers for Belgian Fruit Lines. Their hulls were built by Valmet O/Y, Helsinki and the vessels were towed to Uddevallavarvet A/B in Sweden for completion. They had steel hulls and aluminium superstructures. For Crusader they were painted all-over in an eau-de-nil colour and had a yellow funnel bearing a black crest. A red and white Crusader shield and yellow sword was painted on the black background, making the ships quite distinctive.

Seasonal demand meant that it was not long before the *Crusader* and *Saracen* had to be supplemented with smaller vessels from the fleets of the four lines. Vessel utilisation was covered

An exact sister to the *Crusader*, the *Saracen* came into the Crusader services in 1958. Painted all over with an eau-de-nil colour, the Crusader ships had a yellow funnel with a black shield on which a white, red and yellow crusader shield was affixed. She is photographed passing Port Chalmers in April 1961. BAIN-WRIGHT COLLECTION

in a charter party, but a formula relating to the freight earned on particular voyages or trades determined the actual charter rate, which invariably favoured the ship-owner and was in reality the only form of income, as Crusader, as a company, never made any profits. This arrangement enabled the Lines to emphasise the losses by the company on the 'development trades' to the producer boards. Each shareholder contributed 25 per cent of the cost of the three ships owned by Crusader Line and received a proportionate amount when the vessels were sold. Initially operating costs were sought in the form of interest-free calls from each shareholder.

Blue Star's *Napier Star* was the first Lines' vessel to be employed, making a round voyage to Japan at the end of 1959. In 1960 the *Port Montreal* and *Turakina* were brought in on a more or less continuous basis for several years. Shaw Savill's *Amalric* also entered the Japanese trade from 1961. The *Canterbury Star* made a voyage to WCNA ports in 1961 and thereafter several ships, the *Devon* and the chartered *Norefjell*, supplemented the two services as required.

The company also decided to mount what it called a 'development service' to Noumea, Port Moresby, Singapore, Port Swettenham, Manila, Shanghai and Hong Kong. The *Saracen* made the initial voyage. The *Port Adelaide* followed her with three round voyages and the *Turakina* one voyage until the company's third ship, *Knight Templar*, entered service in 1963. Formerly the Swedish *Arctic Ocean*, she made only three voyages on the development service before being switched to the Japanese run with an occasional voyage to North America. For some years from 1964 Crusader Shipping operated a joint monthly service from New Zealand to Manila, Shanghai, Japanese ports and Hong Kong with the China Navigation Co. The company chartered China Navigation's *Kwangtung* in 1965-66 and later the *Kweichow* in 1966-68. Both were renamed *Norman,* with 14 voyages being made between 1965 and 1968 before Crusader abandoned the service. In one unique situation the *Norman* had slipped so far back on her schedule that by arrangement with the owners, she was handed back in New Zealand and reverted to *Kwangtung*

The only other vessel owned by the Crusader Line, was the 15-year old *Knight Templar* which was purchased in 1963 to mount a service from New Zealand to East Asian ports. She was not altogether suitable for the mix of services, and was sold five years later. She is shown in Otago Harbour. BAIN-WRIGHT COLLECTION

in September 1966, while in Hong Kong, *Kweichow* was renamed *Norman* at much the same time as the previous *Norman* was being re-delivered. The development service, however, was just too much steaming for too little cargo; even worse, light southbound offerings made it very much a one-way trade.

In 1968 Crusader had 18 voyages to Japan and nine to WCNA, two years later there were 25 Japanese sailings and 12 to North America. Apart from *Crusader* and *Saracen* mainly being employed on the American service, larger ships were brought in to handle the increasing volumes of refrigerated cargoes moving to Japan. These included the *Port Alfred, Townsville Star* (1957, 10,632), *Carnatic* (1957, 11,144), *Port Macquarie, Devon* (1946, 9,940), *Northumberland* (1955, 10,144), *Caledonia Star* (1942, 9,141), *Rakaia* (1945, 7,934), *Colorado Star* (1952, 8,230), and *Port Albany.* The North American service was supplemented with the *Amalric* (1960, 7,791) and *Turakina* (1960, 7,707).

When vessels were transferred to the Crusader Line for a series of voyages, their funnels were invariably painted cream and a Crusader crest was affixed. The *Port Adelaide* made only three voyages on the development service to South East Asia, Hong Kong and China but was given a Crusader funnel, as was the *Port Alfred* which undertook 12 Japanese round voyages. *Port Montreal* made 28 round voyages to Japan and three to the West Coast of the USA, but remained throughout entirely in Port Line colours. The *Port Townsville, Port Albany* and *Port Macquarie* each made one Crusader voyage and retained their Port Line livery. The *Port Montreal* did identify her role with a large Crusader crest welded over the top of her Port Line crest on the bow. 'Outside' tonnage chartered for the Crusader Line service, such as the *Egyptian Reefer* (1936, 3,169), *Zaida* (1972, 6,088) and *Zira* (1972, 6,088) also had their funnels painted in Crusader colours.

On her first Crusader Line voyage from Brisbane to Los Angeles, *Port Montreal* passed through a hurricane on 26 December 1959 which gave the ship a severe battering, damaging a

The *Port Alfred* made 12 round voyages on the Crusader Line berth between New Zealand and Japan, and during this time she was given a Crusader Line funnel. I.G.B. LOVIE

number of deck fittings and taking water in the forepeak. On two occasions the *Port Montreal* was in Japan when a typhoon blew through. Under Captain Arthur Kensett in September 1960 when she was in the Tokyo Bay area, typhoon Nancy struck and gave everyone some anxious moments when the anchors dragged in the soft mud, and engine power had to be maintained until the weather eased. Fortunately the typhoon centre was 150 miles north and the ship was not subjected to extreme conditions. In late 1964 when she was lying at buoys in Kobe harbour, typhoon Wilda struck and winds reached 115 miles per hour.

Crusader Shipping was never profitable and by 1971 Cunard, under financial pressure from all directions, instructed Port Line to withdraw. Operationally no further Port Line ships were employed after the *Port Montreal* made a voyage to North America in March 1972 and the withdrawal from the company itself was effective from 29 September 1972. The other three companies bought Port Line's shares. The services had been coming under increasing competition. Two Japanese lines, Nitto Shosen Kaisha and Osaka Shosen Kaisha, had started direct services between Japan and New Zealand in 1952 and 1953 respectively and some Japanese importers sent small refrigerated ships to New Zealand to lift their own cargoes. The Danish firm of J. Lauritzen had commenced a refrigerated cargo service from New Zealand to Honolulu and West Coast of North America ports in November 1957 and shortly afterwards developed a similar service to Japan. In 1960 the Columbus Line, a division of the Hamburg based Hamburg-Sud group, had commenced a service from WCNA ports to New Zealand and return. Lauritzen and Columbus used smaller refrigerated ships which enabled them to provide better service frequency than the larger Conference Line ships seconded to Crusader.

In January 1961 the British Conference Lines ceased the way-port service to the West Indies on their UK-bound vessels and commenced a six weekly round voyage service from New Zealand to Matarani/Mollendo in Peru, Callao, Kingston, Bridgetown, Port of Spain, La Guiara, and Aruba. If demand exceeded capacity of the ships employed, a main line ship was introduced to cover the shortfall. The first vessels were taken from the Lines' fleets. They included the *Amalric, Canterbury Star* (1960, 7,437), *Crusader, Pipiriki* (1944, 10,057), *Gloucester* (1941, 8,532), *Knight Templar, Westmorland* (1966, 11,011) and *Taupo* (1966, 8,219) up to 1965. Port Line contributed the *Port Quebec* for four voyages 1966-7, *Port Lyttelton* four voyages 1969-70 and *Port Sydney* four voyages in 1971-72. The service was still run as a Lines service and not part of Crusader Shipping, although following the withdrawal of Port Line from Crusader the other lines decided to change the operations of that company and the remaining three lines took over one of the services in their own right. The Crusader Line, therefore, ceased operations. The *Knight Templar* had proved too small and too slow, so she had been sold to Philippine buyers in 1968, the *Saracen* was sold to Shaw Savill & Albion in 1970 but the *Crusader* was retained until 1972.

The New Zealand Shipping Co, now renamed P&O NZ Ltd, assumed responsibility for the Japan service and employed its own, or chartered tonnage, until the advent of a container service in 1976. The trade share gained through the Crusader Line was later linked to the Crusader Swire Container Service. Blue Star Line assumed responsibility for the trade to the West Coast North America and introduced pallet-friendly refrigerated ships such as the *Canterbury Star, Timaru Star* (1967, 8,366) and *Montreal Star* (1963, 7,365). In 1977 Blue Star converted the conventional refrigerated ships *Southland Star* (1967, 11,300) and *New Zealand Star* (1967, 11,300) into cellular container ships and placed them on regular service between New Zealand and West Coast North American ports via Fiji and Honolulu. The *New Zealand Star* was renamed *Wellington Star* on conversion. The vessels could also handle breakbulk cargo, bulk liquids and heavy lifts. Shaw Savill & Albion took over the management of the service to the north west coast of South America, Panama, Caribbean and the West Indies and ran vessels either owned or chartered until 1977 when the company merged the service with the Bank Line to form the Bank & Savill Line. Vessels suitable for breakbulk cargo and containers were employed until 1980 when three container ships were introduced – one vessel being owned by Shaw Savill & Albion, another by Bank Line and the third by the Shipping Corporation of New Zealand – with the service operating as the Australia New Zealand Container Line (ANCL).

It is likely that after Port Line withdrew from Crusader Line, the other three lines, using more specialised ships, directly targeting costs and improving efficiencies of operation, would have achieved greatly improved financial results. Certainly in the early years of the Crusader Line, the close links the Lines enjoyed with the producer boards through the main line trades, provided a valuable link in securing meat and dairy cargoes for the various Crusader services.

ASSOCIATED CONTAINER TRANSPORTATION (AUSTRALIA) LIMITED.

The establishment of Associated Container Transportation Ltd (ACT) and the associated ACT(A) has been covered in chapter six. Once its rival, Overseas Containers Ltd (OCL) had decided to containerise the Australian trade, ACT(A) had to follow suit to keep up. The three container pioneers – Sea-land, Matson and the Australian company, Associated Steamships had all developed containers of difference lengths. Sea-land boxes were 35 feet long, Matson's were 24 feet and Associated Steamships 16 feet 8 ins. The International Standards Organisation pressed for universally standard-sized containers to be introduced worldwide, by means of legislation through the various governments. The two British consortia quickly decided to adopt ISO standard size containers, either 8ft or 8ft 6 ins in height, 20 foot or 40 foot in length general cargo containers, or 8 foot high, 20 foot insulated port hole containers for refrigerated cargoes, and to order gearless cellular container ships with refrigerated ducting in the holds, relying on the various ports to provide the cranage to handle the containers.

The ships ordered by OCL were six 26,800 ton steam turbine vessels each with a nominal container capacity of 1,300 TEUs. ACT(A) placed orders on 31 July 1967 for three 24,800-ton steam turbine vessels with a capacity of 1,130 TEUs. British shipyards were un-competitive and with the experience of delays in the building of conventional tonnage and the later contracts for the first four ships ordered for the New Zealand trade, eight of the ships were built in two German yards with only one of the OCL ships (*Jervis Bay* (1970, 26,876) built in the UK. The ACT(A) vessels were built by Bremer Vulkan at Vegesack.

The single-screw, all aft, configuration was chosen for the first generation container ships and this placed severe restrictions on the type of proven propulsion systems then available, so only geared steam turbines and direct drive diesel engines were considered. At the time of ordering, the power required (30,000 shp) was near the limit in the diesel range. Using diesel would also have meant the loss of space for 70 containers because of the space required for the engine while another disadvantage was the limitation of shaft speed to about 119 revolutions per minute for the particular engines available. As the vessels were designed with engines right aft in order to maximise the beam available for containers there were other factors concerning the depth of propeller immersion and propeller tip clearances. The strict scheduling of the ships in service would pose significant maintenance problems and the alternator capacity would need to be greater for a diesel powered vessel. Allowing 14 days per year for dry-docking, repairs and maintenance, the ships would be required to operate throughout the year at a continuous speed at sea of 22 knots, so geared steam turbine propulsion was deemed more efficient.[1] Would the decision in favour of steam have been made if the price of oil fuel, which dramatically rose a few years after the ships entered service, had been known at the time of ordering?

Because of the high volumes of refrigerated cargo involved in the Australian, and eventually the New Zealand trades, it was decided that it would be more economic to have the ship and shore units supplying the cold air refrigeration, than each container having its own built-in refrigerated unit. This was a very important consideration because of the significant increase in power required for individual container refrigeration and the ventilation of under deck spaces. Each insulated container had two port holes at one end for receiving cold air in at the bottom and out at the top. Ducting systems were built in the holds of the vessels to accommodate the eight foot high containers and in New Zealand on-shore tower units capable of taking containers stacked two high were built. Melbourne and Tilbury had specially built installations, similar to the ships' holds. ACT(A) purchased sufficient on-shore tower units to cope with its trade share within each conference grouping, but all lines in the group used each other's towers as required. The cheaper 'port hole' type insulated containers provided more cargo capacity per container as space was not needed for an integral refrigerated unit.

As the ships were being built there was great activity on shore preparing the on-shore transport and terminal systems. In the UK it was logical and cost effective for OCL and ACT to operate from the same container bases and a number of facilities, under the name Containerbases, were set up around the country, as depots to receive cargo, pack and dispatch containers. The shareholding in this company was 75.6 per cent to OCL and 24.4 per cent to ACT. Special contractual arrangements were made with British Rail for the transport of containers and terminal facilities were developed at Tilbury (London). ACT London set up a subsidiary company called ACT Services (commonly abbreviated to ACTS) to handle transport control, container control systems, manifesting, documentation, and research and development for all the partners in the parent ACT to avoid duplication of effort by individual companies. ACT Services handled much of the work for ACT(A) and overall it had a staff of 700. Brian Graves was the first staff member of Port Line seconded to ACT but in the following months further staff transferred to new positions within ACT Services and ACT(A). However as conventional services had to keep operating for several more years there was a limit to the number of staff that could be moved and as many of the senior management of ACT(A) came from outside the shipping industry there was a definite tendency to hire staff, whose thinking was not still firmly inclined towards conventional cargo handling systems.

Although the five ACT shareholders (Ben Line, Blue Star Line, Cunard, Ellerman & T.& J. Harrison) had equal 20 per cent shareholdings in ACT Services, the cost of work done was apportioned against the individual requirements of the line requesting the services. In September 1973 ACTS completed a move from London to a large ten-storey building in Southampton (Richmond House) to be closer to the terminal port for the Far East and South African services. ACT(A) developed the first 'through transport' bill of lading for use in the Australian trade. Previously with conventional shipping, bills of lading covered shipment from port to port, but with containers, the shipping lines would be picking up containers from depots or shipper's premises all over the UK and Europe and the containers would have to be delivered to sites throughout Australia for unpacking. The 'through transport' bill of lading became the standard for container services. ACT Services also undertook contract work, mainly documentation, for other shipping companies. The company was not a major profit centre and between 1972-91 dividends paid to the parent company totaled £535,000 and its last six years as an operating company, from 1986 to 1991, losses almost offset the modest profits made. Its annual turnover throughout its history ranged from £23 million to £36 million.

In Australia the agency companies for the various partners were combined into a separate company, Trans Ocean Containers Pty Ltd, in April 1966 and terminal facilities came under Trans Ocean Terminals at Fremantle, Melbourne and Sydney with depot facilities called Freightbases, at the other main ports. Port Line had a 40 per cent interest in the new Australian agency company called Joint Cargo Services Pty Ltd, which was established with the other ACTA partners, Blue Star Line and Ellermans holding 42 per cent and 18 per cent shareholdings respectively. In line with the parent company policy, Joint Cargo Services was replaced by Port Line Australia and Blue Star Line, with their own offices in Sydney from 1 March 1973. ACT(A) Pty Ltd was also registered, and this company and another, Terminal Properties of Australia Pty Ltd were incorporated as ACT(A) Investments Australia Ltd, on 3 January 1978. The historic association between Port Line and Gibbs, Bright and Company Pty Ltd was terminated in 1968 although some of the shipping staff employed by Gibbs, Bright were taken by the new companies. Gibbs Bright was paid $A550,000 in compensation for early termination of the agency agreement from 1 January 1968 instead of 31 March 1969.

ACT(A) came under considerable criticism from the shipping fraternity when the first ship was launched by Mrs Mary McEwen, wife of the Rt. Hon. J. McEwen, Deputy Prime

The first container ship built for the ACT (A)/ANL service of Associated Container Transportation Company (Australia) Ltd., was the *ACT 1,* which entered service in 1969. Despite increasing fuel prices, *ACT 1* was never re-engined with diesels, although she was employed in the main line trade for 29 years. She is shown outward bound from Port Chalmers. BAIN-WRIGHT COLLECTION

Minister of Australia, on 18 October 1968 with the unimaginative name of *ACT 1.* She was followed by *ACT 2* on 3 January 1969. The management of ACT(A) had little heed of historical sentiment in devising names which provided a link with Port Line, Blue Star Lines or Ellermans. The remaining ship of the series was launched as *ACT 3* on 16 April 1969 but taken over and completed as *Australian Endeavour* for the Australian National Line, under the agreement concluded with the Australian government. Blue Star Line crewed *ACT 1,* Port Line *ACT 2* while Australian seafarers joined *Australian Endeavour.*

Initially OCL and ACT(A) agreed to mount a joint service to Australia with each group sharing container space in every sailing, although each company had developed its own systems and did its own marketing. The first cargo for the new service was accepted on 10 February 1969 and the first ship, *Encounter Bay* (1969, 26,756), sailed from Rotterdam on 6 March 1969 and arrived Fremantle on 28 March. She was closely followed by *ACT 1* on 22 March. A labour dispute at Tilbury prevented calls at a UK port and until May 1970 all cargo to and from the United Kingdom was transhipped over up to nine UK ports to Antwerp, Rotterdam and Zeebrugge at considerable cost to the British consortia. Although an agreement was concluded with the London workforce in April 1970 it was not until 22 May that the first container ship, *Jervis Bay,* berthed at Tilbury. The European Lines, who had previously operated conventional shipping to Australia had elected to follow the two British Lines, and five further container ships were built – one each for Hamburg-Amerika Linie and Norddeutscher Lloyd (both German companies that merged their interests into Hapag Lloyd in 1970), Holland Australia Line, which became part of the Netherlands Shipping Union group in 1970 and was renamed Nedlloyd Group in 1977, Messageries Maritimes of France and Lloyd Triestino of Italy. There was a steady build up of ships coming into service in 1969 and soon there were 14 ships in the trade, all co-ordinated in scheduling under the trade banner of Australia Europe Container Service (AECS) which came into effect on

From her completion in 1973 until 1977, ACT(A) took the 42,007 ton *Remuera* on charter. She was the largest container ship to visit Australian and New Zealand ports and during the four year charter she had a white funnel with a black top and a blue ACT motive on the white. The photograph shows her about to pass under the Sydney Harbour bridge, with the Sydney Opera House in the background. FREEMAN-PRIEST

1 September 1970. The three Scandinavian Lines elected not to participate with cellular container ships but retained their geared Skandia unit-load vessels in the Australasian trade and then from 1972 built several large roll-on, roll-off vessels for the Australian service, extending to New Zealand in 1978.

Four ports were served in Europe (Rotterdam, Hamburg, Antwerp & Bremerhaven, with Zeebrugge or Flushing being used for northbound calls). Tilbury remained the designated United Kingdom port. The ships proceeded through the Suez Canal to Fremantle, Melbourne and Sydney, with an additional loading call at Fremantle on the return voyage. In the early years of the service ACT(A) vessels also called Liverpool as well as Tilbury. ACT(A) also handled the residual conventional cargoes from 1969 by forming ACTANZ Lines and chartering in any conventional ships from the ACT(A) shareholders. The Dolphin Line performed a similar role for OCL.

While Australia was enjoying the benefits of containerisation, New Zealand did not. The potential four container ship service had been dropped in 1971 and since then major shippers had become bitter at their treatment by the lines. In 1971 ACT(A)/ANL signaled its intention to provide New Zealand with a separate container service and thus steal a march on OCL. The company advised it would withdraw from the AECS (Australia Europe Container Service) consortium from 1 November 1971 and would mount a service, marketed as the Independent service, to Australia and New Zealand from September 1972. The ships to be employed were the *ACT 1, Australian Endeavour,* and *ACT 5* seconded from the American PACE Line service. They would load at Liverpool and Tilbury, proceed to Melbourne and Sydney and then on to Wellington and Auckland, returning via the Panama Canal on a 67-day round voyage. The sailing frequency would be every 17 days. A feeder service for Continental containers was to be handled through

Tilbury. *Australian Endeavour* sailed Liverpool on 26 September 1972 to inaugurate the Independent service.

The first of the four large container ships ordered for the proposed New Zealand container service which was abruptly cancelled, was too far advanced in her construction to be scrapped. Owned by P&O (OCL), and named *Remuera* when she was finally completed in December 1973, she had 1,131 of her 1,813 TEU capacity designed to carry insulated containers, so she was really only suitable for employment in the New Zealand trade. ACT(A) took her on charter and was thus able to improve the sailing frequency of the Independent service to fortnightly. In return, the charter of the P&O vessel into the New Zealand trade, enabled the OCL partners to have container space in all the ships employed in the new service. When she arrived in New Zealand in February 1974, *Remuera* broke several records as she was the largest refrigerated ship in the world, and being built to the maximum dimensions allowed by the Panama Canal, she was the largest container ship to visit New Zealand. For her ACT(A) charter she had a black hull and a blue ACT motif on a white funnel with black top.

The Independent service proved very popular in New Zealand as it provided a container service earlier than would have been the case, had the planned four ships finally escaped from the dispute-ridden Swan Hunter & Wigham Richardson shipyard. Overall, container shipping was going through a difficult period. In 1970 bunker prices rose by over 50 per cent and this was a massive increase for the fuel-hungry steamers. Growing inflation pushed up operating costs and a further rise in oil prices in 1974 forced freight rates even higher. The early 1970s also saw a 35 per cent increase in imports to Australia and both container consortia had difficulty locating surplus container tonnage to supplement their existing services. Invariably there were long delays in meeting demand for space and in 1973 ACT(A)/ANL chartered 22 additional sailings and an even greater number were taken in 1974.

Shortly after container services were introduced, freighting structures were changed from rates per kilo or per cubic metre to a rate per container. This provided shippers with the incentive to improve the space utilisation of containers and instead of stowing 6.5 tonnes of carcass lamb in a 20ft container, 12 tonnes of cartonned lamb could be packed. Wet salted pelts, previously shipped in casks, were placed on pallets which would provide good stowage in a container. Initially New Zealand bales of wool were double-dumped (two bales pressed together) to ship a total of 56 bales per 20ft container, but with improved triple-dumping, it was possible to take an average of 108 bales of wool in an 8ft 6in high 20 ft container. Agency staff in Australia and New Zealand, experienced in cargo handling and stowage, worked with exporters to help them stow more into every box. A number of former Port Line staff with sea experience were involved in this work as well as being employed at the various terminals in ship planning and looking after the interests of ACT(A) with the various terminal operators who were now the stevedoring contractors for the container services.

With terminals already available in the North American East Coast ports and the main Australian ports, Wellington and Auckland were already preparing container facilities for a planned container service from North America by Columbus Line, a subsidiary of the Hamburg-Sud group. ACT(A) saw the potential to develop a container service to maintain the trade links that had been started by Ellerman & Bucknall and Tyser Lines in 1898 and which were incorporated into the MANZ Line from 1936. Four further container ships were ordered from Bremer Vulkan,

The *ACT 3*, laden with empty ACT containers, is shown about to arrive at Port Chalmers on 23 March 1977 to inaugurate the extension of the PACE Line service to the South Island. She was the first ACT(A)/ ANL container ship to call Port Chalmers. She was also crewed by former Port Line personnel. BAIN-WRIGHT COLLECTION

being slightly smaller than the European/Australia trade vessels and with a break-bulk hatch right forward and 40-ton deck crane to handle non-containerisable bulky items and heavy lifts. As in the European trade, ANL was invited to purchase one of them. The New Zealand Shipping Company, which had withdrawn from the MANZ Line service in 1966, but had been running a conventional refrigerated service from Australia from January 1969, decided to order a container ship and participate in a joint service with ACT(A)/ANL. With four out of the five ships in the proposed service, ACT(A)/ANL was very much in control and in April 1971, New Zealand Shipping arranged for ACT(A)/ANL to take over its proposed *Chesapeake Bay*, and at the same time secured an undertaking from ACT(A) that the partners would not exercise the 'rights' obtained by the Atlas Line in 1967, and mount a container service from Australia to the Far East.

The ships initially carried up to 556 refrigerated containers under deck and 710 general containers, but due to demand for refrigerated space, capacity for refrigerated cargo was increased in 1975 by 102 boxes to 658. Apart from the cold air systems in the holds, additional refrigerated cargo could be handled by the use of 'clip-on units' attached to each container for on-deck stowage.

The new service was marketed under the name PACE Line (Pacific America Container Express) and the keel of the first ship was laid 30 June 1970. She was launched as *ACT 3* on 26 February 1971. The first Columbus Line container ship, *Columbus New Zealand* (1971, 19,146), arrived in New Zealand in June and when the ship sailed from Port Chalmers on 28 June 1971 she was the first cellular container ship to leave that country. *ACT 3* arrived in Australia in August 1971 and at Wellington 16 August. There she lay at anchor for 12 days while an industrial agreement to work her was hammered out. She finally left Wellington on 30 August direct for the United States and abandoned a call at Auckland in order to reach the eastern seaboard before the projected commencement of a strike by Atlantic coast longshoremen.

The *ACT 3* was followed by *ACT 4*, launched on 11 May 1971. The third ship intended to

In 1977 ACT(A)/ANL partners took delivery of two larger container ships to enable the Australia/New Zealand trade to United Kingdom and Europe to be fully containerised. The first was the *Australian Venture* for the Australian National Line, shown here in Otago Harbour. BAIN-WRIGHT COLLECTION

be *Chesapeake Bay* went into the water as *ACT 5,* and was delivered on 15 February 1972. She was transferred to the Independent service. The fourth vessel was launched on 29 March 1971 as the *Australian Exporter.* Ports of call in America were St. John, Boston, New York and Norfolk and the ships then sailed to Melbourne, Sydney and Brisbane, before crossing to Wellington and Auckland. Philadelphia was added in 1972 and soon became the principal cargo port for the service. Columbus Line also called at Port Chalmers as its vessels had a gantry crane, and Port Chalmers was added to the PACE Line service from March 1977. The final vessel in the North American service, laid down as *ACT 5,* was delivered on 22 December 1972 as the *ACT 6.* She differed from the others in that she had no break-bulk hatch, or crane, so she replaced *ACT 5* in the Independent service. Port Line provided officers and crew for *ACT 3* and *ACT 6* while Blue Star Line took care of *ACT 4* and *ACT 5.*

In order to containerise the total Australian and New Zealand trades between United Kingdom/Europe, five 2,100 TEU motor ships were ordered from Bremer Vulkan – two of which went to OCL, and one each to ACT(A), Australian National Line and the Shipping Corporation of New Zealand. The ships were built to the maximum Panama Canal specifications and after the oil shocks of earlier years were powered by slow speed Sulzer diesel engines. The refrigerated container capacity of the ACT(A)/ANL vessels was 993 while the other three had under deck space for 1,228 port hole type insulated containers.

The first, the *Australian Venture* entered service on 3 March 1977, followed by *ACT 7* on 29 June. With the introduction of this extra capacity, the charter of the *Remuera* was terminated, and the ship then locked in to OCL schedules as the *Remuera Bay.* Trade scheduling came under a group called ANZECS (Australia/New Zealand/Europe Container Service) which comprised OCL, the Continental Lines under the banner of Seabridge and the Shipping Corporation of New Zealand. ACT(A)/ANL sailings were closely linked to ANZECS, although the group still retained its individual schedules until 1984. Of the 14 ship service, four of the smaller ships went out to New Zealand and Australia via the Panama Canal and returned to Europe via Mediterranean

The other 1977 vessel was the *ACT 7*, owned by the ACT(A) partners and crewed by Blue Star Line. She had a capacity for approximately 2100 TEU of which 993 slots were available for refrigerated cargoes. Renamed *Palliser Bay* after the sale of ACT(A) to P&O Containers in 1991, she was delivered to Chinese shipbreakers in 2002.

ports. The other four smaller vessels were captive to a European/Australia/Europe service, while the six large vessels operated an around the world service calling at Tilbury, Hamburg, Rotterdam, Genoa, Fremantle, Melbourne, Sydney, Auckland, Wellington, Lyttelton and Port Chalmers, and back through the Panama Canal to Zeebrugge. Refrigerated handling equipment was set up in Piraeus and this port became a regular port of call in the Mediterranean service from 1979. Also in 1979 ACT(A)/ANL made arrangements with the German line, Hamburg-Sud, to provide container space for the German company's trade share entitlement in the European/New Zealand/European trade. The New Zealand terminals at Auckland, Lyttelton and Port Chalmers were owned and managed by the respective harbour boards, but in Wellington the Shipping Corporation of New Zealand had gained a 51 per cent shareholding in the terminal facility, called Container Terminals Limited. Other lines using the port also gained minor shareholdings and this included ACT(A). Following ACT New Zealand's purchase of the Shipping Corporation of New Zealand in 1989 it briefly held a majority holding in the terminal until 1991.

In New Zealand, Blue Star Port Lines (Management) Limited was merged with Associated Container Transportation (N.Z.) Ltd. in 1976 to form Blueport ACT (N.Z.) Limited. When it came to crewing *ACT 7*, Port Line interests, now represented by Cunard-Brocklebank, were somewhat taken aback when Blue Star Line provided the crew. Although the senior line in the trade, the situation tended to reflect the weak financial position of Port Line, and was a further demoralising element for former Port Line sea staff.

In 1978 the ships shifted to a new London terminal at Northfleet Hope, funded by OCL, ACT(A), and the Port of London Authority. In that year the six large vessels changed their rotation to abandon canal transits and travelled outward via the Cape of Good Hope and back via Cape Horn. Although there was some concern about the dangers of icebergs and poor visibility in the southern oceans on the passage around Cape Horn, it was found in practice that this was no longer a problem. Satellite navigation and radar overcame the many overcast days on that route and as the service was every ten days, the reports positioning icebergs did not vary greatly between sailings.

When bunker costs again rose in 1978, ACT(A)/ANL looked at ways to reduce costs and ship speeds were reduced by three knots, which saved about 30 tons of fuel per vessel per day. During the next dry-docking the ships were painted in high performance epoxy resin oblative (self polishing) paints which kept the hulls clear of weed growth. An exercise was done to re-engine the steamers with diesels but as it was estimated there would have been no payback for eight years, it was decided to re-gear the ships and replace the propellers. Instead of burning 115 tons of fuel per day for 21.5 knots, the vessels would burn only 85 tons per day for a speed of 18.5 knots and the costs of this plan would recover the outlay in two years. OCL elected to re-engine three of its early ships and in retrospect re-engining *ACT 1* and *ACT 2* would have been justified as they remained in service for a further 20 years from 1978. On an index cost of 100 in 1973, bunker prices had risen to 600 by 1979 and by 1990 the index was 2,200.

With the container services, the various pooling agreements with the lines remained in place and on wool sale cards and Conference Line forms for cargo contracts, the names of the original companies, like Port Line Limited, were still listed, even though it had no other identity to the shippers. From 1980 competition on most trades from companies seeking to claim a share of the container traffic intensified. The most significant competitor for ACT(A)/ANL was the ABC Container Line owned by Belgian national, Tsvi Rosenfeld.[2] He employed bulk carriers lifting parcels of synthetic rutile and ilmenite sand under a long-term contract from Geraldton in Western Australia to Gulfport, Missisippi. He devised a plan to put the ships 'full and down' by only partially filling two or three holds with sand and loading the remaining holds and on deck with containers. His service, which commenced in September 1978, came out from Europe via Suez and went back via Panama Canal, picking up the sand on the way. Although the ships were slow, the shippers found that freight rates 10/15 per cent lower than the conference offset this, and ABC received considerable support. In addition the Australian Wool Board awarded the line a contract, at a very low rate of freight, for 1200 TEUs of wool to Egypt.

Rosenfeld tried legal means to break the producer board controls on freight contracts. For the first sailing of an ABC Line vessel from New Zealand in 1979 22 containers of frozen meat were railed to Auckland for shipment. The Meat Producers' Board took out an injunction preventing the loading and the board's right to control the movement of all frozen meat exports was subsequently upheld in court. He also challenged the Wool Board in the courts for denying his company a share of the wool cargoes to United Kingdom and America. Again he failed. However, his very presence, offering to ship the entire New Zealand wool export at 15 per cent below Conference Lines freight rates, helped the producer boards keep down freight rates across the board. His presence also affected the PACE Line service as he won a contract to carry beef to the east coast of North America and was also an approved Wool Board carrier on that route. The Australian Meat Board in 1981 authorised ABC Line as an approved meat carrier from Australia. The average ABC freight charge for a container of wool from Australia to Europe in 1978 was $US4,300. By 1983 it was down to $US 3,800, $US2,100 in 1987 and as low as $US1,993 in 1993. It was therefore no surprise when ABC went into receivership on 5 April 1996 with the five vessels of the fleet being arrested at ports around the world, and the legal ramifications taking years to finalise.

In addition to ABC taking both Australian and New Zealand cargoes, the Polish Ocean Line, the Russian Balt-Australia Line, Eagle Container Line and Zim Lines were all active in the

The *Port Victor, Port Hobart* and *Port Townsville* at Port Chalmers on 23 October 1963.

Port Line had a 25 per cent interest in the Crusader Shipping Company vessel *Crusader* from 1957 to 1972. Her distinctive eau-de-nil colour scheme is shown to advantage as she passes down Otago Harbour.

The *ACT 6* outward bound from Port Chalmers to Wellington in July 1978. GARRY BAIN

The *ACT 7*, shown here outward bound from Port Chalmers to Zeebrugge via Cape Horn, was one of the five large container ships built for the New Zealand-UK-Europe trade in 1977-79. GARRY BAIN

The former *City of Durban*, renamed *ACT 8*, was the largest container ship employed by ACT(A).

ACT(A) operated several chartered container ships on the service from Australia to and from the West Coast of North America. This illustration shows the *ACT 9* at Brisbane on her maiden voyage under this name in November 1986. PORT OF BRISBANE AUTHORITY

Australian trade. In 1986 the New Zealand based Scales Line also tried its hand at re-gaining the wool cargoes of earlier years, and in partnership with Norwegian owned Jebsens, formed the New Zealand Euro Line Limited, operating six self-sustaining container ships on charter in the New Zealand/Europe trade on an 18 day frequency. The New Zealand Conference Lines reduced their wool freights to meet the competition and in the year to June 1988, NZESA Lines carried 71.9 per cent of the European wool, with ABC lifting 21.4 per cent and N.Z. Euro Line only 6.7 per cent over the same period. N.Z. Euro Line collapsed the following year with losses in excess of Scales' share capital and reserves. Two other outsiders, Atlanttrafik Express Service and later Oceanstar Container Line mounted northbound services from New Zealand to Europe in the 1980s but both had little impact as the northbound trade was still very much controlled by the Conference. In addition to these erosions of the northbound trade, a number of other lines, such as Wilhelmsen Lines, Ocean Star Container Line/Contship and N.Z. Euro Line, put their ships into ports on the east coast of North America to pick up southbound cargoes for Australia and New Zealand. In the late 1970s Conference Line services had been carrying almost 100 per cent of the European/Australian trade liner traffic but ten years later the conference carriers had lost 30 per cent of their business to outsiders. Southbound rates of freight from Europe in 1988 were about 60 per cent of the rate per container ten years earlier. Through their contractual arrangements with shipper groups, and better-earning refrigerated cargoes, the conference carriers did not fare so badly with northbound shipments over the same comparative period. Even so, the pool shares of the Conference Line vessels were seldom achieved and the various groups ACT(A)/ANL and OCL came together to operate a joint schedule to reduce costs and unused capacity. In addition there was a space rationalisation with the Scandinavian Lines to ensure all the Conference Lines were competitive against the increasing competition. For six months from September 1983, *ACT 1* was withdrawn from service and laid up at Burnie, while *ACT 2* was chartered out from September 1983 until March 1984. ANL had decided to withdraw from the PACE line service, effective from 1 June 1985 and with the loss of the *Australian Exporter*, ACT(A) carried on with a four-ship service. ANL, which had a 16 per cent trade share in the UK/Europe/Australian service, also withdrew from the ACT(A) partnership entirely from 1 July 1987. ANL had sought to gain a pool share of the New Zealand cargoes, both north and south, but this was initially denied by the respective Conferences. *ACT 8*, formerly the *City of Durban*, was brought into the ACT(A) service to make up for the loss of the *Australian Venture*. With a nominal capacity for 2436 TEUs she became the largest container ship ever operated by ACT(A). Prior to ANL's departure, ACT(A) had developed a joint scheduling arrangement with the Columbus Line in the East Coast North American service. All vessels in the rationalised service carried each others containers although the cargo was very competitively marketed by each line as before.

In 1984 the ANZECS/ACT(A)/ANL grouping improved its Mediterranean service by utilising six ships on a 70-day round voyage cycle from Australian ports, Auckland Wellington and Port Chalmers, returning via Melbourne and Fremantle (with occasional calls at Burnie or Adelaide) to Jeddah, Piraeus, Genoa (later Livorno and La Spezia in place of Genoa), Fos and Barcelona and sailing back directly to Australia, rather than extending to ports in northern Europe.

In the mid 1980s a decision was taken to re-engine the four PACE trade steamers with slow-speed diesels and the conversion was progressively carried out in the IHI (Ishikawa-Jima-Harima) yards at Yokohama and Nagoya. The Stal Laval turbines of 32,000 shaft horse power,

The former Shipping Corporation of New Zealand container ship *New Zealand Caribbean* was acquired by Blue Star Line interests in 1989 and for a brief time in 1990-1 she was employed on the PACE WEST service as the ACT 10. IAN EDWARDS

capable of driving the ships at 22.5 knots, were replaced by IHI Sulzer diesel engines operating at 88 revolutions per minute for a service speed of 18 knots. The £27 million cost of re-engining was financed by a long-term US dollar loan. During the engine conversions, and as a result of crewing reductions making space available, high quality passenger accommodation was installed for up to 11 passengers. The *ACT 7* was also converted to carry eight passengers while a few berths were provided on the *ACT 1* and *ACT 2.* The conversions were all completed in the first half of 1987.

In April 1986 P&O announced that it had bought out the remaining partners in OCL, effective from 28 May 1986, and it now became a wholly-owned subsidiary. OCL became P&O Containers Limited from 1 January 1987. The Furness Withy shareholding in OCL had earlier been split amongst the three remaining partners who had exercised their pre-emptive rights when Furness Withy was going to be sold to Chinese buyer, C.Y. Tung in 1980. Following the sale of the Furness Withy interests, the shareholdings in OCL were Ocean 40.49 per cent, P&O 36.70 per cent and British & Commonwealth 22.81 per cent. The 1986 acquisition also gave P&O the minority trade shares which Clan Line Steamers and Ocean Steam (Blue Funnel Line) had held in the Australian trade. ACT(A), in contrast, was still very much 'locked in' to the views of its individual partners, each with its own agenda, for the long-term future of its shipping investments. The company depended on its trade partners and relied on the space sharing agreements with the ANZECS partners in the UK-Europe trades and in a similar arrangement from May 1985 with Columbus Line in the PACE Line service.

When ACT(A) withdrew from the partnership with the Transatlantic Steam Ship Company of Gothenburg in the roll-on, roll-off service to and from the West Coast of North America to Australia in 1986, the company decided to retain a presence in the trade using chartered lift-on, lift-off vessels. Three modern vessels of between 750/850TEU were chartered from German owners and renamed *ACTs 9, 10* and *11.* The service from Australia to WCNA was marketed as PACE WEST and the ships calling at Fiji were designated PACE PACIFIC. The first sailing took place

In 1989, ACT(A) acquired the Shipping Corporation of New Zealand, including the company's flagship *New Zealand Pacific*, then trading as the *Tui*. A similar vessel to *Australian Venture* and *ACT 7*, she remained in her Shipping Corporation livery and her bright orange hull. She was only under ACTA ownership for a little over two years before being sold to P&O Containers. The photograph shows her coming alongside at Cashin Quay, Lyttelton. I.J. FARQUHAR

with *ACT 9* sailing from Vancouver for Australia on 25 October 1986 and a space sharing agreement with Columbus Line, similar to the ECNA service, was introduced. Noumea was added to the Pacific calls in August 1987. As part of the slot chartering arrangements with Columbus Line, the *Columbus California* was renamed *ACT 12* in 1988 and a replacement *ACT 10* in 1990 was formerly the *New Zealand Caribbean*, which had become the *Abacus* under the control of Blue Star Line. *ACT 9* was renamed *Columbus Oregon* in March 1990 to better reflect the balance with the space sharing arrangements between ACT(A) and Columbus Line.

A move to gain some benefit from economy of scale was taken when ACT (N.Z.) Ltd, a wholly owned subsidiary of ACT(A), purchased the vessels and trade shares of the Shipping Corporation of New Zealand Ltd on 3 April 1989. Having lost over $NZ150 million, the New Zealand government was anxious to exit from shipping. After lengthy negotiations with several bidders, ACTNZ was successful with a bid of $NZ35/40 million subject to contingencies. The final price paid was $NZ33.5 million.[3] The acquisition gave ACT(A) the former New Zealand Line trade shares to the UK, Europe, Red Sea, Japan, Korea and Australia, as well as the ships *New Zealand Pacific* and *New Zealand Mariner* (which was engaged on the trans-Tasman service). These trade share gains were made with only a modest increase in staffing. The purchase also saw Blueport ACT (New Zealand) Ltd in Wellington responsible for the Cunard-Ellerman management contract for the provision of New Zealand crews for the two ships, as well as a ship management contract for the *Tarihiko*, a small LPG tanker operating between New Plymouth, Dunedin, Lyttelton and Onehunga. To better reflect the New Zealand Line element within the enlarged

The other Shipping Corporation ship purchased in 1989 was the trans-Tasman vessel *New Zealand Mariner*. After a few more months on the Tasman service, she was renamed *Marin* and put on feeder services in and out of Singapore. BAIN-WRIGHT COLLECTION

company, Blueport ACT was renamed New Zealand Line Ltd from 1 October 1989.

The ACT(A) partners continued to seek further economies and in early 1991 they announced plans to transfer the registry of the PACE Line ships to Nassau, Bahamas and to use Filipino crews instead of the mixture of British and West Indian crews then prevailing. Some schedule disruptions occurred with industrial stoppages from British seafarers, but the change was implemented throughout 1991, which left only a British master and chief engineer on each ship. This further eroded seagoing positions for former Port Line staff.

ACT(A) had demonstrated since its inception that its personnel had performed exceptionally well in the development of containerisation, particularly in respect to the specialised knowledge and skill in the handling and transport of refrigerated cargoes. ACT(A), with its several services, carried more refrigerated cargo than any other container shipping line. The extent of the involvement was shown in 1978 when ACT(A) became the first container operator to accept an order of 5,000 insulated containers from a single manufacturer. Some of the company's technical people, including former Port Line personnel, were leaders in their field. Despite this degree of enthusiasm and high attainment achieved within ACT(A), the future direction of the consortium was still very much subject to the interest and commitment of its three shareholders, all of whom had differing viewpoints and cultures.

Blue Star Line could be considered the only dedicated ship owner amongst the three, and as a private company, was probably content to accept a lower rate of return, consistent with tight control of costs on the ships it managed. Blue Star Line had long experienced the cyclical nature of shipping and was prepared to accept that returns varied from year to year. Ellerman Lines, had been sold in 1983 to hotelier M.F. North Plc, a group controlled by D.R. and F.H. Barclay. Two years later, on 13 December 1985, the Barclay brothers accepted a management buy-out offer of the Ellerman shipping interests, from Endobrand Limited, a company comprising the executive directors of Ellermans and a consortium of institutional investments led by Charterhouse Developments Ltd. All the Ellerman directors were involved, and they were keen to pay off their indebtedness promptly by maximising cash flows. The ACT(A) container interests were only part of the purchase, as Ellermans had services from the United Kingdom to the Far East, South Africa, Mediterranean and Middle East. Most of the smaller ships in the Mediterranean trades were chartered so the capital commitment was not as high in ratio to the Blue Star Line and Cunard/Port Line interests in ACT(A). Ellermans had also contracted out their ship management requirements. Their objective was to reduce operating costs and create efficiencies which would provide the best financial return as it was extremely hard to secure additional freight increases because of the competition prevailing in all trades. They were very successful with this management style.

Cunard, as a subsidiary of the publicly-listed Trafalgar House Investments Ltd, was directed more at business which would create a strong investment group with shareholders seeing growth through a strengthening share price and gains made by share trading rather than increasing annual dividends. Since the company acquired Cunard in 1971 the overall results from cargo shipping had been disappointing and there had also been a continual need for capital investment in container ships and equipment. Being tied to ACT(A) in partnership with other lines restricted opportunities for either expansion or withdrawal. Further growth in ACT(A) could only be achieved through heavy capital investment. Any prospect of a better financial return on the existing level of investment was constantly being eroded as more and more 'outsiders' tried their hand in the various services, always at bargain freight rates lower than the rates charged by the conference groupings in each trade.

Trafalgar House had made a takeover bid for P&O in 1983, but an eight-month delay in getting approval from the UK Monopolies and Mergers Commission dulled its interest, since the P&O share price had risen, greatly inflating the cost of any successful bid. In the submissions made by Cunard Line to the Commission it stated that 'deep sea cargo and consortia interests are not high on the list of priorities' – a statement that reinforced the perception that Trafalgar House was only interested in shipping as an investment, rather than as a long-term ship owner. It was also stated that further rationalisation of the container trades was desirable and that 'the acquisition of the P&O Group could be the catalyst for opening up discussions with the parties concerned' – a statement that became a reality in reverse some years later!

Although most of its conventional fleet had been sold, it was ironic that Port Line had its most successful financial years in the mid 1970s. Largely as a result of its 42.5 per cent shareholding in ACTA it paid a record dividend of £6,709,000 to Trafalgar House Investments in 1977, and £6,735,000 in 1978. The majority of the surpluses generating the record dividends came from profits on the charter hire of the ACT(A) container ships which were paid directly to each ACT(A) partner. These were the highest dividends paid in the history of Port Line. Results were spasmodic from 1980 and after a dividend of £4,236,000 in 1986, Port Line never paid another dividend before P&O Containers took over the company and its assets in 1991. The downward path in the profitability of ACT(A) was driven by increased competition, particularly in the Europe/Australia trade with freight rates dropping to compete and erosion of Conference Line trade shares as a result. Other factors were the rise of the Australian/New Zealand/West Coast North American land-bridge to the United States for all time-sensitive cargoes, leaving the PACE East Coast service with lower paying cargoes and reducing volumes of frozen meat as a result of two conventional shipping lines (Lauritzen to WCNA and Kyokuyo to ECNA) providing palletised services to both coasts of North America at reduced freight rates. ACT(A), as a company, never paid a dividend to its shareholders, and with a modest capital of £200,000 was probably not intended to. The highest ACT(A) profit was £10,187,000 in 1989 but generally years of modest profits were interspersed with losses. As with Crusader Shipping Co, the ships were chartered from the individual shareholders and profits would ensue from this directly to the three partners. The 42.5 per cent Port Line shareholding in ACT(A) was apportioned against each ship with *ACTs 1* and *2* assessed at 45 per cent, *ACT 3* at 37 per cent, *ACT 4* at 24 per cent, *ACT 6* at 100 per cent and *ACT 7* at 42 per cent, with no interest in *ACT 5* which was wholly owned by Blue Star Line.

After nearly 20 years of constantly refining and restructuring the cargo shipping interests through Port Line to ACT(A), Trafalgar House realised it would have to improve the returns from shipping, if this segment was to be retained as a unit of the group. It saw potential in securing the Ellerman share, because with the 57.5 per cent stake it would then possess, the company would be in a much stronger position to either on-sell or to have a greater influence in any future investment proposals.

On 1 July 1987 Trafalgar House acquired the whole of the issued share capital of the Ellerman Group for £24.1 million. This also provided the Cunard Cargo Division with a wide spread of services to the Red Sea, Arabian Gulf, East Africa, the Mediterranean, Portugal, Sweden and Eire. More importantly Cunard had also purchased the 15 per cent Ellerman share in ACT(A), and the sudden announcement took the industry by surprise, including the remaining ACT(A) shareholder, Blue Star Line. Trafalgar House had also long been critical of the management skills that had come to it through the acquisition of Cunard and its subsidiary Port Line, so the company also took over the Ellerman management team to manage the enlarged ACT(A) interest. With the transfer of the Ellerman shareholding to Cunard, the crewing of the *ACT 4* would come under Cunard control, but the company elected to retain the Ellerman management company of Denholm Ship Management, as a yardstick against the performance of Cunard management of the *ACT 2, ACT 3* and *ACT 6.*

In 1991 Trafalgar House reported a pre-tax profit 42 per cent below that of the previous year, and the chief executive of Cunard-Ellerman, as the cargo shipping division was then named, said shipping had achieved an operating profit but not an adequate return on the assets employed. The returns for the ensuing six months to March 1991 showed an even more dismal picture with the group profit 75 per cent lower than the 1989/90 result. Port Line Limited, with its 42.5 per cent share in ACT(A), reported a loss of £438,000 in 1989 and an even larger loss of £7,309,000 in 1990. A few months later, there were reports that the Cunard-Ellerman cargo interests were up for sale, and that P&O was the likely bidder. On 1 July 1991 both P&O and Trafalgar House confirmed discussions were taking place and on 18 July, P&O announced the acquisition for £62.5 million. Cunard-Ellerman had initially discussed a sale with Blue Star Line, but the complexities of dealing with all the Ellerman Line side trades had no interest for Blue Star Line. The company was keen to stay in the American trades but would be reluctant to remain in the main line trade where it would now have a minor share compared to P&O.

The takeover of Cunard Ellerman interests, effective from 30 September 1991 and operationally from 11 October, resulted in a major reorganisation of British shipping. P&O sold the ACT(A) North American trades to Blue Star and passed the Cunard-Ellerman interests in the

Mediterranean, Middle East, India and East Africa to Andrew Weir Shipping Limited, operators of Bank Line Limited, United Baltic Corporation and MacAndrew and Company Limited. The *ACT 1, ACT 2* and *ACT 7,* along with the *New Zealand Pacific* and *Marin* (ex *New Zealand Mariner*) came into the P&O fleet on 11 October 1991. At the same time the container ships on the East Coast North American service, *ACTs 3* to *6,* transferred to Blue Star Line. The company acquired £12,898,000 of the ACT(A) assets. Blue Star Line also took over the *Columbus Louisiana* (1979, 19,193) on the PACE Line west coast of North America service under the terms of the rationalised services between Blue Star and Columbus and she was renamed *Oregon Star* on 23 October 1991, instead of the intended name of *ACT 9.* The Blue Star Line owned vessel *ACT 10* was renamed *Columbia Star* in December 1991. ACT(A)'s reefer container stocks at the time of the sale to Trafalgar House interests to P&O included 13,353 porthole containers, 767 insulated containers with integral units, and 2,768 clip-on generator units, plus general cargo leased containers. They were divided between P&O and Blue Star Line as they became available in accordance with the sale agreement. ACT(A) had a brief life of 24 years and with its passing all the historical connections of Tyser Line and Port Line cargo shipping from 1886 disappeared.

Of the other two shipping lines which made up the five original shareholders in ACT when it was formed in 1966, The Ben Line Steamers was forced to buy the 20 per cent Ellerman share in Ben Line Containers to prevent it going to P&O in 1991. From January 1992 Ben Line developed a joint Far East container service with the East Asiatic Company of Copenhagen, trading as EAC-Ben, but within six months massive losses saw Ben Line sell its 24 per cent interest in the consortium to its Danish partner and exit shipping entirely. The other original ACT shareholder, Charente Steam-Ship Company, managed by T.&J. Harrison, continued to operate as a slot charterer to South Africa with a 35 per cent share of the ownership in the *City of Durban,* and with its own container ships to the West Indies and adjacent areas. However in July 1998, P&O Containers acquired the shareholding in the *City of Durban* and in October 2000, P&O Nedlloyd purchased the remaining Harrison interests in the West Indies services, then operating as the CAROL (Caribbean Overseas Lines) service.

The P&O Containers acquisition of the Cunard-Ellerman interests in 1991 made ACT Services in Southampton redundant as P&O integrated its functions into its own systems and trades. However since then, ACT Services has been retained as a dormant company within P&O Containers Ltd, and later P&O Nedlloyd Container Line Ltd.

P&O became the dominant player in the Australian/New Zealand/United Kingdom and Europe trade and strengthened conference control by bringing into the service the long-time 'outsider' Contship Container Line, initially with a three year agreement commencing from 1 January 1994. The ANZEC name was dropped in favour of P&O/Contship. ANL, Hapag Lloyd, Hamburg Sud, Lloyd Triestino and Wilh.Wilhelmsen remained in this grouping as slot charterers, with only P&O and Contship providing the ships, with the exception of the *Australian Venture,* until it was sold in January 1996, when ANL also withdrew from the consortium entirely.

Over the five years following the acquisition of ACT(A), P&O had looked for a suitable partner in which to strengthen the company in the various trades and also achieve a greater economy of scale in its operations. On 9 September 1996 it announced a merger of the container fleet with ailing Nedlloyd Lines of the Netherlands, to form P&O Nedlloyd Container Lines. It was hoped the resulting economies of merging the fleets would slash costs and create better profits. The new company commenced operations from 1 January 1997.

Blue Star Line continued in the American trades but at the end of 1997 the company also succumbed to a P&O offer to acquire the ships and services and this became effective from May 1998. Blue Star Line could see no long term viability for the container services and the elderly ships they employed. Competition in all trades was increasing, not only with new direct services, but through other lines relaying cargoes to 'hub' ports like Singapore. The cost of building new tonnage was prohibitive. The Vestey Group decided to offer its liner services for sale, and despite strong interest from the Company's North American trade joint-service partner, Hamburg-Sud, through its Columbus Line subsidiary, and from CP Ships of Canada, P&O Nedlloyd won the day.

Over a period of years P&O had acquired the interests of all the historic British shipping companies engaged in the New Zealand trade. The Shaw Savill & Albion trade share was acquired by OCL exercising its pre-emptive rights when the parent Furness Withy was about to be sold to Hong Kong interests in 1980. Port Line and Blue Star Line main line trading interests were purchased in 1991, and of course the former New Zealand Shipping Co/Federal Steam Navigation Co interests had been owned since 1916. P&O Nedlloyd was itself swallowed up in 2005 when the world's largest container company, A.P. Moller-Maersk of Copenhagen, made a successful takeover bid. This takeover also spelt the end of the historical shipping conferences in the main line trades from Australia and New Zealand and after the notice period expired on 14 March 2006 the conference arrangements were dissolved.

With so much competitive shipping, including feeder services from New Zealand to the ëntrepot port of Singapore, and later to Tanjung Pelepas in Malaysia, and then using these ports' network of shipping services to relay containers to literally anywhere in the world, the producer boards had started to move aside from their earlier powerful status and allow the market place to steadily reduce freight rates. There had also been much change in the marketing of New Zealand refrigerated cargoes overseas and the amount of meat and dairy exports going to the UK was continuing to decline. In 1960 it had been 70 per cent of the meat but ten years later it was only 57 per cent, by 1980 31 per cent, 1990 22 per cent and in 1995 it was only 16 per cent. However 16 per cent still represented 123,531 tonnes compared 152,827 tons shipped to the UK in the 1923/24 season. Even 57 per cent in 1970 represented 365,163 tonnes.

The New Zealand Meat Producers' Board had vigorously protected its control of freight negotiations, but pressure from within the meat industry became more intense, and there were calls to examine all aspects of the freight chain, from works to market. Only the meat companies could do this effectively. In 1980, the consultancy company, Manalytics of San Francisco, was commissioned by the board to examine all aspects of freighting and handling methods, as well as recommending procedures for negotiating continuity of freight contracts. The report, presented in 1982, was kept confidential from the industry – the board arguing that keeping its recommendations confidential would be beneficial in negotiating new contracts with the shipping lines.

Finally in 1988 the board set up the Meat Industry Freight Council to act as a united industry approach to freight negotiations. The council comprised three board representatives and three members nominated by the meat companies. For the very first time, exporters became involved with the lines' representatives in freight negotiations and, as a result, the council achieved substantial freight reductions. Virtually all negotiations were now conducted in New Zealand. In earlier years, board negotiators going to London for freight talks had often been seen at Ascot, Wimbledon and other British 'establishments', as the guests of the Lines. Under the Meat Industry Freight Council, all these trimmings were abandoned in favour of tough talking. It was only when the meat industry itself had more say in board affairs that efficiencies were developed between the parties. Incredibly, it was not until 1996 that some chief executive officers of major meat companies were appointed to the Meat Board.

When the two-year contract between the board and the Lines expired in October 1993, exporters were finally allowed to negotiate direct with individual shipping lines. The boards retained a measure of control in that they would approve a group of shipping lines in each trade as 'designated carriers'. Following the passing of the Meat Board Act in December 1997, the board lost its transport control and other powers. The larger meat companies, in concluding their own freighting arrangements, achieved significant volume discounts over the smaller players in the industry. The other producer boards were also dismantled and producer board control of the transport of cargoes from New Zealand was over. The efficiencies of modern container transportation also eliminated the vast numbers of staff engaged on conference affairs both in New Zealand and the UK. The protection enjoyed between the boards and the Conference Lines had created a 'cosy' atmosphere and it was only the reality of competition which created a climate that forced both parties to look more intensely at bringing down costs.

Many New Zealanders will say that the four British shipping lines held their country to ransom. Despite that, it is questionable if the farmer 'politicians' heading the producer boards had sufficient business abilities to match the collective negotiating skills of four experienced shipping company leaders. We have already seen where one Meat Board chairman described freight negotiations as resembling a 'good old horse trade'! It is futile to try to apply the competitive free market style of today to the business climate of the past, which balanced wartime strategy and imperial loyalties against short-term profits. There is no doubt that in the period from 1922 up to the mid 1950s New Zealand enjoyed a very good shipping service to the UK and Europe. However, as outside competition emerged in many trades from the 1970s, it is clear that the producer boards were slow to respond. While New Zealand had regular sailings from all ports and standard freight rates, the system did not provide any real incentive to boldly tackle costs or improve handling methods. We have already seen how the meat industry quickly adapted to benefit from the change in the meat freight tariff from a rate per kilo to a rate per container and in later years the benefit of having meat company managers directly involved in the freight talks. A few more incentives of this nature and a more crucial examination of the producer boards' transport systems might have generated even more benefits. In simplistic terms the producer boards tight control of the freight contracts were appropriate for the first 40 years or so, but board control went on for much longer than was justified as a more competitive climate developed, hastened by the benefits of container transport which gave greater flexibility for cargoes to be shipped direct, or conveniently trans-shipped at hub ports, to destinations all over the world.

PACIFIC AUSTRALIA DIRECT LINE

Pacific Australia Direct Line (PAD) was established by the Transatlantic Steam Ship Company of Gothenburg in 1921 when the company's steamer *Anten* (1920, 5,135) sailed from West Coast North American ports to Australia. The line operated without interruption throughout World War II and by 1968, after an exhaustive study into future trade patterns, ordered two roll-on, roll-off ships (RORO) to replace the six fast conventional motorships then operating the service. A third RORO vessel was required to maintain a three weekly schedule and agreement was reached with ACT(A) in December 1969 to build it at Eriksbergs Mekaniska Verkstads AB., Gothenburg. In line with the Australian government's desire to have a direct involvement in the main overseas trades, Transatlantic agreed that the second ship would be jointly owned by the Australian National Line (50 per cent), Elder Smith & Co Ltd (25 per cent), and Trans-Austral Shipping Pty Ltd (Transatlantic agents in Australia) (25 per cent) under a separate company called PAD Shipping Australia Pty Ltd.

The first vessel owned by Transatlantic, and under the Swedish flag, entered service as *Paralla* (1971, 13,355) in March 1971; the second, the *Allunga* (1971, 13,217), Australian-flagged, came into service in June 1971. The ACT(A) vessel was launched as *Dilkara* on 6 May 1971. She was under the British flag and registered to the ownership of Blue Star Line, Port Line and Ellerman Lines. Each company within ACT(A) held a one third share, rather than the 42.5/42.5/15 per cent shareholding percentages of the three partners within ACT(A). She was initially managed by Blue Star Port Line Management and over the 15 years she was in service, several Port Line officers served on her and the experience gained saw them transferring to the Cunard Line roll-on, roll-off vessels in the Atlantic Container Line. Her first master was Port Line's Captain Ian North, and from the experience in *Dilkara* he transferred to Cunard Line RORO vessels in the Atlantic Container Line. It was while he was master of the *Atlantic Conveyor* (1970, 14,946) that he was lost when she was struck by Exocet missiles in the South Atlantic Ocean on 25 May 1982 during the Falklands conflict. The *Dilkara* entered PAD service in December 1971. Sailors for the vessel came from Kiribati, formerly the Gilbert and Ellice Islands in the Pacific. A nautical school had been established there and the *Dilkara* was the first British-registered ship to accept crew from the school.

The vessels had Australian aboriginal names with *Paralla* meaning the moon, *Allunga* the sun and *Dilkara* a rainbow. The PAD line had a distinctive house flag with the design of a rainbow serpent coiled around its eggs set on a light yellowish bunting, representative of the colour of a desert. The ships had an angled stern ramp, seven metres wide, with each vessel having a large sign over the stern door reading 'The PAD Highway'. They had four interconnecting decks as well as the weather deck and had the equivalent capacity for 1200 TEUs. Through the 20-ton fork lifts carried on the vessels they could handle ISO containers, large items of break bulk cargoes, heavy machinery and bulk liquids. At the time Sweden and Norway were prominent in the development of roll-on, roll-off, unit load, palletised cargo handling systems and did not believe the ISO container or cellular container systems were the most efficient forms of sea transport.

The ships worked through New Westminster, Tacoma, Portland, Oakland and Los Angeles

ACT(A) was a partner with the Transatlantic Steam Ship Company of Gothenburg, and the Australian National Line in the operation of a roll-on, roll-off container and break-bulk service from Australia to and from the West Coast of North America. The ACT(A) contribution to the three-ship service, known as the PAD Highway, was the *Dilkara*. BAIN-WRIGHT COLLECTION

for Sydney, Melbourne, Adelaide and Brisbane and from 1982 regular calls were made at Portland, Oregon. Wayport calls at Noumea, Fiji and Honolulu were later introduced. The chartered *Skauboard* (1979, 31,070) was added to provide a 12-day frequency and she was soon replaced by the 1,787 TEU RORO *Lillooet* (1979, 22,094). Overall profitability eluded the line and in order to reduce overheads, the costly Australian-registered *Allunga* was withdrawn in January 1985 and laid up at Portland. Her huge crewing costs of 72 men (one crew on, one crew off) were bleeding the company. *Paralla* was sold in March 1986 and the larger RORO *Elgaren* (1979, 21,721) maintained the service with the *Dilkara* and *Lilloet*. Increasing competition was another significant factor and in October 1986, ACT(A) and Transatlantic amicably agreed to end their partnership. By this time Transatlantic and ACT(A) were in a 50/50 pool as the Australian National Line and Elder Smith had resigned from the PAD partnership in 1985. The *Dilkara* was withdrawn and sold to Taiwan shipbreakers, and another Swedish RORO, *Kolsnaren* (1978, 21,722), was brought in to maintain the three-ship service.

ACT(A) was keen to remain in the trade with lift-on, lift-off container ships and made overtures to Blue Star Line to combine with that company's New Zealand Pacific coast container service. The proposal was initially rejected and ACTA carried on with chartered tonnage, *ACTs 9* to *12* under the marketing name of PACE WEST. In 1991 PACE WEST and Columbus line rationalised their west coast service, similar to the East Coast and the *ACT 12* was withdrawn. Later in the year PACE WEST was caught up in the Cunard Ellerman sale to P&O and *Columbus Louisana,* which was intended to be another *ACT 9,* was taken over by Blue Star Line and renamed *Oregon Star.*

The PAD Line struggled on, merging its sailings with the Australia-New Zealand Container Line (ANCL) from 1 January 1988, the combined service being known as ANZDL. ANCL was a subsidiary of the Shipping Corporation of New Zealand. Shortly after the two companies had combined their schedules, the Compagnie General Maritimes of Paris signed an agreement on 31 March 1988 to buy out Transatlantic. On 21 April 1988, the Shipping Corporation of New Zealand announced the sale of its share of ANZDL to Sofrana Unilines, another French company with links to CGM. Overall control came under Groupe Bollore Technologies of Paris, whose largest shareholder was Delmas Vieljeux of Paris. In 1997 Brierley Investments Limited, owner of New Zealand's Union Shipping Group, purchased 50 per cent of ANZDL but 18 months later, CP Ships (a division of Canadian Pacific), purchased ANZDL and took operational control from 18 December 1998. It remained in the trade, extending US coverage by slot chartering container space direct to East Coast North American ports in sailings of the P&O Nedlloyd/Contship service from December 2002.

OTHER ASSOCIATED COMPANIES

The Commonwealth & Dominion Line/Port Line sometimes invested in other smaller companies, mainly agencies, stevedoring or wool dumping companies. In Australia, many of the investments were undertaken jointly with principal agents, Gibbs Bright, and included such companies as the Sydney Stevedoring & Wool Dumping Co, which in 1948 split into the Port Jackson Stevedoring Pty Ltd and the Port Jackson Wool Dumping Pty Ltd. The former was sold by Trafalgar House Investments in 1979 and the Wool Dumping Co was later sold when it merged with others to become Osmarine (Australia) Pty Ltd. Other Sydney companies set up for specific activities were Waterside Services Pty Ltd, in which Port Line had an interest from 1947-72, Port Jackson Mechanical Services Pty Ltd 1961-74, and the company also briefly held an interest in Sydney Australport Pty Ltd in the early 1970s. A shareholding was also held in Northern Tasmanian Stevedoring Pty Ltd, but this was sold in the early 1970s as container shipping took over from conventional cargo handling. Port Line also purchased a shareholding in Tasmanian shipbrokers, Staley, Radford & Co Ltd in December 1948.

In New Zealand, apart from shareholdings in some of the meat exporting companies, dating from Tyser & Company, Port Line purchased the Christchurch agency company of Kinsey & Co Ltd in 1948. It was an important agency with many of the New Zealand wool buyers domiciled in Christchurch and the purchase also included a stevedoring company, and later a road transport company, E.H. Boyce & Co Ltd. The group was sold on 6 June 1973. Port Line had a small shareholding in Tapley Swift Shipping Agencies Ltd in Dunedin from when it was formed in 1949, but this was disposed of in 1970 as part of the Cunard policy to divest itself of minority interests of this nature. Between 1956 and 1958 Port Line also briefly owned H.R. Beauchamp & Co of Wanganui.

Port Line had a long time interest in the stevedoring companies contracted for the company's work at Auckland and Wellington. In 1965 Wellington stevedore Gannaway & Co was jointly purchased by Blue Star Line and Port Line and a similar arrangement prevailed with the Auckland Stevedoring Co. The latter company was sold 31 December 1972 and Gannaway & Co on 16 January 1975. Port Line also had shareholdings in Southland Stevedoring Co Ltd., in Bluff, Dominion Stevedoring and Wharfingering Co Ltd, in Wellington and Napier Stevedoring Co Ltd, in Napier. All these companies were sold in the 1970s, with the advent of containers, although Port Line, in partnership with the other British lines, was a part-owner of the New Zealand Stevedoring Co Ltd. In 1967 Port Line became a shareholder in Cargo Equipment Services Co

Ltd (CESCO) which was established by the lines for the provision of on-board forklifts and other mechanical equipment. The creation of these two companies followed the recommendations of the "Streamlining Report" of 1965. The interest in CESCO was sold to P&O on 8 January 1975 and Port Line's involvement in stevedoring ceased on 1 October 1976 when N.Z. Stevedoring and Wharfingering Co was sold to the Owens Group Ltd in Tauranga.

1 *Fairplay International Shipping Journal,* 15 Oct 1971.
2 *New Zealand Marine News,* Vol. 50, No. 4, 2002.
3 Ian Farquhar, *Jack of all Trades, Master of None: The Shipping Corporation of New Zealand Limited 1973-1989,* New Zealand Ship & Marine Society, Wellington, 1996.

The most important northbound cargo for the PACE Line container service from Australia and New Zealand to the east coast of North America was frozen beef. The ACTUSA marketing caricature was designed to convey to importers the care and attention the company gave to its carriage.

APPENDIX 2

Fleet Lists

NOTES TO FLEET LISTS

1. Technical details are taken from *Lloyd's Register*. Official numbers are first recorded. Gross and net tonnages can vary over the life of a vessel and the tonnages recorded are generally those after completion. Length between perpendiculars is given, with overall lengths shown where known. Dimensions shown in feet and inches for vessels built up to 1968, with metric equivalents in brackets.
2. With the Tyser/C&D Line and Port Line fleets, vessels were mainly involved in the carriage of refrigerated cargoes and the initial insulated capacity is provided, but with enhancements, and in some cases reductions, the second figure represents changes in the refrigerated capacity over the life of the vessel. Metric equivalents are in brackets.
3. Incidents which occurred in the careers of vessels are not necessarily complete and are only those that have been found in the course of researching the histories of the vessels and the companies. Minor accidents, scrapes with dock walls and the like, have been excluded. Dates used generally relate to local time where the incident occurred.

Section 1

SAILING SHIPS OWNED BY THE TYSER FAMILY

Wooden ship ***NORTHUMBERLAND*** 4651
812t, 133.0 x 38.7 x 21.9, (40.5 x 11.8 x 6.7).
Built 1838 at Moulmein, Burma.
R&H Green, London, 1838-59.
G.D. Tyser & partners, London, 1859-67.
W. Pile Ltd, London, 1867-9.
Abdool Hossain, Moulmein, 1869-79.
9/1879: Broken up at Calcutta, India.

Wooden ship ***BOMBAY*** 29383
937t, 186.0 x 33.4 x 20.9, (56.7 x 10.2 x 6.3).
Built 1861 at Harwich, Essex, England.
G.D. Tyser & partners, London, 1861-72.
6.3.1872: On passage Iloilo to Singapore, foundered on reef, NNW of the Mangsee Islands, Balabac Strait, Philippines and became total loss.

Iron ship *TREVELYAN* 47368
1,042t, 203.6 x 33.4 x 21.2, (62.0 x 10.2 x 6.5); barque-rigged 1885-8.
Built 1863 by Pile, Hay & Co, Sunderland.
G. D. Tyser & partners, London 1863-73.
Shaw Savill & Company, London 1873-82, Shaw Savill & Albion Co Ltd London, 1882-8.
23.3.1888: Sailed Glasgow for Port Chalmers, and went missing off the South African coast, believed to have foundered early June 1888.

Iron ship *BERAR* 48529
906t, 188.5 x 32.4 x 20.3, (57.5 x 9.8 x 6.2); barque-rigged 1895-6.
Built 1863 by Pile & Co, Sunderland.
G.D. Tyser and partners, London, 1863-84.
G.W. & W.H. Tyser, London, 1884-5.
Foley and Co, London, 1885-95.
G. Bertolotto, Genoa, 1895-6.
6.10.1896: Blown ashore in fog during heavy gale near Seaton, Charton Bay, Devon, in position 50.42.10N, 2.59.48W and shortly after broke in two. On passage from Borga to Seville.

Iron ship *HIMALAYA* 48594
1,088t, 201.2 x 33.0 x 20.4, (61.3 x 10.1 x 6.2); barque-rigged 1880-1926.
Built 1863 by Pile, Hay & Co, Sunderland.
G.D. Tyser & partners, London, 1863-74.
Shaw Savill & Co, London, 1874-1882, Shaw Savill & Albion Co Ltd, London, 1882-97.
J.J. Moore & Co, Honolulu, and registered Valparaiso, Chile, 1897-1902.
Alaska Packers' Association, San Francisco, 1902-26 and r/n *Star of Peru* (USA) 1906-26.
1926: Sold through Burns Philp & Co, Sydney, to Comptoirs Francais des Nouvelles Hebrides, Noumea. 1926 and r/n *Bougainville* (French). Later towed from Noumea to Espiritu Santo and anchored in the Second Channel where she was employed as a copra hulk. 1942 the hulk sunk as a target by U.S. aircraft.

Himalaya, pictured here at Wellington, was a sister ship to the *Trevelyan*. Built for G.D. Tyser in 1863, she was also acquired by Shaw Savill, and ran for 23 years in the New Zealand trade. She ended her days as a copra hulk in the Pacific. DE MAUS, ALEXANDER TURNBULL LIBRARY

Iron ship ***HOWRAH*** 50033
1,098t, 207.7 x 33.6 x 21.2, (63.3 x 10.6 x 6.6); barque-rigged 1903-11.
Built 1864 by Pile, Hay & Co, Sunderland.
G.D. Tyser & partners, London, 1864-84.
G.W. & W.H. Tyser, London, 1884-90.
Verdeaux & Cie, Bordeaux 1890-9 and r/n *Tourny* (French) 1890-1904.
G. Dor, Marseilles 1899-1903 (same name).
L. Mortola fu A., Genoa 1903 and r/n *Agostino M* (Italian) 1904-11.
Broken up at Genoa 1911.

Iron ship ***POONAH*** 56889
1,199t, 223.5 x 34.9 x 21.8, (68.1 x 10.6 x 6.6).
Built in 1867 by W. Pile & Company, Sunderland.
G.D. Tyser and partners, London, 1867-84.
G.W. & W.H. Tyser, London, 1884-93.
R.N. Smith & Co Ltd, London, 1893-4 (same name).
H. Janentsky, Rostock, 1894 -1902 (same name).
Th. Nordaas, Egersund, Norway, 1902, and r/n *Leif* (Norway) 1902-5.
5.12.1905: While loading at Bridgewater, Nova Scotia, struck rock on shifting berth in the La Havre River and half-submerged. Declared a constructive total loss and condemned.

The iron ship *Poonah*, built for G.D. Tyser in 1867, was successful and was owned by the family interests for 26 years before being sold to new owners for further trading. MONTEREY MARITIME MUSEUM

Iron ship ***ARCOT*** 60684
1,191t, 223.3 x 34.8 x 21.8, (68.1 x 10.6 x 6.6).
Built 1868 by W. Pile & Co, Sunderland.
G.D. Tyser & partners, London, 1868-71.
10.4.1871: Sailed Calcutta for London and went missing and last sighted 4.6.1871 off Cape of Good Hope in position 36S, 24E.

Iron ship ***NORTH*** 58907
1,333t, 220.4 x 37.1 x 22.6, (67.2 x 11.3 x 6.9); barque-rigged 1895-1906.
Built 1868 by G.R. Clover & Co, Birkenhead.
Coubrough & Co, Liverpool, 1868-72.
G.D. Tyser and partners, London, 1872-84.
G.W. & W.H. Tyser, London, 1884-95.
G. Casabona and Co, Genoa, 1895; r/n *Casabona* (Italian) 1895-1906.
Broken up Genoa 1906.

Iron ship ***LIGHTNING*** 48506
1,248t, 210.8 x 35.0 x 23.0, (64.2 x 10.7 x 7.0); barque-rigged 1878-81.
Built 1863 by M. Samuelson & Co, Hull.
Joshua Bros., Liverpool, 1863.
Kendall Brothers, Liverpool, 1863-6.
Guion & Co, Liverpool, 1866-8.
J. Morison, London, 1868-72.
G. D. Tyser and partners, London 1872-81.
6.11.1881: Sailed New York for London and went missing.

Iron ship ***PLASSEY*** 70579
1,764t, 258.5 x 40.1 x 23.7, (75.7 x 12.2 x 7.2).
Built 1874 by W. Pile & Co, Sunderland.
G.D. Tyser & Partners, 1874-83.
23.12.1882: Sailed Demerara for London and stranded at Sandgate, between Folkstone & Hythe, 29.1.1883-1.2.1883 strained by the tide, and the following day fell over and broke up.

Steel ship ***LUCKNOW*** 87113
1,492t, 245.3 x 37.1 x 22.4, (74.8 x 11.3 x 6.8).
Built 1883 by Wm. Doxford and Sons, Sunderland.
William Haviside Tyser, London, 1883-9.
22.2.1889: Sailed Newcastle, N.S.W. for San Francisco and went missing. Last reported 12.3.1889 in approximate position 33S, 179E.

Section 2

COLONIAL UNION LINE LTD

TSS ***VLISSINGEN*** 91946
221gt, 150n, 147.0 x 21.0 x 7.7, (44.8 x 6.4. x 2.3).
1872 by J & K Smit, Kinderdyk.
T 3cyl 40 nhp by Koninklijke Maatschappij de Schelde, Flushing.
Completed as non-propelled lighter for Belgian owners 1872-86.
Rebuilt 1886 by K.M. de Schelde, Holland and fitted with engines.
25.7.1886: Delivered to Tyser & Co and sailed for London to be equipped with refrigeration for cross-channel service London to Antwerp.

1886: G.W. & W.H. Tyser, London, as *Rouen* (British) 1886-87, r/n *Vlissingen* (Br) 1887-98.
1887: Ownership registered to Colonial Union Line Ltd (G.W. & W.H. Tyser, mgr) 1887-90, transferred Tyser Line Ltd, London, 1890-95.
4.1895: Sold Andrew McIlwraith, and registered to a subsidiary, Walter Reid & Co Ltd, Brisbane (same name-Australian registry) (later Hunter, Reid & Co Ltd).
13.6.1898: In collision in Fitzroy River with steamer *Leichardt* (1865, 690) broke her back and became total loss, while on passage Port Alma to Rockhampton. Remains removed in sections and broken up by 1.1899.

Section 3

TYSER LINE LTD

SSS ***HAWKES BAY*** 98893
4,583 gt, 2960 n, 383.1 x 48.0 x 22.2, (116.8 x 14.6 x 6.8), 10k.
1891 by Wm. Doxford & Sons, Sunderland.
T3-cyl 495 nhp by North Eastern Marine Engineering. Co Ltd, Newcastle.
Ins. cap 155,000 cf (4,390).
Tyser Line Lrd, London 1891-1912.
1912: Sold The Chasehill Steam Ship Co Ltd, London (Kaye, Son & Co Ltd, mgr); r/n *Chasehill* (Br) 1912-16.
22.2.1915: Captured by German Auxiliary cruiser *Kronprinz Wilhelm* (1901, 14,908) in position 6.15S 28.15W. Later filled with prisoners from captured and sunken ships and released 9.3.1915.
1915: Sold Essex Chase Steamship Co Ltd, London (Meldrum & Swinson, mgr) (same name).
18.1.1916: Following steering gear failure, foundered in position 40N, 63W on passage New York to Le Havre.

The clipper-bowed *Hawkes Bay* was the first steamer built for the Tyser Line. Pictured here at Tysers' Wharf (formerly Moores' Wharf) in Sydney, she had 20 years with the company, with her last year in the River Plate trade. She burned 30-33 tons of coal per day for a service speed of 10 knots. Two of her holds were refrigerated with a capacity for 65,000 carcasses of mutton. WM. LIVERMORE

SSS ***TOMOANA*** 110136
5,987 gt, 3,905 n, 440.0 x 54.3 x 29.6, (134.1 x 16.5 x 9.0), 10.5k.
1899 by Sir James Laing & Sons Ltd, Sunderland.
T3-cyl 515 nhp, by G. Clark Ltd, Sunderland.
Ins. cap 252,711 cf (7,156)
Tomoana Steam Ship Co Ltd, London (Tyser and Company, mgr) 1899-03.
27.7.01: Struck uncharted rock at Gisborne – slight damage.
1903: Ownership transferred to Tyser Line Ltd, London, 1903-12.
1912: Sold Brodvale Steam Ship Co Ltd, London (Blue Star Line Ltd, mgr) and r/n *Brodvale* (Br) 1912-20.
1920: Ownership transferred Union Cold Storage Co Ltd, London (Blue Star Line (1920) Ltd, mgr) and r/n *Tudorstar* (Br) 1920-29.
19.12.1922: Bridge damaged in severe Atlantic storm and vessel reached Greenock 28.12.1922.
1929: R/n *Tudor Star* (same owners) but registered to Blue Star Line Ltd, 1930-4.
1934: Sold Italian shipbreakers, arrived Savona 6.10.1934 for demolition by S.A. Ricuperi Metallici.

SSS ***MIMIRO*** 112681
6,225 gt, 4,025n, 440.0 x 55.1x 29.9, (134.1 x 16.8 x 9.1), 12k.
1900 by Workman, Clark & Co Ltd, Belfast.
T3-cyl 570 nhp by Workman Clark & Co Ltd, Belfast.
Ins. cap. 237,000 cf (6,712).
Mimiro Steam Ship Co Ltd, London (Tyser and Co, mgr) 1900-3.
29.8.1902: Picked up steamer *Taviuni* (1890, 1,465) with broken tail shaft (28.8.1902) off Tolaga Bay and towed her to Gisborne.
1903: Ownership transferred Tyser Line Ltd, London, 1903-14.
Transferred C&D Line Ltd, London, 1914 and r/n *Port Hacking* 1916-28.
16.9.1916: On passage London to New York in collision with *Clermiston* (1895, 1,282) in the Straits of Dover, near the South Goodwin lighthouse and returned for repairs.
1928: Sold Andrea Zanchi fu Giovanni, Genoa and r/n *Capo Nord* (Italian) 1928-33.
1933: Sold Italian shipbreakers and broken up Genoa.

Port Hacking was the name given to the Tyser Line *Mimiro* in 1916, after a non-commercial port south of Port Botany in New South Wales. Then already 16 years old, she was sold to Italian buyers in 1927. E. FLUCK

TSS *NIWARU* 114854
6,444 gt, 4,170n, 450.0 x 55.2 x 30.2, (137.2 x 16.8 x 9.2), 12k.
1902 by Workman, Clark & Co Ltd, Belfast.
T6-cyl 583 nhp by Workman, Clark & Co Ltd, Belfast.
Ins. cap 252,000 cf (7,137).
Tyser Line Ltd, London, 1902-14.
16.3.1903: Grounded outward bound from Las Palmas, damaged five of six propeller blades and required new starboard shaft and stern tube.
19.7.1903: Struck rocks near Pania Reef when entering Napier Harbour on passage Auckland to Napier, holed and beached to prevent sinking. Some cargo and coal bunkers discharged, refloated 23.7.1903 and sailed 8.8.1903 for Auckland for dry-docking and repairs.
Transferred C&D Line Ltd, 1914 and r/n *Port Lyttelton* 1916-24.
22.1.1924: Outward-bound Launceston for Hobart, grounded outside Low Head, mouth of Tamar River and suffered bottom damage. Refloated 26.1.24, portion of cargo discharged Launceston. Proceeded to Sydney to complete discharge. Sailed to Batavia (Jakarta), arriving 5.8.24 and after dry-docking owners decided to sail to Genoa for demolition.
17.10.1924: Sold Angelo Bertorello, Genoa for scrapping and then resold L.E. Conti, Genoa.
12.12.1925: Fire broke out and all timberwork destroyed while being broken up.

TSS *MARERE* 115941
6,443 gt, 4,160 n, 450.0 x 55.2 x 30.4, (137.2 x 16.8 x 9.3), 12k.
1902 by Workman, Clark & Co Ltd, Belfast.
T6-cyl 583 nhp by Workman, Clark & Co Ltd, Belfast.
Ins. cap 252,000 cf (7,137).
Tyser Line Ltd, London, 1902-14.
1914 Transferred C&D Line Ltd, London 1914-16 (not r/n).
18.1.1916: While on passage Fremantle to UK, captured by *U-35*, 236 miles east of Malta and sunk by gunfire in position 35.51N, 19.70E.

A sister ship of the *Niwaru*, the *Marere*, was given a Maori name denoting 'to go swiftly'. After a short life of just 14 years, she was sunk in the Mediterranean in 1916 before she could be given a 'Port' name. WM. LIVERMORE

TSS ***WHAKARUA*** 125591
6,534 gt, 4198 n, 450.3 x 55.3 x 30.4, (137.2 x 16.9 x 9.3), 12k.
1907 by Workman, Clark & Co Ltd, Belfast.
T6-cyl 650 nhp by Workman, Clark & Co Ltd, Belfast.
Ins. cap 255,697 cf (7,241).
Tyser Line Ltd, London, 1907-14.
16.2.1908: Put into Cape Town on fire, on passage London to Australia.
16.2.1913: Caught fire on passage London to Australia and had to put into Cape Town for repairs 22.2.1913 and resumed voyage 28.2.1913.
Transferred to C&D Line Ltd, 1914 and r/n *Port Chalmers* 1916-26.
12.3.1917: Chased by U-boat off South West Ireland and escaped.
1926: Sold Andrea Zanchi, Genoa and r/n *Norge* (Italian) 1926-40.
21.12.1940: Sunk by torpedo while under Allied air attack from Swordfish aircraft from HMS *Illustrious,* 35 miles southwest of Kerkenah Island, Tunisia. (34.39N, 10.48E) on passage Palermo to Tripoli.

The Tyser Line *Whakarua* became the *Port Chalmers* in 1916 and remained in the fleet until sold to Italian owners in 1926. E. FLUCK

TSS *NEREHANA* 125633
6,533 gt, 4,196 n, 450.3 x 55.3 x 30.4, (137.2 x 16.9 x 9.3), 12k.
1907 by Workman, Clark & Co Ltd, Belfast.
T6-cyl 650 nhp by Workman, Clark & Co Ltd, Belfast.
Ins. cap 252,000 cf (7,137).
Tyser Line Ltd, London, 1907-14.
1914: Transferred C&D Line Ltd, London, and r/n *Port Hardy* 1916-18.
6.7.1918: Torpedoed and sunk by *U-91* 78 miles west by north off Cape Spartel, Morocco on passage Buenos Aires to Genoa.

The *Nerehana* at Wellington. Nerehana was the Maori name for William Nelson, the man who had influenced Tyser & Company to commence a shipping service from Napier to London. J. DICKIE, ALEXANDER TURNBULL LIBRARY

TSS ***MURITAI*** 129099
7,280 gt, 4,645 n, 470.0 x 58.2 x 31.7, (143.3 x 17.7 x 9.7), 12k.
1910 by Workman, Clark & Co Ltd, Belfast.
T6-cyl 727 nhp by Workman, Clark & Co Ltd, Belfast.
Ins. cap 298,000 cf (8,439).
Tyser Line Ltd, London, 1910-14.
Transferred C&D Line Ltd, London 1914 and r/n *Port Victor* 1916-35.
26.9.1917: Torpedoed 30 miles south of St. Catherine's Point by *UC 69* but made port (Southampton).
1935: Sold T.W. Ward Ltd, Sheffield and broken up by P & W McLellan, arriving Bo'ness in tow 10.11.1935.

Direct from the Workman Clark shipyard and empty of cargo, the *Muritai* is shown on trials in 1910. Muritai is Maori for 'sea breeze'. PORT LINE ARCHIVES, UNIVERSITY OF LIVERPOOL

TSS ***MAKARINI*** 132703
8,418 gt, 5,442 n, 490.2 x 61.4 x 32.9, (149.4 x 18.7 x 10.0), 13k.
1912 by Workman, Clark & Co Ltd, Belfast.
T6-cyl 804 nhp by Workman, Clark & Co Ltd, Belfast.
Ins. cap 106,000 cf, increased to 330,000 cf. (3,002-9,346).
Tyser Line Ltd, London, 1912-14.
Transferred to C&D Line Ltd 1914 and r/n *Port Nicholson* 1916-17.
15.1.1917: Mined and sunk in position 51.02N, 01.58E, 15 miles west by north from Dunkirk, from mines laid by *UC-1* the previous day.

TSS ***HAWKES BAY*** 135175
8,491 gt, 5,430 n, 490.2 x 61.4 x 32.9, (149.4 x 18.7 x 10.00), 13k.
1912 by Workman, Clark & Co Ltd, Belfast.
T6-cyl 805 nhp by Workman, Clark & Co Ltd, Belfast.
Ins. cap 330,000 cf (9,346).
Tyser Line Ltd, London, 1912-14.
Transferred to C&D Line Ltd, 1914 and r/n *Port Napier* 1916-36.
17.8.1920: Explosion occurred in No 3 hold when 150 miles from Panama Canal on passage New York to Auckland, and on arrival Colon, some cargo discharged and voyage resumed 24.8.1920.
10.1.1922: On passage London to Sydney lost blades of port propeller, 450 miles from Simonstown and reached that port on one engine 13.1.1922.
24.8.1928: Fire broke out in No 4 shelter deck and as it was quickly gaining, vessel diverted to Pago Pago arriving 24.8.1928. Fire extinguished 25.8.1928. Vessel on passage London to Suva.
1936: Sold T. & J. Brocklebank Ltd, Liverpool and r/n *Martand* (Br) 1936-8.
1938: Sold Andrea Zanchi, Genoa and r/n *Martano* (Italian) 1938, *Mar Bianco* (Italian) 1938-43 (same owner).
8.9.1943: Taken by Germany at Ancona following capitulation of Italy.
7.12.1943: Bombed and heavily damaged by Allied aircraft off Zara, Adriatic, while under German control. Sank in shallow water and capsized 2.2.1944.

The *Port Napier*, formerly the Tyser Line *Hawkes Bay*, was a very successful vessel and was in the fleet until 1936 before being transferred to T. & J. Brocklebank Ltd, a Cunard sister company. She was bombed and sunk while under the German flag in 1943. A.C. GREEN

Section 4

JAMES P. CORRY & COMPANY, BELFAST

(All the James. P. Corry steamers were employed on Tyser Line services)

SSS *STAR OF VICTORIA* 93164
3,240 gt, 2,116 n, 361.7 x 42.7 x 26.4, (110.2 x 13.0 x 8.0), 10k.
1887 by Workman, Clark & Co, Belfast.
T3-cyl 325 nhp by J.&J. Thomson, Glasgow.
Ins. cap 108,847 cf (3,083).
Star of Victoria Steam Ship Co Ltd, Belfast (J.P. Corry & Co, mgr) 1887-1903.
The Star Line Ltd, London (J.P. Corry & Co, mgr) 1903-11.
1911: Sold Fratelli Cosulich, Trieste and r/n *Frigida* (Italian) 1911-15. Registered to Unione Austriaca di Nav, Trieste (F. Cosulich, Mgr) 1911-15.
1915: Sold Soc.Anon de Nav.Sud Atlantica, Buenos Aires (N.Mihanovich, Mgr) and r/n *Moinho Fluminense* (Argentine) 1915-16.
1916: Sold Soc. Nationale d' Affretments, Le Havre and r/n *Marseille* (French) 1916-17.
20.3.1917: Lost in collision with *Easingwold* (1898, 3,107) off Ile d'Yeu, France in position 46.0N, 2.0W on passage Bordeaux to Cardiff.

SSS *STAR OF ENGLAND* 93180
3,584 gt, 2,271 n, 371.8 x 44.2 x 27.2, (113.3 x 13.5 x 8.3), 11k.
1889 by Workman, Clark & Co Ltd, Belfast.
T3-cyl 361 nhp by J.&J. Thomson, Glasgow.
Ins. cap 115,209 cf (3,263).
Star of England Steam Ship Co Ltd, Belfast (J.P. Corry & Co, mgr) 1889-1903.
The Star Line Ltd, London (J.P. Corry & Co, mgr) 1903-13.
13.3.1890: Outward bound from London for Australia in collision with *Vesper* (1878,679) at Sea Reach, English Channel. *Vesper* badly damaged and *Star of England* returned to Gravesend with hole below waterline for repair.
25.10.1893: On passage Wellington to Bluff, stranded in fog off Cape Saunders, Otago Peninsula, but not damaged.
1913: Sold T. Gazzolo fu A, Genoa and r/n *Purificazione* (Italian) 1913-15.
1915: Sold Societa Anonima Ilva, Genoa (same name)
8.9.1915: Sprang a leak and abandoned in North Atlantic on passage Genoa to Norfolk.

SSS *STAR OF NEW ZEALAND* 104459
4,417 gt, 2,833 n, 393.5 x 46.8 x 28.0, (119.9 x 14.3 x 9.2), 12k.
1895 by Workman, Clark & Co Ltd, Belfast.
T3-cyl 457 nhp by Workman, Clark & Co Ltd, Belfast.
Ins. cap 149,440 cf (4,232).
Star of New Zealand Steam Ship Co Ltd, Belfast (J.P. Corry & Co, mgr) 1895-1903.
The Star Line Ltd, London (J.P. Corry & Co, mgr) 1903-15.
31.3.1899: In collision off Beachy Head, English Channel with *Pontos* (1895, 2,710), the *Pontos* sinking after being cut in two, with *Star of New Zealand* having her boats stove in, stern and upperworks damaged.

21.9.1912: On passage La Plata to Liverpool in collision with *Slieve Bloom* (1906, 1,106) 4 miles SE of South Stack, near Holyhead, beached, refloated 27.9.12, temporary repairs and resumed voyage 30.9.1912.
13.5.1914: When manoeuvring to take pilot, collided with and sank Cardiff pilot cutter *W.W. Jones*.
5.12. 1915: Ran aground in dense fog on Balosquet Rock, one mile south of Molene, near Ushant, on passage Montevideo to Le Havre and abandoned as total wreck.

SSS ***STAR OF AUSTRALIA*** 110507
6,179 gt, 3,985 n, 440.0 x 55.1 x 29.7, (134.1 x 16.8 x 9.0), 12k.
1899 by Workman, Clark & Co Ltd, Belfast.
T3-cyl 579 nhp by Workman, Clark & Co Ltd, Belfast.
Ins. cap 217,442 cf (6,158).
Star of Australia Steam Ship Co Ltd, Belfast (J.P. Corry & Co, mgr) 1899-1903.
The Star Line Ltd, London (J.P. Corry & Co, mgr) 1903-14.
2.7.1904: Crew of Canadian barque *Swansea* abandoned in North Atlantic in sinking condition, and picked up by *Star of Australia* with the master and 9 officers and crew receiving an award from the Canadian government.
28.10.1912: On passage Sydney to Dunkirk, broke tail shaft 600 miles east of Aden. Boat's crew located 4.11.1912 by *Glenlochy* (1896, 4,654) and vessel towed to Aden 5–10.11.1912.
Transferred C&D Line Ltd, 1914 and r/n *Port Stephens* 1916-24.
2. 8.1918: On passage London to Hampton Roads, collided and sank *North Cambria* (1907, 4,635) 70 miles west of Ushant.
3.1920: Stripped of refrigeration machinery and insulation.
26.4.1920: Met with disabled freighter *Tashmoo* (1919, 3,283) 1200 miles west of Ireland and over five days towed her to Queenstown, arriving 1.5.1920.
6.3.1924: Sold shipbreakers G.B. Amedeo Lombardo, Genoa, resold L.E. Conti & Figli, Genoa and arrived Genoa for demolition 4.5.1924.

The *Star of Australia* was renamed *Port Stephens* in 1916, and as she dated from 1899, was sold in 1924, replaced by newer tonnage. She is alongside the company's berth in Sydney. WM. LIVERMORE

SSS ***STAR OF IRELAND*** 116006
4,331 gt, 2,743 n, 380.0 x 48.7 x 28.3, (115.8 x 14.8 x 8.6), 12k.
1903 by Workman, Clark & Co Ltd, Belfast.
T3-cyl 452 nhp by Workman, Clark & Co Ltd, Belfast.
Ins. cap 211,129 cf (5,979).
The Star Line Ltd, London (J.P Corry & Co, mgr) 1903-16.
1916: Sold Nelson Steam Navigation Co Ltd, London (H.&W. Nelson Ltd, mgr) 1916 and r/n *Highland Star* 1916-30.
4.1930 Sold T. W. Ward Ltd for demolition. Sailed the Tyne for Inverkeithing 3.5.1930 with work commencing 12.5.1930.

The smaller 4,331-ton steamer *Star of Ireland*, built in 1903. was often employed on the Tyser Line service from New York to Australian and New Zealand ports. She is photographed at Sydney. WM. LIVERMORE

SSS ***STAR OF SCOTLAND*** 120702
6,230 gt, 4,001 n, 440.3 x 55.3 x 30.3, (134.2 x 16.8 x 9.2), 12k.
1904 by Workman, Clark & Co Ltd, Belfast.
T3-cyl 579 nhp by Workman, Clark & Co Ltd, Belfast.
Ins. cap 238,792 cf (6,763).
The Star Line Ltd, London (J.P. Corry & Co, mgr) 1904-14.
2.1.1914: Damaged above waterline in Long Reach, in the Thames following collision with tug *Lady Curzon* (1904, 253). Resumed voyage after repairs 6.1.1914.
Transferred C&D Line Ltd, 1914 and r/n *Port Campbell* 1916-18.
7.4.1918: Torpedoed on passage London to New York by *U-53*, 115 miles WSW from Bishop Rock and sunk 9.4.1918.

Similar to the *Star of Australia*, the *Star of Scotland* is shown at Port Chalmers. She had a refrigerated capacity for 100,000 carcases of mutton. DE MAUS

SSS ***STAR OF JAPAN*** 120717
6,236 gt, 4,000 n, 440.3 x 55.3 x 30.3, (134.2 x 16.8 x 9.2), 12k.
1906 by Workman, Clark & Co Ltd, Belfast.
T3-cyl 601 nhp by Workman, Clark & Co Ltd, Belfast.
Ins. cap 248,498 cf (7,037)
The Star Line Ltd, London, (J.P. Corry & Co, mgr) 1906-8.
2.4.08: Wrecked on Islote Piedra Galha rock, (22.12N, 16.50W) St. Cyprian's Bay, West Africa, on passage London to Napier; several thousand tonnes of cargo salvaged but vessel was total loss.

The *Star of Japan* had a very short life, being wrecked in St. Cyprians Bay, West Africa in 1908, less than two years after she was built. The photograph shows her in Auckland on her maiden voyage in 1906. ALEXANDER TURNBULL LIBRARY

TSS ***STAR OF CANADA*** 129627
7,280 gt, 4,623 n, 470.3 x 58.4 x 31.6, (143.3 x 17.8 x 9.6), 12.5k.
1909 by Workman, Clark & Co Ltd Belfast.
T6-cyl 749 nhp by Workman, Clark & Co Ltd, Belfast.
Ins. cap 293,774 cf (8,320).
The Star Line Ltd, London (J.P. Corry & Co, mgr) 1909-12.
23.6.1912: While lying in Gisborne roadstead, dragged anchors during heavy gale, ran ashore at Kaiti Beach, Gisborne, New Zealand. Quantity of cargo lightered ashore but vessel caught between the ridge on a reef of rock with forepart submerged. Vessel broke her back 3.7.1912 and was total loss.

The *Star of Canada* in Sydney Harbour. She had a short career from 1909 to 1912 before she became a total loss in the Gisborne roadstead. WM. LIVERMORE

TSS ***STAR OF INDIA*** 129635
7,316 gt, 4,602 n, 470.1 x 58.4 x 31.6, (143.3 x 17.8 x 9.6), 12.5k.
1910 by Workman, Clark & Co Ltd, Belfast.
T6-cyl 756 nhp by Workman, Clark & Co Ltd, Belfast.
Ins. cap 299,727 cf (8,488).
The Star Line Ltd, London (J.P. Corry & Co, mgr) 1910-14.
Transferred C&D Line Ltd, London 1914 and r/n *Port Pirie* 1916-35.
1935: Sold T.W. Ward Ltd, Sheffield and arrived Briton Ferry for demolition 11.11.1935.

A sister ship to the *Star of Canada*, the *Star of India* entered service two years later. She was renamed *Port Pirie* in 1916 and remained in service until 1935. ALDERSLEY, ALEXANDER TURNBULL LIBRARY

Absorbed into the Commonwealth & Dominion Line, the *Star of India* became the third *Port Pirie* in 1916. She is shown fully laden, outward bound from Adelaide. E. FLUCK

TSS ***STAR OF VICTORIA*** 132046
9,152 gt, 5,852 n, 501.3 x 63.3 x 33.6, (152.8 x 19.3 x 10.2), 14k.
1914 by Workman, Clark & Co Ltd, Belfast.
T6-cyl 979 nhp by Workman, Clark & Co Ltd, Belfast (Bauer-Wach turbines fitted 1929).
Ins. cap 387,100 cf increasing to 410,549 cf (10,963-11,626).
Laid down for the J.P. Corry & Co and initially registered to the Star Line Ltd but completed for the C&D Line Ltd, London, 1914 and r/n *Port Melbourne* 1916-48.
18.5.1948: Arrived Blyth, following sale to British Iron & Steel Co for demolition by Hughes Bolckow Ltd.

Corry's *Star of Victoria* was renamed *Port Melbourne* in 1916 and survived until scrapped in 1948. A.C. GREEN

TSS ***STAR OF ENGLAND*** 136660
9,136 gt, 5,835 n, 501.3 x 63.3 x 33.6, (152.8 x 19.3 x 10.2), 14k.
1914 by Workman, Clark & Co Ltd, Belfast.
T6-cyl 979 nhp by Workman, Clark & Co Ltd, Belfast (Bauer-Wach turbines fitted 1929).
Ins. cap 387,100 cf increasing to 409,680 cf (10,963-11,602).
Laid down for the J.P. Corry & Co, Star Line, but completed for the C&D Line Ltd, London, 1914 and r/n *Port Sydney* 1916-48.
1948: Sold British Iron & Steel Co, allocated to T. W. Ward Ltd, and arrived Preston for demolition 19.12.1948.

The sister ship to the *Star of Victoria*, the *Star of England* was renamed *Port Sydney* in 1916 and, like her sister, served until 1948. A.C. GREEN

Section 5

T.B. ROYDEN & SONS, LIVERPOOL

(Only those vessels employed on Tyser Line services, and although *Indrani* (1894, 4,994), *Indra* (1897, 6,057), *Indravelli* (1897, 5,805) *Indradeo* (1902, 5,315) and *Indramayo* (1902, 5,200) made voyages to and from Australia/New Zealand the vessels were on charter to other companies)

SSS ***INDRA*** 93769
3,582 gt, 2,333 n, 361.8 x 44.3 x 27.1, (110.3 x 13.5 x 8.3), 11k.
1888 by T. Royden & Sons, Liverpool.
T3-cyl 256 nhp by Fawcett, Preston & Co, Liverpool.
The Indra Steamship Co Ltd, Liverpool (MacVicar, Marshall, mgr 1888-94, T.B. Royden & Sons, mgr 1894-96).
1896 Sold S.S. Kildona Co Ltd, Dundee (W. Thomson & Sons, mgr) and r/n *Kildona* 1897-07.
14.12.1907: Struck Brazil Rocks, Cape Sable on passage Halifax, Nova Scotia to Portland, Maine and by 17.12.1907 had completely sunk.

The first Royden steamer employed on a Tyser Line berth was the *Indra* in 1891 when she was sent out to Australia for a homeward wool and general cargo. She made only one round voyage for Tysers. ALAN B. DEITSCH COLLECTION

SSS *INDRAMAYO* 96302
4,110 gt, 2,662 n, 400.2 x 45.1 x 28.2, (122.0 x 13.7 x 8.6), 11k.
1889 by London & Glasgow Engineering & Iron SB Co. Ltd, Govan.
T3-cyl 421 nhp by London & Glasgow Engineering & Iron SB Co Ltd, Govan.
Ins. cap 160,795 cf (4,554).
The Indramayo Steamship Co Ltd, Liverpool (MacVicar, Marshall, mgr 1889-94, (TB. Royden & Sons mgr 1894-01).
28.3.1899: Cargo in No 1 hold caught fire when vessel 5 miles off Hen & Chicken Islands, New Zealand and fire extinguished in Auckland.
1901: Sold Houlder Line Ltd, London, and r/n *Thorpe Grange* 1901-30.
29.5.1930: Sailed Liverpool for Troon for demolition by West of Scotland Shipbreaking Co Ltd.

SSS *INDRALEMA* 102,133
3,150 gt, 2,020 n, 330.0 x 41.5 x 25.1, (100.6 x 12.6 x 7.6), 12k.
1894 by C.S. Swan & Hunter, Newcastle.
T3-cyl 264 nhp by Central Marine Engineering Works, West Hartlepool.
The Indralema Steam Ship Company Ltd, Liverpool (T.B. Royden, Mgr) 1894-1900.
2.12.1896: Sailed Penarth for Newport News and subsequently broke propeller and towed to St Thomas, West Indies by *Texan* (1883,3,258) arriving 17.1.1897.
1900: Sold Ulster Steamship Co Ltd, Belfast, (G. Heyn & Sons, mgr) and r/n *Bray Head* 1900-17.
14.3.1917: Captured and sunk by shellfire from *U-44* 375 miles northwest by west from the Fastnet in position 52.04N, 18.50W, on passage from St.John, New Brunswick to Belfast.

Built in 1894, the *Indralema* entered Tyser Line service on completion and remained with the company until her sale in 1900. She is photographed at Port Chalmers. DE MAUS, ALEXANDER TURNBULL LIBRARY

SSS ***INDRAGHIRI*** 105384
4,927 gt, 3,070 n, 400.4 x 48.2 x 29.0, (122.0 x 14.7 x 8.8), 12k.
1896 by Chas. Connell & Co, Glasgow.
T3-cyl 485 nhp by D. Rowan & Son, Glasgow.
Ins. cap 191,716 cf (5,429).
The Indraghiri Steamship Co Ltd, Liverpool, 1896-02, The Indra Line Ltd, Liverpool, 1902-10 (T.B. Royden, mgr).
2.6.1897: On passage London to Wellington collided with *Bamburgh* (1895, 647) in Sea Reach, English Channel. Bow damaged and resumed voyage after repairs 20.6.1897.
16.4.1907: Stranded off Ismailia, west bank of Suez Canal, on passage Australia to London.
21.8.1907: Fire in Melbourne in No 1 Lower Hold, although quickly extinguished serious damage to insulation and cargo.
1910: Sold Brodstone Steamship Co Ltd, London, (Blue Star Line Ltd, mgr) 1910-17.
15.8.1917: Torpedoed and sunk by *UB-40* , 95 miles west, quarter south, from Ushant on passage Cardiff to Zarate, Argentine.

Built in 1896, the *Indraghiri* spent 14 years on Tyser Line services. She had capacity for 75,000 carcasses of frozen mutton and dry cargo space for 3,900 tons of general cargo. J. DICKIE, ALEXANDER TURNBULL LIBRARY

SSS *INDRADEVI* 110639
5,683 gt, 3,702 n, 420.6 x 53.2 x 29.4, (128.2 x 16.2 x 9.0), 12k.
1900 by Sir James Laing & Sons Ltd, Sunderland.
T3-cyl 520 nhp by J. Dickinson & Son Ltd, Sunderland.
Ins cap 218,293 cf reducing to 213,905 cf. (6,182-6,058).
The Indradevi Steamship Co Ltd, Liverpool (T.B. Royden, Mgr) 1900-11.
11.5.1906: Fire while lying Wanganui Roadstead – minor damage confined to ship.
27.6.1910: Caught fire at Auckland, No 1 hold flooded, fire extinguished after 23 hours.
1911: Sold Furness Withy & Co Ltd, West Hartlepool, and r/n *Chase Side* 1911-12.
1912: Transferred British & Argentine Steam Navigation Co Ltd, London, (Furness Withy & Co Ltd, mgr) and r/n *El Cordobes* 1912-26.
1926: Sold M. Querci & O. Rosini, Genoa and r/n *Pratomagno* (Italian) 1926-31.
30.4.1931: Sold Italian shipbreakers and arrived Savona for demolition.

The *Indradevi* was built in 1900 to the requirements of the Tyser Line and remained on that company's services until sold in 1911. She is shown at the Tyser berth in Sydney. WM. LIVERMORE

SSS *INDRALEMA* 113469
6,669 gt, 4,344 n, 450.6 x 55.0 x 30.8, (137.3 x 16.8 x 9.4), 12k.
1901 by Chas. Connell & Co, Glasgow.
T3-cyl 615 nhp by D. Rowan & Son, Glasgow.
Ins. cap 238,549 cf (6,756).
The Indra Line Ltd, Liverpool, (T.B. Royden, mgr) 1901-14.
15.11.1904: In collision in Mersey River with *Manchester Corporation* (1899, 5,474), holed, beached & repaired, sailing Liverpool 4.2.1905.
23.4.1911: On passage Southampton to Tyne in ballast, collided with, and sank steamer *Trooper* (1902, 958) off Dungeness, English Channel, on passage London to Liverpool.
1914: Transferred C&D Line Ltd, London, r/n *Port Alma* 1916-23.
1923: Sold Vianda Steam Ship Co Ltd, (Wm. H. Muller & Co (London) Ltd, mgr) London, r/n *Vianda* (Br) 1923-6.

1926: Sold Pietro Ravano fu Marco, Genoa and r/n *Fidelitas* (Italian) 1926-32.
1927: Transferred Societa Anon de Navigazione "Unione", Genoa 1927-32.
16.5.1932: Sold Italian shipbreakers and arrived Savona for demolition.

Royden's *Indralema*, which came into the C&D Line fleet, was renamed *Port Alma* in 1916, and sold in 1923 as new ships were built. She is getting under way in Sydney Harbour. WM. LIVERMORE

TSS ***INDRABARAH*** 131279
7,396 gt, 4,664 n, 471.0 x 58.4 x 31.6, (143.6 x 17.8 x 9.6), 13k.
1910 by Swan, Hunter & Wigham Richardson Ltd,, Newcastle.
T6-cyl 755 nhp by Richardsons Westgarth & Co Ltd, Hartlepool.
Ins. cap 289,337 cf (8,194).
The Indra Line Ltd (T.B. Royden, Mgr) 1910-14.
10.5.1913: On passage Gisborne to Wanganui, stranded 5 miles north of Rangitikei River, New Zealand, refloated 6.7.1913 and reached Wellington 7.7.1913.
12.12.1913: On passage Sydney to London, grounded in Habret section, Suez Canal, and lightered cargo to refloat on 16.12.1913.
1914: Transferred C&D Line Ltd, London. and r/n *Port Elliot* 1916-24.
12.1.1924: Stranded on reef between Horoera Point and Te Araroa Point, East Cape, 80 miles north of Gisborne, New Zealand, on passage Auckland to Wellington. Leaking badly in Nos 2 & 3 holds and with the engine room flooded, became a total loss.

The four-masted *Indrabarah* was a solidly-built vessel and in 1913 she spent nearly two months ashore before being refloated. She stranded again on the New Zealand coast in 1924 but this time, under the name of *Port Elliot*, became a total wreck. W. HILLSDON

TSS *INDRAPURA* 131403
8,144 gt, 5,147 n, 490.6 x 61.3 x 32.4, (149.5 x 18.7 x 9.9), 13k.
1911 by Swan, Hunter & Wigham Richardson Ltd, Newcastle.
T6-cyl 924 nhp by Wallsend Slipway & Engineering Co Ltd, Wallsend-on-Tyne.
Ins. cap 313,000 cf increasing to 332,210 cf. (8,864 – 9,408).
Refitted as migrant carrier 1912.
The Indra Line Ltd, Liverpool (T.B. Royden, mgr) 1911-14.
1914: Transferred C&D Line Ltd, and r/n *Port Adelaide* 1916-17.
3.2.1917: Torpedoed and sunk by *U-81,* 180 miles SW of Fastnet Rock in position 48.49N, 11.40W, on passage London to Sydney.

The Royden Line also converted a sister ship of the *Indrabarah* to carry up to 1000 migrants from London to Melbourne. This was the *Indrapura* and she made the second sailing under the migrant contract in October 1912 carrying 300 men and 700 women and children. She was one of the first steamers fitted with acetylene lighting. Renamed *Port Adelaide* in 1916, she was torpedoed and sunk a year later. D.M.H. LITTLE, STATE LIBRARY OF VICTORIA

Section 6

WILLIAM MILBURN & COMPANY LTD

Milburn Line steamers employed on the Anglo Australasian Steam Navigation Co Ltd service to Australia and 'Port' vessels registered to the ownership of that company and designated for the Australian service.

SSS *HANKOW* 68510
3,594 gt, 2,332 n, 389.0 x 42.1 x 28.8, (118.6 x 12.8 x 8.8).
1873 by C. Mitchell & Co, Newcastle.
Compound 2-cyl 500 nhp by R.&W. Hawthorn, Newcastle.
Watts, Milburn & Company, London 1873-9, (E.H. Watts shown as the registered owner 1873-5)
Wm. Milburn & Co, London, 1879-97.

1897: Sold Aberdeen Atlantic Shipping Co, Aberdeen (J. Rust & Son, mgr) (same name) 1897-98.
1898: Sold Acties Dunnet, Tonsberg, (Wilh Wilhelmsen, mgr) and r/n *Dunnet* (Norway) 1898-9.
6.4.1899: Sailed Barry for Genoa and believed to have foundered in the Bay of Biscay.

SSS *TEDDINGTON* 82817
2,016 gt, 1,310 n, 287.0 x 36.1 x 23.9, (87.5 x 11.0 x 7.3).
1880 by C.S. Swan & Hunter, Newcastle.
Comp. inverted 2-cyl 235 nhp by T. Clark & Co, Newcastle.
Wm. Milburn & Company, London 1880-7.
9.6.1887: Foundered after striking Avocet Rock, Aden in position 14.24.5N, 42.42.5E on passage Bombay to Gibraltar (for orders).

SSS *CONISTON* 82818
2,258 gt, 1,491 n, 300.0 x 36.4 x 25.2, (91.4 x 11.1 x 7.7).
1880 by A. Leslie & Company, Newcastle.
Comp. inverted 2-cyl 250 nhp by R.&W. Hawthorn, Newcastle.
Wm. Milburn & Company, London 1880-84.
24.12.1884 Sailed Liverpool for New York in ballast and went missing.

SSS *ASCALON* 85178
2,351 gt, 1,523 n, 290.0 x 37.2 x 27.4, (88.4 x 11.3 x 8.3).
1882 by Campbell, McIntosh & Bowstead, Scotswood-on-Tyne, Newcastle.
Comp. inverted 2-cyl 300 nhp by R. & W. Hawthorn, Newcastle.
W. Milburn & Company, London, 1882-7.
26.5.1884: Ran aground Cape Romania, Red Sea in position 1.26N, 104.20E on passage Hong Kong to Calcutta. Refloated 27.5.1884.
13.10.1887: On passage Aden to Calcutta, ran ashore 14 miles west of Galle, Ceylon (Sri Lanka) and became total wreck.

SSS *NORMANTON* 87017
2,367 gt, 1,533 n, 291.2 x 37.3 x 27.3, (88.8 x 11.4 x 8.3).
1882 by Campbell, McIntosh & Bowstead, Scotswood–on-Tyne, Newcastle.
Comp. inverted 2-cyl 250 nhp by R.&W. Hawthorn, Newcastle.
Wm. Milburn & Co, London, 1882-6.
24.10.1886: Wrecked off Izu Ohshima in position 34.45N, 139.20E, Japan on passage Yokohama to Hiogo (Kobe).

SSS *HAVERTON* 87073
2,531 gt, 1,645 n, 300.0 x 37.3 x 27.5, (91.4 x 11.4 x 8.4).
1883 by Tyne Iron Shipbuilding Co Ltd, Newcastle.
Compound 2-cyl 300 nhp by R.&W. Hawthorn, Newcastle.
Wm. Milburn & Co, London 1883-94.
3.7.1894: Struck Ecureuil Shoal, St Lawrence River and beached Sainte Croix, 15 miles upriver from Quebec, on passage Sydney, Cape Breton Island to Montreal, suffering severe bottom damage.
24.7.1894: Sold for $C7000 and coal cargo sold for $C500.
18.8.1894: Refloated and towed to Quebec.
5.1895: Sold 'as is' for scrapping, Quebec.

SSS *CHOLLERTON* 87079
2,650 gt, 1,734 n, 317.2 x 37.1 x 27.25, (96.7 x 11.3 x 8.3).
1883 by A. Leslie & Company, Hebburn.
Compound 2-cyl 300 nhp by Wigham Richardson & Company, Newcastle.
Wm. Milburn & Co, London, 1883-96.
11.6.1883: On passage London to Adelaide (sailed London 7.5.1883) lost her propeller in position 11.36S, 70.22E, Indian Ocean and had to proceed to Bombay under sail to fit spare. Sailed Bombay for Adelaide 4.8.1883.
1896: Sold S.S. Nyassa Co Ltd, Glasgow (Maclay & McIntyre, mgr) 1896-99.
1899: Transferred S.S. Everilda Co Ltd, Glasgow (Maclay & McIntyre, mgr) 1899-01.
1901: Sold A. Parodi fu B of Genoa and r/n *Jolanda* (Italian) 1901-09.
1909: Broken up at Genoa.

SSS *TIVERTON* 87168
2,673gt, 1,743 n, 320.1 x 37.6 x 27.4, (97.6 x 11.5 x 8.4).
1883 by Campbell, McIntosh & Bowstead, Scotswood-on-Tyne.
Compound 2-cyl 350 nhp by T. Clark & Co, Newcastle.
Wm. Milburn & Co, London, 1883-96.
1896: Sold S.S. Nyassa Co Ltd, Glasgow (Maclay & McIntyre, mgr) 1896-99.
1899: Transferred Glasgow Navigation Co Ltd, Glasgow (Maclay & McIntyre, mgr)1899.
1899: Transferred S.S. Inverleith Co Ltd, Glasgow (Maclay & McIntyre, mgr) 1899-01.
1901: Sold A.S. Vagliano, Piraeus and r/n *K.Paskhalidis* (Greece) 1901-04.
3.6.1904: While on passage Stratoni to Marseilles ran aground off Cape Lavra on south eastern tip of Mt. Athos Peninsula, Aegean Sea and sank 4.6.1904.

SSS *ANGERTON* 89529
2,794 gt, 1,823 n, 320.0 x 38.0 x 27.4, (97.5 x 11.6 x 8.4).
1884 by W. Dobson & Company, Newcastle.
Compound 2-cyl 375 nhp by Wallsend Slipway Co, Newcastle.
Laid down as *Port Stephens* but launched as *Angerton*.
Wm. Milburn & Co, London 1884-96.
1.12.1895: On passage Palermo to USA, stranded at Eastern Beach, Gibraltar. Following lightering cargo, refloated 13.12.1895 and proceeded to Gibraltar. Structurally damaged and taken over by hull insurers as a compromised total loss (67 per cent).
1896: Sold Northumbrian Shipping Company, Newcastle (L. Macarthy, mgr) (same name) 1896-9.
9.3.1899: Went ashore 15 miles west of Alexandria on passage Cardiff to Alexandria and became total wreck.

SSS HUNTINGDON 82874
2,224 gt, 1,463 n, 300.0 x 36.3 x 24.7, (91.4 x 11.1 x 7.5).
1881 by A. Leslie & Company, Newcastle.
Compound 2-cyl 275 nhp by R.&W. Hawthorn, Newcastle.
Wm. Milburn & Co, London, 1881-97.
1897: Sold Foscolo, Mango and Co, Piraeus (E.J. Oliver & Co, mgr) and r/n *Norbertos* (Greek) 1897-01.
1901: Transferred P.G. Foscolo, Trieste 1901-02, (same name), then following the death of Foscolo,

ownership transferred. Executors P.G. Foscolo, Trieste (T. Cossovich, mgr) and r/n *Huntingdon* (Austro-Hungary) 1902-3, under ownership of Rougier & Company (J. Pitts, mgr).
1903: Sold Salonikli Mustapha Bey of Constantinople, and r/n *Bassorah* (Turkey) 1903-5.
1905: Sold S.A. Siderides, Piraeus and r/n *Alexandra* (Greek) 1905-24.
1916: Sold Jean Carras & Sons, Piraeus, transferred Carras Bros, Piraeus 1919-24 (same name).
1924: Sold Hadji Zade Mehmed Kiazim Bey, Istanbul and r/n *Istambol* (Turkey) 1924-8.
1928: Sold Kir Zade Chevki & Company, Istanbul and r/n *Istanbul* (Turkey) 1928-34.
1934: Sold Italian shipbreakers and broken up in Genoa in second quarter 1934.

SSS *PORT JACKSON* 87178
2,644 gt, 1,728 n, 317.0 x 37.2 x 27.4, (96.6 x 11.3 x 8.4).
1883 by A. Leslie & Company, Newcastle.
Compound 2-cyl 350 nhp by T. Clark & Co, Newcastle.
Anglo-Australasian Steam Navigation Co Ltd, London (Wm. Milburn & Co, mgr) 1883-92.
14.3.1891: On passage Sydney to London grounded off Cape Elba, Red Sea in position 22.50N, 36.48E, refloated 16.3.1891 with structural damage to forepeak.
1892: Ownership transferred to A. Coote & J.H. Ridley, directors of R.&W. Hawthorn, Leslie & Co as part payment towards *Port Melbourne* 1892-95.
1895: Sold A. Mancini, Genoa and r/n *Agordat* (Italian) 1895-1903.
1903: Sold F. Schiaffino fu G, Genoa and r/n *Beppe* (Italian) 1903-5.
1905: Sold Calame & Cortese, Genoa and r/n *Jeanne Marcelle* (Italian) 1905-7.
1907: Sold L. Pittaluga, Genoa (same name) 1907-10.
1910: Sold Italian shipbreakers and broken up at Genoa 2nd quarter 1910.

SSS *PORT PHILLIP* 89488
2,671 gt, 1,732 n, 317.0 x 37.2 x 27.5, (96.6 x 11.3 x 8.4).
1883 by A. Leslie & Company, Newcastle.
Compound 2-cyl 350 nhp by Wallsend Slipway Co Ltd, Newcastle.
Anglo-Australasian Steam Navigation Company Ltd, London,(Wm. Milburn & Co, mgr) 1883-96.
1896: Sold Blyth Steam Shipping Co Ltd, London (Petersen, Tate & Co, Mgr) and r/n *Blyth* 1896-7.
17.10.1897: On passage Lulea to Rotterdam stranded at Holmo Gadd, near Umea, Gulf of Bothnia in position 63.39N, 20.55E, and abandoned as total loss. Wreck subsequently raised and broken up.

SSS *PORT DARWIN* 89546
2,517 gt, 1,628 n, 300.1 x 37.4 x 27.1, (91.5 x 11.4 x 8.3), 10k.
1884 by A. Leslie & Co, Newcastle.
Compound 2-cyl 350 nhp by R.&W. Hawthorn, Newcastle.
Anglo-Australasian Steam Navigation Co Ltd, London (Wm. Milburn & Co, mgr) 1884-92.
1892: Ownership transferred to A. Coote & J.H. Ridley, directors of R.&W. Hawthorn, Leslie & Co in part payment for *Port Hunter* 1892-7.
1897: Sold E. Morgan & Co, (Evan Morgan, mgr) 1897-1905 (same name).
15.11.1905: Struck rocks 3 miles off La Guardia, south of Vigo, Spain on passage Honaine, Algeria to Rotterdam and became total loss.

SSS ***PORT ADELAIDE*** 89560
2,751 gt, 1,783 n, 332.0 x 38.1 x 27.5, (101.2 x 11.6 x 8.4), 10k.
1884 by A. Leslie & Company, Newcastle.
Compound 2-cyl 400 nhp by Wigham Richardson & Co, Newcastle.
Anglo-Australasian Steam Navigation Co Ltd, London (Wm. Milburn & Co, Mgr) 1884-98.
1898: Sold G. Brailli, Orebich, Austria-Hungary and r/n *Sofia Brailli* (Austro-Hungary) 1898-1909.
1909: Sold A. Merveille and broken up Dunkirk 11.1909.

The *Port Adelaide* built in 1884 had a raked bow and a more speedier look than the early 'Port' steamers.
THE MARINERS' MUSEUM, NEWPORT NEWS

SSS ***PORT VICTOR*** 91872
2,793 gt, 1,828 n, 336.0 x 38.2 x 27.5, (102.4 x 11.6 x 8.4), 10k.
1885 by A. Leslie & Company, Newcastle.
T3-cyl 400 nhp by Wigham Richardson & Company, Newcastle.
Ins. cap. 29,428 cf (833).
Wm. Milburn & Co, London, 1885-1898.
8.7.1889: On passage Newcastle to Batavia grounded on Restoration Island, Queensland. Refloated undamaged 11.7.1889 after jettisoning 260 tons of coal.
4.6.1897: On passage London to Jamaica, in collision with *Roecliff* (1894, 3,263) off Beachy Head, 6 miles south of Sovereign Light off the Hastings. *Roecliff* sunk and *Port Victor* towed to Tilbury by 3 tugs, 10 feet by the head and forward hold full of water.
1898: Sold U.S. Army and r/n *McClellan* and employed as U.S. Army Transport 1898-1917.
1917: Transferred to U.S. Shipping Board (same name) 1917-19.
1919: Sold Lloyd Royal Belge Soc. Anon, Antwerp and r/n *Hastier* (Belgium) 1919-22.
3.11.1920: Caught fire at Antwerp while discharging, and scuttled clear of the berth. Raised 1921 and sold 11.12.1922 to Soc. Metallurgique de Merxem, Antwerp and broken up.

The fine lines of the three-masted *Port Victor* of 1885 are emphasized in this photograph, taken at Gravesend. She sailed from London on her maiden voyage to Australia on 21 October 1885. F.C. GOULD & SON

SSS ***PORT PIRIE*** 91932
3,109 gt, 2,040 n, 353.5 x 39.4 x 27.5, (107.7 x 12.0 x 8.4), 10k.
1886 by R.&W. Hawthorn, Leslie & Co Ltd, Newcastle.
T3-cyl 450 nhp by Wigham Richardson & Company, Newcastle.
Ins. cap. 30,755 cf. (871)
Wm. Milburn & Company, London, 1886-87 and transferred to Anglo-Australasian Steam Navigation Co Ltd, London (Wm. Milburn & Co, mgr) 1887-97.
1897: Sold Prince Steam Shipping Co Ltd, Newcastle (J. Knott, mgr) 1897-98, Prince Line Ltd, London (J. Knott, mgr) 1898-00 and r/n *Spanish Prince* 1897-00.
1900: Sold Cia. Cantabrica de Nav. (Orbe y Gobeo, mgr), Bilbao, Spain and r/n *Guernica* 1900-02.
10.2.1902: Sprang leak and foundered 11.2.1902 off Galicia, Spain, in position 45N, 8W on passage Cardiff to Genoa. Crew taken off by German steamer *Nestor* (1894, 1,229).

A sister of the *Port Victor,* the first *Port Pirie* sailed from London on 21 October 1886 for Australia via Las Palmas, Cape Town carrying general cargo and 104 passengers in steerage. At this time the Milburn sailings alternated between the Cape of Good Hope and the Suez Canal route. F.C. GOULD & SON

SSS *PORT AUGUSTA* 91971
2,833 gt, 1,856 n, 347.0 x 38.7 x 27.5, (105.8 x 11.8 x 8.4), 10k.
1886 by Tyne Iron Shipbuilding Co Ltd, Newcastle.
T3-cyl 450 nhp by Wigham Richardson & Co, Newcastle.
Wm. Milburn & Co, London 1886-91.
1891: Sold Russkoye obshchestvo parolhodstva I torgovli (R.O.P.I.T) Odessa and r/n *Czaritza* (Russian) 1891-15.
10.3.1915: Commissioned by Russian Navy as troopship *N75* 1915-16.
19.10.1916: Torpedoed and sunk north east of Cape Midia, Black Sea by *UB 42.*

The *Port Augusta* of 1886 had only five years under the Milburn Line before being sold to Russian owners as the *Czaritza.* Her distinctive silhouette is shown in this photograph taken during her two years under the Russian flag. P. WARNECKE COLLECTION

SSS *PORT DENISON* 94316
3,505 gt, 2,289 n, 375.0 x 42.2 x 28.5, (114.3 x 12.9 x 8.7), 10k.
1887 by R.&W. Hawthorn, Leslie & Company, Newcastle.
T3-cyl 650 nhp by Wigham Richardson & Company, Newcastle.
Wm. Milburn & Co 1887-8, Anglo-Australasian Steam Navigation Co Ltd, London, (Wm. Milburn & Co, Mgr) 1888-93.
1893: Sold J. Jover y Costas, Barcelona and r/n *Miguel Jover* (Spanish) 1893-1918.
1918: Sold Hijos de Jose Taya S. en C., Barcelona and r/n *P Claris* (Spanish) 1918-26.
1926: Broken up in La Spezia, Italy and awaiting demolition 5.4.1926.

Four vessels bore the name *Port Denison*. This was the first, one of the *Port Victor* class built in 1887. Port Denison was the original name for Bowen in Queensland. F.C. GOULD & SON

SSS *PORT FAIRY* 94340
2,539 gt, 1,645 n, 330.0 x 38.3 x 26.2, (100.6 x 11.7 x 8.0), 11k.
1887 by Wigham Richardson & Company, Newcastle.
T3-cyl 450 nhp by Wigham Richardson & Co, Newcastle.
J.D. Milburn, 1887-8, Wm. Milburn & Co, London, 1888-93.
1893: Sold J.H. Andresen, Oporto and r/n *Dona Maria* (Portugal) 1893-07.
1896: Ownership registered to Successors of J.H. Andresen. Oporto 1896-07 (same name).
1907: Sold The Booth Steam Ship Co Ltd, Liverpool, and r/n *Port Fairy* (British) 1907-09.
1909: Sold The Ellerman Lines Ltd, London, and r/n *Italian* (British) 1909-13.
6.5.1913: Arrived Preston for demolition by T.W. Ward Ltd.

One of the last of the three-masted, clipper bowed Milburn steamers was the *Port Fairy* of 1887. She was sold to Spanish owners six years later. F.C. GOULD & SON

SSS *PORT CAROLINE*
3,513 gt, 2,291 n, 375.0 x 42.2 x 28.5, (114.3 x 12.9 x 9.0), 11k.
1888 by R.&W. Hawthorn, Leslie & Co Ltd, Newcastle.
T3-cyl 600 nhp by Wigham Richardson & Co, Newcastle.
Laid down and launched as *Port Caroline* for Wm. Milburn & Co, but sold before completion to the Russian Volunteer Fleet Association, Odessa and r/n *Kostroma* (Russia) 1888-1913.
25.5.1905: Captured as Russian hospital ship in Tsushima Strait during Russian-Japanese war and released by Japanese 12.6.1905.
7.9.1913: Wrecked at Karantinskaia Kosa (Kamchatka) on passage Vladivostok to the east coast of Kamchatka.

SSS *PORT CAROLINE* 95529
3,528 gt, 2,130 n, 378.5 x 44.1 x 28.2, (115.4 x 13.4 x 8.6), 11k.
1889 by W. Dobson & Co, Newcastle.
T3-cyl 600 nhp by Wigham Richardson & Co, Newcastle.
Wm. Milburn & Co, London, 1889-90, Anglo-Australasian Steam Navigation Co Ltd, London (Wm. Milburn & Co, mgr) 1890-3.
1893: Sold Hijo de J. Jover y Serra, Barcelona and r/n *J. Jover Serra* (Spanish) 1893-1918.
1894: Ownership transferred to J. Jover y Costas, Barcelona (same name).
1918: Ownership transferred Hijos de Jose Taya S. en C., Barcelona and r/n *Roger de Lluria* (Spanish) 1918-20.
11.4.1920: Caught fire in No 3 hold on passage Havana to Barcelona and grounded at Santa Cruz de Teneriffe 13.4.1920. By 15.4.1920 all holds full of water, back broken 18.6.1920, and abandoned as total loss.

SSS *PORT ALBERT* 98966
4,140 gt, 2,652 n, 371.4 x 46.2 x 26.1, (113.2 x 14.1 x 8.0), 10k.
1891 by W. Dobson & Company, Newcastle.
T3-cyl 297 nhp by Wallsend Slipway & Engineering Co, Newcastle.
Wm. Milburn & Co, Newcastle 1891-4.
1894: Sold Japanese Government (Ministry of the Navy) and r/n *Kagoshima Maru* (Jopan) 1894-18.
1896: Ownership transferred Nippon Yusen Kabushiki Kaisha, Tokyo 1896-10 (same name).
1910: Sold Harada Shoko, Osaka, later Harada Kisen Kaisha, Osaka (same name).
1.1918: Went missing on passage Saigon to Port Said.

The *Port Albert,* built in 1891, was a new design, but only had three years on the Australian run before becoming one of the early ships of the Nippon Yusen Kaisha, of Tokyo. F.C. GOULD & SON

SSS *PORT CHALMERS* 98973
4,154 gt, 2,667 n, 371.0 x 46.1 x 27.7, (113.1 x 14.1 x 8.4), 11k.
1891 by J.L. Thompson & Sons, Sunderland.
T3-cyl 459 nhp by J. Dickinson, Sunderland.
Ins. cap 91,120 cf (2,581)
W. Milburn & Co, London, 1891-96.
27.7. 1895: Struck iceberg in position 44.55S, 52.23E, bowsprit, figurehead and damage to bow plating. Vessel was on passage from London to Adelaide and pumps were continuously in service until arrival in Adelaide. Repairs at Sydney involved stripping 32 plates, taking out 12 frames and reverse frames from keel to top-gallant as well as considerable other steelwork, fitting new bowsprit and figurehead.
1896: Sold Federal Steam Navigation Co Ltd, London, 1896-8.
1898: Sold United States Government and r/n *Delmonico* 6.8.1898, *Glacier* 12.8.1898-41.
1922: Sold Barde Steel & Machinery Co, Seattle (same name) 1922-4.
1924: Sold Northern Fisheries Inc., San Francisco (same name) 1924-38.
1938: Sold Alaska Salmon Co, San Francisco (same name) 1938-41.
1941: Sold Carbella Steam Ship Co, Panama (Bulk Carriers Corp, New York, mgr) and r/n *Carbella* (Panama) 1941-44.
1944: Sold Cia. Continental de Navegacion S.A.de C.V., Vera Cruz and r/n *Presidente Juarez* (Mexico) 1945-51.
1949: Sold Cia. Mexicana de Navegacion, Vera Cruz 1949-51 (same name).
1951: Sold Cia de Exportacion e Importacion Mexicana S.A., Vera Cruz.
28.11.1955: Beached Shelley Bay, Bermuda when cargo shifted in heavy weather while on passage to Rotterdam. Vessel had been sold to British Iron & Steel Corp, London, for demolition on completion of discharge.
3.3.1956: Left Bermuda for Rotterdam under tow of tug *Tyne* (1944, 386), arriving 4.1956. Following discharge of cargo vessel towed to Inverkeithing by tug *Rode Zee* (1949, 500) allocated by BISCO to T.W. Ward Ltd. Arrived Inverkeithing for demolition 22.4.1956.

The *Port Chalmers* was a sister ship to the *Port Albert*. She is shown here at Sydney as the United States Government store ship *Glacier*. Originally built in 1891, she saw service under several owners and flags and was not broken up until 1956. WM. LIVERMORE

SSS *PORT DOUGLAS* 99000
4,285 gt, 2,744 n, 371.5 x 46.1 x 26.3, (113.2 x 14.1 x 8.0), 11k.
1891 by Sir James Laing, Sunderland.
T3-cyl 529 nhp by G. Clark & Co, Newcastle.
Ins. cap circa 90,000 cf (2,549).
W. Milburn & Co, London, 1891-2.
27.11.1891: On passage London to Melbourne, in position 40.30S, 88.30E, three blades of propeller broke off, and completed balance of voyage under canvas arriving Melbourne 15.12.1891.
24.5.1892: Stranded on reef off Cape Verde Island, on passage London to Melbourne and became total loss.

SSS *PORT MELBOURNE* 101940
4,670 gt, 3,011 n, 360.4 x 48.0 x 26.2, (109.8 x 14.6 x 8.0), 11k.
1892 by R.&W. Hawthorn, Leslie & Co Ltd, Newcastle.
T3-cyl 529 nhp by R.&W. Hawthorn, Leslie Co Ltd, Newcastle.
Ins. cap 96,112 cf (2,722).
Anglo-Australasian Steam Navigation Co Ltd, London (Wm. Milburn & Co, mgr) 1892-9.
1899: Went missing on passage New York to London, while under charter to National Line, Liverpool Last reported 27.1.1899.

The *Port Melbourne* (1892) was the first of a new class of steamer for the Australian trade. She is shown passing Port Chalmers in January 1895 on her only visit while on a voyage from Calcutta to New Zealand. Four years later she disappeared at sea. DE MAUS

SSS *PORT HUNTER* 101958
4,670 gt, 3,011 n, 360.4 x 48.0 x 26.2 , (109.8 x 14.6 x 8.0), 11k.
1892 by R.&W. Hawthorn, Leslie & Co Ltd, Newcastle.
T3-cyl 529 nhp by R.&W. Hawthorn, Leslie & Co Ltd, Newcastle.
Anglo-Australasian Steam Navigation Co Ltd, London (Wm. Milburn & Co, mgr)1892-4.
1894: Sold Japanese Government (Ministry of the Navy) and r/n *Riojun Maru* (Japan) 1894-21.
1896: Ownership transferred Nippon Yusen Kabushiki Kaisha, Tokyo 1896-09.
1909: Sold Harada Shoko Goshi Shosen Kaisha, Osaka 1909-13.
1913: Transferred Harada Shoko Goshi Kaisha, Osaka 1913-7.
1917: Transferred Harada Kisen Kabushiki Kaisha, Osaka1917-21.
28.5.1921: Stranded on reef and sank 45 miles north of Gaspar Strait, on passage Dairen to Batavia (Jakarta).

SSS *PORT ELLIOT* 102848
3,556 gt, 2,295 n, 345.5 x 44.1 x 27.5, (105.3 x 13.4 x 8.4), 11k.
1894 by W. Dobson & Co, Newcastle.
T3-cyl 288 nhp by Wallsend Slipway Co Ltd, Newcastle.
W. Milburn & Co, London, 1894-95, Anglo-Australasian Steam Navigation Co Ltd, London, 1895-06.
25.5.1905 Broke propeller blade during gale on passage London to Adelaide and had to reduce speed to 3-6 knots arriving Adelaide 20.6.1905, a fortnight overdue.
1906: Sold Cie Royal Belgo-Argentine, Antwerp (Armement Adolph Deppe, mgr) and r/n *Republica Argentina* (Belgium) 1906-33.
1933: Sold Orazio Rossini, for breaking up and arrived Genoa 25.7.1933 for demolition.

The *Port Elliot*, built in 1894, was named after an historic port on Encounter Bay, approximately 91 kilometres south of Adelaide. The photograph was taken in Adelaide. F.E. WEAR

SSS ***PORT STEPHENS*** 102853
3,554 gt, 2,278 n, 345.0 x 44.1 x 26.0, (105.2 x 13.4 x 7.9), 11k.
1894 by J.L. Thompson & Sons, Sunderland.
T3-cyl 287 nhp by J Dickinson, Sunderland.
Wm. Milburn & Co, London, 1894-95, Australasian Steam Navigation Co Ltd, London (Wm. Milburn & Co, mgr) 1895-06.
3.10.1906: Tail shaft broke on passage Oamaru, New Zealand, to Newcastle, N.S.W., in position 45.50S, 164.04E. After drifting 229 miles south to latitude 49.20S, crew taken off by barque *Ravenscroft* 8.10.1906 and vessel abandoned drifting south in position 49.21S, 164.48E.

SSS ***PORT HUNTER*** 105734
3,552 gt, 2,297 n, 346.0 x 44.0 x 18.3, (105.5 x 13.4 x 5.6), 11k.
1895 by W. Dobson & Company, Newcastle.
T3-cyl 289 nhp by North Eastern Marine Co Ltd, Newcastle.
Wm. Milburn & Co, London, 1895-7.
1897: Sold Gordon Steam Shipping Co Ltd, London (R. Gordon & Co, London, mgr) and r/n *Dargai* (British) 1897-14.
28.8.1914: Stranded on English Bank, Montevideo on passage Hull to Montevideo; became total loss.

SSS ***PORT DENISON*** 105896
3,435 gt, 2,188 n, 345.0 x 46.0 x 17.0, 105.2 x 14.0 x 5.2), 11k.
1896 by Tyne Iron Shipbuilding Co Ltd, Newcastle.
T3-cyl 322 nhp by J. Dickinson & Sons, Sunderland.
Wm. Milburn & Co, London, 1896-07.
1907: Sold The Bede Steam Ship Co Ltd, Newcastle (Frew, Elder & Co, mgr) and r/n *Bedeburn* (British) 1907-18.
1915: Sold the Kent Steam Ship Co Ltd, London, (S. Walton, London, mgr) (same name).
1918 Sold Britain Steamship Co Ltd London (Watts, Watts & Co Ltd, mgr) and r/n *Chiswick* (British) 1919-29.
1929: Sold Sea & Land Securities Ltd, London (same name) and resold Jaunsem & Co, Riga. R/n *Zigurds* (Latvia) 1929-31. Arrested and sold by Admiralty order to Felipe F. Aguado, Santander, 1931, and r/n *Santa Marta* (Panama) 1931-34.
10.3.1934: Left Ravenna, Italy in tow for Venice for demolition.

A second *Port Denison* entered service in 1896 and remained in the Australian trade until sold to other British owners in 1907. She is pictured here at Adelaide. F.E. WEAR

SSS *PORT ALBERT* 108207
3,514 gt, 2,250 n, 345.0 x 46.0 x 26.0, (105.2 x 14.0 x 7.9), 11k.
1897 by Tyne Iron Shipbuilding Co Ltd, Newcastle.
T3-cyl 297 nhp by North Eastern Marine Co Ltd, Newcastle.
W. Milburn & Company, London, 1897-06.
1906: Sold Aktiebolaget Sydafrikanska Handels Komp. Stockholm (M. Wallenberg, mgr) and r/n *Delagoa* (Swedish) 1906-10.
11.4.1910: Ran ashore on Minicoy Island, Laccadives on passage Singapore to Gothenburg; became total wreck.

The name of *Port Albert* was also repeated and this is the 1897 ship. Sold to Swedish owners in 1906, she was wrecked four years later.

SSS *PORT PHILLIP* 108243
3,103 gt, 1,971 n, 324.8 x 48.5 x 22.8, (99.0 x 14.8 x 6.9), 11k.
1897 by Tyne Iron Shipbuilding Co Ltd, Newcastle.
T3-cyl 279 nhp by North Eastern Marine Co Ltd, Newcastle.
W. Milburn & Co, London, 1897-00.
1900: Sold Buenos Ayres Great Southern Rail Co, London (Arthur Holland & Co, mgr) and r/n *Sola* (British) 1900-12.
23.12.1912 Sailed Newport, Mon. for Buenos Aires and went missing. A lifeboat and three bodies were found near the Lizard and the official inquiry believed she had foundered in a strong westerly gale off the southern coast of England 26.12.1912.

SSS *PORT VICTORIA* 108266
3,378 gt, 2,195 n, 354.0 x 48.5 x 23.8, (107.9 x 14.8 x 7.3), 11k.
1897 by J.L. Thompson & Sons, Sunderland.
T3-cyl 326 nhp by J. Dickinson & Sons Ltd, Sunderland.
Anglo-Australasian Steam Navigation Co Ltd, London (Wm. Milburn & Co, mgr) 1897-07.
1907: Sold Russian Commercial Steam Ship Co, Mariupol (Peter Regier & Sons, mgr) and r/n *Belorossia* (Russian) 1908-18. Requisitioned by Imperial Russian Navy 3.1915 in the Black Sea as *Transport N10.*
25.3.1918: Adrift in Black Sea after engine breakdown in bad weather and drifted towards Bulgarian coast; captured by Bulgaria.
1918: Bulgarian government as *Dobrudzha* (Bulgaria) 1918, returned to owners and r/n *Belorossia* (Russia) 11.1918-1920.
1920: Transferred to Anglo-Commercial Shipping Co Ltd, Newcastle upon Tyne (E.P. Martin, Newcastle, mgr 1920, William S. Walton, London 1920-26) and r/n *Balderton* (British) 1920-26.
1926: Sold to Parabrodarsko Akcionarske Drustvo 'Progres', Split, r/n *Poredak* (Yugoslavia) 1927-33.
4. 3.1933 Arrived Savona, Italy for demolition.

This family gathering in Adelaide in June 1906 has the first steamer named *Port Victoria* in the background. *Port Victoria* was a port on the south east of the Spencer Gulf, South Australia. F.E. WEAR

SSS *PORT PHILLIP* 118499
5,561 gt, 3,550 n, 420.7 x 54.0 x 28.6, (128.2 x 16.5 x 8.7), 11k.
1904 by R.&W. Hawthorn, Leslie & Co Ltd, Newcastle.
T3-cyl 518 nhp by North Eastern Marine Engineering Co Ltd, Newcastle.
Laid down as *Port Phillip* for Wm. Milburn & Company for employment on the Anglo-Australasian Steam Navigation Co Ltd, berth but sold prior to completion to the Federal Steam Navigation Co Ltd, London (Allan Hughes, mgr) and r/n *Durham* 1904-24.
10.3.1906: Collision with steamer *Indian* (1900, 9,121) off Bardsley Heads, on passage Liverpool to Australia and returned for repairs.
1924: Sold Andrea Zanchi, Genoa and r/n *Augusta* (Italian) 1924-41.
10.6.1940: Interned at Bahia and seized by Brazilian government 12.1941. Allocated to Lloyd Brasileiro, Rio de Janiero and r/n *Minasloide* (Brazil) 1941-50.
1950: Returned to Andrea Zanchi, Genoa and r/n *Augusta* (Italian) 1950.
15.5.1950: Arrived La Spezia in tow and subsequently demolished by S.A. Cantieri de Portovenere from 6.8.1950.

SSS ***PORT JACKSON*** 119128
5,505 gt, 3,512 n, 420.6 x 54.0 x 28.6 (128.2 x 16.5 x 8.7), 11k.
1904 by R.&W. Hawthorn, Leslie & Co Ltd, Newcastle.
T3-cyl, 505 nhp by North Eastern Marine Engineering Co Ltd, Newcastle.
Launched as *Port Jackson* for Wm. Milburn & Co for employment on the Anglo-Australasian Steam Navigation Co Ltd, berth but sold prior to completion to British India Steam Navigation Co Ltd, London, r/n *Waipara* (1904-24).
25.8.1909: Struck Smith's Rock, 2 miles north of Cape Moreton, Queensland, beached and refloated a week later and taken to Brisbane for repairs.
23.5.1914: Grounded on reef, between Hannibal Island and Great Barrier reef and after jettisoning 300 tons of cargo was towed clear on 27.5.1914 by HMS *Fantome* and proceeded to Townsville.
4.8.1918: Torpedoed by *UC 71*, 16 miles off Dunnose Head, English Channel, on passage Havre to Southampton. Abandoned but later reboarded and beached off Netley. Salved and repaired.
28.8.1923: Sold shipbreakers and left London 7.9.1923 in tow for Rotterdam for demolition by T.C. Pas in 1924.

SSS ***PORT CAROLINE*** 120587
4,076 gt, 2,640 n, 380.6 x 49.0 x 25.7, (116.0 x 14.9 x 7.8), 11k.
1905 by R.&W. Hawthorn, Leslie & Co Ltd, Newcastle.
T3-cyl 434 nhp by North Eastern Marine Engineering Co Ltd, Newcastle.
Anglo-Australasian Steam Navigation Co Ltd, London (Wm. Milburn & Co,mgr) 1905-14.
1914: Sold Soc. Veneziana di Nav.a Vapore., Venice and r/n *Loredano* (Italian) 1914-32.
1932: Sold Industrie Navali Soc. Anon (I.N.S.A.), Genoa and r/n *Parisina* (Italian) 1932-4.
1934: Sold Italian shipbreakers and arrived Savona for demolition 14.4.1934.

This photograph of the *Port Caroline* (1905) at Adelaide also has the tall chimney (1889-1910) of the Junction Smelting Works in the background. She was named after Port Caroline, a non-commercial port in Lacepede Bay, South Australia. F.E. WEAR

SSS *PORT CHALMERS* 120598
4,077 gt, 2,602 n, 380.5 x 49.0 x 25.7 (116.0 x 14.9 x 7.8) 11k.
1905 by R.&W. Hawthorn, Leslie & Co Ltd, Newcastle.
T3-cyl 434 nhp by North Eastern Marine Engineering Co Ltd, Newcastle.
Anglo-Australasian Steam Navigation Co Ltd, London (Wm. Milburn & Co, mgr) 1905-12.
15.8.1906: On passage Newcastle to Manila, stranded Ulrua reef, entrance to Albany Pass, Torres Strait, refloated 23.8.06. Repairs completed and resumed voyage 1.9.1906.
6.5.1907: Struck submerged wrecks of *Norma* & *Jessie Darling* off Semaphore, South Australia, causing hull damage which was repaired Sydney.
12.9.1909: Bound Tees for London, in collision with *Ailsa Craig* (1890, 3,451) off Great Yarmouth with extensive damage to No 5 hold on *Port Chalmers.*
25.4.1910: Struck by tidal wave rounding Cape of Good Hope, causing extensive on deck damage.
1912: Sold Thos. Law & Co, Glasgow (William Law, mgr) 1912-14 and r/n *Duns Law* 1912-14.
27.1.1913: In collision with *Miramichi* (1902, 3,624) 20 miles south of Portland Bill, with *Miramichi* beached at Portland.
4.8.1914: Seized by Germany at Nordenham and abandoned to insurers. Under German control she became the naval auxiliary *Senta,* and fitted out as auxiliary minelayer in 2.1917.
1918: Recovered and sold by the North of England P&I Club, to The Dalgliesh Steam Shipping Company Ltd, Newcastle (R.S. Dalgliesh, mgr) and r/n *Ravensworth* 1919-29.
20.4.1928: Arrived Shields and laid up. Sold shipbreakers and left in tow for Inverkeithing, arriving 3.5.1929 for demolition. Believed resold to Maison Grosos Fils of France 4.1929 and likely broken up Le Havre 1929-30.

SSS *PORT HUNTER* 123689
4,062 gt, 2,589 n, 380.5 x 49.1 x 25.7, (116.0 x 15.0 x 7.8), 11k.
1906 by R.&W. Hawthorn, Leslie & Co Ltd, Newcastle.
T3-cyl 442 nhp by R.&W. Hawthorn, Leslie & Co Ltd, Newcastle.
W. Milburn & Co Ltd, London, 1906-14.
16.12.1909: On passage Adelaide to London, propeller seized, Red Sea, north of Farisan Islands in position 18.4N,40.9E and towed 833 miles by *Ambon* (1901,3,598) to Suez 16-22.12.1909.
1914: Transferred to C&D Line Ltd, London 1914-18 (same name).
2.11.1918: Sunk in collision with U.S. tug *Covington* (1899, 401) off Vineyard Haven, Nantucket Sound in position 41.29N, 70.33W on passage Boston to St. Nazaire, subsequently beached and salvage abandoned.

The *Port Hunter*, anchored in Sydney harbour, was one of six similar ships built in 1905-6. Port Hunter was the original name for Newcastle. WM. LIVERMORE

SSS ***PORT AUGUSTA*** 123696
4,063 gt, 2,587 n, 380.6 x 49.1 x 25.7, (116.0 x 15.0 x 7.8), 11k.
1906 by R.&W. Hawthorn, Leslie & Co Ltd, Newcastle.
T3-cyl 481 nhp by R.&W. Hawthorn, Leslie & Co Ltd, Newcastle.
Anglo-Australasian Steam Navigation Co Ltd, London, 1906-14.
1914: Transferred to C&D Line Ltd, London, 1914-25.
2.5.1916: In gun battle with German submarine in Bay of Biscay, but escaped with minor damage.
19.9.1921: On passage New York to Fremantle, had serious fire in No 2 Hold bunker in position 27.0S, 9.0E, 700 miles northwest of Cape Town, arriving 23.9.1921, where the fire was not extinguished until 27.9.1921.
13..9.1924: On passage Port Pirie to Antwerp arrived Port Natal leaking in No 2 ballast tank since off Cape Leeuwin, believed to have been caused by earlier grounding at Port Pirie. Resumed voyage 16.9.1924.
7.10.1925: Sold William Thomas Shipping Co Ltd, London, (R.J. Thomas & Co Ltd, London, mgr) and r/n *Cambrian Countess* 1925-31.
1931: Broken up by P & W McLellan at Bo'ness 7.1931.

SSS ***PORT PHILLIP*** 123708
4,060 gt, 2,586 n, 380.4 x 49.1 x 25.7, (115.9 x 14.7 x 7.8), 11k.
1906 by R.&W. Hawthorn, Leslie & Co Ltd, Newcastle.
T3-cyl 442 nhp by R.&W. Hawthorn, Leslie & Co Ltd, Newcastle.
W. Milburn & Co Ltd, London, 1906-14.
1914: Transferred C&D Line Ltd, London 1914-18.
16.10.1918: On passage New York to Le Havre sunk in collision with USS *Proteus* (1900, 10,653) in Ambrose Channel, New York; beached in shallow water in Gravesend Bay and became total loss.

The *Port Phillip* of 1906, lies anchored in Sydney harbour on 27 January 1908, fully dressed for the annual regatta day which is now linked to the annual Australia Day on 26 January. The P&O liner *Macedonia* on the right of the photograph was flagship for the regatta. WM. LIVERMORE

SSS *PORT PIRIE* 125615
4,068 gt, 2,574 n, 380.3 x 49.0 x 25.7,(115.9 x 14.9 x 7.8), 11k.
1907 by R.&W. Hawthorn,Leslie & Co Ltd, Newcastle.
T3-cyl 435 nhp by North Eastern Marine Engineering Co Ltd, Newcastle.
Anglo-Australasian Steam Navigation Co Ltd, London, (Wm. Milburn & Co, mgr) 1907-14.
1914: Transferred C&D Line Ltd, London, 1914-15.
1915: Sold Glasgow Steam Shipping Co Ltd, Glasgow (J. Black & Co, mgr), r/n *Kelvinbrae* 1915-24.
1920: Sold Romney Steamship Co Ltd, London (Fawcett, Coverdale & Co, mgr), r/n *Darnley* 1924-5.
1925: Sold Britain Steamship Co Ltd, London (Watts, Watts & Co Ltd, mgr), r/n *Laleham* 1925-6.
31.3.1926: Sprang a leak in North Atlantic on passage San Antonio, Chile to UK via Norfolk, Va. and abandoned sinking in position 37.06N, 55.18W. Crew taken off by steamer *Shirvan* (1925, 6,017). Sank 1.4.1926.

The last of the series of six, the *Port Pirie*, was the first ship sold by the Commonwealth & Dominion Line. With the high prices prevailing for second hand tonnage during World War I, she passed to other British owners in 1915. A.C. GREEN

SSS *PORT CURTIS* 129118
4,710 gt, 2,998 n, 400.6 x 52.7 x 26.2, (122.1 x 16.1 x 8.0), 11k.
1910 by R.&W. Hawthorn, Leslie & Co Ltd, Newcastle.
Q4-cyl 590 nhp by North Eastern Marine Engineering Co Ltd, Newcastle.
C.T. Milburn, London (W.Milburn & Co) 1910-14.
1914: Transferred C&D Line Ltd, London 1914-17.
7.8.1917: Captured by *UC 71* and sunk by time bombs in position 47.30N, 6.00W, 70 miles west of Penmarch, France on passage Bahia Blanca to Brest.

No further Milburn ships were built for the Australian trade from 1907 until the *Port Curtis* in 1910. This first 'Port' steamer was named after an historic coal port in Queensland, near Gladstone.

SSS ***PORT KEMBLA*** 129131
4,700 gt, 2,990 n, 400.6 x 52.7 x 26.2, (122.1 x 16.1 x 8.0),12k.
1910 by R.&W. Hawthorn, Leslie & Co Ltd, Newcastle.
Q4-cyl 590 nhp by North Eastern Marine Engineering Co Ltd Newcastle.
Ins. cap 129,000 cf (from 1914) (3,653).
Anglo-Australasian Steam Navigation Co Ltd, London 1910-14.
1914: Transferred C&D Line Ltd, London 1914-17.
18.9.1917: Struck mine laid by German commerce raider *Wolf* (1913, 5,809) 11 miles off Cape Farewell, New Zealand, on passage Melbourne (sailed 12.9.1917) to London.

SSS ***PORT LINCOLN*** 132733
7,243 gt, 4,638 n, 426.0 x 54.1 x 29.3, (139.7 x 16.5 x 8.9), 12.5k.
1912 by R.&W. Hawthorn, Leslie & Co Ltd, Newcastle.
Q4-cyl 777 nhp by North Eastern Marine Engineering Co Ltd, Newcastle.
Ins. cap 4,850 cf (137).
Wm. Milburn & Co Ltd, London 1912-14.
1914: Transferred C&D Line Ltd, London 1914-27.
1927 Sold William Thomas Shipping Co Ltd, London (R.J. Thomas & Co Ltd, mgr) and r/n *Cambrian Baroness* 1927-9.
1928: Sold C.W. Kellock & Co Ltd, London (same name).
1929: Sold Clan Line Steamers Ltd, Glasgow and r/n *Clan Graham* 1929-38.
1935: Transferred British & South American Steam Nav. Co Ltd, (Houston Line (London) Ltd, mgr).
1938: Sold Neill & Pandelis Ltd, (G.O. Till, mgr) London and r/n *Maritima* 1938-42.
2.11.1942: On passage New York to Glasgow torpedoed and sunk by *U-522*, 500 miles NE of St Johns, Newfoundland in position 52.20N, 45.40W.

SSS *PORT MACQUARIE* 135132
7,236 gt, 4,638 n, 426.0 x 54.1 z 29.3, (129.8 x 16.5 x 8.9), 12.5k.
1912 by R.&W. Hawthorn, Leslie & Co Ltd, Newcastle.
Q4-cyl 777 nhp by North Eastern Marine Engineering Co Ltd, Newcastle.
Ins. cap 4,850 cf (137).
Anglo-Australasian Steam Navigation Co Ltd, London. (Wm. Milburn & Co, mgr) 1912-14.
1914: Transferred C&D Line Ltd, London, 1914-27.
6.4.1920: Broke adrift at Newport News, colliding with *Lake Inaha* (1919, 2,622), grounded on sandbank and later refloated with damage to hull plating.
1927: Sold William Thomas Shipping Co Ltd, London (R.J. Thomas & Co Ltd, mgr); r/n *Cambrian Marchioness* 1927-9.
1928: Sold C.W. Kellock & Co Ltd, London (same name).
1929: Sold Clan Line Steamers Ltd, Glasgow (Cayzer, Irvine & Co Ltd, mgr); r/n *Clan Grant* 1929-38.
1935: Transferred British & South American Steam Nav. Co Ltd, (Houston Line (London) Ltd, mgr).
1938: Sold Stanhope Steamship Co Ltd, London (J.A. Billmeir & Co Ltd, mgr); r/n *Stangrant* 1938-40.
13.10.1940: On passage Hampton Roads to Belfast torpedoed and sunk by *U-37,* 220 miles west of the Butt of Lewis in position 58.27N, 12.36W.

The *Port Lincoln*'s sister ship, the *Port Macquarie* entered service in September 1912. E. FLUCK

SSS *PORT ALBANY* 136676
5,714 gt, 3,620 n 426.3 x 54.1 x 29.3 (129.9 x 16.5 x 8.9) 13k.
1914 by R.&W. Hawthorn, Leslie & Co Ltd, Newcastle.
Q 4-cyl 767 nhp by North Eastern Marine Engineering Co Ltd, Newcastle.
Ins. cap 229,870 cf (6,510).
Laid down for W. Milburn & Co, London, but completed for the C&D Line Ltd, London, 1914-29.
7.11.1923: While lying at Hull had serious fire in coal bunker.
1929: Sold Union Cold Storage Co Ltd, London (Blue Star Line (1920) Ltd, 1929-30, Blue Star Line Ltd 1930-34, mgr) and r/n *Oregonstar* 1929, then *Oregon Star* 1929-34.
13.11.1932: Caught fire while under repair at Palmer's Shipbuilding & Iron Co Ltd, Hebburn.
17.11.1932: Fire finally extinguished and declared constructive total loss on 24.11.1932. Lay idle in the River Tyne until she was sold to Hughes Bolckow Ltd for demolition at Blyth (arriving 1.5.1934).

Section 6

COMMONWEALTH & DOMINION LINE LTD, LONDON 1914-1937, PORT LINE LTD, LONDON, 1937-1991

(Vessels built for the company or on long term charter)

TSS *PORT DARWIN* 140446

8,179 gt, 5,137 n, 500.5/480.4 x 60.3 x 40.8, (152.5/146.4 x 18.4 x 12.4), 14k, 10p.
1918 by Workman, Clark & Co, Belfast
T2-3cyl 809 nhp by Workman, Clark & Co Ltd, Belfast (Bauer-Wach turbs fitted 1929).
Ins. cap 316,690 cf increasing to 351,772 cf (8,969-9,962).
C&D Line Ltd, London, 1918-37, Port Line Ltd, London, 1937-49.
28.8.1940: Collided with, and sank, *Driebergen* (1923. 5,231) in position 55.25N, 1.22W and returned to Shields for repair of bow damage.
18.10.1941: On passage Methil to New York, caught fire at sea, proceeded to New York where repairs took 3 weeks.
1949: Sold British Iron & Steel Corp; arrived Barrow for demolition by T.W. Ward & Co, 5.8.1949.

TSS *PORT DENISON* 142397

8,191 gt, 5,152 n, 500.5/480.4 x 60.3 x 32.3,,(152.5/146.4 x 18.4 x 9.8), 14k, 10p.
1918 by Workman, Clark & Co, Belfast.
T2-3 cyl 809 nhp by Workman, Clark & Co Ltd, Belfast (Bauer-Wach turbs fitted 1929).
Ins. cap 316,676 cf increasing to 352,656 cf (8,968-9,987)
C&D Line Ltd, London, 1918-37, Port Line Ltd, London, 1937-40.
26.9.1940: Bombed and sunk 27.9.1940 by a German aircraft in position six miles NE of Peterhead, Scotland on passage Methil, Fife to New Zealand.

A sister ship of the *Port Darwin*, delivered in April 1918 as the *Port Denison*, is shown outward bound from Adelaide, fully laden, with the last derricks being dropped for the passage home. E. FLUCK

TSS *PORT NICHOLSON* 143058
8,402 gt, 5,338 n, 481.2 x 62.3 x 33.0, (146.7 x 19.0 x 10.0), 14k, 12p.
1919 by Hawthorn, Leslie & Co, Newcastle.
4 steam turbs SR geared to 2 screw shafts, 967 nhp by Hawthorn, Leslie & Co Ltd, Newcastle.
Ins. cap 328,593 cf increasing to 386,997 cf. (9,306-10,960).
C&D Line Ltd, London, 1919-37, Port Line Ltd, London. 1937-42.
23.10.1924: On passage London to Sydney, struck rock off Isleta, Las Palmas, refloated 3.11.1924, grounded again and refloated 6.11.1924.
22.12.1924: Left Las Palmas for Shields under tow of tug *Roode Zee* (1908, 573) arriving Tilbury en route 9.1.1925.
21.7.1928: On passage Brisbane to London, put into Gibraltar with frozen meat cargo in No 5 hold heating. Fire extinguished 22.7.1928.
9.6.1938: Collided with, and sank tug *Ocean Cock* (1932,182) off Gravesend outward bound London to Australia.
16.6.1942: Torpedoed by *U-87* east of Cape Cod in position 42.11N, 69.25W on passage Halifax, Nova Scotia to Boston and vessel sank 17.6.1942.

TSS *PORT BOWEN* 143202
8,267 gt, 5,110 n, 480.7 x 62.4 x 32.9, (146.5 x 19.0 x 10.0), 14k, 12p.
1919 by Workman, Clark & Co, Belfast.
4 steam turbs SR geared to 2 screw shafts, 1001 nhp by Workman, Clark & Co, Belfast (conv. 6 steam turbs 1922).
Ins. cap 316,665 cf increasing to 375,225 cf. (8,968-10,626).
C&D Line Ltd, London, 1919-37, Port Line Ltd, London. 1937-39.
13.10.1933: Slight damage in collision with *Tanimbar* (1930, 8,169) off Wandelaar Light Vessel, River Schelde inward bound to Antwerp from Adelaide.
19.7.1939: Grounded in Wanganui Roadstead, off Castlecliff Beach, Wanganui on passage Picton to Wanganui; abandoned to the underwriters 10.1939. Wreck progressively removed and work completed 8.1943.

TSS *PORT CAROLINE* 143790
8,263 gt, 5,108 n, 480.7 x 62.4 x 32.9, (146.5 x 19.0 x 10.0), 14k, 12p.
1919 by Workman, Clark & Co, Belfast.
4 steam turbs DR geared to 2 screw shafts. 1001 nhp by Workman, Clark & Co, Belfast (Conv. 6 Steam turbs 1922).
Ins. cap 326,719 cf increasing to 378,483 cf. (9,253-10,719).
C&D Line Ltd, London, 1919-37, Port Line Ltd, London, 1937-50.
31.10.1949: Employed as floating frozen meat storage vessel at London until 5.2.1950.
1950: Sold British Iron and Steel Corp and allocated to Hughes Bolckow Shipbreaking Co Ltd, arriving Blyth under tow 21.2.1950 for demolition.

The third *Port Caroline* entered service in November 1919 and survived World War II, being finally broken up 31 years later. The photograph shows her at Liverpool. B. & A. FIELDEN

TSS ***PORT ADELAIDE*** 143949
8,422 gt, 5,350 n, 481.2 x 62.3 x 33.0 (146.7 x 19.0 x 10.0), 14k, 12p.
1919 by Hawthorn, Leslie & Co, Newcastle .
4 steam turbs DR geared to 2 screw shafts, 967 nhp by Hawthorn, Leslie & Co, Newcastle (conv. 6 steam turbs 1922).
Ins. cap 327,228 cf increasing to 377,217 cf. (9,267-10,683).
C&D Line Ltd, London 1919-37, Port Line Ltd, London 1937-49.
1.1944: Collided with *Julesburg* (1943, 10,172) in New York Harbour; repairs took 16 days.
1949: Sold British Iron & Steel Corp and arrived Inverkeithing 21.8.1949 for demolition by T.W. Ward Ltd, with work commencing 14.10.1949.

The *Port Adelaide*, led by a tug, in her name port of Adelaide. E. FLUCK

SSS ***PORT CURTIS*** 144533
8,287 gt, 5,155 n, 450.2 x 58.4 x 37.1, (137.2 x 17.8 x 11.3), 12k, 4p.
1920 by Workman, Clark & Co, Belfast.
2 steam turbs DR geared to 1 screw shaft. 892 nhp by Workman, Clark & Co, Belfast.
Re-engined 1936 T. 3 cyl 729 nhp by Palmer's Shipbuilding & Iron Co, Newcastle, with engine from tanker *San Manuel* (1922 5,923) and refrigerating machinery and insulation removed at the same time.
Ins. Cap 215,561 cf. (6,105).
Standard G class refrigerated meat carrier with intended name *War Thalia,* sold under construction to C&D Line Ltd, London, and completed as *Port Curtis* 1920-36.
1935: Sold Downs Steamship Co Ltd, London, (Counties Ship Management Co Ltd, mgr) and r/n *Tower Dale* (British) 1936-7.
1937: Sold to J. A. Zachariassen & Co, Nystad and r/n *Kronoborg* (Finland) 1937-45. Taken by USSR as war reparation from Finland. R/n *Kronshtadt* (USSR) 1945-70 and operated by Baltic State Shipping Co, Leningrad 1945-7, Far Eastern State Shipping Co, Vladivostok, 1947-67. (State dropped from name 1964).
1967: Sold Nav. Mar. Bulgare, Varna, and r/n *Algeneb* (Bulgaria) 1967-70.
25.4.1970: Arrived Bilbao for demolition by Spanish shipbreakers, Hierros Eduardo Varela, with work commencing 26.5.1970.

TSS ***PORT KEMBLA*** 144631
8,435 gt, 5,345 n, 481.2 x 62.3 x 33.0, (146.7 x 19.0 x 10.0), 14k, 12p.
1920 by Hawthorn, Leslie & Co, Newcastle.
4 Steam turbs DR geared to 2 screw shafts, 967 nhp by Hawthorn, Leslie & Co Ltd, Newcastle (Conv. 6 Steam turbs 1922).
Ins. cap 326,553 cf. (9,248).
C&D Line, London, 1920-6.
8.7.1926: Ran ashore on reef at San Salvador Island (Watling Island), West Indies, on passage London to Lyttelton via Norfolk, Va. Abandoned to underwriters 27.8.1926. All attempts at salvage failed and by 22.9.1926 *Port Kembla* had broken her back.

TSS ***PORT CAMPBELL*** 146580
8,308 gt, 5,123 n, 480.8 x 62.4 x 32.9, (146.5 x 19.0 x 10.0), 14k, 12p.
1922 by Workman, Clark & Co Ltd, Belfast.
T2-3-cyl, 1040 nhp by Workman, Clark & Co Ltd, Belfast (Bauer-Wach turbs fitted 1929).
Ins. cap 329,665 cf, increasing to 401,369 cf. (9,376-11,366).
C&D Line Ltd, London, 1922-37, Port Line Ltd, London, 1937-53.
1953: Sold British Iron & Steel Corp; allocated to T.W. Ward Ltd, arriving Briton Ferry 12.5.1953 for demolition.

TSS ***PORT AUCKLAND*** 146606
8,308 gt, 5,123 n, 480.8 x 62.4 x 32.9, (146.5 x 19.0 x 10.0), 14k, 12p.
1922 by Workman, Clark & Co Ltd, Belfast.
T2-3-cyl 859 nhp by Workman, Clark & Co Ltd, Belfast (Bauer-Wach turbs fitted 1928).
Ins. cap 330,576 cf increasing to 403,563 cf (9,362-11,429).

C&D Line Ltd, London, 1922-37, Port Line Ltd, London, 1937-43.
20.6.1923: Sailed Lyttelton for London and in position 51.8S, 146W encountered very heavy weather which buckled deck plates. Fully laden and down to her marks, the vessel was forced to return to Wellington for repairs, and arrived 30.6.1923. Sailed 8.7.1923, but put back to restow 3000 tons concentrates stowed No 3. Sailed for London 2.8.1923.
22.10.1923: In collision with *Fernhill* (1908, 2,399) near Blankenese, Hamburg. *Fernhill* sank but *Port Auckland* remained seaworthy. *Fernhill* later refloated and repaired.
6.7.1930: Coastwise out of London for Middlesbrough, was in collision with *Nutfield* (1919, 1,561) near Cross Sand Lighthouse, English Channel and *Nutfield* was badly damaged above the waterline on the starboard side.
15.9.1940: Shot down Junkers Ju-88 aircraft when manoeuvring in King George V dock, London.
3.5.1941: Suffered minor bomb damage at Liverpool.
7.6.1942: Holed in collision with *Historian* (1924, 5,074) while travelling in convoy and put into Falmouth for repairs.
17.3.1943: Torpedoed and sunk by *U-305* in North Atlantic, SE of Cape Farewell, in position 52.25N, 30.15W on passage Brisbane to Avonmouth in convoy.

TSS ***PORT HUNTER*** 146641
8,437 gt, 5,296 n, 481.2 x 62.3 x 33.0, (146.7 x 19.0 x 10.0), 14k, 12p.
1922 by Hawthorn, Leslie & Co Ltd, Newcastle.
6 Steam turbs DR geared to 2 screw shafts. 967 nhp by Hawthorn, Leslie & Co Ltd, Newcastle.
Ins. cap 315,843 cf, increasing to 390,597 cf. (8,945-11,062).
C&D Line Ltd, London ,1922-37, Port Line Ltd, London, 1937-42.
15.4.1940: While travelling in convoy, in collision with *Queen Maud* (1936, 4,976) and arrived Southampton 17.4.1940 for repairs.
11.7.1942: Torpedoed and sunk by *U-582* 500 miles NW of Canary Islands in position 31N, 24W while travelling independently on passage Liverpool to New Zealand.

TSS ***PORT HARDY*** 146697
8,705 gt, 5,431 n, 481.2 x 62.3 x 33.0, (146.7 x 19.0 x 10.0), 14k, 12p.
1923 by Hawthorn, Leslie & Co Ltd., Newcastle.
T2-3-cyl, 856 nhp by Hawthorn, Leslie & Co Ltd, Newcastle (Bauer-Wach turbs fitted 1928).
Ins. cap 302,886 cf increasing to 380,453 cf. (8,578-10,774).
C&D Line Ltd, London, 1923-37, Port Line Ltd, London, 1937-41.
27.3.1935: In collision with *Ville de Mostaganem* (1901, 966) in Dunkirk roads while on passage Geelong to Hull. Stem and several plates damaged and forecastle flooded. No cargo damage.
22.4.1940: In collision with *New Sevilla* (1900, 13,801); hull damage.
28.4.1941: Torpedoed and sunk by *U-96* north of Rockall in position 60.14N, 15.20W on passage Nova Scotia to United Kingdom in convoy.

TSS *PORT BRISBANE* 147563
8,315 gt, 5,077 n, 480.7 x 62.4 x 32.9, (146.5 x 19.0 x 10.0), 14k, 12p.
1923 by Workman, Clark & Co Ltd, Belfast.
T2-3-cyl 860 nhp by Workman, Clark & Co Ltd, Belfast (Bauer-Wach turbs fitted 1930).
Ins. cap 326,051 cf increasing to 401,715 cf. (9,234-11,377).
C&D Line Ltd, London, 1923-37, Port Line Ltd,London 1937-40.
21.11.1940: Captured in Indian Ocean by German commerce raider *Pinguin* and sunk with time bombs 22.11.1940 in position 29.29S, 95.35E on passage Adelaide to United Kingdom.

TSS *PORT WELLINGTON* 147589
7,868 gt, 4,784 n, 470.1 x 60.4 x 32.3, (143.3 x 18.4 x 9.8), 14k, 12p.
1924 by Workman, Clark & Co Ltd, Belfast.
T2-3-cyl 806 nhp by Workman, Clark & Co Ltd, Belfast (Bauer-Wach turbs fitted 1930).
Ins. cap 304,121 cf increasing to 380,453 cf. (8,613-10,774).
C&D Line Ltd, London, 1924-37, Port Line Ltd, London, 1937-40.
17.1.1937: Major fire in Victoria Dock, Melbourne, which extended to several outbreaks onboard and vessel towed clear of the berth and fires extinguished.
30.11.1940: Captured in South Indian Ocean by German commerce raider *Pinguin* and sunk with time bombs 1.12.1940 in position 32.10S, 75.00E (German position recorded as 31.10S, 70.37E) on passage Adelaide to UK.

The *Port Dunedin*, photographed at Brisbane in later years with her shorter funnel. W. ELLIOTT, V.H. YOUNG & L.A. SAWYER

TSMV *PORT DUNEDIN* 148599
7,463 gt, 4,453 n, 484.4/466.9 x 59.8 x 31.3, (147.6/142.3 x 18.2 x 9.5), 14k , 12p.
1925 by Workman, Clark & Co Ltd, Belfast.
2 S. C.S.A. 2- 4 cyl. 1,112 nhp by Wm. Doxford & Sons Ltd, Sunderland.
Ins. cap 297,644 cf, increasing to 347,690 cf., (8,429- 9,847).
C&D Line Ltd, London, 1925-37, Port Line Ltd, London, 1937-62.
7.12.1937: On passage London to Newcastle in ballast, in collision with *Australia Star* (1935, 11,122) in the Thames, causing extensive damage above waterline.
25.9.1962: Sold Cantieri Navali del Golfo S.p.A., Genoa and arrived La Spezia for demolition with work commencing 12.1962.

TSMV *PORT HOBART* 148631
7,448 gt, 4,493 n, 484.4/ 466.9 x 59.7 x 31.3, (147.6/142.3 x 18.2 x 9.5), 14k, 12p.
1925 by Swan, Hunter & Wigham Richardson Ltd, Newcastle.
2S. C.S.A.2 -4 cyl 1,112 nhp by Wm. Doxford & Sons Ltd, Sunderland.
Ins. cap 297,850 cf, increasing to 344,233 cf (8,435-9,749).
C&D Line Ltd, London, 1925-37, Port Line Ltd, London, 1937-40.
4.4.1931: Struck submerged object off Cape Turakirae, Wellington, on passage Auckland to Wellington, incurring bottom damage and a broken starboard propeller.
18.5.1938: On passage Hobart to Hull, starboard engine scavenge pump broke and vessel proceeded to Durban on one engine at half speed. Arrived Durban 27.6.38 and resumed voyage after repairs 3.6.1938.
24.11.1940: Captured and sunk by German heavy cruiser *Admiral Scheer* south east of Bermuda in position 24.44N, 58.21W on passage Liverpool to New Zealand.

TSMV *PORT FREMANTLE* 149807
8,072 gt, 4,960 n, 495.0/477.4 x 63.4 x 31.0, (150.8/145.5 x 19.3 x 9.4), 14.5k, 12p.
1927 by Workman, Clark & Co Ltd, Belfast.
2S. C.S.A.2- 4 cyl 1,281 nhp by Wm. Doxford & Sons Ltd, Sunderland.
Ins. cap 331,993 cf increasing to 406,130 cf, (9,402 11,502).
C&D Line Ltd, London, 1927-37, Port Line Ltd, London, 1937-60.
26.1.1932: Fire broke out in wool cargo No 5 hold at Wanganui roadstead, vessel proceeded to Wellington, arriving 28.1.1932, where hold was flooded and fire extinguished 29.1.1932.
1.9.1960: Sold Japanese shipbreakers and arrived Osaka, with work commencing 15.10.1960.

TSMV *PORT HUON* 149842
8,021 gt, 4,956 n, 496.7/477.2 x 63.3 x 31.0, (151.4/145.5 x 19.3 x 9.4), 14.5k ,12p.
1927 by Swan, Hunter & Wigham Richardson Ltd, Newcastle.
2S. C.S.A. 2-4 cyl 1,495 nhp by Wallsend Slipway Co Ltd, Newcastle.
Ins. cap 330,287 cf increasing to 408,720 cf.
C&D Line Ltd, London, 1927-37, Port Line Ltd, London, 1937-61
10.11.1961: Sold Japanese shipbreakers, Toyo Menka Kaisha, Tokyo and arrived Yokosuka for work commencing 20.11.1961.

With the second series of motorships, the company insisted on engining one of the ships with Sulzer rather than Doxford diesels, and the *Port Huon* was so fitted. The photograph shows her about to come through the moles at Lyttelton. D. JONES

TSMV ***PORT GISBORNE*** 149874
8,001 gt, 4,952 n, 496.7/477.2 x 63.3 x 31.0, (151.4/145.4 x 19.3 x 9.4), 14.5k, 12p.
1927 by Swan, Hunter & Wigham Richardson Ltd, Newcastle.
2S. C.S.A. 2-4 cyl 1,281 nhp by Wm. Doxford & Sons Ltd, Sunderland.
Ins. cap 330,957 cf, increasing to 397,636 cf, (9,373-11,261)
C&D Line Ltd, London, 1927-37, Port Line Ltd, London, 1937-40.
11.10.1940: Torpedoed and sunk by *U-48* south west of Rockall in position 56.38N, 16.40W on passage Bermuda to UK in convoy.

TSMV ***PORT FAIRY*** 160590
7,980 gt, 4,927 n, 495.0/477.3 x 63.2 x 31.0, (150.9/145.5 x 19.3 x 9.4), 14.5k, 12p.
1928 by Swan, Hunter & Wigham Richardson Ltd, Newcastle.
2S. C.S.A. 2-4 cyl 1,374 nhp by Wm. Doxford & Sons Ltd, Sunderland.
Ins. cap 335,430 cf, increasing to 413,660 cf, (9,499-11,715).
C&D Line Ltd, London, 1928-37, Port Line Ltd, London, 1937-65.
28.2.1940: Sustained damage following collision with *Loch Dee* (1937, 5,252) while travelling in convoy with both vessels returning to Halifax for repairs.
22.10.1940: Due to inexplicable turn by convoy escorting destroyer, HMCS *Margaree* across the bows of *Port Fairy,* destroyer cut in two, 450 miles west of Ireland, in position 53.47N, 23.01W and she sank

The *Port Fairy* had a series of incidents in World War 11 but survived. She was in service for a remarkable 37 years. The photograph shows her about to berth at Dunedin, direct from London, on 26 August 1936.
EVENING STAR

with the loss of 141 lives.
5.2.1941: While undergoing major hull repairs at Wellington, a fire broke out in the engine room and the area was flooded, requiring holes to be cut in the shell plating to pump out the water.
12.7.1943: Bombed off the coast of North Africa in position 37.18N, 14.37W, while on passage Glasgow to Buenos Aires, causing fires to break out, with repairs at Casablanca taking six weeks.
22.12.1952: Engines failed through contaminated fuel oil and vessel drifted for three days towards Fatu Hiva Atoll, Marquesas, until one engine repaired and vessel was able to proceed at half speed.
24.6.1954: Fire in engine room when completing refit at Swan, Hunter & Wiigham Richardson's Yarrow yard.
14.1. 1954: Sailed Cristobal for Hull, but engines broke down and returned for repairs. Sailed again 5.2.1954, but again broke down and finally reached Hull 3.3.1954.
29.12.1955: Serious engine room fire at Piraeus, causing considerable damage to ship and cargo. Vessel towed to Palermo for temporary repairs 10-15.1.1956.
13.2.1958: Lost propeller entering Port Said on passage Avonmouth to New Zealand and returned to Southampton on one engine.
1965: Sold Embajada Cia. Nav. S.A., Piraeus (Rethymnis & Kulukundis, Mgr) and r/n *Taishikan* (Greece) 1965 for positioning voyage and resale to shipbreakers.
4.6.1965: Arrived Hong Kong for demolition at Cheoy Lee Shipyard, Ngau Tau Kok, for Fourseas Enterprises Ltd, with demolition commencing 7.7.1965.
22.7.1965: While being broken up, vessel caught fire, setting off a number of explosions, with the fire extinguished three days later.

TSMV ***PORT ALMA*** 160615
7,983 gt, 4,926 n, 495.0/477.3 x 63.2 x 31.0, (150.9/145.5 x 19.3 x 9.4), 14.5k, 12p.
1928 by Swan, Hunter & Wigham Richardson Ltd, Newcastle.
2S. C.S.A. 2-4 cyl. 1,374 nhp by Wm. Doxford & Sons Ltd, Sunderland
Ins. cap 335,607 cf, increasing to 413,030 cf, (9,504-11,697).
C&D Line Ltd, London, 1928-37, Port Line Ltd, London, 1937-64.
20.12.1940: During bombing raid at Liverpool, badly shaken and leak started.
24.7.1964 :Arrived Auckland with a damaged port crankshaft and decided to sell the vessel for scrap.
30.8.1964: Arrived Onomichi, Japan for demolition by Tokyo Tsusho Kaisha, Onomichi with work commencing 14.9.1964.

The final vessel in the second series of motorships was the *Port Alma*, the first and only Port Line ship to be named after the deepwater port for Rockhampton in Queensland. She also was fortunate to survive in World War II and remained in service for 36 years. She is shown at Wellington in the early 1950s. V.H. YOUNG & L.A. SAWYER

TSS ***ARGYLLSHIRE*** 129581
11,916 gt, 7487 n, 526.2 x 61.4 x 33.3, (160.4 x 18.7 x 10.1), 14k.
1911 by John Brown & Company Ltd, Clydebank.
Q2-4 cyl 1264 nhp by John Brown & Company Ltd, Glasgow.
Ins. cap 442,856 cf (12,542).
Scottish Shire Line Ltd, Glasgow (Turnbull, Martin & Co, Mgr) 1911-29.
5.2.1917: On passage London to Barry struck a mine laid by *UC46*, 3 miles south west of Start Point but safely made Plymouth.

1927-9: Laid up off Southend.
1929: Purchased by the three British Lines in the New Zealand trade as part settlement in a pooling agreement dispute. The C&D Line had a 22.5 per cent share in the vessel, which was registered to the ownership of the Federal Steam Navigation Co Ltd, London, 1929-32.
1932: Sold to The Clan Line Steamers Ltd, Glasgow (Cayzer, Irvine & Co, mgr) and r/n *Clan Urquhart* (British) 1932-7.
1936: Sold T.W. Ward Ltd, Sheffield and arrived Briton Ferry for demolition 30.10.1936.
14.3.1937: Caught fire while being broken up and scuttled in shallow water nearby.

TSMV ***PORT CHALMERS*** 163429
8,535 gt, 5,204 n, 506.8/488.8 x 65.3 x 31.6, (154.5/149.0 x 19.9 x 9.6), 15k, 12p.
1933 by Swan, Hunter & Wigham Richardson Ltd, Newcastle.
2S. C.S.A. 2-4 cyl 1,579 nhp by Barclay, Curle & Co Ltd, Glasgow.
Ins. cap 442,151 cf, increasing to 447,810 cf, (12,522-12,682).
C&D Line Ltd, London, 1933-37, Port Line Ltd, London, 1937-65.
2.9.1937: In collision with *City of Oran* (1915, 7,323) in dense fog off Portugal, and returned Falmouth for repairs to extensive bow damage.
14.5.1962: On passage London to Philadelphia, 400 miles west of Lands End, starboard engine explosion caused considerable damage and vessel proceeded on one engine to Falmouth 18.5.1962, thence Newcasle for repairs, eventually resuming voyage 7.9.1962.
1965: Sold Hong Kong Salvage & Towage Co Ltd, Hong Kong and arrived Kaohsiung, Taiwan 15.11.1965 for demolition by Nan Feng Steel Enterprises Co Ltd, with work commencing 17.11.1965.

TSMV ***PORT WYNDHAM*** 163561
8,580 gt, 5,233 n, 511.0/494.5 x 65.2 x 30.6, (155.8/150.7 x 19.9 x 9.3), 15.5k, 12p.
1935 by John Brown & Co Ltd, Clydebank.
2S.C.S.A. 2- 4 cyl 1882 nhp by John Brown & Co Ltd, Clydebank.
Ins. cap 427,187 cf, increasing to 457,520 cf, (12,098-12,957).
C&D Line Ltd, London, 1935-37, Port Line Ltd, London, 1937-67.
8.9.1937: Grounded inside breakwater leaving Townsville, propeller damaged. Refloated and proceeded Sydney for repairs.
1.3.1943: Attacked by German aircraft 400 miles northwest of Finisterre but escaped damage.
11.4.1945: Torpedoed by *U5070* (Seehund two-man submarine) 5 miles off Dungeness Light, but towed stern-first to Southampton, arriving 15.4.1945, where repairs took 15 months.
9.5.1956: Collided with *Esso Cheyenne* (1942, 9,798) off Dover, minor damage, on passage Port Chalmers to London.
27.1.1958: Caught fire at Timaru, damaging electrical installations and causing five-day delay.
12.5.1966: Engine room fire at New Plymouth, extinguished after four hours but repairs at Wellington until 22.6.1966.
23.1.1967: Arrived Osaka, Japan for demolition by Okadagumi Ltd; work commenced at Funamachi, Osaka on 1.2.1967.

TSMV *PORT TOWNSVILLE* 164519
8,661 gt, 5,228 n, 496.4 x 65.2 x 31.0, (151.3 x 19.9 x 9.4), 15.5k, 12p.
1935 by Swan, Hunter & Wigham Richardson Ltd, Newcastle.
2S. C.S.A.2-8 cyl 2237 nhp by Wallsend Slipway & Engineering Co Ltd, Newcastle.
Ins. cap, 410,321 cf, (11,620).
C&D Line Ltd, London, 1935-37, Port Line Ltd, London, 1937-41.
12.1.1941: Ashore Jamaica but refloated without damage.
3.3.1941: Bombed and set on fire in St. George's Channel, off Pembrokeshire by German aircraft in position 51.57N, 05.43W. Abandoned sinking 52.05N 05.24W on passage Newport, Mon. to Melbourne and sank 4.3.1941.

TSMV *PORT JACKSON* 165383
9,687 gt, 5,826 n, 521.2/500.6 x 68.2 x 29.8, (158.9/152.6 x 20.8 x 9.1), 16.5k, 12p.
1937 by Swan, Hunter & Wigham Richardson Ltd, Newcastle.
2S.C.S.A. 2-4 cyl 2025 nhp by Barclay Curle & Co Ltd, Glasgow.
Ins. cap 494.751 cf, increasing to 502,160 cf, (14,011-14,221).
C&D Line Ltd, London, 1937-37, Port Line Ltd, London, 1937-67.
27.8.1942: Attacked by gunfire from submarine, slight damage, and attack broken off.
7.6.1950: Extensive bottom damage repairs required following grounding at Stockholm.
26.8.1952: Arrived Cape Town on fire in No 4 Hold which had been burning for nine days.
11.3.1959: In collision with *Jalavikram* (1958, 4,573), in the River Elbe off Pagen Sand, subsequently grounded. Refloated, and with extensive bow damage towed Hamburg for repairs.
1967: Sold Embajada Cia. Nav. S.A., Piraeus (K Stergiopulos of Rethymnis & Kulukundis, mgr) and r/n *Legation* (Greece) 1967 for positioning voyage and resale to shipbreakers. Sold Iwai & Company and arrived Kure, Japan 13.4.1967 for demolition at Etajima; work commenced 26.4.1967.

SSMV *PORT MONTREAL* 165587
5,882 gt, 3,458 n, 438.9 x 58.9 x 25.7, (133.8 x 18.0 x 7.8), 13k.
1937 by Wm. Doxford & Sons Ltd, Sunderland.
2S.C.S.A. 1-4 cyl 861 nhp by Wm. Doxford & Sons Ltd, Sunderland.
Ins. cap 17,981 cf (509).
C&D Line Ltd, London, 1937, Port Line Ltd, London, 1937-42.
10.6.1942: Torpedoed and sunk by *U-68* in Caribbean Sea in position 12.17N, 80.20W on passage Halifax to Melbourne.

SSMV *PORT HALIFAX* 165611
5,820 gt, 3,350 n, 456.7/440.1 x 59.0 x 25.8, (139.2/134.1 x 18.0 x 7.9), 13k.
1937 by Swan, Hunter & Wigham Richardson Ltd, Newcastle.
2S.C.S.A. 1-4 cyl, 861 nhp by Swan, Hunter & Wigham Richardson Ltd, Newcastle.
Ins. cap 18,247 cf, increasing to 41,597 cf, (517-1,178).
Port Line Ltd, London, 1937-62.

1962: Sold Olistim Navigation Co, Beirut, Lebanon (Franco Shipping Co Ltd, Athens, mgr) and r/n *Ilena* (Lebanon) 1962-73.
1969: Transferred Sanspyridon Shipping Co, Famagusta (Franco Shipping Co Ltd, Athens, mgr) (same name, but Cyprus registry).
1973: Sold Detel Malatya Demir Sanayii Ltd, Turkish shipbreakers. Sailed Alexandria 10.2.1973 and arrived Istanbul prior to 15.2.1973 for demolition by Detel Malatya Demir Sanayii Ltd, Istanbul-Halic, with work commencing 4.5.1973.

The second MANZ Line ship, the *Port Halifax*, was launched a month earlier than the *Port Montreal* in 1937, but was completed a month later. The bridge fronts on both *Port Halifax*, and the *Port Saint John* were very low and were raised by another deck in 1952. The *Port Halifax* is shown sailing out of Sydney Harbour. DR E.M. HUMPHERY

SSMV ***PORT SAINT JOHN*** 166332
5,668 gt, 3,306 n, 465.1/448.4 x 59.0 x 25.2, (141.8/136.7 x 18.0 x 7.7), 13k.
1938 by J.L. Thompson & Sons Ltd, Sunderland.
2S.C.S.A., 1-4 cyl, 861 nhp by Richardsons, Westgarth & Co Ltd, Hartlepool.
Ins. cap 16,820 cf increasing to 37,319 cf. (476-1,057).
Laid down as *Port Quebec* but launched as *Port Saint John.*
Port Line Ltd, London, 1938-61.
17.1.1938: On passage Halifax to Melbourne, grounded near Sydney, Nova Scotia, refloated 8 hours later with extensive bottom damage. Following repairs vessel sailed 2.3.1938 but returned to port with defective thrust block 3.3.1938. Finally resumed voyage 10.3.1938.
4.5.1938: On passage New Plymouth to Gladstone in ballast, grounded on coral reef off Lady Elliot Island, refloated 13.5.1938, and arrived Sydney, N.S.W. for temporary repairs 16.5.1938. Final repairs

undertaken at Newcastle-on-Tyne.
7.4.1939: On passage Saint John to Brisbane, arrived Cristobal with No 2 crosshead beam side rod damaged and proceed to Balboa for repairs. Sailed 12 .4.1939 but returned and finally resumed passage 14.4.1939.
22.12.1944: Rescued entire crew *Michael J Goulandris* (1921, 6,590) which had run aground on d'Entrecasteaux Point, West Australia 21.12.1944 and became total loss.
1961: Sold Cia.Lamia de Nav. S.A., Piraeus (Fafalios Ltd, London, mgr); r/n *Redestos* (Greece) 1961-9.
1969: Sold Chinese shipbrokers and arrived Hsinkang 28.7.1969 with delivery to breakers 9.8.1969.

SSMV ***PORT QUEBEC*** 167532
6,294 gt, 3,625 n, 468.0/451.0 x 59.7 x 25.2, (142.6/137.5 x 18.2 x 7.7), 14.5k.
1939 by J.L. Thompson & Sons Ltd, Sunderland.
2S.C.S.A. 1-5 cyl, 1076 nhp by Wm. Doxford & Co Ltd, Sunderland.
Ins. cap 19,084 cf increasing to 301,170 cf. (540-8,529)
Port Line Ltd, London, 1939-68.
1939: Requisitioned incomplete and fitted out by Furness Ship Building Co Ltd, Haverton Hill as minelayer HMS *Port Quebec* 1939-43.
1943: Delivered to John Brown & Co Ltd, Clydebank for conversion to aircraft maintenance repair vessel, being commissioned 1.1.1945 as HMS *Deer Sound* 1945-7.
20.12.1947: Delivered Port Line Ltd as *Port Quebec* following conversion to merchant ship by Swan, Hunter & Wigham Richardson Ltd, Newcastle.
23.6.1968: Arrived Kaohsiung for demolition by Chous Iron and Steel Company, but broken up at the company's facility at Keelung, with work commencing 12.1968.

TSMV ***PORT NAPIER*** 167578
9,847 gt, ———-, 523.9/503.5 x 68.2 x 38.3, (159.7/153.5 x 20.8 x 11.7), 16k.
1940 by Swan, Hunter & Wigham Richardson Ltd, Newcastle.
2S.C.S.A.2-5 cyl 2,152 nhp by Swan, Hunter & Wigham Richardson Ltd, Newcastle.
Port Line Ltd, London, 1940.
30.1.1940: Requisitioned incomplete and completed as mine-layer HMS *Port Napier.*
26.11.1940: Blown across the Kyle of Loch Alsh into shallow water and during bunkering from a barge on 27.11.1940 she caught fire and subsequently blew up.

TSMV ***PORT PHILLIP*** 168257
12,439 gt, 7,587 n (tonnage openings closed); 9,936 gt 5,362 n 523.9/503.5 x 68.2 x 38.3 (159.7/153.5 x 20.8 x 11.7), 16k, 24/12p.
1942 by Swan, Hunter & Wigham Richardson Ltd, Newcastle.
2S. C.S.A. 2-5 Cyl 2,152 nhp by Swan, Hunter & Wigham Richardson Ltd, Newcastle.
Ins. cap 522,633 cf. (14,801).
Port Line Ltd, London, 1942-71.

8.9.1942: While berthed at Port Tewfik, Egypt, in collision with *Seatrain Texas* (1940, 8,108) causing above waterline hull damage.
22.9.1942: During gun practice, on passage Aden to Bombay, the gun burst killing the 3rd officer, one DEMS gunner and injuring seven other members of the gun crew.
22.10.1947: Steering gear disabled during severe storm and towed into Kingston, Jamaica.
31.1.1971: Arrived Shanghai for demolition and delivered China National Machinery Import & Export Corp, Beijing, 10/2/1971.

The Port Line had ordered another improved *Port Jackson* class vessel in February 1939. This vessel was requisitioned and completed as HMS *Port Napier* in 1940 but she caught fire and blew up in November that year. Completion of a further *Port Jackson* class ship was delayed due to urgent wartime shipyard work, but the *Port Phillip* was completed in 1942. She is shown here in Wellington Harbour. Her short wartime masts were retained throughout her career. G.C. HERON

TSMV ***PORT VICTOR*** 168324
12,411 gt, 7,433 n (tonnage openings closed)
523.9/503.5 x 68.2 x 38.3, (159.7/153.5 x 20.8 x 11.7), 16k.
1942 by Swan, Hunter & Wigham Richardson Ltd, Newcastle
2S.C.S.A. 2-5-cyl, 2,152 nhp by Swan, Hunter & Wigham Richardson Ltd, Newcastle.
Ins. cap 527,390 cf (14,936)
Port Line Ltd, London, 1942-3.
30.4.1943: Torpedoed and sunk by *U-107* 600 miles SW of Ireland in position 47.49N, 22.02W on passage Buenos Aires to UK.

SSMV *PORT MACQUARIE* 169750
9,072 gt, 5,485 nt (tonnage openings closed) 1944-7, 7,308 gt, 4,302 n.
487.9/470.9 x 62.2 x 37.2, (148.7/143.5 x 19.0 x 11.3), 15k, 2p.
1944 by Swan, Hunter & Wigham Richardson Ltd, Newcastle.
2S.C.S.A., 1-6-cyl 1,291 nhp by Swan, Hunter & Wigham Richardson Ltd, Newcastle.
Ins. cap 376,406 cf reducing to 364,578 cf. (10,660 -10,325).
Port Line Ltd, London, 1944-68.
13.6.1957: Towed disabled *Captain Hobson* (1920, 8,173) 400 miles east of East Cape, NZ, to Auckland, arriving 18.6.1957.
13.9.1968: Arrived Kaohsiung for demolition by Tai Kien Industry Co Ltd, Taipeh, with work commencing 12.1968.

Building berths were hard to obtain for merchant ships during the war and the only other ship completed for Port Line during that time was the single screw motorship *Port Macquarie*, in February 1944. She retained her short wartime masts throughout her 24 years in service. BAIN-WRIGHT COLLECTION

SSMV *PORT LINCOLN* 180808
7,246 gt, 4,196 n, 487.9/470.9 x 62.2 x 28.6, (148.7/143.5 x 19.0 x 8.7), 15k, 2p.
1946 by Swan, Hunter & Wigham Richardson Ltd, Newcastle.
2S.C.S.A. 1- 6-cyl, 1,291 nhp by Swan, Hunter & Wigham Richardson Ltd, Newcastle.
Ins. cap 386,040 cf reducing to 372,455 cf. (10,933-10,548).
Port Line Ltd, London, 1946-71.
11.12.1952: While anchored between Holehaven & North Foreland, raked by *Pacific Reliance* (1951, 9,442) but suffered only superficial damage.
27.10.1971: Arrived Castellon for demolition by I.M. Varela Davalillo, Spanish shipbreakers, with work commencing 2.1972.

TSMV ***PORT HOBART*** 180937
11,877 gt, 7,036 n, 540.5/521.4 x 70.5 x 30.9,(164.7/158.9 x 21.5 x 9.4), 16.5k , 128p reducing to 12p 1950.
1946 by Harland & Wolff Ltd, Belfast.
2S.C.D.A.2-8-cyl, 4,000 nhp by Harland & Wolff Ltd, Glasgow.
Ins. cap 492,570 cf increasing to 497,189 cf. (13,948-14,080)
Launched as *Empire Wessex* for Ministry of War Transport but sold Port Line and r/n *Port Hobart* prior to completion 1946-70.
22.3.1954: Explosion in engine room on passage Bluff to Hull, killing jnr 4th engineer.
17.9.1970: Arrived Shanghai for demolition by China National Machinery Import & Export Corp, Beijing.

TSMV ***PORT WELLINGTON*** 180911
10,644 gt, 6,247 n, 528.8/508.5 x 68.4 x 30.2, (161.2/155.0 x 20.8 x 9.2), 16k, 12p.
1946 by John Brown & Co Ltd, Clydebank.
2S.C.S.A.2-5-cyl 2,200 nhp by John Brown & Co Ltd, Clydebank.
Ins. cap 542,342 cf reducing to 539,508 cf. (15,359-15,279).
Port Line Ltd, London, 1946-71,
13.8.1951: Sailed Wellington for London, after being delayed 14 weeks with engine repairs.
21.7.1971: Arrived Castellon for demolition by I.M. Varela Davalillo, Spanish shipbreakers, with work commencing 15.9.1971.

Another vessel of the *Port Jackson* class was launched in February 1946 by Lady Freyberg, wife of Sir Bernard Freyberg, governor-general-designate of New Zealand, as the *Port Wellington*. She is shown lying at the roadstead port of Gisborne in May 1952, with a lighter alongside No 3 hatch.

SSS *PORT ALBANY* 169933
7,271 gt, 5,174 n, 441.7/423.9 x 57.0 x 27.9, (134.6/129.2 x 17.4 x 8.5), 11k.
1943 by Oregon Ship Building Corp, Portland, Oregon.
T.3-cyl 450nhp by Iron Fireman Manufacturing Co Ltd, Portland, Oregon.
13.7.1943: Launched as *William C Lane* for United States War Shipping Administration.
21.7.1943: Delivered on bare-boat charter to Ministry of War Transport, London (Port Line, mgr) and r/n *Sampler* (British) 1943-7.
18.4.1947: Sold Port Line Ltd, London, r/n *Port Albany* 1947-51.
1951: Sold Cia. Naviera Vista Dorada S.A., Panama (Capeside Shipping Co, London, mgr), r/n *Teni* (Panama) 1951-3.
1953: Sold Mid-Atlantic Shipping Company, Piraeus, r/n *Gloriana* (Liberia) 1953-9.
1959: Placed under Greek registry (same owners, same name 1959-68); (John Livanos & Sons Ltd, London mgr 1951-59, General Marine Agency Ltd, London, 1959-68.
1968: Sold Chinese shipbreakers, arrived Shanghai 3.6.1968 for demolition.

TSMV *PORT PIRIE* 181562
10,561 gt, 6,163 n, 529.0/508.5 x 68.4 x 30.2, (161.2/155.0 x 20.8 x 9.2), 16k, 12p.
1947 by Swan, Hunter & Wigham Richardson Ltd, Newcastle.
2S.C.S.A. 2-5-cyl, 2,130 nhp by Swan, Hunter & Wigham Richardson Ltd, Newcastle.
Ins. cap 540,960 cf reducing to 536,616 cf. (15,320-15,197).
Port Line Ltd, London, 1947-72.
2.7.1972: Arrived Castellon for demolition by I.M. Varela Davalillo, Spanish shipbreakers, with work commencing 10.1972.

The last in the series of twin screw motorships which started with the *Port Jackson* in 1937 was the *Port Pirie*, completed in January 1947. R.A. PRIEST

OPPOSITE PAGE: The first of a new postwar series of large twin screw refrigerated ships was the *Port Napier*, delivered in September 1947. For many years she was the largest refrigerated ship in the world, with an insulated capacity of 16,508 cubic metres. PHILIPSON

SSMV ***PORT LYTTELTON*** 181590
7,413 gt, 4,352 n, 487.8/470.9 x 63.7 x 28.6, (148.7/143.5 x 19.4 x 8.7), 15k, 5p.
1947 by Hawthorn, Leslie & Co Ltd, Newcastle.
2S.C.S.A.1- 6 cyl 1,321 nhp by Hawthorn, Leslie & Co Ltd, Newcastle.
Ins. cap 391,026 cf reducing to 380,937 cf. (11,074-10,788).
Port Line Ltd, London, 1947-72.
19.12.1953: Grounded when sailing from Fernandina, Florida, and pulled off 36 hours later with extensive structural damage. Spent 63 days at Savannah discharging and undergoing repairs.
11.4.1959: Serious engine room fire at Brisbane, repairs taking a fortnight to complete.
7.6.1972: Arrived Faslane for demolition by Shipbreaking Industries Ltd; work commenced 8/6/1972

The third of the single screw ships, the *Port Lyttelton*, came into service in March 1947. Shortly after she was built, a deck crane was added to work either No 5 hatch or the poop, and this photograph of the ship passing Port Chalmers in August 1952 shows the crane in its unusual stowed position. BAIN-WRIGHT COLLECTION

TSMV ***PORT NAPIER*** 181707
11,879 gt, 6,824 n, 559.5/536.9 x 70.3 x 30.6, (170.5/163.6 x 21.4 x 9.3), 17k, 12p.
1947 by Swan, Hunter & Wigham Richardson Ltd, Newcastle.
2S.C.S.A. 2-6-cyl, 2,674 nhp by Wallsend Slipway Co Ltd, Wallsend.
Ins. cap 582,920 cf. (16,508) Port Line Ltd, London, 1947-70.
2.1.1958: In collision with *Proteus* (1951, 2,860) in Empire Reach, Panama Canal. Minor damage.
10.2.1970: Arrived Kaohsiung for demolition by Nan Feng Steel Enterprises Co Ltd, Taipeh; work commenced 1.4.1970.

TSMV *PORT BRISBANE* 182957
11,942 gt, 6,836 n, 559.9/538.4 x 70.3 x 30.7, (170.7/164.1 x 21.4 x 9.4), 17k, 12p.
1949 by Swan, Hunter & Wigham Richardson Ltd, Newcastle.
2S.C.S.A. 2-6-cyl 2,674 nhp by Wallsend Slipway Co Ltd, Wallsend.
Ins. cap 569,953 cf reducing to 568,886 cf. (16,141-16,111).
Port Line Ltd, London, 1949-75.
2.11.1975: Arrived Hong Kong for demolition by Loy Kee Shipbreaking Co; work commenced 23.12.1975.

The next two ships of the *Port Napier* class were very distinctive ships with their streamlined bridge fronts and swept back funnels. The *Port Brisbane* was delivered from the Swan Hunter & Wigham Richardson yard in February 1949 and attracted international attention, as well as receiving a visit from the Queen Elizabeth and Princess Margaret prior to commencing her maiden voyage. She is shown fully laden, outward bound from Port Chalmers. BAIN-WRIGHT COLLECTION

TSMV *PORT AUCKLAND* 183007
11,945 gt, 6,817 n, 559.9/538.4 x 70.3 x 30.7, (170.7/164.1 x 21.4 x 9.4), 17k, 12p.
1949 by Hawthorn, Leslie & Co Ltd, Newcastle.
2S.C.S A., 2-6 -cyl 2,704 nhp by Hawthorn, Leslie Co Ltd.
Ins. cap. 573,920 reducing to 571,250 cf (16,253-16,185).
Port Line Ltd, London, 1949-76.
3.7.1976: Arrived Singapore for conversion into a live sheep carrier for Gulf Fisheries W.L.L.,Kuwait, (Cunard Line held 39 per cent share) (Cunard Steam-Ship Co Ltd, mgr) and r/n *Mashaallah* (Kuwait) 1976-9.
1979: Following engine inspections Hong Kong, sold to shipbreakers.
30.9.1979: Arrived Kaohsiung for demolition by Chien Cheng Iron & Steel Co Ltd, Taiwan; work commenced 25.10.1979.

TSMV ***PORT VINDEX*** 183031
10,489 gt, 5,884 n, 523.9/503.7 x 68.4 x 30.3, (159.7/153.5 x 20.8 x 9.2), 16k, 12p.
1943 by Swan, Hunter & Wigham Richardson Ltd, Newcastle.
2S.C.S.A. 2-5 cyl 2206 nhp by Swan, Hunter & Wigham Richardson Ltd, Newcastle.
Ins. cap 538,764 cf reducing to 528,360 cf. (15,258-14,963)
Laid down for Port Line, intended to be *Port Sydney*, but taken over by the Admiralty and commissioned as aircraft carrier HMS *Vindex* 15.11.1943.
2.10.1947: Repurchased by Port Line, returned to builders for conversion to cargo liner; delivered 1.6.1949.
Port Line Ltd, London, 1949-71.
23.8.1971: Arrived Kaohsiung for demolition by Zui Fat Steel & Iron Co Ltd, Taiwan; work commenced 15.9.1971.

TSMV ***PORT VICTOR*** 181935
10,409 gt, 5,863 n, 524.0/505.3 x 68.4 x 30.2, (159.7/154.0 x 20.8 x 9.2), 16k, 12p.
1943 by John Brown & Co Ltd, Clydebank.
2S.C.S.A. 2-5 cyl, 2203 nhp by John Brown & Co Ltd, Clydebank.
Ins. cap. 527,390 cf reducing to 520,520 cf. (14,936-14,741).
Laid down for Port Line, intended to be *Port Pirie,* but taken over by the Admiralty 2.11.1941 and completed as aircraft carrier HMS *Nairana* 12.12.1943.
On loan to Royal Netherlands Navy 20.3.1946-28.5.1948 and r/n *Karel Doorman.*
29.5.1948 Returned to Royal Navy and r/n HMS *Nairana.*
6.1948: Repurchased by Port Line, returned to builders for conversion to cargo liner; delivered 16.9.1949.
Port Line Ltd, London, 1949-69, Cunard Steam-Ship Company Ltd, London, 1969-7, reverting to Port Line Ltd 1971.
21.7.1971: Arrived Faslane for demolition by Shipbreaking Industries Ltd; work commenced 7.8.1971.

The second converted escort carrier was completed as the *Port Victor* in September 1949. She had been commissioned in December 1943 as HMS *Nairana* and was later taken by the Royal Netherlands Navy for two years as the *Karel Doorman* before returning the Royal Navy in 1948. The photograph shows her at Cape Town. V.H.YOUNG & L.A. SAWYER

SSMV *PORT ADELAIDE* 184435

8,106 gt, 4,565 n, 490.0/473.0 x 64.7 x 28.9, (149.4/144.2 x 19.7 x 8.8), 15.5k, 10p.

1951 by Hawthorn, Leslie & Co Ltd, Newcastle.

2S.C.S.A. 1-6-cyl 1500 nhp by Hawthorn, Leslie & Co Ltd, Newcastle.

Ins. cap. 364,250 cf reducing to 354,760 cf, (10,316-10,047).

Port Line Ltd, London, 1951-72.

19.12.1966: Rescued 12 crew of American tuna clipper *Belle of Portugal* (1937, 369) on fire off Punta Mala on the SW Pacific coast of Panama and landed them at Balboa.

19.8.1972: Arrived Kaohsiung for demolition by Jui Fa Steel & Iron Company, Taiwan; work commenced 23.11.1972.

SSMV *PORT TOWNSVILLE* 184519

8,070 gt, 4,479 n, 489.1/471.1 x 64.7 x 29.4, (149.1/143.6 x 19.7 x 9.0), 15.5k,10p.

1951 by Swan, Hunter & Wigham Richardson Ltd, Newcastle.

2S.C.S.A. 1- 6-cyl, 1500 nhp by Wallsend Slipway & Engineering Co Ltd, Wallsend.

Ins. cap. 316,180 cf increasing to 350,730 cf. (8,954-8,933).

Port Line Ltd, London, 1951-72.

29.10.1960: Engine breakdown on passage Levuka to Dunedin and after temporary repair failed, towed 170 miles to Auckland by *Port Fairy*.

21.11.1965: Main engine breakdown off Cape Hatteras; towed by *Port Alfred* to Newport News 22-23.11.1965.

1972: Sold Isaac Manuel Varela Davalillo, Spain and passed Gibraltar 27.6.1972 on passage to Castellon for demolition; work commenced 8.1972.

The second of the three single-screw motorships was the *Port Townsville*, completed by Swan, Hunter & Wigham Richardson in October 195, seen here on a windy day in Cape Town. C.R.V. SOLOMON

SSMV ***PORT NELSON*** 184526
8,375 gt, 4,667 n, 490.0/472.0 x 64.8 x 28.9, (149.4/143.9 x 19.8 x 8.8), 15.5k, 10p.
1951 by Harland & Wolff Ltd, Belfast.
2S.C.S.A., 1-7-cyl, 1390 nhp by Harland & Wolff Ltd, Belfast.
Ins. cap. 315,110 cf, increasing to 348,060 cf. (8,924-9,857).
Port Line Ltd, London, 1951-72.
1972 Sold Isaac Manuel Varela Davalillo, Spain, and arrived Castellon 11.5.1972 for demolition; work commenced 6.1972.

The *Port Nelson* completed the series, being delivered from Harland & Wolff, Belfast in late October 1951. All three vessels had streamlined bridge fronts. The *Port Nelson* is shown in Otago Harbour outward bound from Dunedin. BAIN-WRIGHT COLLECTION

SSMV ***PORT MONTREAL*** 186004
6,843 gt, 3,717 n, 468.9/440.0 x 64.3 x 26.9, (142.9/134.1 x 19.6 x 8.2), 16.25k, 4p.
1954 by Harland & Wolff Ltd, Govan.
2S.C.S.A. 1-7-cyl, 7,700 bhp by Harland & Wolff Ltd, Belfast.
Ins. cap. 88,060 cf increasing to 271,960 cf. (2,494-7702).
Port Line Ltd, London, 1954-72.
1972: Sold Maritime Company Overseas Inc, Liberia (Cia. Maritima, Manila, mgr) and r/n *Puerto Princesa* (Liberia) 1972-8. From 1977 Philippine registry under ownership Maritime Company of the Philippines Inc, Manila.
27.9.1978: Dragged anchor and damaged in collision with *Fides Orient* (1958, 4,850) Manila Harbour during typhoon 'Lola'. Decision taken not to repair the vessel.
27.11.1978: Arrived Kaohsiung for demolition by Nan Long Steel & Iron, Co, Taiwan,; work commenced 17.12.1978.

TSMV ***PORT HARDY*** 168872
8,311 gt, 4,870 n, 492.5/471.7 x 64.3 x 30.0, 150.1/143.8 x 19.6 x 9.1), 15.5k
1944 by Barclay, Curle & Co Ltd, Whiteinch, Glasgow.
2S.C.S.A. 2-4-cyl, 9000 bhp by Barclay, Curle & Co Ltd, Glasgow.
Built as *Herefordshire* for Bibby Line Ltd, Liverpool (Bibby Bros. & Co, mgr) 1944-54.
Taken on long term charter by Port Line Ltd, 1951-61 and r/n *Port Hardy* 1954-61.
Returned to owners 1961 and r/n *Herefordshire* 1961-9.
1969 Sold Meritath Cia. Nav. S.A., Famagusta (Troodos Shipping & Trading Ltd, London, mgr) and r/n *Merryland* (Cyprus) 1969-73.
7.2.1973 Arrived Kaohsiung for demolition by Chia Tai Steel & Iron Works, Taiwan shipbreakers,; work commenced 9.3.1973.

From 1954 the Port Line took several dry-cargo vessels on long term charters, starting with the Bibby Line's *Herefordshire*. She was chartered in 1951, renamed *Port Hardy* in 1954 and was employed on the main line trade until 1961 when she was re-delivered and reverted to her original name. The *Port Hardy* is shown in Otago Harbour. BAIN-WRIGHT COLLECTION

SSMV ***PORT CURTIS*** 181155
5,635 gt, 3,071 n, 449.8/431.4 x 59.6 x 25.1, (137.1/131.5 x 18.2 x 7.7), 14k.
1953 by J.L. Thompson & Sons Ltd, Sunderland.
2S.C.S.A. 1-4-cyl, 4,400 bhp by Wm. Doxford & Sons Ltd, Sunderland.
Built as *Thistledowne* for the Albyn Line Ltd, Sunderland (Allan, Black & Co, mgr) 1953-5.
Taken on 5-year charter by Port Line Ltd, and r/n *Port Curtis* 1955-61.
Returned to owners 1961 and r/n *Thistledowne* 1961-6.
Albyn Line sold Chapman & Willan Ltd, Sunderland, 2.1966 and *Thistledowne* registered to the ownership of Somerston Shipping Co Ltd, Hamilton, Bermuda 2.1966 but transferred 4.1966 to Carlton S.S. Co Ltd, Bermuda.
6.1966: Sold Ratnakar Shipping Co Ltd, Calcutta and r/n *Ratna Jyoti* (India) 1966-72.
15.11.1972: Arrived Bombay for demolition by Great Steel Corp, Bombay and delivered 25/11/1972; work commenced 1.1.1973.

A second five-year charter in 1954 was the Albyn Line *Thistledowne*, which became the *Port Curtis*. Chartered ships were left in their owners' colours but had their funnel repainted in Port Line colours. Her smaller cargo capacity made her more suitable for the MANZ Line service. Re-delivered in 1961, she is shown in Adelaide River. N.J. KIRBY

TSMV ***PORT STEPHENS*** 169879

6,597 gt, 3,861 n, 490.3/469.8 x 63.5 x 26.0, (149.4/143.2 x 19.4 x 7.9), 15k.
1944 by J.L. Thompson & Sons Ltd, Sunderland.
2S.C.S.A.2-4-cyl., 1374 nhp by Wm. Doxford & Sons Ltd, Sunderland.
Built as *Silveroak* for Silver Line Ltd, London, 1944-55.
Taken on charter by Port Line Ltd, and r/n *Port Stephens* 1955-6.
Returned to owners and immediately on sold The Ben Line Steamers Ltd, Leith (Wm. Thomson & Co, Edinburgh, mgr) 1956 and r/n *Benvannoch* 1956-69.
11.1.1969: Arrived Kaohsiung for demolition by Chin Ho Fa Steel & Iron Co, Taiwan; work commenced 4.1969.

The *Silveroak* of the Silver Line was taken on five-year charter in 1955 and renamed *Port Stephens*. She was returned to her owners after two years and was immediately resold to The Ben Line steamers as the *Benvannoch*. She is shown at Wellington on her first visit in December 1955. V.H. YOUNG & L.A. SAWYER

TSMV ***PORT SYDNEY*** 186201
10,166 gt, 5,585 n, 532.9/498.0 x 70.3 x 28.10, (162.4/151.8 x 21.4 x 8.6), 17.75k, 12p.
1955 by Swan, Hunter & Wigham Richardson Ltd, Newcastle.
2S.C.S.A., 2-6 cyl., 13,200 bhp by Wallsend Slipway & Engineering Co Ltd, Wallsend.
Ins. cap. 427,040 cf reducing to 413,741 cf (12,094-11,717)
Port Line Ltd, London, 1955-72.
1972: Sold Chion Naftiliaki A.E., Piraeus (J.C. Carras & Sons, mgr), r/n *Akrotiri Express* (Greek) 1972-4: Ownership transferred Akrotiri Express Shipping Co, Piraeus (same mgr).
1974-5: Converted to cruise ship at Chalkis Shipyard, and ownership to Delian Athina Cruises Inc., Monrovia (J.C. Carras & Sons remaining mgrs) and r/n *Daphne* (Greek) 1974-84.
1979-1984: On charter to Costa Line, Genoa.
1984: Sold Independent Continental Lines S.A., Panama (Costa Armatori S.P.A. (Linea C), Genoa, Mgr) (same name, but Panamanian registry).
2.7.1986: Fire in generator room in Frederick Sound, 80 miles SW Juneau during Alaskan cruise. Returned to Vancouver under own power and then to Genoa for repairs arriving 22.8.1986.
1988-90: Management transferred to Costa Crociere S.P.A., Genoa.
1990: Sold Prestige Cruises N.V. Netherlands Antilles (Prestige Cruises Management, Monaco, mgr) (same name but Liberian registry). (Prestige Cruises a joint venture between Costa and Sovcomflot).
1996: Sold Leisure Cruises S.A., Switzerland (Joint venture between Reiseburo Mittelthurgau and International Cruise & Hotel Management) r/n *Switzerland* (Liberia) 1996-02. Registered to Arminter S.A.M., Monte Carlo (Martinoli S.A.M. mgr 1996-02). Ownership transferred Dreamline Cruises, Monrovia (same mgr) 2000-02.
2001: Laid up Marseilles due to collapse of Swiss Air, the principal of the Swiss charterer.
2002: Sold Oceanic Cruising Corp., Panama (Chartworld Shipping Corp, Athens, Mgr, later Majestic International Cruises Inc) and r/n *Ocean Odyssey* (Panama) 2002, *Ocean Monarch (Panama)* 2002-03.
2003: Ownership transferred to Madeira International Shipping Register, Madeira (Madeira registry)
2004: Ownership reverted to Majestic International Cruises Inc 2004-05, Oceanic Cruising Corp. (Majestic International Cruises Inc., Mgr) 2005- (same name)
(Still extant 2006)

In 1955 the Port Line took delivery of two 17.75 knot motorships with 16,990 cubic metres of cargo space. Designed for the Australian trade, the *Port Sydney* entered service in March. Sold in 1972, she was subsequently converted into a cruise liner, and after several conversions, she remains in this role in 2006, but with the same hull and main engines she had when completed in 1955. The photograph shows her at full speed in the Bay of Biscay. CAPTAIN D. SINCLAIR, SNR

The former *Port Sydney* in Otago Harbour on 12 January 1998 as the cruise liner *Switzerland*. I.J. FARQUHAR

TSMV ***PORT MELBOURNE*** 186263
10,470 gt, 5,457 n, 532.6/498.0 x 70.0 x 28.10, 162.3/151.8 x 21.3 x 8.6), 17.75k, 12p.
1955 by Harland & Wolff Ltd, Belfast.
2S.C.S.A. 2-6-cyl 13,200 bhp by Harland & Wolff Ltd, Belfast.
Ins. cap. 413,120 cf reducing to 412,180 cf. (11,700-11,673).
Port Line Ltd, London, 1955-72.
1972: Sold Chion Naftiliaki A.E., Piraeus (J.C. Carras & Sons, mgr); r/n *Therisos Express* (Greek) 1972-4: Ownership transferred Therisos Express Shipping Co, Piraeus 1973 (same name).
1974-5: Converted to cruise ship at Chalkis Shipyard, and ownership to Delian Artemis Cruises Inc, Monrovia (J.C. Carras & Sons, remaining as mgr) 1975. Intended to be r/n *Chloe* but entered service as *Danae* (Greece) 1975-84.
1979-84: Chartered to Costa Line, Genoa.
1984: Sold Independent Continental Lines S.A., Panama (Costa Armatori S.P.A. (Linea C), Genoa, Mgr) (same name, Panamanian registry).
1988-90: Management transferred to Costa Crociere S.P.A., Genoa.
1990: Sold Prestige Cruises N.V., Netherlands Antilles (Prestige Cruises Management, Monaco, mgr). (Prestige Cruises a joint venture between Costa and Sovcomflot).
10.12.1991: Damaged by fire while undergoing repair in dry dock at Genoa and declared constructive total loss. Sold Harbour Maritime Ltd, Monrovia and r/n *Anar* (Liberia) and towed 9.7.1992-20.7.1992 for Piraeus.
1992: Hulk repurchased by Prestige Cruises Marine S.A., Monaco and unofficially r/n *Danae* during her rebuilding as a cruise liner.
1993: Re-entered service as *Starlight Princess* (St. Vincent & Grenadines), ownership registered to Capricorn Maritime Inc.
1994: Sold Flax International Co Ltd, Monrovia (Antonios Lekakis subsidiary) (Ellice Marine Co Ltd, Piraeus, mgr) and r/n *Baltica* (Panama) 1994-6.
1996: Sold Waybell Cruises Inc., (Arcalia Shipping Co Ltd, Lisbon, mgr) and r/n *Princess Danae* (Panama 1996-03, Portugal 2003-)
(Still extant 2006)

The second of the two vessels followed in July 1955 as the *Port Melbourne*. Like the *Port Sydney*, she was converted to a cruise liner and although declared a constructive total loss following a fire at Genoa in December 1991, was rebuilt and continues cruising. This shows her outward-bound from Port Chalmers on passage to Wellington in April 1965. BAIN-WRIGHT COLLECTION

Photographed in Adelaide on 16 February 1986, the cruise liner *Danae* was originally the *Port Melbourne*. N.J. KIRBY

SSMV *PORT LAUNCESTON* 187546
8,957 gt, 5,006 n, 490.6/461.0 x 65.6 x 28.8, (149.3/140.5 x 20.0 x 8.8), 15.5k, 10p.
1957 by Harland & Wolff Ltd, Belfast.
2S.C.S.A. 1-7-cyl, 7,700 bhp by Harland & Wolff Ltd, Belfast.
Ins. cap 365,180 cf increasing to 417,640 cf., (10,342-11,828).
Port Line Ltd, London, 1957-77.
3.2.1964: Collided with, and sank tug *Kingsgarth* (1938, 181) off the entrance to Avonmouth Docks.
1977: Sold Woburn Shipping Co Ltd, Monrovia (Gulf Shipping Lines Ltd, London, mgr); r/n *United Vantage* (Singapore) 1977-80.
23.1.1980 Arrived Kaohsiung for demolition by Nan Long Steel & Iron Co Taiwan; work commenced 20.2.1980.

SSMV ***PORT WANSTEAD*** 183130

5,664 gt, 2,745 n, 475.9/440.8 x 64.3 x 25.1, (145.1/134.4 x 19.6 x 7.7), 15k.
1949 by Caledon Shipbuilding & Engineering Co Ltd, Dundee.
2S.C.S.A. 1-5-cyl by Scotts' Shipbuilding & Engineering Co Ltd, Greenock.
Built as *Wanstead* for Britain Steam Ship Co Ltd, London (Watts, Watts & Co Ltd, mgr) 1949-57.
1957: Time-chartered by Port Line Ltd, and r/n *Port Wanstead* 1957-60.
Returned to owners 1960 and r/n *Wanstead* 1960-63, *Raeburn* 1963-64 (while on charter to Lamport & Holt Line), *Wanstead* 1964, *Wanliu* 1964-75 (while on charter to China Navigation Co Ltd (John Swire & Sons Ltd, London, mgr).
1969: Purchased by charterers;ownership registered to China Navigation Co Ltd, London, 1969-75.
1975: Sold Maldives Shipping Ltd, Male and r/n *Maldive Explorer* (Maldives) 1975-78.
11.6.1978: Arrived Gadani Beach for demolition by Pakistani shipbreakers.

The Watts, Watts & Company general cargo freighter *Wanstead* was chartered from 1957 to 1960. The *Port Wanstead*, a distinctive looking vessel with a high cubic capacity to deadweight, is shown in Otago Harbour. BAIN-WRIGHT COLLECTION

SSMV ***PORT INVERCARGILL*** 187753

8,847 gt, 5,005 n, 490.5/461.0 x 65.6 x 28.8, (149.5/140.5 x 20.0 x 8.8), 15.5k, 10p.
1958 by Harland & Wolff Ltd, Belfast.
2S.C.S.A. 1-7-cyl, 7,700 bhp by Harland & Wolff Ltd, Belfast.
Ins. cap. 353,440 cf increasing to 401,690 cf. (10,009-11,376).
Port Line Ltd, London, 1958-69.
5.6.1967: Trapped in Great Bitter Lakes, Suez Canal, during Egypt/Israeli war while on passage Australia to the UK. Port Line claimed for loss of the vessel and ownership assumed by the London Shipowners Mutual Insurance P&I Club from 19.2.1969 and ownership registered to Invercargill Shipping Co Ltd, London (same name).
30.5.1975: Released and sold Defteron Corp, Monrovia (Gourdomichalis Maritime S.A., Piraeus, Mgr) and r/n *Kavo Kolones* (Greek) 1975-9.
22.8.1979: Arrived Kaohsiung for demolition by Shyeh Sheng Huat Steel & Iron Works, Taiwan; work commenced 12.9.1979.

TSMV *PORT NEW PLYMOUTH* 301251
13,085 gt, 7,218 n , 561.4/526.10 x 73.9 x 30.9, (171.1/160.3 x 22.5 x 9.4), 18k, 12p.
1960 by Swan, Hunter & Wigham Richardson Ltd, Newcastle.
2S.C.S.A. 2-6 cyl, 15,600 bhp by Wallsend Slipway & Engineering Co Ltd, Wallsend.
Ins. cap. 575,920 cf. (16,309).
Port Line Ltd, London, 1960-79. (Cunard Shipping Services Ltd, mgr 1979).
1979: Sold Tex-Dilan Shipping Co, Panama (S.L. Sethia Liners Ltd, London, mgr); r/n *Plymouth* (Panama) 1979.
3.10.1979: Arrived Kaohsiung for demolition by Chi Yung Steel Enterprises Co, Taiwan; work commenced 6.11.1979.

SSMV *PORT DENISON* 301402
6,227 gt, 3,294 n, 485.0/440.0 x 61.9 x 26.1, (147.8/134.1 x 18.9 x 8.0), 15.5k.
1959 by A/B Ekensbergs Varv, Stockholm.
2S.C.S.A., 1-7 cyl, 6,300 bhp by Burmeister & Wain, Copenhagen.
Laid down and launched for A/S Lise (W. Holter-Sorensen, Mgr) as *Fair Lady* (Norway) but sold and completed for the Dornoch Shipping Co Ltd, Glasgow (Harrisons (Clyde) Ltd, mgr) and named *Vimeira* 1959-60.
1960: Taken on 5-year time charter by Port Line Ltd; r/n *Port Denison* 1960-5.
1965: Returned to owners r/n *Vimeira* 1965.
1965: Sold to Johnson & Co. H.A.B., Stockholm (Johnson Line) and renamed *Star Altair* (Sweden) 1965-78.
1978: Sold Laertes Shipping Corp, Monrovia (A. Bacolitsas Cia. Nav. S.A., Piraeus, mgr); r/n *Laertes* (Greek) 1978-85.
1982: Ownership transferred Genesis Shipping Corp Ltd, Valletta (same managers but registry to Malta. (Laid up Piraeus 28.1.1983-16.12.1985)
1985: Ownership transferred Contessa Shipping Ltd of Valletta (same mgrs); r/n *Tessa* (Malta) 1985-6.
23.2.1986: Arrived Gadani Beach for demolition by Pakistani shipbreakers.

An almost new dry-cargo vessel, *Vimeira*, was taken on long-term charter in 1960 and renamed *Port Denison*, the fourth vessel to bear this name. She was returned to her owners in 1965. In immaculate condition, and with a Port Line funnel, she is shown in Otago Harbour. BAIN-WRIGHT COLLECTION

SSMV ***PORT WIMBLEDON*** 300765

9,223 gt, 5,126 n, 487.6/460.0 x 63.4 x 27.9, 148.6/140.2 x 19.3 x 8.5), 15.5k.

1958 by Barclay, Curle & Co Ltd, Glasgow.

2S.C.S.A., 1-6-cyl, 6,700 bhp by Barclay, Curle & Co Ltd, Glasgow.

Britain Steam Ship Co Ltd, London, (Watts, Watts & Co Ltd, mgr) 1958-67 as *Wimbledon* 1958-60.

Taken on 5-year time charter by Port Line and r/n *Port Wimbledon* 1960-5.

1965: Returned to owners and r/n *Wimbledon* 1965-7.

1967: Sold National Shipping Corp., Karachi and r/n *Swat* (Pakistan) 1967-82.

1978: Owners r/n Pakistan National Shipping Corp. Karachi 1978.

27.9.1982: Arrived Gadani Beach for demolition by Pakistani shipbreakers.

Another more modern vessel from Watts, Watts & Company was chartered for five years from 1960 and renamed *Port Wimbledon*. With the Port Line flag prominent from her mainmast she is shown slipping past Port Chalmers in Otago Harbour. BAIN-WRIGHT COLLECTION

SSMV ***PORT ALFRED*** 302596

9,044 gt, 5,034 n, 500.2/470.10 x 67.6 x 31.3, (152.5/143.3 x 20.6 x 9.5), 17k , 10p.

1961 by Harland & Wolff Ltd, Belfast.

2S.C.S.A. 7-cyl, 11,500 bhp by Harland & Wolff Ltd, Belfast.

Ins. cap 430,910 cf. (12,203).

Port Line Ltd, London, 1961-75.

1975: Ownership transferred Cunard Steam-Ship Co Ltd, Liverpool (Cunard-Brocklebank Bulkers Ltd, mgr 1975-79, Cunard Shipping Services Ltd, Mgr 1979-82) and r/n *Masirah* 1978-82.

19.7.1981-23.2.1982: Laid up Falmouth

1982 Sold Orpheus Ltd, Gibraltar (A. Bacolitsas, Mgr) and r/n *Masir* (British) 1982-6.

22.7.1982-8.3.1986: Laid up Piraeus

24.7.1986: Arrived off Sriracha, near Bangkok, for demolition by Thailand shipbreakers at Chon Buri.

SSMV ***PORT CAMPBELL*** 301408
7,683 gt, 3,949 n, 505.0/466.0 x 65.9 x 27.7, (153.9/142.0 x 20.1 x 8.4), 14k.
1960 by Lithgows Ltd, Port Glasgow.
2S.C.S.A. 6-cyl by J.G. Kincaid & Co Ltd, Greenock.
H. Clarkson & Co Ltd, Glasgow (J & J Denholm (Management) Ltd, Mgr) 1960-61 as *Clarkspey*
1961: Time-chartered for 5 years by Port Line Ltd, London: r/n *Port Campbell* 1961-6.
1966: Returned to owners and sold Counties Steam Navigation Co Ltd, London (Counties Shipping Ltd, mgr) and r/n *Kings Reach* (British) 1966-70.
1970: Sold Alderminster Shipping Co Ltd, Gibraltar (Mullion & Co (Shipping) Ltd, London, mgr) and r/n *Alderminster* (British) 1970-6.
1976: Transferred Joli Shipping Inc, Monrovia (same mgrs) and r/n *Joli* (Liberia) 1976.
1976: Sold Kyklops Cia. Nav. S.A. Panama (Omega Maritime Enterprises S.A., Athens, mgr) and r/n *Flora C* (Panama 1976-7, Greek 1977-82)
1982: Sold Bangladesh shipbreakers, Burhani Metal Works, Bhatiari Beach, and sailed Kakinda 24.9.1982 and arrived Chittagong prior to 22.10.1982.

The final vessel taken by on long-term charter was the *Clarkspey*, which entered service as the *Port Campbell* in 1961. She was returned to her owners in 1966.

SSMV ***PORT ST.LAWRENCE*** 302814
9,040 gt, 5,018 n, 500.2/470.10 x 67.8 x 28.3, (152.5/143.3 x 20.7 x 8.6), 17k, 10p.
1961 by Harland & Wolff Ltd, Belfast.
2S.C.S.A. 7-cyl 11,500 bhp by Harland & Wolff Ltd, Belfast.
Ins. cap 441,490 cf (12,503)
Port Line Ltd, London, 1961-75
1975: Ownership transferred to Cunard Steam-Ship Co Ltd, London (Cunard Brocklebank Bulkers Ltd, mgr 1975-9, Cunard Shipping Services Ltd, mgrs 1979-82) and r/n *Matangi* 1975-82.
1982: Sold Armier Shipping Co Ltd, Valletta (Diana Shipping Agencies S.A., mgr) and r/n *Nordave* (Malta) 1982-3.
30.4.1983: Arrived Gadani Beach for demolition by Pakistani shipbreakers.

The sister ship of the *Port Alfred* entered service as the *Port St Lawrence* in October 1961. She was also transferred to Cunard Shipping Services and was renamed *Matangi* in 1975 and was employed by Cunard until 1982. The photograph shows her in Cape Town. V.H. YOUNG & L.A. SAWYER

TSMV ***PORT NICHOLSON*** 304378
13,847 gt, 7,771 n, 573.6/541.8 x 76.2 x 30.9, (174.8/165.1 x 23.2 x 9.4), 18.5k, 12p.
1962 by Harland & Wolff Ltd, Belfast.
2S.C.S.A. 12-cyl 17,000 bhp by Harland & Wolff Ltd, Belfast.
Ins. cap 603,810 cf. (17,098).
Port Line Ltd, London, 1962-79. (Cunard Shipping Services Ltd, mgr 1979).
9.10.1979: Arrived Kaohsiung for demolition by Dah Yung Steel Manufacturing Co Ltd Taiwan; work commenced 5.11.1979.

SSMV ***PORT HUON*** 306501
6,081/8,362 gt, 2,669/4,663 n (dual tonnage)
489.3/450.0 x 67.10 x 30.7, (149.1/137.2 x 20.5 x 9.4), 19k.
1965 by Caledon Shipbuilding & Engineering Co Ltd, Dundee.
2S.C.S.A., 1-8-cyl 13,100 bhp by Wallsend Slipway & Engineering Co Ltd, Wallsend.
Ins. cap. 361,060 cf. (10,225).
Ownership registered to Cunard Steam-Ship Co Ltd, Liverpool, for financing purposes. (Port Line Ltd, London, mgr 1965-72).
Sold Afromar Inc., Monrovia (N. Vernicos-Eugenides,Piraeus, mgr) and r/n *Julietta* (Greek) 1972-84.
1984: Transferred Egyptian Reefer & General Cargo Shipping Co Ltd, Alexandria (same mgrs); r/n *Amana* (Egyptian) 1984-93.
2.8.1991-23.11.1993: Laid up Piraeus.
1993: Sold Universal Ltd, St Vincent & Grenadines (Incom Shipping Ltd, London, mgr); r/n *Mana* (St.Vincent & Grenadines) for delivery voyage to breakers.
31.1.1994: Anchored off Alang for demolition by Jaibharat Steel Co and beached 10.2.1994, with work commencing 4.5.1994.

SSMV *PORT ALBANY* 308652
6,081/8,362 gt, 2,669/4,663 n (dual tonnage).
489.3/450.0 x 67.10 x 30.7 (149.1/137.2 x 20.5 x 9.4), 19k.
1965 by Caledon Shipbuilding & Engineering Co Ltd, Dundee.
2S.C.S.A. 1-8 cyl' 13,100bhp by Wallsend Slipway & Engineering Co Ltd, Wallsend
Ins. cap. 361,060 cf. (10,225).
Ownership registered to Cunard Steam-Ship Co Ltd, Liverpool, for financing purposes.
(Port Line Ltd, London, 1965-72, mgr).
Sold Afromar Inc., Monrovia (N. Vernicos-Eugenides, Piraeus, Mgr) and r/n *Marietta* (Greek) 1972-90.
1990: Ownership transferred Greek Regular Lines Special Shipping Co Inc. Piraeus (same managers) and r/n *Artemon* (Greek) 1990-2.
15.5.1992: Arrived Alang for demolition by Indian shipbreakers which commenced 15.6.1992.

SSMV *PORT BURNIE* 308012
6,156/8,374gt, 2,722/4,682 n (dual tonnage).
489.4/450.0 x 67.10 x 30.7 (149.2/137.2 x 20.5 x 9.4), 19k.
1966 by Barclay, Curle & Co Ltd, Glasgow.
2S.C.S.A., 1-8 cyl. 13,100 bhp by Wallsend Slipway & Engineering Co Ltd, Wallsend.
Ins. cap. 334,700 cf, increasing to 350,780 cf. (9,479-9,934).
Port Line Ltd, London 1966-72.
Sold Afromar Inc., Monrovia (N. Vernicos-Eugenides, Piraeus, Mgr) and r/n *Angeliki* (Greek) 1972-92.
1992: Sold Niverco Inc. (Reefer & General Shipmanagement Co Inc, Panama, subsidiary of N. Vernicos-Eugenides, Piraeus, Mgr) and r/n *Skopelos* (Greek) 1992-3.
1993: Sold Emerald Navigation Ltd, St Vincent & Grenadines (Incom Ltd, London, mgr) and r/n *Skopelo* (St. Vincent & Grenadines) for delivery voyage to breakers.
21.8.1993: Arrived Alang for demolition by Indian shipbreakers.

TSMV *PORT CHALMERS* 335667
12,398/16,283 gt, 6,766/9,217 n (dual tonnage).
612.2/570.0 x 81.5 x 39.9 (186.6/173.7 x 24.8 x 12.2), 21.5k, 12p.
1968 by A. Stephen & Son Ltd, Linthouse, Glasgow.
2S.C.S.A. 2-6 cyl, 26,000 bhp by George Clark & N.E.M. Ltd, Wallsend, Sunderland.
Ins. cap. 606,940 cf, increasing to 663,170 cf. (17,186-18,779).
Port Line Ltd, London, 1968-83.
24.7.1979-22.11.1979: Laid up Falmouth. Cunard Shipping Services Ltd, London, mgr 1979-83 and r/n *Manaar* 10.1981-83
13.7.1981-2.10.1981: Laid up Falmouth
1.7.1982-15.3.1983: Laid up Opua, New Zealand
2.6.1983: Sold Mint Crown Shipping Corp., Monrovia (Kappa Maritime Inc.,Piraeus, mgr) and r/n *Golden Glory* (Greek) 1983-5.
31.5.1983-1.1985: Laid up Piraeus
13.6.1985: Arrived Shanghai for demolition by Chinese mainland shipbreakers.

TSMV ***PORT CAROLINE*** 335944
12,398/16,283 gt, 6,766/9,217 nt (dual tonnage)
612.2/570.0 x 81.5 x 39.9 (186.6/173.7 x 24.8 x 12.2), 21.5k, 12p.
1968 by Upper Clyde Shipbuilders Ltd, (r/n from A. Stephen & Sons Ltd) Linthouse, Glasgow
2S.C.S.A., 2-6 cyl, 26,000 bhp by George Clark & N.E.M. Ltd, Wallsend, Sunderland.
Ins. cap. 606,940 cf, increasing to 663,170 cf. (17,186-18,779).
Port Line Ltd, London, 1968-83.
13.2.1978 Struck bank while transiting Panama Canal, damaging propeller and requiring vessel proceed Avonmouth on one engine.
28.6.1979-1.12.1979: Laid up Falmouth.
2.8.1981-31.12.1981: Laid up Rabaul; Cunard Shipping Services Ltd, London, mgr 1979-83 and r/n *Matra* 12.1981-3.
14.7.1982: Laid up Falmouth and remained there until sold.
2.6.1983: Sold Dolphin Crown Shipping Corp, Monrovia (Kappa Maritime Inc, Piraeus, mgr); r/n *Golden Dolphin* (Greek) 1983-5.
31.1.1985: Sailed Fujairah on sale to Chinese mainland shipbreakers, arrived Shanghai prior to 1.4.1985.

Section 7

VESSELS MANAGED BY THE COMPANY

WORLD WAR I

TSS ***WAR HECUBA*** 143286
7,920 gt, 4,908 n, 450.0 x 58.4 x 37.1, (137.2 x 17.8 x 11.3).
1919 by Workman, Clark & Company Ltd, Belfast.
T2-3-cyl, 1138 nhp by Workman, Clark & Co Ltd, Belfast.
Laid down as *War Hecuba* for the Shipping Controller; management allocated to C&D Line Ltd, mgr, 10.1918-3.1919.
3.1919: Sold prior completion to Albionstar Steam Ship Co Ltd, London (Blue Star Line Ltd, mgr) and completed as *Albionstar* (British) 1919-29
1920: Ownership transferred Union Cold Storage Co Ltd, London (Blue Star Line (1920) Ltd, mgr)
1929: R/n *Albion Star* (British) 1929-48 (same owners but managers Blue Star Line Ltd)
1948: Sold T.W. Ward Ltd, Sheffield and delivered to Briton Ferry 23.4.1948 for demolition.

SSS ***VALENCIA*** 143225
5,227 gt, 3,198 n 364.9 x 50.9 x 30.1, (111.2 x 15.5 x 9.2).
1913 by Act. Ges. 'Neptun', Rostock, Germany.
T3-cyl 398 nhp by Act. Ges. 'Neptun', Rostock.
Hamburg-Amerikanische Packetfahrt, A.G., Hamburg 1913-19 as *Valencia* (German) 1913-19.
21.5.1919: Surrendered to British Govt, and placed under C&D Line Ltd, London, management 1919-20 (same name)
1920: Sold James Nourse Ltd, London, and r/n *Hughli* (British) 1920-7.
1927: Sold Bank Line Ltd, Glasgow (Andrew Weir & Co, mgr) and r/n *Tinhow* (British) 1927-40.
11.5.1943: Torpedoed and sunk by *U-181,* off Lourenco Marques in position 25.15S, 33.30E on passage Durban to Calcutta via Beira.

WORLD WAR II

TSMV ***LOWLANDER*** 168281
8,059 gt, 4,977 n 467.6 x 57.2 x 32.3, (142.5 x 17.4 x 9.8).
1925 by Stabilimento Tecnico S.A., Trieste.
2SC.S.A. 2-6 cyl 1500 nhp by Soc. Anon. 'Fiat' S.G.M., Turin.
Built as *Leme* (Italian) for Navigazione Libera Triestina S.A., Trieste (E. Pollich, mgr).
1937: Ownership transferred to 'Italia' Societa Anon. Di Nav., Genoa (same name).
10.6.1940: At Astoria, Oregon and subsequently moved to Portland and laid-up. Detained by Executive order from 2.1941, and taken up by U.S. government 25.7.1941.
21.12.1941: Transferred under Lend Lease to Britain under Ministry of War Transport with Port Line Ltd management and r/n *Lowlander* (British) 1941-8.
4.9.1947: Returned to US Maritime Administration at New York, and laid-up under management of American Export Lines, being finally redelivered to owners 31.5.1948.
'Italia' Societa per Azioni di Nav, Genoa and r/n *Leme* (Italian) 1948-61.
1960: Transferred Lloyd Triestino Soc per Azioni di Nav, Trieste (same name) 1960.
1961: Sold Sidemar, Italian shipbreakers for demolition at Trieste with work commencing 4.1961.

The captured Italian cargo and passenger freighter *Leme* was under Port Line management as the *Lowlander* from 1941 to 1947. She is shown with a Port Line funnel in New York Harbour in August 1946. R. SCOZZAFAVA, W.A. SCHELL COLLECTION

SSS ***FORT CHAMBLY*** 168820
7,130 gt, 4,256 n, 441.8/424.5 x 57.2 x 34.9, (134.7/129.4 x 17.4 x 10.6), 11k.
1942 by Davie Shipbuilding & Repairing Co Ltd, Lauzon, Quebec, Canada.
T3-cyl 505 nhp by Dominion Engineering Works Ltd, Montreal.
Purchased on completion by U.S. War Shipping Administration and transferred on bare-boat charter to Ministry of War Transport with management by Port Line Ltd, London. (Liverpool registry).
18.4.1942: Delivered to Port Line Ltd, London and managed 1942-7.

1947: Returned to U.S. Maritime Commission and laid up.
1959: Sold Commercial Metals Co, Dallas and broken up at Mobile, Alabama, by Pinto Island Metals Company.

SSS *FORT STIKINE* 168351
7,142 gt, 4,261 n 441.5/424.2 x 57.2 x 34.9, (134.6/129.3 x 17.4 x 10.6), 11k.
1942 by Prince Rupert Drydock & Shipyard, Prince Rupert, Canada.
T3-cyl 505 nhp by Dominion Engineering Works Ltd, Montreal.
Purchased on completion by U.S. War Shipping Administration and transferred on bare-boat charter to Ministry of War Transport with management by Port Line Ltd, London, (London registry).
31.7.1942: Delivered to Port Line Ltd, London and managed 1942-4.
14.4.1944: Caught fire while discharging at Victoria Dock, Bombay, and subsequently blew up with devastating force, completely destroying the vessel and much of the port area, with the total loss, or constructive total loss, of 12 other ships ranging in size from *Tinombo* (1930, 872) up to sister ship *Fort Crevier* (1943, 7,131) with several other ships suffering damage.

SSS *EMPIRE TREASURE* 168992
7,022 gt, 4,908 n, 447.6/432.7 x 56.2 x 34.2, (136.4/131.9 x 17.1 x 10.4), 11k.
1943 by Lithgows Ltd, Port Glasgow.
T3-cyl 558 nhp by J.G. Kincaid & Co Ltd, Greenock.
28.12.1942: Launched for Ministry of War Transport as *Empire Treasure.*
9.3.1943: Delivered to Port Line Ltd, London and managed 1943-6.
15.1.1944: Disabled from damaged propeller and subsequently taken in tow by HMS *Bustler* and towed 1091 miles to Newport, Wales.
10.5.1946: Sold Donaldson Line Ltd, Glasgow, (Donaldson Bros. & Black Ltd, mgr) and r/n *Gracia* 1946-54.
3.1954: Sold Blue Star Line Ltd, London and r/n *Oregon Star* 1954-55.
1955: Sold Williamson & Co Ltd, Hong Kong and r/n *Inchleana* (Hong Kong) 1955-66.
1966: Sold National Shipping Corporation, Karachi and r/n *Tetulia* (Pakistan) 1966-9.
21.7.1968: Arrived Chittagong and utilised as a lighter.
1969: Sold to Mohamadi Iron Traders for demolition at Chittagong; work commenced 18.9.1969.

SSS *SAMPLER*
(see *Port Albany* page 298)

SSS *SAMBLADE* 169670
7,219 gt, 4,380 n 441.6/ 422.8 x 57.0 x 34.8, (144.9 /128.9 x 17.4 x 10.6), 10.5k.
1943 by California Shipbuilding Corp, Los Angeles.
T3-cyl by Joshua Hendy Works, Sunnyvale, California.
Launched as *Augustus H. Garland* but completed for the U.S. War Shipping Administration as *Samblade* and placed under bare-boat charter to the British Ministry of Transport.
8.8.1943: Delivered to the management of Port Line Ltd, London, 1943-7.
25.7.1947: Returned to U.S. Maritime Commision, r/n *Augustus H. Garland* and laid up James River.
29.10.1959: Arrived Baltimore under tow for demolition by Patapsco Scrap Company.

SS *SAMLEVEN* 169817
7,210 gt, 4,395 n, 441.6/ 423.1 x 57.1 x 34.8, (134.6/129.0 x 17.4 x 10.6), 10.5k.
1943 by Bethlehem-Fairfield Shipyard Inc, Baltimore.
T3-cyl by General Machinery Corporation, Hamilton.
Completed for the U.S. War Shipping Administration as *Samleven* and placed under bare-boat charter to the British Ministry of Transport.
14.2.1944: Delivered to the management of Port Line Ltd, London 1944-7.
31.7.1947: Returned to USMC and subsequently sold to Sold Bury Hill Shipping Co Ltd, London, then transferred Tramp Shipping Development Co Ltd, London (Counties Ship Management Co Ltd, mgr) and r/n *Bisham Hill* (British) 1947-52.
1951: Transferred London & Overseas Freighters Ltd, London (same managers/name).
1952: Sold Global Carriers Inc, Monrovia (N.K.Venizelos, mgr) and r/n *Nausica* (Liberia)1952-6.
1956: Sold Panormitana Nav. S.p.A., Palermo (Leonardo Arrivabene, Venice, mgr) and r/n *Praglia* (Italian) 1956-60.
1960: Sold Olisman Cia. Naviera S.A., Beirut (Purvis Shipping Ltd, London, 1960-1, Franco Shipping Ltd, London, 1961-70, mgr) and r/n *Vassiliki* (Lebanon 1960-7, Cyprus 1967-70.)
1967: Transferred Franco Shipping and Managing Co Ltd, Limassol, under Cypriot registry (same name) 1967-70.
31.3.1970: Grounded on rocks off Mayaguana Island, Bahamas in position 22.28N, 73.08W on passage from Augusta, Sicily to Havana and became total loss.

SSS *SAMEDEN* 169851
7,210 gt, 4,395 n, 441.6/423.1 x 57.1 x 34.8, (134.6/129.0 x 17.4 x 10.6), 10.5k.
1944 by Bethlehem-Fairfield Shipyard Inc, Baltimore.
T3-cyl by Filer & Stowell Co, Milwaukee.
Completed for the U.S. War Shipping Administration as *Sameden* and placed under bare-boat charter to the British Ministry of Transport.
14.3.1944: Delivered to the management of Port Line Ltd, London, 1944-7.
1947: Sold Mill Hill Steam Ship Co Ltd, London (Counties Ship Management Co Ltd, mgr) and r/n *Mill Hill* (British) 1947-51. Transferred London & Overseas Freighters Ltd, London (same name/ managers) 1951.
19.8.1950: While on passage Whyalla to Thevenard, cargo of pig iron shifted and a 70 degree list developed causing abandonment of the ship 20.8.1950. *Mill Hill* was taken in tow 22.8.1950 for Port Lincoln and arrived safely 25.8.1950.
1951: Sold Costa de Marfil Cia. Nav. S.A., Monrovia (Diamantis Pateras Ltd, London, mgr) and r/n *Educator* (Liberia) 1951-61.
1961: R/n *Kanaris* (Greek) 1961-6 (same owners).
1964: Transferred Compania Nav. Kanaris S.A., Pireaus (same name).
1966: Sold Active Steam Ship Co S.A., Panama (Shipping & Financial S.A., Lausanne, mgr) and r/n *Splendid Sky* (Panama) 1966-9.
4.10.1969: Grounded in River Schelde, leaving Antwerp for Spezia and broke her back 6.10.1969. Refloated and broken up Antwerp by Jos.de Smedt, with work commencing 8.1.1970.

SSS ***EMPIRE MOULMEIN*** 180219
7,047 gt, 4,741 n, 446.4/430.9 x 56.2 x 35.2, (136.1/131.3 x 17.1 x 10.7), 13k.
1944 by J. Readhead & Sons Ltd, South Shields.
T3-cyl 542 nhp by J. Readhead & Sons Ltd, South Shields.
Completed for Ministry of War Transport and placed under Port Line Ltd management as *Empire Moulmein* 1944-45.
1945: Sold French Republic and r/n *Colonel Vieljeux* (French) 1945-48 under management of Nouvelle Cie Havraise Peninsulaire de Nav., Havre.
1948: R/n *Ville de Diego-Suarez* (French) 1948-62 and sold previous managers NCHP.
1962: Sold Soc. Monegasque d'Armement et de Navigation, Monaco and r/n *Vimy* (Monaco).
1962: Sold Riza ve Aslan Sadikoglu ve Ortagi Adi. Komandit Sirketi, Istanbul and r/n *Demirhan* (Turkey) 1962-6.
1966: Sold Manizade Vapuru Donatma Istiraki, Istanbul and r/n *Manizade* (Turkish) 1966-76.
1973: Ownership re-styled Sevket Manioglu Denizcilik Isletmesi Donatma Istiraki, Istanbul.
1976: Arrived Aliaga for demolition by Zeki Veren with work commencing 20.3.1976.

Associated Companies

MONTREAL AUSTRALIA NEW ZEALAND LINE LTD, MONTREAL

SSS ***CANADIAN BRITISHER*** 150578
5,370 gt, 3,244, 400.0 x 52.0 x 28.5, (121.9 x 15.8 x 8.7), 11k.
1921 by Wallace Shipbuilding & Dry Dock C. Ltd, North Vancouver.
T3-cyl 369 nhp by J. Inglis & Sons Ltd, Toronto.
Laid down as *Canadian Thrasher*, then launched as *Canadian English* by Prince Rupert Drydock & Engineering Co, Prince Rupert., but completed as *Canadian Britisher* by Wallace Shipbuilding & Dry Dock Co Ltd, North Vancouver.
Canadian Britisher Ltd, Montreal (Canadian Government Merchant Marine Ltd, 1921-8, Canadian National Steamships, 1928-36 mgrs).
1936: sold Montreal Australia New Zealand Line Ltd, Montreal 1936.
1936: sold Fan Shien Ho., Tsingtao, China and renamed *Ping An* (China) 1936-8.
1938: sold Amakasu Sangyo Kisen, Yokohama and renamed *Heian Maru* (Japan).
1944: sold Toyo Kaiun K.K., Tokyo (same name)
13.11.1944: Bombed by U.S. aircraft and sunk in position 14.35N, 120.55E while lying 1 mile off north pier at Cabcaben, Bataan Peninsular.

SSS *CANADIAN CHALLENGER* 150366
5,439 gt, 3,331 n, 400.1 x 52.2 x 28.3 (122.0 x 15.9 x 8.6), 11k.
1921 by Davie Shipbuilding & Repairing Co.Ltd, Levis, Quebec.
T3-cyl 522 nhp by Tidewater Shipbuilders Ltd, Three Rivers, Quebec.
Canadian Challenger Ltd, Montreal (Canadian Government Merchant Marine Ltd, 1921-8, Canadian National Steamships, 1928-36, mgrs).
1936: Sold Montreal Australia New Zealand Line Ltd, Montreal.
1939: Sold Ernels Shipping Co Ltd, London (Counties Ship Management Co Ltd, London, mgrs) and renamed *Barn Hill* (British) 1939-40.
20.3.1940: Bombed and sunk by German aircraft, 3 miles SSW from Beachy Head while on passage Halifax to London. Abandoned aground and subsequently broke in two, 25.3.1940.

When Port Line and the other two British companies established the Montreal Australia and New Zealand Line in 1936, one of the conditions imposed by the Canadian government merchant marine was that ten of that company's freighters would be taken over to maintain the service until the new owners built new tonnage. The *Canadian Challenger*, photographed at Brisbane in 1938, continued with MANZ Line until she was sold in 1939. W. ELLIOTT, V.H. YOUNG & L.A. SAWYER

SSS *CANADIAN CONQUEROR* 141831
5,448 gt, 3,336 n, 400.4 x 52.3 x 28.5, (122.0 x 15.9 x 8.7), 11k.
1920 by Canadian Vickers Ltd, Montreal.
T-3 cyl 520 nhp by Canadian Vickers Ltd, Montreal.
Canadian Conqueror Ltd, Montreal, (Canadian Government Merchant Marine Ltd, 1920-8, Canadian National Steamships, 1928-36 mgrs)
1936: Sold Montreal Australia New Zealand Line Ltd, Montreal.
1938: Sold Imprese Nav. Commerciale Soc. Anon, Rome and renamed *Ada* (Italian) 1938-41.
On charter to Japanese shipowners from 1940 and subsequently placed under ownership Teikoku Kisen K.K., Tokyo and renamed *Ataka Maru* (Japan) 1941-3.
23.8.1943: Torpedoed and sunk by USS *Paddle* about 10 kms SSW of Kaketsuka Lighthouse, Shizuoka Ken in position 34.35N, 137.54E on passage Yokohama to Keelung.

The *Canadian Conqueror*, outward-bound from Dunedin, after loading wool, and rabbit skins, remained in MANZ Line service for two years. All the former Canadian government ships had been built in Canada between 1920 and 1922 under a government shipbuilding programme. OTAGO DAILY TIMES

SSS *CANADIAN CONSTRUCTOR* 150465
7,178 gt, 4,413 n, 430.0 x 56.2 x 34.8, (131.1 x 17.1 x 10.6), 12k.
1922 by Halifax Shipyards Ltd, Halifax, Nova Scotia.
T3-cyl 705 nhp by Tidewater Shipbuilders Ltd, Three Rivers, Quebec.
Canadian Constructor Ltd, Montreal (Canadian Government Merchant Marine Ltd, 1922-8, Canadian National Steamships, 1928-36 mgrs)
1936: Sold Montreal Australia New Zealand Line Ltd, Montreal 1936-9.
1939: Sold Ernels Shipping Co.Ltd, London (Counties Ship Management Co Ltd, mgrs) and renamed *Argos Hill* (British) 1939-45.
7.8.1945: Abandoned on fire southeast of Halifax in position 41.30N, 54.54W but later towed into St. Johns, Newfoundland. Declared constructive total loss, towed to Sydney, Nova Scotia and broken up there 1947.

SSS *CANADIAN CRUISER* 150463
7,178 gt, 4,413 n, 430.0 x 56.2 x 34.8, (131.1 x 17.1 x 10.6), 12k.
1921 by Halifax Shipyards Ltd, Halifax, Nova Scotia.
T3-cyl 705 nhp by Tidewater Shipbuilders Ltd, Three Rivers, Quebec.
Canadian Cruiser Ltd, Montreal (Canadian Government Merchant Marine Ltd, 1921-8, Canadian National Steamships, 1928-36 mgrs)
1936: Montreal Australia New Zealand Line Ltd, Montreal 1936-40.
1940: Sold Canadian Tramp Shipping Co Ltd, Montreal (Counties Ship Management Company Ltd, London, Mgrs) (same name).
21.2.1941: Shelled, boarded and scuttled by German heavy cruiser *Admiral Scheer* in position 06.36S, 47.18E, off Mombasa while on passage Port Sudan to West Indies via Durban.

A sister ship to the *Canadian Constructor*, the *Canadian Cruiser*, outward-bound from Adelaide, was the last of the ten ships to be sold. Sold to other Canadian buyers in 1939, she was sunk by the German heavy cruiser *Admiral Scheer* in February 1941. W. BURCH

SSS *CANADIAN HIGHLANDER* 150265
5,370 gt, 3,260 n, 400.0 x 52.4 x 28.8, (121.9 x 16.0 x 8.8), 11k.
1921 by Wallace Shipbuilding & Drydock Co Ltd, Vancouver.
T3-cyl 540 nhp by Wallace Shipbuilding & Drydock Co Ltd, Vancouver.
Canadian Highlander Ltd, Montreal (Canadian Government Merchant Marine Ltd, 1921-8 Canadian National Steamships, 1928-36 mgrs).
1936: Sold Montreal Australia New Zealand Line Ltd, Montreal 1936-8.
1938: Sold St. Quentin Shipping Co Ltd, Newport, Wales (B & S Shipping Co Ltd, mgrs) and renamed *St. Lindsay* (British) 1938-41.
13.6.1941: Reported missing while on passage Glasgow to Buenos Aires and believed torpedoed and sunk by *U-751* in position 51.00N, 30.00W 13.6.1941.

SSS *CANADIAN LEADER* 141833
5,492 gt, 3,342 n, 400.3 x 52.4 x 28.5, (122.0 x 16.0 x 8.7), 11k.
1921 by Canadian Vickers Ltd, Montreal.
T3-cyl, 520 nhp by Canadian Vickers Ltd, Montreal.
Canadian Leader Ltd, Montreal (Canadian Government Merchant Marine Ltd, 1921-8, Canadian National Steamships, 1928-36 mgrs)
1936: Montreal Australia New Zealand Line Ltd, Montreal 1936.
1936: Sold Fan Shien Ho, Tsingtao and renamed *Ta An* (Japan) 1936-8.
1938: Sold Amakasu Shoten Senpaku, Yokohama and renamed *Taian Maru* (Japan) 1938-49.
1949: Sold Toyo Kaiun K.K., Yokohama (same name) 1949-51.
1950: Allocated to the Indonesian government as war reparations.
1951: Sold Republiek Indonesia Serikat, (Indonesian government) Djakarta, and renamed *Mawar* (Indonesia) 1951.
9.1951: Sold to shipbreakers, believed to be Japanese buyers.

SSS *CANADIAN PLANTER* 141482
5,399 gt, 3,333 n, 400.3 x 52.4 x 28.6, (122.0 x 16.0 x 8.7), 11k.
1920 by Canadian Vickers Ltd, Montreal.
T3-cyl 520 nhp by Canadian Vickers Ltd, Montreal.
Canadian Planter Ltd, Montreal (Canadian Government Merchant Marine Ltd, 1920-8, Canadian National Steamships, 1928-36 mgrs)
Intended to be sold to Montreal Australia New Zealand Line Ltd, Montreal, but was involved in collision 3.5.1936 with *City of Auckland* (1914, 8,336) in Nantucket Sound, off the Massachusetts coast. Subsequently sold 'as is' under Court Order to Zetska Plovidba A.D., Yugoslavia (Lale N. Zuber, mgr). Repaired Bethlehem Shipbuilding Corporation, Baltimore and renamed *Boka* (Yugoslavia) 1936-40.
1940: Placed under Cia. Centroamericano de Navegacion Ltda, Panama with Panamanian registry 1940.
20.9.1940: Torpedoed and sunk by *U-138* in convoy OB 216 in position 55.54N, 7.24W while on passage Barry to Sierra Leone. Eight crew lost.

SSS *CANADIAN SCOTTISH* 150573
5,334 gt, 3,242 n, 399.9 x 52.2 x 28.5, (121.9 x 15.9 x 8.7), 11k.
1920 by Wallace Shipbuilding & Dry Dock Co.Ltd, North Vancouver.
T3-cyl 369 nhp by John Inglis Co Ltd, Toronto.
Launched as *Canadian Reaper* by Prince Rupert Shipbuilding & Dry Dock Co, Prince Rupert but completed by Wallace Shipbuilding & Drydock Co Ltd North Vancouver.
Canadian Scottish Ltd, Montreal (Canadian Government Merchant Marine Ltd, 1920-8, Canadian National Steamships, 1928-36 mgrs).
1936: Sold Montreal Australia New Zealand Line Ltd, Montreal.
1937: Sold Kulukundis Bros., Piraeus and renamed *Mount Parnassus* (Greek) 1937-9.
1939: Sold Atlas Reederi A.G.(Schulte & Bruns, Mgrs) Emden and renamed *Johann Schulte* (German) 1939-40.
1.1.1940: While on passage Narvik to Germany, lost propeller, and abandoned off Kya LH, Folla, Norway' and subsequently drifted ashore at Rodoya, south of Buholmraasa.

The *Canadian Scottish* was one of three of the ten vessels quickly sold off in 1937. Fairly utilitarian vessels, they were a familiar sight in New Zealand and Australian ports from 1920 to 1936. She was photographed in the Brisbane River in May 1934. W. ELLIOTT, V.H. YOUNG & L.A. SAWYER

SSS *CANADIAN VICTOR* 141765
5,454 gt, 3,340 b, 400.0 x 52.4 x 28.5 (121.9 x 15.9 x 8.7), 11k.
1920 by Canadian Vickers Ltd, Montreal.
T3-cyl 520 nhp by Canadian Vickers Ltd, Montreal.
Canadian Victor Ltd, Montreal (Canadian Government Merchant Marine Ltd, 1920-8 Canadian National Steamships, 1928-36 mgrs).
1936: Sold Montreal Australia New Zealand Line Ltd, Montreal.
1937: Sold Chang Shu Chang, Tsingtao and renamed *Foo Shong* (China) 1936-8.
1938: Sold Taiheiyo Gyogyo K.K., Tokyo and renamed Fukusei *Maru,* (sometimes records as *Hukusei Maru* (Japan) 1938-42.
17.1.1942: Stranded off mouth of Yangtze River and became total loss in approximate position 31.0N, 122.0E.

SSS *OTTAWA VALLEY* 175604
7,164 gt, 4,295 n, 424.6 x 57.2 x 34.9 (134.5/129.4 x 17.4 x 10.6), 11k.
1944 by Victoria Machinery Depot Co Ltd Victoria, Canada.
T3-cyl 628 nhp by Dominion Engineering Works Ltd, Montreal.
Laid down as *Fort Behrens* and completed as *Mission Park.* Canadian Government, (Park Steam Ship Co Ltd, Montreal, mgrs) 1944-7.
16.2.1947: Sold Montreal Australia New Zealand Line Ltd, Montreal, and renamed *Ottawa Valley* (Canada 1947-50, British 1950-4) (Trinder, Anderson & Co., London, mgrs 1950-4).
1954: Sold Splosna Plovba, Yugoslavia and renamed *Rog* (Yugoslavia) 1954-66.
1966: Sold Wm Brandts (Leasing) Ltd, Hong Kong,and renamed *Millstrident* (Hong Kong) 1966-9.
6.2.1969: Arrived Kaohsiung in tow (prior to 6.2.1969) for demolition by Taiwan shipbrokers, Keun Hwa Iron & Steel Works & Enterprise Ltd.

Vessels managed by Montreal Australia New Zealand Line Limited, Montreal

SSS *RONDEAU PARK* 175382
7,138 gt, 4,221 n, 424.5 x 57.2 x 34.9 (129.4 x17.4 x 10.6), 10k.
1944 by United Shipyards Ltd, Montreal.
T3-cyl by Dominion Engineering Works Ltd, Montreal.
Canadian Government (Montreal Australia New Zealand Line Ltd, mgrs for Park S.S. Co, Montreal) 1944-6.
Placed on bare-boat charter by Canadian Government to British Ministry of Transport (The Aviation & Shipping Co Ltd, London (Noel W. Purvis, mgr) 1946-50.
1950: Sold Halifax Overseas Freighters Ltd, London (Counties Ship Management Co Ltd, mgrs) and renamed *Sycamore Hill* (British) 1950-66. Ownership to Antarctic (Bermuda) Shipping Co Ltd (same mgrs, same name) 1965-6.
24.6.1966: Arrived Hong Kong for demolition by Fuji Marden & Co Ltd, with work in progress at Junk Bay by 1.7.1966.

SSS ***RUNNYMEDE PARK*** 175393
7,139 gt, 4,209 n, 424.5 x 57.2 x 34.9 (129.4 x 17.4 x 10.6), 10k.
1944 by United Shipyards Ltd, Montreal.
T3-cyl by Dominion Engineering Works Ltd, Montreal.
Canadian Government (Montreal Australia New Zealand Line Ltd, mgrs for Park S.S. Co, Montreal) 1944-6.
Placed on bare-boat charter by Canadian Government to British Ministry of Transport (St. Quentin Shipping Co Ltd, Cardiff - The South American Saint Line Ltd, mgrs) 1946-8. Baltic Shipping Co Ltd, Newcastle-on-Tyne, mgrs 1948-51).
1951: Sold Runnymede Steam Ship Co Ltd, London, (Ships Finance and Management Co Ltd, mgrs) and renamed *Lake Michigan* (British) 1951-7.
1957: Sold Marempressa Cia. Nan. S.A., Monrovia (George Nicolau Ltd, mgrs) and renamed *Karaostasi* (Liberia) 1957-64.
1964: Sold Fraternity Maritime Transport Ltd, Famagusta (Fraternidad Cia. de Nav. Ltd, mgrs) and renamed *Adelphos Petrakis* (Cyprus) 1964-6.
24.12.1966: Badly damaged by fire in engine room while lying at Niihama, Japan and subsequently sold Japanese shipbreakers.

SSS ***FAIRMOUNT PARK*** 176004
7,145 gt, 4,210 n, 424.6 x 57.2 x 34.9 (129.4 x 17.4 x 10.6), 10k.
1945 by Burrard Dry Dock Co Ltd, Vancouver.
T3-cyl by Canadian Allis-Chalmers Ltd, Montreal.
Canadian Government (Montreal Australia New Zealand Line Ltd, mgrs for Park S.S. Co, Montreal) 1945-6.
1946: Sold Bristol City Line (Canada) Ltd, Montreal and renamed *Montreal City* (Canada) 1946-8.
1948: Managed by Charles L. Hill & Sons, Bristol (same owners/name) but British registry 1948-59.
1959: Sold Polish Government (Polish Steamship Co, mgrs) and renamed *Huta Baildon* (Polish) and subsequently converted 1967 into storage warehouse at Gdansk.

SSS ***HIGHLAND PARK*** 176025
7,150 gt, 4,214 n, 424.6 x 57.2 x 34.9 (129.4 x 17.4 x 10.6), 10k.
1945 by North Van Ship Repairs Ltd, North Vancouver.
T3-cyl by Canadian Allis-Chalmers Ltd, Montreal.
Canadian Government (Montreal Australia New Zealand Line Ltd, mgrs for Park S.S. Co, Montreal) 1945-6.
1946: Sold Saguenay Terminals Ltd, Port Alfred, Quebec and renamed *Sunjewel* (Canada 1948-54, British 1954-60)
1960: Sold Dah Kiu Shipping Co Ltd, Hong Kong (Shipping Managers (Hong Kong) Ltd, mgrs) and renamed *Leefoon* (Hong Kong) 1960-3.
1962: Vessel damaged, repairs not undertaken and class suspended 11.1962.
1963: Broken up at Hong Kong.

CRUSADER SHIPPING CO LTD, LONDON

SSMV ***CRUSADER*** 187691
3,338 gt, 1,131 n, 406.1/370.0 x 53.6 x 29.8 (123.8/112.8 x 16.3 x 9.1).
1957 by Valmet O/Y, Helsinki, but fitted out and completed by Uddevallavarvet A/B, Uddevalla.
2SA 10 cyl by Uddevallavarvet A/B, Uddevalla.
Ins. cap 210,479 cf (5,964).
Laid down as *Edith Thorden* for Thorden Lines A/B, Uddevalla (Gustav B. Thorden, mgr) but completed as *Crusader* for N.Z. Shipping Co Ltd, Blue Star Line Ltd, Port Line Ltd, & Shaw Savill & Albion Co Ltd, all of London (Shaw Savill & Albion Co Ltd, mgrs) 1957.
1972: Sold Everett Orient Line, Monrovia, 1972 and renamed *Rentoneverett* (Liberia) 1972-83.
1983: Sold Taiwan shipbreakers and arrived Kaohsiung 19.10.1983 for demolition.

SSMV ***SARACEN*** 187829
3,441 gt, 1,245 n, 406.1/370.0 x 53.6 x 29.8, (123.8/112.8 x 16.3 x 9.1).
1958 by Valmet O/Y, Helsinki but fitted out and completed by Uddevallavarvet A/B, Uddevalla.
2SA 10-cyl by Uddevallavarvet A/B, Uddevalla.
Ins. cap 219,303 cf (6,210).
Ordered for Gustav B. Thorden, Uddevalla, but launched and completed as *Saracen* (British) for N.Z. Shipping Co Ltd, Blue Star Line Ltd, Port Line Ltd, & Shaw Savill & Albion Co Ltd, all of London (Shaw Savill & Albion Co Ltd, mgrs) 1958-70.
1970: Sold Shaw Savill & Albion Co Ltd, London and renamed *Langstone* (British) 1971-5.
1975: Sold Petries Cia. Nav.S.A., Piraeus (D. Cosmas, C. Karafotias & E. Karelias, mgrs) and renamed *Dimitrios K* (Greek) 1975-81.
1981: Sold Indian shipbreakers. Sailed Cochin 14.3.1981 and arrived Bombay prior to 1/4/1981 with demolition under way 8/1981.

TSMV ***KNIGHT TEMPLAR*** 304456
3,971 gt, 2.007 n, 394.1/365.8 x 53.0 x 34.0 (120.1/111.5 x 16.2 x 10.4).
1948 by Eriksbergs Mekaniska Verkstads A/B., Gothenburg.
2SA each 9 cyl by Burmeister & Wain, Copenhagen.
Ins. cap 232,035 cf (6,571).
Built as *Arctic Ocean* (Swedish) for A/B Oceankompaniet, Gothenburg (E. Wetter, mgrs 1948-52, William Thoren, mgr 1952-63).
1963 Sold N.Z. Shipping Co Ltd, Blue Star Line Ltd, Port Line Ltd, & Shaw Savill & Albion Co Ltd, all of London (Shaw Savill & Albion Co Ltd, mgrs) and renamed *Knight Templar* 1963-8.
1968: Sold Litton & Co In., Manila and renamed *Mindanao Sea* (Philippine) 1968-73.
1968: Sold Linda Mar. Corp, Manila (same name).
1968: Sold Sea Transport Co Inc, Manila (same name).
26.1.1973: Caught fire while discharging at Bislig, Philippines, 18.4.1973 refloated, towed clear, and beached 20.5.1973 at Toledo, Cebu Island. Wreck sold to Atlas Consolidated Mining & Development Corp, Rizal for demolition at Toledo.

SSMV ***NORMAN*** 315043

5,957 gt, 3,245 n, 422.1/390.0 x 55.9 x 33.6 (128.7/118.9 x 17.0 x 10.2), 14.5k.

1959 by Taikoo Dockyard & Engineering Co Ltd, Hong Kong.

2SA4-cyl by Taikoo Dockyard & Engineering Co Ltd, Hong Kong.

Ins. cap 24,215 cf (686).

China Navigation Co Ltd, London, (John Swire & Sons Ltd, mgrs) 1959 as *Kwangtung* 1959-65.

Time chartered by Crusader Shipping Co Ltd, London, renamed *Norman* (British) 10.3.1965-30.10.1966.

Reverted to owners 1966 and renamed *Kwangtung* (British) 1966-77 (Hong Kong (1977-9).

1977-9: Transferred Taikoo Navigation Co Ltd, Hong Kong (John Swire & Sons Ltd, mgrs)

1979: Sold Gordon Navigation Co S.A., Panama (Johnson Co (Asia) Ltd, Hong Kong, mgrs) and renamed *California* (Panama) 1979-83. Transferred Juniper Shipping Co S.A., Panama (same mgrs) and renamed *Wayful* (Panama) 1983-4.

1984: Sold to Chinese shipbreakers and arrived Shanghai for demolition about 2.5.1984 but not finally demolished until 1985.

To supplement its own ships and those of its owners, the Crusader Shipping Company, sometimes chartered other ships to meet demand. The China Navigation Company's *Kwangtung* was taken on charter in 1965 and was renamed *Norman* as shown here. She was re-delivered to her owners in New Zealand in October 1966 and about the same time in Hong Kong, her sister ship *Kweichow* was renamed *Norman* and resumed the charter until 1968. BAIN-WRIGHT COLLECTION

SSMV ***NORMAN*** 315052

5,957 gt, 3,147 n, 422.1/390.0 x 55.9 x 33.6 (128.7/118.9 x 17.0 x 10.2).

1959 by Taikoo Dockyard & Engineering Co Ltd, Hong Kong.

2SA 4 cyl by Taikoo Dockyard & Engineering Co Ltd, Hong Kong.

Ins. cap 24,215 cf (686).

China Navigation Co Ltd, London (John Swire & Sons Ltd, mgrs) 1959 as *Kweichow* 1959-66. Time-chartered by Crusader Shipping Co Ltd, London, and renamed *Norman* (British) 4.11.1966-20.5.1968.

Reverted to owners 1968 and renamed *Kweichow* (British) 1968-74.

1974: Sold Compania de Navegacion 'Orient Victory' S.A., Mogadishu (Phoenix Enterprises Co Ltd, mgrs) and renamed *Orient Victory* (Somali Rep.) 1974-7.

1977-84: Ownership transferred Phoenix Enterprises S.A., Panama and renamed *Fortune Victory* (Panama). Ownership reverted to Compania de Navegacion 'Orient Victory' S.A., Panama (same name) 1982-84.

1984: Sold Chinese shipbreakers. Sailed Qinhuangdao 28.4.84 and arrived Shanghai for demolition prior 2.5.1984.

ASSOCIATED CONTAINER TRANSPORTATION (AUSTRALIA) LTD, LONDON

With the container vessels of ACTA/ANL and PAD Lines, the TEU (twenty foot container equivalents) figure from *Lloyd's Register* is shown. Container capacities, however, are deceptive and in many cases, on-deck capacities varied as a result of stability issues and the maximum weight allowed on hatch covers. Although container vessels may have had a designated number of slots for refrigerated containers, this could be increased by additional containers, with clip-on units, being carried on deck. When the *ACT 1* class was ordered a nominal capacity of 1,130 TEU was quoted but within a short time the vessels were carrying up to 1,414 of which 960 were general and 454 insulated (the original reefer capacity was increased from 326 to 454 containers in 1973). The PACE vessels were designated 1,067 TEU, and the *AUSTRALIAN VENTURE* and *ACT 7*, 1,782TEU when first ordered, but all were enhanced through experience in the trades; the ratio of weight and measurement cargoes was another factor, as well as structural alterations. Originally the PACE vessels had no container capacity abaft the bridge, but the after deck was later cleared to allow the carriage of 26 empty containers stowed four-high.

SSS *ACT 1* 337032
24,821 gt, 14,771 n, 217.25/205.75 x 28.96 x 15.93, 1,414 TEU, 22k/19.5k.
1969 by Bremer Vulkan, Vegesack.
2 S turbs dr geared to 1 shaft 30,000 shp by Bremer Vulkan, Vegesack.
Blue Star Line Ltd, Port Line Ltd, & Ellerman Lines Ltd, London (Blue Star Line Ltd, mgrs) 1969-91.
1991: Sold P&O Containers Ltd, London, and renamed *Discovery Bay* (British) 1992-8.
1997: Ownership registered to P&O Nedlloyd Limited, London 1997-98 (same name).
12.2.1998: Arrived Singapore with engine trouble and subsequently sold Indian shipbreakers, being renamed *Discovery* (St. Vincent & Grenadines) for the delivery voyage.
7.9.1998: Arrived Alang for demolition.

SSS *ACT 2* 337172
24,821 gt, 14,771 n, 217.25/206.75 x 28.96 x 15.93, 1,414 TEU, 22k/19.5k.
1969 by Bremer Vulkan, Vegesack,
2 S turbs dr geared 1 shaft 30,000 shp by Bremer Vulkan, Vegesack.
Blue Star Line Ltd, Port Line Ltd, Ellerman Lines Ltd, London (Cunard-Brocklebank Ltd 1969-79, Cunard Shipping Services Ltd 1979-87, Cunard Ellerman Shipping Services Ltd, mgrs 1987-91);
Time-chartered to Johnson Scanstar Line 9.1983-3.1984 and renamed *Los Angeles* (British).
1991: Sold P&O Containers Ltd, London and renamed *Moreton Bay* (British) 1991-8
1997: Ownership transferred to P&O Nedlloyd Ltd, London, 1997-8.
28.5.1998: Arrived Alang for demolition following sale to Indian shipbreakers.

The *ACT 2*, the second of the ACT(A)/ANL vessels with the unimaginative names, was crewed by former Port Line and Cunard personnel throughout her 22 years with ACT(A). She is shown in Wellington harbour in 1986. V.H. YOUNG & L.A. SAWYER

SSS ***AUSTRALIAN ENDEAVOUR*** 332298
25,144 gt, 14,403 n, 217.25/206.75 x 28.96 x 15.93, 1,223 TEU, 22k/19.5k.
1969 by Bremer Vulkan, Vegesack.
2 S turbs dr geared to 1 shaft 30,000 ship by Bremer Vulkan, Vegesack.
Laid down as *ACT 3* for Blue Star Line Ltd, Port Line Ltd & Ellerman Lines Ltd, London, but sold prior to completion to the Australian Coastal Shipping Commission, Melbourne, and completed as *Australian Endeavour* (Australia) 1969-85.
Ownership transferred Australian Shipping Commission (Australian National Line, mgrs) 1974-85.
10.6.1985: Arrived Kaohsiung for demolition following sale to Taiwan shipbreakers.

The Australian flagged and crewed container ship was originally intended to be the *ACT 3*, but when the Australian government agreed to take over one of the ACT(A) vessels she was completed as the *Australian Endeavour* in 1969 for the Australian National Line. She is about to pass under the Sydney Harbour Bridge.

SSS/SSMV *ACT 3* 341451
23,818 gt, 14,166 n, 217.25/206.75 x 28.96 x 15.93, 1,254/1,472 TEU, 22k/19.5k.
1971 by Bremer Vulkan, Vegesack.
2 S turbs dr geared 1 shaft – 30,000 shp by Bremer Vulkan, Vegesack.
Re-engined 2SA 8-cyl 17,100 bhp by IHI, Nagoya 4.1987.
Blue Star Line Ltd, Port Line Ltd, Ellerman Lines Ltd, London (Cunard-Brocklebank Ltd, 1971-9, Cunard Shipping Services Ltd, 1979-87, Cunard Ellerman Shipping Services Ltd, 1987-91, mgrs) (British registry 1971-91, Bahamas 1991-9).
1991: Sold P&O Containers Ltd, London, resold to Blue Star PACE Ltd, London (Blue Star Ship Management Ltd, mgrs) and renamed *America Star (*Bahamas*)* 1991-03.
Ownership transferred Blue Star (North America) Ltd, London 1995, Star Offshore Ltd, London 1995, Blue Star Marine Ltd, London, 1995-8 (same managers).
1998: Blue Star Marine Ltd, sold P&O Nedlloyd Ltd, London (same name) 1998-03 (London registry 1999-2003).
20.2.2003: Arrived Jiangyin for demolition by Jiangyin Shipbreaking Co.

SSS/SSMV *ACT 4* 342859
24,216 gt, 14,262 n, 217.25/205.75 x 28.96 x 15.93, 1,254/1,308 TEU, 22k/19.5k.
1971 by Bremer Vulkan, Vegesack.
2 S turbs dr geared to 1 shaft 32,000 shp by Bremer Vulkan, Vegesack.
Re-engined 2SA 8-cyl 17,100 bhp by IHI, Yokohama 2.1987.
Blue Star Line Ltd, Port Line Ltd, Ellerman Lines Ltd, London (Blue Star Line Ltd, mgrs 1971-87, Denholm Ship Management Ltd 1987-91). (British registry 1971-87, Isle of Man 1987-91, Bahamas 1991-9).
1991 Sold P&O Containers Ltd, London, resold to Blue Star PACE Ltd, London, (Blue Star Ship Management Ltd, London. mgrs) and renamed *Melbourne Star* (Bahamas) 1992-03. Ownership transferred to Blue Star (North America) Ltd, London 1995, Star Offshore Ltd, London 1995, Blue Star Marine Ltd, London 1995-8 (same managers).
1998: Blue Star Marine Ltd sold P&O Nedlloyd Ltd, London, (same name/owners) 1998-03 (London registry 1999-03).
12.2.2003: Arrived Jiangyin for demolition by Jiangyin Shipbreaking Co.

The second of the ACT(A)/ANL East Coast North American PACE Line trade container ships, the *ACT 4*, entered service in 1971. Three of the ships in this service had a 40-ton deck crane right forward to handle heavy lifts and bulky non-containerisable cargo. BAIN-WRIGHT COLLECTION

SSS *AUSTRALIAN EXPORTER* 344010
23,486 gt, 15,326 n, 217.25/205.75 x 28.96 x 15.93, 1,168/1,208 TEU, 22k/19.5k.
1972 by Bremer Vulkan, Vegesack.
2 S turbs dr geared to 1 shaft 32,000 shp by Bremer Vulkan, Vegesack.
Australian Coastal Shipping Commission, Melbourne, 1972-4, then Australian Shipping Commission (Australian National Line) 1974-90. Withdrawn from ACTA/ANL service 1987.
19.10.1990: Arrived Hong Kong and subsequently sold Red Riband Corp, Monrovia (Triton Shipping, mgrs) 1.12.90 but resold later that month to Indian shipbreakers and renamed *Ali* (St Vincent & Grenadines) 1990.
1991: Sold Mediterranean Shipping Co, S.A. Geneva and renamed *MSC Mirella* (Panama) 1991-9 with ownership registered to Raisun Investments Inc S.A., Panama.
17.4.1999: Arrived Alang for demolition by Indian shipbreakers.

The Australian National Line container ship in the PACE line service was the *Australian Exporter*. The photograph shows her outward bound from Wellington in August 1984. V.H. YOUNG & L.A. SAWYER

SSS/SSMV *ACT 5* 343036
24,212 gt, 14,234 n, 217.25/205.75 x 28.96 x 15.93, 1,254/1,308 TEU, 22k/19.5k.
1972 by Bremer Vulkan, Vegesack.
2 S turbs dr geared to 1 shaft 32,000 shp by Bremer Vulkan, Vegesack.
Re-engined 2SA 8-cyl 17,100 bhp by IHI, Yokohama 3.1987.
Ordered by Overseas Containers Limited, London as *Chesapeake Bay* but sold to Blue Star Line Ltd, & Port Line Ltd, London, 26.9.1972 with Port Line Ltd, transferring interest solely to Blue Star Line Ltd, 26/9/1972.
1987-91: Ownership transferred to Blue Star Line Ltd, Port Line Ltd, and Ellerman Lines Ltd, (Blue Star Line Ltd, mgrs) (British registry 1972-91, Bahamas 1991-9).
1991: Sold P&O Containers Ltd, London, which sold to Blue Star PACE Ltd, London, (Blue Star Ship Management Ltd London, mgrs) and renamed *Sydney Star* (Bahamas) 1991-9, London 1999-03.
Ownership transferred to Blue Star (North America) Ltd, London 1995, Star Offshore Ltd, London, 1995: Blue Star Marine Ltd, London, 1998 (same managers).
1998: Blue Star Marine Ltd sold P&O Nedlloyd Ltd, London (same name/owners) 1998-03.
(London registry 1999-2003).
24.1.2003: Arrived Jiangyin for demolition by Jiangyin Shipbreaking Co.

ACT 5, laid down as the *Chesapeake Bay*, was taken over in 1971 by ACT(A) when Overseas Containers withdrew from the East Coast North American-Australasian service. BAIN-WRIGHT COLLECTION

SSS/SSMV ***ACT 6*** 358737
25,162 gt, 15,004 n, 17.25/205.75 x 28.96 x 15.93, 1316 TEU, 22k/19.5k.
1972 by Bremer Vulkan, Vegesack.
2 S turbs dr geared to 1 shaft 32,000 shp by Bremer Vulkan, Vegesack. Re-engined 2SA 8-cyl 17,100 bhp by IHI, Nagoya 5.1987.
Blue Star Line Ltd, Port Line Ltd, Ellerman Lines Ltd, London, 1972 with Blue Star Line and Ellerman Lines Ltd, transferring their interest to Port Line Ltd 1972-1987.
1987: Blue Star Line Ltd, Port Line Ltd, Ellerman Lines Ltd, London 1987-91 (Cunard-Brocklebank Ltd, mgrs 1972-79, Cunard Shipping Services Ltd, Mgrs 1979-87, Cunard Ellerman Shipping Services Ltd, mgrs 1987-91.) (British registry 1972-91, Bahamas 1991-9).
1991: Sold P&O Containers Ltd, London, who sold to Blue Star PACE Ltd, London (Blue Star Ship Management Ltd, mgrs) and renamed *Queensland Star* (Bahamas) 1992-03.
1993: Ownership transferred Blue Star (North America) Ltd, London, 1995, Star Offshore Ltd, London, 1995, Blue Star Marine Ltd, London, 1995-03 (both same managers).
1998: Blue Star Marine Ltd sold P&O Nedlloyd Ltd, London (same name/owners) 1998-2003. (London registry 1999-2003).
14.2.2003: Arrived Jiangyin for demolition by Jiangyin Shipbreaking Co.

TSS/SSMV ***REMUERA*** 360840
42,007 gt, 24,806 n, 252.03/236.02 x 32.06 x 20.73, 1655/2074 TEU, 21k.
1973 by Swan Hunter Shipbuilders Limited, Walker shipyard, Newcastle.
4 S turbs dr geared to 2 shafts, 48,660 shp by English Electric-A.E.I., Manchester. Re-engined 2SA 9-cyl single screw 29,610 bhp by Mitsubishi Heavy Industries Ltd, Kobe, 12.1983.
P &O Steam Navigation Co, London 1973-7. On charter to ACT(A) 14.12.1973-5.6.1977.
1977: Renamed *Remuera Bay* (same owners) and ownership registered to P&O Containers Ltd, London 1987-96, Abbey National March Leasing (1) Ltd, London, 1996-7.
1994-02: Re-named *Berlin Express* (same owners/registry) in recognition Hapag Lloyd trade share. Ownership transferred to P&O Nedlloyd Lines, London, 1997-02.
2002: Re-named *Press* (same owners/registry).
3.6.2002: Sailed Hong Kong for Shanghai and demolition commenced at Jiangyin Shipbreaking Co. 10.6.2002.

The final vessel for the PACE Line series of container ships was delivered in December 1972 as the *ACT 6*. She had no crane or breakbulk hatch like the other vessels built for the American service, so she was mainly employed on the main line service from United Kingdom/Europe to Australia and New Zealand. BAINWRIGHT COLLECTION

TSMV *AUSTRALIAN VENTURE* 374582
43,878 gt, 32,011 n, 248.6/238.36 x 32.24 x 21.62, 1,700 TEU, 22k.
1977 by Bremer Vulkan, Vegesack.
2SA 16-cyl 53,360 bhp by Bremer Vulkan, Vegesack.
Australian Shipping Commission (Australian National Line), Melbourne 1977-84, then ownership registered Lombard Leasing Company & HBZ Finance AG, Melbourne (Australia National Line) 1984-96.
1987: Withdrawn from ACTA services and operated with ANZECS consortium 1987-96.
1996: Sold Lavicer Investments Corp, Panama (Mediterranean Shipping Co S.A., Geneva, mgrs), renamed *MSC Nuria* (Panama) 1996-
(Still extant 2006)

TSMV *ACT 7* 377322
43,992 gt, 31,962 n, 248.6/238.36 x 32.24 x 21.52, 1,822/2,451 TEU, 22k.
1977 by Bremer Vulkan, Vegesack.
2SA 16-cyl 53,280 bhp by Bremer Vulkan, Vegesack.
Blue Star Line Ltd, Port Line Ltd, Ellerman Lines Ltd, London (Blue Star Ship Management Ltd, mgrs) 1977-91.
Sold P&O Containers Ltd, London, 1991 and renamed *Palliser Bay* (British) 1991-02. Ownership transferred to P&O Nedlloyd Limited, London 1997-02.
2002: Sold Jiangyin Shipbreaking Co, and arrived Jiangyin 10.8.2002 for demolition.

TSMV *ACT 8* 377052
52,055 gt, 21,263 n, 258.55/248.22 x 32.26 x 20.65, 2,436/2,870 TEU, 23k.
1978 by A.G. Weser, Bremen.
2SA 16-cyl 32,000 bhp by Masch. Augsburg-Nuernberg (MAN), Augsburg.
Ellerman Lines Ltd, & The Charente Steam Ship Co Ltd, London, (Ellerman Lines Ltd, mgrs) as *City of Durban* (British) 1978-85 (apart from three round voyages UK/NZ/UK for Overseas Containers Ltd, London in 1983, when she was renamed *Portland Bay*.)

1985: Renamed *Act 8* (Isle of Man) under charter to ACT(A) (Denholm Ship Management Ltd, mgrs) 1985-91.
1990: Reverted to owners and renamed *City of Durban* (Isle of Man) 1990-6.
1991: P&O Containers Ltd, London purchase Ellerman Lines interests and ownership registered to P&O Containers Ltd & The Charente Steam Ship Co Ltd, London and renamed *Pegasus Bay* (Isle of Man 1996-02.
1997: P&O Nedlloyd Ltd, London & The Charente Steam Ship Co Ltd, London (same name).
1999: P&O Nedlloyd Ltd, London (same name).
19.10.2002: Arrived Jiangyin for demolition by Jiangyin Shipbeaking Co.

TSMV *ACT 9* 14530
9,764 gt, 5,509 n, 148.55/133.79 x 21.71 x 11.26, 856 TEU.
1984 by J.J. Sietas GmbH & Co K.G. Schiffsw., Hamburg.
2 4SA 16-cyl 9,514 bhp by Kloeckner Humboldt Deutz, Voerde.
Bugsier-Reederei und Bergungs GmbH, Hamburg as *Hannoverland* (German) 1984-6 apart from period 1985-6 on charter to Lloyd Brasileiro, Rio de Janiero as *Lloyd Londres* (German).
1986: Under charter to ACTA for PACE WEST service and renamed *Act 9* (German) 1986-90, *Columbus Oregon* (German) 1990-1 (under space sharing with Hamburg-Sud)
1991: Reverted to owners and renamed *Hannoverland* (German) 1991.
1991: Renamed *Sea Beach* (German) (same owners) 1991-3
1993: Reverted to owners and renamed *Hannoverland* (German) 1993-4.
1994: Renamed *Maersk La Plata* (German) (same owners) 1994-7.
1997: Reverted to owners. Sold Reederei m.s. 'Christine Eberhardt' GmbH & Co, Hamburg (Carl F. Peters GmbH & Co., Hamburg, mgrs) and renamed *Christine Eberhardt* (Antigua & Barbuda) 1997.
1997: Renamed *CGM de Lesseps* (Antigua & Barbuda) (same owners) 1997-8.
1998: Renamed *Melbridge Christine* (Antigua & Barbuda) (same owners) 1998-9.
1999: Reverted to owners and renamed *Christine Eberhardt* (Antigua & Barbuda) 1999.
1999: Renamed *Horizon* (Antigua & Barbuda) (same owners) 1999-2000.
2000: Renamed *Christine Eberhardt* (Antigua & Barbuda) 2000 (same owners).
2000: Renamed *Coral Christine* (Antigua & Barbuda) 2000-01 (same owners).
2001: Renamed *MSC Christine* (Antigua & Barbuda) 2001-02 (same owners).
2002: Renamed *Christine Eberhardt* (Antigua & Barbuda) 2002-03 (same owners).
2003: Renamed *P&O Nedlloyd Christine* (Antigua & Barbuda) 2003 (same owners).
2004: Sold Feeder Associate Systems S.a.r.L, Malta (CMA CGM (The French Line) Mgrs) and renamed *CMA CGM North Africa 2* (Malta) 2004-
(Still extant 2006)

SSMV *ACT 10* 15170
8,106 gt, 4,088 n, 132.7/119.41 x 22.7 x 10.8, 885 TEU.
1986 by Martin Jansen GmbH & Co, K.H. Schiffswft u F., Leer.
4SA 7-cyl 4,622 bhp by MAN B & W Diesel GmbH, Augsburg.
Launched as *Maria Sibum* (German) for Sibum GmbH & Co KG ms 'Maria Sibum' (Sibum GmbH & Co, Hamburg, mgrs) and completed as *Act 10* (German) under charter to ACTA for PACE WEST service 1986-8.

The chartered self-sustaining container ship *ACT 10* which was for the PACE WEST service in 1986. IAN EDWARDS

1988: Reverted to owners and renamed *Karaman* (German) 1988-93.
1993: Renamed *Independent Concept* (German) (same owners) 1993, *Kent Trader* (German) (same owners) 1993-7.
1997: Reverted to owners and renamed *Maria Sibum* (German) 1997-01.
2000: Sold Nimmrich & Prahm Reed. GmbH & Co KG ms 'Maria' (German) and renamed *APL Belem* (German) 2001.
2001: Renamed *Maria* (German) 2001-02 (same owners).
2002: Renamed *Tiger Sun* (German) 2002 (same owners).
2002: Renamed *Maria* (German) 2002 (same owners).
2002: Ownership transferred to Cirksena Shipping Co.Ltd, Antigua & Barbuda (Nimmrich & Prahm Reed GmbH & Co., Hamburg (same name but Antigua & Barbuda registry)
2004: Sold Compania Naviera Shirley S.A., Panama (Mediterranean Shipping Company, mgrs) and renamed *MSC Shirley* (Panama) 2004-
(Still extant 2006)

SSMV *ACT 11* 15180
8,641 gt, 4,079 n, 133.38/120.07 x 21.71 x 11.31, 754 TEU.
1986 by J.J. Sietas K.G. Schiffswft GmbH & Co., Hamburg.
4SA 9-cyl 4,044 bhp by MAN B&W Diesel GmbH, Augsburg.
Launched as *Jan Ritscher* (German) for Partenreederi ms 'Jan Ritscher' GmbH & Co, Hamburg. and completed as *Act 11* (German) under charter to ACTA for PACE WEST service 1986-8.
1988: Reverted to owners and renamed *Jan Ritscher* (German) 1988.
1988: Renamed *Independent Pursuit* (German) (same owners) 1988-93.
1993: Reverted to owners and renamed *Jan Ritscher* (German) 1993-6
1996: Sold Mild Lin Shipping Corp, Panama (Moon Keung Shipping & Transportation Ltd, Hong Kong, Mgrs 1996-97, Sunscot & Co (1991) Ltd, Hong Kong mgrs 1997-) and renamed *Mild Lin* (Panama) 1996-03.
(Still extant 2006)

The third German-built geared container ship chartered from German owners in 1986 for the PACE WEST service was named *ACT 11* for the period of the time charter 1986-88. IAN EDWARDS

SSMV ***ACT 12*** 141 (Tonga)
12,188 gt, 7,096 n, 162.31/144.02 x 24.21 x 13.39, 531 TEU
1975 by Kherson Shipyard, Kherson, Russia.
2SA6-cyl, 11,600 bhp by Bryansk Engineering Works, Bryansk, Russia.
Hamburg-Sud Dampsf ges. Eggert abd Amsinck, Hamburg 1975 as *Santa Rita* (German) 1975-9.
1979: Converted to container ship, renamed *Columbus Taranaki* (German) (same owners) 1979-80.
1980: Renamed *Monte Olivia* 1980-2, *Columbus California* 1982-3, *Saxon Star* 1983-6 (all German registry and same owners).
1986: Renamed *Columbus California* (German) (same owners) under charter to Blue Star Line Ltd, London 1986-8 (in accordance with space-sharing agreement with Hamburg-Sud).
1988: Renamed *ACT 12* (German 1988-9, Tonga 1989-91) under charter to ACTA for PACE WEST service 1988-91. Owner under Tongan flag was Tongaocean Limited, Tonga (Shipping Corporation of Polynesia, mgrs) 1989-91.
1991: Reverted to owners and sold Pacific International Lines (Pte) Ltd, Singapore and renamed *Kota Sabas* (Singapore) 1991-03.
27.8.2003: Beached Alang for demolition by Indian shipbreakers.

SSMV ***ACT 10*** 388269
19,613 gt, 10,712 n, 169.4/159.7x 27.79 x 16.31, 18.5k, 852 TEU.
1980 by Bremer Vulkan AG, Bremen.
Built for the Shipping Corporation of New Zealand Ltd, but registered to Lloyd's Leasing Equipment Ltd, London, 1980-9 as *New Zealand Caribbean* (London 1980-5, New Zealand 1985-9).
1989: Sold Bass World International Ltd, Limassol (Columbia Ship Management Ltd, mgrs) and renamed *Abacus* (Bahamas) 1989-90.
1990: Transferred NWS9 Ltd, UK (same mgrs) and renamed *ACT 10* (Bahamas) 1990-1.
1991: Sold Claire Navigation S.A. Panama (Blue Star Ship Management Ltd, London, mgrs) and renamed *Colombia Star* (Bahamas) 1991-2000.
1994: Ownership transferred NWS9 Ltd, UK (same name/mgrs).

When two of the smaller German chartered ships on the PACE WEST service came off charter in 1988, the Russian-built *Columbus California* was renamed *ACT 12* to reflect the space-sharing arrangements between ACT(A) and Columbus Line on the Australian-West Coast North America container service. IAN EDWARDS

2000: Sold Oceanica AGW Comercial e Representatives Ltda. (Mercosul Line), Brazil, and renamed *Mercosul Argentina* (Brazil) 2000.
2000: Sold P&O Nedlloyd Ltd (P&O Nedlloyd B.V. Amsterdam, mgrs) and renamed *P&O Nedlloyd Luanda* (Bahamas) 2000-02.
17.6.2002: Arrived Jiangyin for demolition by Jiangyin Shipbreaking Co.

TSMV *NEW ZEALAND PACIFIC* 380007
42,276 gt, 29,744 n, 248.6/238.36 x 32.24 x 21.52, 1822/2344 TEU, 22k.
1978 by Bremer Vulkan, Vegesack.
2SA 16-cyl 53,280 bhp by Bremer Vulkan, Vegesack.
The Shipping Corporation of New Zealand Ltd, Wellington 1978-89 as *New Zealand Pacific* (New Zealand) 1978-89.
1989: Sold Fuday Ltd, Hong Kong (Denholm Ship Management Ltd, mgrs) and renamed *Tui* (Hong Kong) 1989.
1989: Sold Act New Zealand Ltd and registered to Blue Star Line Ltd., Port Line Ltd, and Ellerman Lines Ltd, London 4.1989. Transferred 8.1989 to NWS9 Ltd, London (Associated Container Transportation (Aust.) Ltd, London and renamed *New Zealand Pacific* (Hong Kong) 1989-91.
1991: NWS9 Ltd sold P&O Containers Ltd, (same name/registry) 1991-8.
1998: Capital Bank Leasing (9) Ltd, London (P&O Nedlloyd Ltd, mgrs) (same name but Bermudan registry) 1998-9.
1991: P&O Nedlloyd Ltd, London 1991-02 (same name/registry).
4.11.2002 Sailed Hong Kong for Shanghai for demolition by Chinese shipbreakers, arriving Jiangyin 11.11.2002.

SSMV *NEW ZEALAND MARINER* 395124
10,991 gt, 7,139 n, 144.86/135.01 x 22.01 x 11.03, 550 TEU, 18.5k.
1977 by Howaldswerke-Deutsche Werft, Hamburg.
4SA 12-cyl 12,660 bhp by Masch. Augsburg-Nuernberg (MAN), Augsburg.
Willner Oltanker GmbH & Cosima Reederei K.G., Hamburg (Poseidon Schiffahrt GmbH, mgrs) and intended to be named *Ulanga* (German) but renamed *Gulf Clipper* (German) before completion under ownership of Kommandit Nord-est Container Linien GmbH & Co (DAL Deutsche Afrika Linien GmbH & Co Hamburg.
1978: Renamed *Ulanga* (German) 1978-85 (same owners).
1985: Sold The Shipping Corporation of New Zealand Ltd, Wellington and renamed *New Zealand Mariner* (New Zealand) 1985-91.
1989: Sold Act New Zealand Ltd and registered Blue Star Line Ltd, Port Line Limited and Ellerman Lines Ltd, London 4.1989. Transferred 9.1989 NWS9 Ltd, London (Associated Transportation Company (Aust) Ltd, London, 1989, Cunard-Ellerman Shipping Services Ltd, 1989-91, mgrs) and renamed *Marin* (Bahamas) 1991-9.
1991: NWS9 Ltd sold P&O Containers Ltd, London and ownership registered National Westminster (Hong Kong) Ltd,(same name/registry) 1991-8.
1998: Ownership registered to Capital Bank Leasing (9) Ltd, London (P&O Nedlloyd Ltd, Mgrs) (same name/registry) 1998-9.
1999: P&O Nedlloyd Ltd, London 1999-02 (same name but London registry)
5.2.2002: Delivered Jiangyin for demolition by Jiangyin Shipbreaking Co.

TSMV *TARIHIKO* 394916
2,169 gt, 650 n, 81.11/75.01 x 13.81 x 6.91, (Liquefied Gas Carrier)
1984 by Ferguson-Ailsa Ltd, Troon, Scotland.
2 4SA 12-cyl 2,800 bhp by Krupp Mak. Maschinebeau GmbH, Kiel.
Ship Leasing (1982) Ltd, Auckland (The Shipping Corporation of New Zealand Ltd, Wellington mgrs) as *Tarihiko* (New Zealand) 1984-99. Owned by Liquigas Ltd, Wellington 1993-99.
1989: Management contract taken over by Blueport ACT (NZ) Ltd, Wellington, later New Zealand Line Ltd, 1989-91 and by P&O Containers Ltd, Wellington 1991-9 (same name/registry).
1999: Sold Kil Shipping Pte Ltd, Singapore (Kil Shipping A/S, mgrs 1999-01, Tschudi & Eitzen A/S, Lysaker, mgrs 2001-03, Camillo Eitzen & Co A/S, Lysaker 2003-) and renamed *Kilgas Centurion* (Singapore) 1999-01, *Sigas Centurion* (Singapore) 2001-
2003: Sold Sigas Singapore (Camillo Eitzen & Co A/S, Lysaker, Mgrs) 2003- (same name)
(Still extant 2006).

One of the responsibilities assumed by Blueport ACT New Zealand on the acquisition of the Shipping Corporation of New Zealand was the management and crewing of the LPG coastal tanker *Tarihiko*. She is seen entering Otago Harbour. I.J. FARQUHAR

PACIFIC AUSTRALIA DIRECT LINE

SSMV ***DILKARA*** 342903
14,144 gt, 8,087 n, 199.02/184.74 x 28.66 x 16.87, 1,212 TEU, 22.5k.
1971 by Eriksbergs M/V A/B, Gothenburg, Sweden.
2 Vee Oil 4SA each 18-cyl 25,920 bhp by Eriksbergs M/V, A/B, Gothenburg.
Blue Star Line Ltd, Port Line Ltd, & Ellerman Lines Ltd, London (Ellerman Lines Ltd, mgrs 1971-86) (British registry 1971-85, Isle of Man 1985-6).
1986: Sold Taiwan shipbreakers and arrived Kaohsiung for demolition 2.12.1986.

APPENDIX 3

Port Line Ltd – Origins of Names

Port Adelaide	34.51S, 138.30E	Port Adelaide on E. side of Gulf of St Vincent, S Australia
Port Albany	35.25S, 117.54E	Albany, historic port in Princess Royal Harbour, King George Sound S coast Western Australia
Port Albert	38.36S,146.40E	Non-commercial port for Alberton, S end Ninety Mile beach Vic., Australia
Port Alfred	48.20N, 70.53W	Commercial port on Saguenay River running into St. Lawrence Seaway, Eastern Canada
Port Alma	23.38S, 150.35E	Port Alma, the deepwater port for Rockhampton, central Queensland, Australia
Port Auckland	36.51S, 174.49E	Auckland, in the Hauraki Gulf, E coast North Island, NZ
Port Augusta	32.29S, 137.54E	Port Augusta, at the head of Spencer Gulf, S Australia.
Port Bowen	20.10S, 148.15E	After Bowen (formerly Port Clinton) on Edgecumbe Bay, N Queensland coast, Australia
Port Brisbane	27.28S, 153.20E	Brisbane, up river from Moreton Bay, South Queensland, Australia
Port Campbell	38.37S, 143.04E	Port Campbell, non-commercial port on Victorian coast, 61 km W of Cape Otway
Port Caroline	36.45S, 139.45E	Port Caroline, non-commercial port in Lacepede Bay, now named Kingston. Approx. 257 km SE of Adelaide, S Australia.
Port Caroline (1968)	44.24S, 179.19E	Caroline Bay, alongside the port of Timaru, S Canterbury, NZ .
Port Chalmers	45.49S,179.39E	Port Chalmers, deep water port for Otago, E coast of South Island, NZ
Port Curtis	23.15S, 151.16E	Port Curtis, Gladstone, central Queensland, Australia
Port Darwin	12.25S, 130.55E	Port Darwin, Northern territory coast, Beagle Gulf, Australia
Port Denison	20.10S, 148.30E	Port Denison, now Bowen, former port in Edgecumbe Bay, 5 km E of Bowen, Queensland, Australia
Port Douglas	16.29S, 145.28E	Port Douglas, N. Queensland coast, approx. 75 kms N of Cairns, Australia
Port Dunedin	45.52S, 170.32E	Dunedin, port of Otago, east coast S Island, NZ
Port Elliot	35.32S, 138.41E	Port Elliot, NNW shore of Encounter Bay, approx 91 km south of Adelaide, Australia
Port Fairy	38.23S,142.16E	Port Fairy, S coast of Victoria, 27 km W of Warrnambool
Port Fremantle	31.10S,115.31E	Fremantle, on SW coast of Western Australia – deepwater port for Perth
Port Gisborne	38.42S, 178.20E	Gisborne, on Poverty Bay, E coast of North Island, NZ
Port Hacking	34.05S, 151.11E	Port Hacking, S of Port Botany, NSW coast, Australia

Port Halifax	44.38N,63.33W	Halifax, central E coast of Nova Scotia, Canada
Port Hardy	40.55S, 173.53E	Port Hardy, bay on N end of D'Urville Island, Marlborough Sounds, NZ
Port Hobart	42.53S, 147.20E	Hobart, capital of Tasmania on Derwent River, in the SE of the island, Australia.
Port Hunter	32.56S, 151.47E	Port Hunter, now Newcastle, at mouth of Hunter River, NSW E coast, Australia
Port Huon	43.10S, 147.00E	Huon, on the Huon River, SE coast of Tasmania, Australia
Port Invercargill	46.23S, 168.25E	Invercargill, city on the southern coast of S Island, NZ
Port Jackson	33.50S, 151.17E	Sydney, capital of New South Wales situated on Port Jackson, (Sydney Harbour), Australia
Port Kembla	34.28S, 150.54E	Port Kembla, deep water port for Wollongong, NSW, 72 km south of Sydney, Australia
Port Launceston	41.27S, 147.70E	Launceston, approx 67 km up the River Tamar, Tasmania, Australia
Port Lincoln	34.43S, 136.51E	Port Lincoln, in Boston Bay, Spencer Gulf, South Australia, 241 km W of Adelaide
Port Lyttelton	43.35S, 172.42E	Lyttelton, deep water port for Christchurch on central E Coast S Island, NZ
Port Macquarie	31.25S, 125.55E	Port Macquarie, at mouth of Hastings River, NSW, 408 km N of Sydney, Australia
Port Melbourne	37.50S, 144.58E	Port Melbourne, situated at head of Port Phillip Bay on S coast of Victoria, Australia
Port Montreal	45.30N, 73.73w	Montreal, on the junction of Ottawa and St. Lawrence rivers, Canada
Port Napier	39.29S, 176.54E	Napier, Hawke's Bay on central E coast N Island, NZ
Port Nelson	41.17S, 173.17E	Nelson, in Tasman Bay, north coast of S Island, NZ
Port New Plymouth	39.30S, 174.30E	New Plymouth, principal port on W coast N Island, NZ near Cape Egmont
Port Nicholson	41.19S, 174.51E	Port Nicholson, now Wellington, on S coast North Island, NZ
Port Phillip	38.70S, 144.45E	Port Phillip, now Melbourne in Port Phillip Bay, S coast of Victoria, Australia
Port Pirie	38.10S, 138.20E	Port Pirie, in the N of Spencer Gulf, 229 km NNW of Adelaide, S. Australia
Port Quebec	46.49N, 71.12W	Quebec, approx 580 km up St.Lawrence River from Gulf of St.Lawrence, Canada
Port Saint John	45.16N, 66.30W	Saint John, in the Bay of Fundy, on the SE coast of New Brunswick, Canada
Port St. Lawrence	46.55N, 55.23W	St.Lawrence, S coast Newfoundland, Canada
Port Stephens	32.43S, 152.12E	Port Stephens, natural harbour 32 km N of Newcastle, NSW, Australia
Port Sydney	33.55S, 151.17E	Sydney in Port Jackson harbour, central NSW coast, Australia
Port Townsville	19.17S, 146.48E	Townsville, on northern Queensland coasr, 372 km S of Cairns, Queensland, Australia

Port Victor	35.33S, 138.37E	Victor Harbour, on NE shore of Encounter Bay, approx 83 km S of Adelaide, Australia
Port Victoria	34.30S, 137.28E	Port Victoria, on SE shore of Spencer Gulf, S. Australia
Port Vindex		Retained from HMS *Vindex,* following distinguished wartime career as an escort aircraft carrier.
Port Wanstead		Chartered vessel *Wanstead* given Port name for period of charter. Wanstead is suburb of London
Port Wimbledon		Chartered vessel *Wimbledon* given Port name for period of charter. Wimbledon is suburb of London
Port Wellington	41.14S, 174.46E	Wellington, in Port Nicholson harbour, southern coast of North Island, NZ
Port Wyndham	15.27S, 128.60E	Wyndham, west-arm of Cambridge Gulf, NW Western Australia

APPENDIX 4

Personalia

COLONIAL UNION LINE LIMITED 1887-90

DIRECTORS

William Haviside Tyser	1887-90	(Chairman 1887-90)
George William Tyser	1887-90	
Henry Benham	1887-90	
Richard W. Shaw	1887-90	
William Wright	1887-90	
Thomas F.M. Parkyns	1888-90	

TYSER LINE LTD 1889-1914

DIRECTORS

William Haviside Tyser	1889-1908	(Chairman 1889-08)
George William Tyser	1889-1915	(Chairman 1908-15)
William Wright	1889-1906	
Richard W. Shaw	1889-1896	
H.W.P. Hoskyns	1890-1915	
Sir Thomas F.M. Parkyns	1890-1915	
Sir E. Montague Nelson KCMG	1892-1915	
Sir William Corry, Bt	1892-1915	
Sir Thomas Royden	1892-1915	
Walter Parkyns Tyser	1896-1915	
Henry Erskine Tyser	1903-1913	

COMMONWEALTH & DOMINION LINE LTD 1914-37
PORT LINE LTD 1937-91

CHAIRMEN

Walter Parkyns Tyser	1914-39
Herbert W. Corry	1939-47
William Donald, CBE	1947-60
Ronald H. Senior DSO, TD	1961-67
Sir Basil Smallpeice KCVO	1968-71
Norman S. Thompson	1971-72
William B. Slater CBE, VRD	1972-85
Alexander J. Macintosh	1985-88
Anthony R.C.B. Cooke	1988-91

DIRECTORS

Walter Parkyns Tyser	1914-40
Charles T. Milburn	1914-22
Sir William Corry Bt	1914-26
Robert Corry	1914-41
Paris K.F. Foot	1914-24
W.H. Moore	1914-20
T. Royden (Lord Royden CH, DL)	1914-50
Sir E. Montague Nelson KCMG	1914-19
H.C. Benson	1915-24
Sir Alfred Booth Bt	1916-45
Sir Percy Bates Bt CBE	1916-46
T. Ashley Sparkes KCMG, KBE	1917-52
Herbert W. Corry	1923-49
John R. Rooper	1926-57
Col. Dennis H. Bates MC, TD	1929-59
William Donald CBE	1938-65
W.D. de Gruchy OBE	1938-53
Warwick E.C. Gregory MC	1940-57
Sir James P.I.M. Corry Bt	1941-55
Ronald H. Senior DSO, TD	1946-67
Frank A. Bates, MC, AFC, DL	1946-57
B.P. Arrowsmith OBE	1947-58
Frank H. Dawson CBE, MC	1951-59
Brigadier J.H. Hardy CBE, MC	1952-61
Sir John Brocklebank Bt	1954-65
Derek G. Hollebone MBE	1954-78
John A. Holt MBE	1954-61
H.E.T. Ross TD	1954-66
R.J.H. Lockett CBE	1957-61
David R. Rooper	1957-68
John S. Corry	1957-67
Robert W. Cromarty	1959-64
A.H. Hume	1962-66
Patrick J. Fuller TD	1963-72
John H. Cook	1963-67
Capt W.S.C. Jenks OBE	1964-69
Sir Basil Smallpeice KCVO	1965-71
E.C. Sutton	1965-72
Hon. Sir Geoffrey Gibbs KCMG	1966-68
Capt A. Gordon Russell	1966-73
P.H. Shirley	1968-71
Philip E. Bates VRD	1968-69
J.D.M. Hearth	1968-71
Norman S. Thompson (CBE 1980)	1969-72
William B. Slater CBE, VRD	1972-85
B.M. Angers	1972-86
L.C. Carrel	1972-73
R.O.P. Grieg	1972-75
Michael S. Lake	1972-78
F. Leach	1972-73
P.M. North	1972-73
J.J.L. Packer	1972-78
John H. Joyce	1973-88
C.R. Moss	1974-74
F.K. Crawford	1974-78
A.J. Macintosh	1985-91
G.A.C. Pribul	1986-91
P.K. Thatai	1986-91
A.R.C.B. Cooke	1988-91

LOCAL DIRECTORS – SYDNEY

H.C. Benson	1914-15
H.W. Corry	1915-23
W.G. de Gruchy	1927-46
F.G. Murdoch	1927-33
D.F.Middleton	1938-61
Warwick E.C. Gregory MC	1946-51
D.G. Hollebone MBE	1950-58
F.J.O. Graham	1956-67
P.J. Fuller, TD	1958-72
G.A. Archer	1966-78

LOCAL DIRECTORS – NAPIER/WELLINGTON

Robert Dobson (Tyser & Co)	1887-93
Capt R.J.C. Todd (Tyser & Co)	1893-14
Capt R.J.C. Todd	1914-16
John R. Rooper	1916-21
Warwick E.C. Gregory MC	1934-39
N. Douglas Binnie	1946-54
John H. Cook	1956-68
David I. Binnie	1968-69

LOCAL DIRECTORS: NEW YORK

T. Ashley Sparks KCMG, KBE	1917-52
Brigadier J.H. Hardy CBE, MC	1952-61

LONDON MANAGERS

John R. Rooper	1921-27
William Donald, CBE	1927-45
Ronald H. Senior, DSO, TD	1945-47
D. Cunningham	1947-48

R.L. Harvey	1948-51
H.E.T. Ross (General Manager)	1951-61
Stephen C. Gibbs	1961-62
H. Kenneth U'Ren	1962-68

COMPANY SECRETARIES

H.O. Goring	1914-24
Sir James P.I.M. Corry Bt, MA	1924-55
E. C. Sutton	1955-71
F. Leach	1971-72
W.A. Stephens	1972-73
A.M.G. Richardson	1973-74
Brian N. Barlow	1974-91

MARINE SUPERINTENDENTS – LONDON

Capt T.B. Linklater	1914-28
Capt W.H. Lea	1928-36
Capt Harold E. Higgs	1936-42
Capt William Gilling, CBE	1942-45
Capt A.R. Martin	1945-53
Capt Hugh S. Datson	1953-60
Capt A. Gordon Russell	1960-66
Capt Thomas S. Paton	1966-68

ENGINEER SUPERINTENDENTS – LONDON

Alexander McDonald	1914-23
H. Glover Dearden	1923-38
B.P. Arrowsmith, OBE	1938-47
Robert W. Cromarty	1947-64
Capt W.S.C. Jenks, OBE, RN (Rtd)	1964-65
R.H. Curry	1965-68

COMMODORE MASTERS

W.G. Higgs OBE	1948-49
T. Kippins OBE, DSC	1949-50
E.J. Syvret OBE	1954-58
F.W. Bailey MBE	1958-59
E.T.N. Lawrey	1959-60
C.R. Townshend	1963-64
P.H. Pedrick OBE	1964-65
F.J. Lavers OBE	1965-67
L.W. Cady	1967-69

COMMODORE CHIEF ENGINEERS

D.C. Jack OBE	1954-55
D. Poston OBE	1958-59
D.N. McLaren	1959-59
J.N. Robertson OBE	1960-64
S.G.L. Bentley DSO	1965-66
T.C. Linklater	1966-66

MARINE SUPERINTENDENTS - SYDNEY

Capt H. Hollis	1916-25
Capt J. M McCaw, MC, Croix de G.	1927-44
Capt A.E. Fishwick	1945-50
Capt A. Gordon Russell	1951-59
Capt Thomas B. Milburn	1959-71

SUPERINTENDENT ENGINEER – SYDNEY

William Fyffe	1956-71

MARINE SUPERINTENDENTS – NAPIER/WELLINGTON

Capt R. Todd (Tyser & Co)	1887-93
Capt T.Q. East (Tyser & Co)	1893-07
Capt T. Sharp (Tyser & Co)	1907-08
Capt J.B. Rainey (Tyser & Co)	1908-13
Capt J.B. Rainey	1914-20
Capt A. West	1920-25
Capt H. Hollis	1925-36
Capt S.E.A. Gregory	1936-47
Capt H. McGregor Post MBE	1947-63
Capt William M Clough	1963-70

SUPERINTENDENT ENGINEER – WELLINGTON

Leonard A. Willoughby	1954-72

MARINE SUPERINTENDENTS - NEW YORK

Capt F. Norman	1914-17
Capt J.C. Alexander	1917-37
Capt W.J. Enright	1937-38
Capt S.W. Hayter	1938-42
(T.& J. Brocklebank superintendents)	1942-59
John R. Peek	1959-69

ASSOCIATED CONTAINER TRANSPORTATION (AUSTRALIA) LTD 1967-91

CHAIRMEN	
R.A. Vestey	1967-71
Sir Basil Smallpeice, KCVO	1971-79
E.H. Vestey	1979-82
W.B. Slater, CBE, VRD	1982-85
E.H. Vestey	1985-88
A.J. Macintosh	1988-91
A.R.C.B. Cooke	1991-91
DIRECTORS	
D.G. Hollebone, MBE, MC, TD	1967-78
R.A. Lloyd	1967-82
J.G. Payne	1967-79
E.H. Vestey	1968-88
P.E. Bates	1968-69
P.H. Shirley	1968-70
R.A. Vestey	1968-71
J.D.M. Hearth	1969-71
N.S. Thompson (CBE in 1980)	1970-74
D.F. Martin-Jenkins	1970-76
W.B. Slater, CBE, VRD	1971-72
Sir Basil Smallpeice KCVO	1971-79
B.R. Hazlitt	1971-74
V.C. Matthews, later Lord Matthews	1972-83
A. J. Macintosh	1974-85
E.C. Sutton	1974-80
I.R. Weatherston	1974-91
W.B. Slater, CBE	1974-85
M.B. Northen	1975-91
B.R. Hazlitt	1976-91
D.A. Lloyd	1976-79
A.R.C.B. Cooke	1979-91
P.G. Pike	1981-91
M.R.F. Cartwright	1981-92
R.H.S. Dilley	1982-85
E.W. Parker	1983-86
P. Fullagar	1985-87
A.J. Macintosh	1985-91
A.G. Kennedy	1986-88
D.J.C. Habgood	1988-91
P.K. Thatai	1988-91
M.G. Parker	1989-90
R.C. Whyte, OBE	1989-91
C.S. Cullen	1989-91
A.S. Humphryes	1990-95

APPENDIX 5

Port Line Tales

The distinctive Port Line house flag came from Tyser and Company, and in a conversation around the beginning of the 20th century between A.W.M. Clarke, a young man in the Tyser London office, and W.H. Piper, a Tyser employee from 1873, Piper explained that originally Tyser vessels flew a white flag with a red St. George's cross superimposed on the white. After a while the partners received a letter from the British Red Cross Society which complained about the use of this flag design, which the Society said was a breach of the Geneva Convention as the design was exclusive to the Red Cross organisation. W.H. Tyser, the chairman of the company, decided to place a blue cross in the style of a St Andrews cross from corner to corner behind the red, and this design was subsequently adopted.

WHALE TALES

There were a number of reports of ships striking whales in the Tyser line days, but in more recent times, the *Port Hobart* struck a whale outward bound to New Zealand in 1947. The whale, about ten metres long, was almost cut in two by the speed of the ship, but remained draped across the bow. When 2nd mate Tony Braund took morning star sights, he found the ship was well behind her expected position. At daybreak he noticed the bow wave was different, investigated and discovered the whale. The ship was stopped after breakfast, and the passengers were invited to go forward to see the whale, but sensing something 'fishy', none did, since it was 1 April. The carcass dropped off after the *Port Hobart* went astern.

Captain Syvret in the *Port Wellington* had a similar experience in 1953. He said the ship had passed through a shoal of whales and no one onboard took much notice although the ship's speed had dropped back to just under 14 knots instead of over 16 knots. This was put down to an adverse current, often experienced in this area. The ship carried on at 14 knots, but when she slowed engines for manoeuvring prior to transiting the Panama Canal, the ship's carpenter looked over the side and found the body of a dead whale, about 7-8 metres in length, jammed under the fore foot and just breaking surface. The ship had apparently killed the whale and carried the body from the previous afternoon.

WITH THE GREY FUNNEL LINE

During the first Malta convoy in 1941, Admiral Troubridge of HMS *Nelson* came on the bridge for a general look around. The officer of the watch happened to remark to the admiral that before joining the Royal Navy, he had been with Port Line spending three years in the *Port Chalmers*. In that case, said the admiral, perhaps you can tell me what light is showing from that ship, which at this hour should have been extinguished. The lieutenant first thought that the light was coming from the cook's pantry but finally decided it was emanating from the apprentices' bathroom. The admiral ordered a message be sent to the *Port Chalmers* instructing the ship to extinguish the light in the apprentices' bathroom immediately. Two years later, Captain Gordon Higgs, master of the *Port Chalmers* in that first convoy, was invited to a reception on board H.M.S. *Nelson* and on entering the wardroom immediately recognised the lieutenant who was his pre-war junior officer. Captain Higgs smiled and turned to Troubridge and said that he now had the answer to the amazingly accurate signal you transmitted to me as we were approaching Malta two years ago!

Rear Admiral J.E.H. McBeath, DSO, DSC, chief of the New Zealand Naval Staff, was shocked to find his admiral's flag flying on the *Port Jackson* on the morning of 9 September 1956. He had made a weekend visit to Napier and was the guest of the commander of the New Zealand frigate *Pukaki.* In the early hours of Saturday morning, fourth officer Jim North of *Port Jackson* dodged behind some railway wagons on the wharf where both vessels were berthed, and while chief steward 'Bunny' Hewitt engaged the officer of the watch on the *Pukaki*, Jim North climbed onto the naval vessel and it was a easy matter to secure the Admiral's flag, stuff it under his jacket and return it to his own ship. At 'flags' at 0800 the same morning the admiral's flag was run up on *Port Jackson.* Within a short time a note was sent from *Pukaki* emphasizing that 'while appreciating the feat', the admiral wanted his flag returned, and a short time later a Royal New Zealand Navy party, headed by a lieutenant, received back the flag, with due solemnity, on the deck of *Port Jackson.* The incident received wide publicity in Napier and the waterside workers loudly cheered as the admiral's flag was raised on *Port Jackson.*

MASTERS AND MARTINETS

Captain Peter Pedrick, later a commodore in Port Line, developed a very smart flag ceremony night and morning. Precisely at 0800 every morning, the gangway Quartermaster would ring eight bells. Through a loud-speaker system, the 4th officer would start playing a bugle recording of 'Colours', to which music the Red Ensign would be slowly raised so that when the music ended the ensign would reach its height. At this moment an apprentice would break out the company house flag on the port yardarm and another apprentice would drop the courtesy flag of the country where the ship was berthed on the starboard yardarm, while another apprentice would raise the stem-jack (small version of the company house flag) on the short mast on the foc'sle. At sunset the same procedure was followed in reverse when all flags were lowered simultaneously. Captain Pedrick later found a piper (Mike McKinnon from Barra in the Outer Hebrides) on board and for a time the bag-pipes replaced the recording of 'Colours'.

On the *Port Curtis* in New York harbour, in the early hours of 18 April 1928, the ship was boarded by a burglar. When he broke into Captain W.J. Enright's cabin the master grabbed his revolver and ordered the man to stop. The intruder ignored the warning and ran off. Captain Enright fired three shots and the 30-year old Spaniard collapsed to the deck and died almost immediately, with some stolen cuff links and shirt studs lying nearby. The master was automatically charged with manslaughter, but the charge was subsequently withdrawn and he was fully exonerated for his actions.

Ten days out from Cape Town on passage to Melbourne, Captain T.H. Rigden, master of the *Port Darwin,* had the misfortune to swallow one of his dentures. It stuck in his larynx and he could not remove it. It was extremely painful and he was forced to subsist on a liquid diet until the ship reached Melbourne and the denture could be surgically removed.

Captain G.W. Hearn was a keen cricketer and in the late 1930s his loyalty to the English team was being frustrated by the famous Australian batsman Don Bradman, who kept knocking up centuries with great ease. He became so excited one day when he briefly heard a radio announcement 'BRADMAN OUT" that he jumped for joy, but coming back down, broke his toe!

Some masters adopted very high standards on their regular inspections around their ship and on occasions nearly drove their chief officers 'up the wall' with their demands. One of the more particular masters was Captain Claude Townshend, and he was very fussy about white paint getting on the rubber insulation strips around doors and invariably mates would have the bosun blacken over any stray white paint. David Sinclair recalls that when he was mate of *Port Auckland,* Captain Townshend was most put out by the smell in the passenger's laundry which was coming up the scupper pipe. This was a tiny compartment directly above the donkey boiler in the engine room and in the tropics, the water in the trap, which would have prevented any smell, quickly evaporated. The mate was told to get it fixed and on the following day's inspection, Captain Townshend went into his usual sniffing routine in the laundry and left all smiles. On asking his chief officer on how he had achieved this, his smile faded when the mate said he had got the chippy to cement up the scupper pipe!

On another occasion, when the *Port Auckland* was loading in London, Captain Townshend advised the assistant cargo superintendent that he wanted the ship EXACTLY two feet by the stern for the voyage out. On the last day of loading the superintendent said he was unable to achieve this and tried to explain the difficulties of achieving an exact trim. Captain Townshend cut him off and said: 'When I am loading in the colonies, my chief officer has no difficulty achieving such a result!'

Another crusty master was a bit of a character during inspections and one day he noted that for two days running there was a bucket containing someone's washing that was being soaked. On the second day, the master pronounced that if that 'dhobey' was still there tomorrow, he would dump it! Sure enough it was there on the third day and the Captain took it to the ship's side and threw it overboard. An irate junior engineer fronted up to the master and told him he could not do that, to which he was told 'The only thing I can't do to you on this ship is put you in the family way … now booger off'(in a strong Lancashire accent)!

Captain P.S. Ball, when he was master of the 1914-built *Port Melbourne,* had fallen out with his tiger (personal steward) and the relationship went from bad to worse. One night, the 'tiger' decided he had had enough, and in making up his master's supper, he filled the door-stop slices of bread with crushed garlic cloves. On his way back down to his cabin, the steward passed the apprentices cabin and said 'I think I've overdone it this time, wait for the explosion'. Sure enough, a few minutes later, there was a bellow from above. 'Tiger where are you?' The Tiger rushed up the stairs to the waiting master standing outside his cabin. 'What did you put in my sandwiches?' 'Garlic, sir'. 'Good, I will have the same tomorrow night'.

Captain David Sinclair recalls the day the Greek marine superintendent came aboard the *Port Sydney* after her sale to Greek shipowners. He asked David about the Ralston stability indicator and how it worked. He said, suppose you were loading 5000 tons of bagged grain, how would you do it? Captain Sinclair went through the procedures and explained it all. Later he discovered that the *Port Sydney,* under her new owners, had gone off to load a part cargo of bagged grain in North France for Greece and that he had unwittingly worked out the stability and the draft for the new owners!

One of the Port Line 'characters' was Captain Ian Harry North and all who came in contact with him enjoyed his exuberant humour, and likewise admired his ability as a shipmaster. He was also something of an artist and the following drawing exemplifies all the trouble he has gone to in preparing the dry dock specifications, and presumably the alligators nipping at his heels are intended to portray his masters in the marine superintendent's department!

Port Line master Ian North reflects the views of many a Port Line master when he makes a mockery in this drawing of the 'blood, sweat and tears' expended in getting the dry-docking specifications drawn up for the superintendent engineers' department. Captain North often conveyed similar messages in pencil drawings showing the 'alligators' of head office nipping at his heels! (I.H. NORTH)

During World War II, a second mate, on joining his new ship found a 70 pound bag of sugar with a cargo brand in his wardrobe, presumably his predecessor had been unable to smuggle it ashore. During the course of the voyage considerable thought was given on how to get it ashore as it would be very useful at home with sugar being a tightly rationed commodity. He decided to discuss his problem with Captain H. McGregor Post, the company's Marine Superintendent in Liverpool. Mac promptly told him to get an apprentice to take it down to his car and he would get it off the dock. The advice worked perfectly!! The only problem was that the Second Mate never saw the sugar again but the Post family sugar rations were greatly augmented!

BILL BAILEY

In the 1930s when former Port Line commodores, Harry Steele and Bill Bailey were chief and second officers respectively, Harry Steele was invited to stay the night at the Bailey home in Kent. There he met Bill's sister and fell in love. As the two had enjoyed a fair bit of hell-raising together, Bailey did not consider Steele a suitable match for his sister, and a bitter enmity developed between the two men. On 21 November 1940, the *Port Brisbane,* in command of Harry Steele, was captured by the German commerce raider *Pinguin* and the ship's company was taken prisoner. Nine days later the *Pinguin* captured the *Port Wellington.* The master of the ship was killed when the raider shelled the bridge and the senior officer was chief officer Bill Bailey, who joined Harry Steele on the raider. Thrown together in a small cabin, the two men finally made up and then spent the next four years together in German prison camps. They stayed friends until they died.

Bill Bailey achieved some notoriety when he was master of the *Port Bowen* when she went ashore at Wanganui in 1939 and for a time afterward, until war intervened, he was demoted to chief officer. Some years later after the war, Port Line junior apprentice Arthur Turnbull remembers being invited to the home of the Fenwick family for Sunday lunch. The Fenwicks' company was the Port Line stevedoring contractor in Napier, and Fenwick senior was a friend of Arthur's grandfather. John Fenwick and his three sisters were at lunch and Arthur was horrified to find his commanding officer, Captain E.J. Syvret, and Captain Bailey, whose ship was also in port, were both there as well. There was also a youth from Wanganui, about Arthur's age. During the meal when the boy realised the conversation centred very much on Port Line, he suddenly announced that he remembered the *Port Bowen* being wrecked at Castlecliff and babbled on about how he expected the captain must have been very embarrassed when his ship ran aground. There was a stunned silence around the table, then Bill Bailey looked at the young man and said two words – 'I was'! For some reason or other the lad from Wanganui never opened his mouth again during the meal.

ASHORE

And then there is the story of the colonial lad working in Port Line London office. He had the task of travelling to the Continent to meet all the Port Line ships going there and acting as owner's representative. He was always given a first class ticket on the boat train from Victoria to Dover. This he would exchange for a third class ticket and drink the difference en route! Apparently the London manager, Bill Donald, got wind of this and followed him on one occasion and waited until he was seated in the third class compartment. He then knocked on the window and asked why he was not in the first class section. The response was 'I couldn't find a seat'! 'Nonsense my boy', says Donald, 'get out and I will find you one'. He then waited until the train pulled out and of course, our traveller had to cough up the extra fare when the ticket collector came along. It certainly cured him from trying that trick again.

Becoming an apprentice with the Port Line involved a lengthy interview with the company's marine superintendent, who generally had the final say. One budding candidate well remembers his interview with Captain A.R. Martin. All was going reasonably well until Captain Martin opened the candidate's *Conway* report book and he asked what 'RN Class' meant. It was explained that he had failed the specialist entry exams for the Royal Navy. Captain Martin closed the file before him, stood up and took the young hopeful to the lift, explaining that whilst he knew the deputy chairman of the company was interested in him, Port Line did not accept any candidate making the merchant navy his second choice of career. The lad, whose father managed a London lighterage company, had to wait a little longer while his father spoke to Ronnie Senior, the deputy chairman, who issued a memo to Captain Martin that the lad was to be taken on, but dropped if not up to standard, as to refuse would be an embarrassment to him. It all worked out. The apprentice eventually rose to command in Port Line and later became a superintendent with the company.

From 1941 British Railways built a series of powerful steam locomotives known as the 'Merchant Navy' class, and each engine was named after a major British shipping company. The concept was to commemorate the role of merchant shipping during World War II and to acknowledge the links between Southern Railway and the various shipping lines. When a new series was introduced in 1947, permission was sought from Port Line to name one of the new locomotives after the company. On 24 April 1950 locomotive number 35027 was named 'Port Line' by Bill Donald, chairman of the company. The ceremony was held at Southampton and Donald briefly drove the locomotive along the wharf. The engine held a plaque denoting Merchant Navy Class with the name Port Line set around a circle with a motif of the company house flag in the centre. 'Port Line' was overhauled and rebuilt in 1956-7, but as steam engines were being steadily replaced in the 1960s, it was withdrawn from service in September 1966 after steaming 872,290 miles. It was saved from scrapping in January 1982 by a preservation group and over subsequent years 1983-8 it was progressively restored and presently remains with the Swanage Railway in Dorset.

UNUSUAL CARGOES

In 1930 the Australian government approached the company to carry several hundred tons of defence equipment, including the spare mounting for an eight-inch [250-mm] gun turret, from Newcastle-upon-Tyne to Sydney. Weighing approximately 90 tonnes, the dimensions of the mounting prevented it being lowered into the hold. Because of the size and weight there was a reluctance to carry it on deck – in any case, it would have been very difficult to securely lash such a heavy item. None of the other lines in the Australian trade were prepared to carry the shipment. Captain Harold Higgs, assistant marine superintendent of the C&D Line, asked for drawings of the gun mounting, and after careful study, suggested that it could be carried if it was suspended over one of the hatches. It was shaped something like an old fashioned bottle top, and the idea was to rest the top on the hatch coaming and the remainder of the mount would be suspended within the hatchway. Long, heavy baulks of timber were placed fore and aft and thwartships over No 3 hatch and the wide portion of the mount was lifted by floating crane and set on top of these which helped to spread the weight of the load more evenly. The hatchway itself was then made watertight with timber framing and canvas tarpaulins. The *Port Gisborne* safely delivered her unusual cargo to Sydney where it was again taken ashore by floating crane. The British Board of Trade had to approve the unusual stowage arrangement and the Australian government actually sent a Royal Australian Navy captain to Britain to check and sanction the proposed method of shipment.

FOREIGN PARTS

On 13 February 1958 whilst approaching the pilot cutter off Port Said, something happened to one of the *Port Fairy*'s propellers. A diver was engaged to inspect the stern area and confirm the actual situation. Captain A.J. 'Snow' Hawkins was master of the ship, and in his characteristic stentorian voice, tinged on this occasion with a little impatience, he asked the diver – Well, do we have a propeller? The Arab diver's unshaven face broadened with a big smile and he replied "Yes, Cap-e-tan, you have no propeller".

As ships passed through the Suez Canal, officers were invariably approached by Egyptian 'traders' seeking to buy any old ropes. One such approach, by a character known as the Prince of the Red Sea, was firmly rejected by the chief officer of one vessel but the Prince said he would like to present him with a briefcase anyway. Nothing appeared by the time ship left Suez but an emissary from the Prince made contact at Ismaillia, apologising for not being able to bring the case, but it would be supplied at Port Said. There, more profuse apologies were made, and the runner said it would be sent on to him. Some weeks later in London, Captain F.R. Gorman, marine superintendent, informed the chief officer there was a parcel for him in his office. The parcel, in torn brown paper wrapping from an Arab source, with a note conveying the compliments of the Prince of the Red Sea, contained a black leather brief case. The marine superintendent made no comment as the red-faced chief officer retrieved his present!

In another incident in Kingston, Jamaica, an officer on the *Port Saint John* noticed a mooring rope was disappearing over the side of the ship and raced forward onto the forecastle to see what was happening. He just had time to slip the inner eye over a bollard and when the small boat heading up the harbour at some speed reached the point where it could go no further, it shot vertically in the air and ejected its two occupants into a shark infested harbour – and with the mooring line coming un-hitched from the boat, it carried on into the night on its own!

INCIDENTS

In 1957 while on passage from Saint John to New York, Captain Albert Brown of *Port Montreal* reported that the ship ran into dense fog. Keeping a close watch on the radar a strong echo appeared on the port bow, which by plotting appeared to be a vessel crossing *Port Montreal*'s path at a collision angle. After a few minutes, the object had doubled back on itself and was heading away. Later it passed in the distance and dropped astern. He said 'having other vessels to contend with, we ceased plotting that echo, but its peculiar antics and high speed in the fog made us keep a watchful eye on it. Some little time later we were amazed to observe the echo closing us rapidly on the starboard quarter. It was heading right for us, at a speed of at least 20 knots. Suddenly the echo disappeared off the radar screen and was last seen still on a dangerously fast closing course'. By this time Captain Brown said, we were wondering what sort of a lunatic we were having to deal with. Here was a subject, bent on our destruction, at the most critical stage of events, suddenly disappearing off the screen for no valid reason. Our problem was eventually solved – we had been trying to dodge an airship!

Some of the long-serving bosuns with the company were quite remarkable characters and their strength and imposing appearance ensured the 'deck crowd' behaved themselves and pulled their weight. One such personality was big Murdo McLeod from the Hebrides. He had been in the Marines during World War II, was over six foot tall and very strong. The stevedore at Lyttelton once asked him if he had any trouble with the sailors. Big Murdo drew himself up and replied 'We never have trouble with the crowd on this ship – EVER'!

Two Port Line ships were crossing the Pacific in different directions and it was expected they would pass close to each other within a few hours. Morning star sight positions were exchanged and by a slight alteration of course the vessels were expected to pass within sight of each other at about 1130 the same morning. The passengers were alerted and everyone was waiting with anxious anticipation for the other ship to come into sight. No ship appeared by noon and the junior third officer on the 8-12 watch was admonished for not keeping a sharp enough look-out. Noon positions were exchanged between the two vessels and amazingly they were both identical! At least the engineers, who were always skeptical at what took place on the bridge, would have had a good laugh at this situation. Nowadays of course the satellite navigation would have ensured a definite sighting

In 1957 while on passage from Cristobal to Brisbane with a MANZ Line cargo of newsprint from Canada, the *Port Fremantle* 'went missing' for almost a week. She radioed her position on 9 February 1957 that she was 975 miles east of Brisbane and nothing further was heard from the ship. After she was two days overdue at Brisbane, a full-scale search was ordered. The Royal Australian Air Force was just about to send out the first search plane when a faint signal was received from the vessel advising her position was 100 miles off Brisbane. Her main radio transmitter was out of action and the emergency transmitter in one of the ship's lifeboats was used to send the message. This emergency transmitter only had a range of 100 miles so it was not possible to send a message earlier. Since her last report, the ship had also come through Cyclone 'Clara', which generated winds in excess of 75 miles an hour, and it was estimated the *Port Fremantle* was within 60 miles of the centre of the storm. It was only when the ship heard on the local shore radio station that a full scale search was about to be mounted that it was decided to use the transmitter from the lifeboat to advise that 'all was well'! The radio operator had also decided to lock himself in the radio room, as well as giving up sending messages. His action prevented the ship being aware of the loss of contact with the shore and he was relieved on the vessel's arrival at Brisbane. Sent home on other Port Line ship, he became sick and had to be landed at Panama.

Before leaving the ship, he gave the master a thick envelope and asked that it be handed to the Port Line marine superintendent in London, as it told his side of the story of the passage out in *Port Fremantle*. When the envelope arrived in London, the superintendent got the Marconi representative around and when they opened the envelope, they found that it was stuffed full of toilet paper!

PASSENGERS

The majority of passengers travelling on Port Line ships were elderly couples wanting to enjoy a restful sea voyage, although quite often the doctor signing on articles as ship's surgeon had his young family with him. In any event there was not the formality of the larger passenger ships, nor did the ships engage in all the activities liner passengers were encouraged to participate in. On one voyage home, two of the *Port Wellington*'s passengers were middle aged spinsters around 50 years of age. Captain Les Kidwell, who was having a drink with the agent prior to sailing deepsea, commented that they would be looking much younger and more attractive, after the 18 days it would take the ship to reach Panama!

The passenger manager of Port Line in Wellington in the post-war years was Robert E. Parsons. He was something of a character and well known throughout the New Zealand travel industry. Most of his salary was paid for by Cunard Line as he was also the Cunard passenger representative in New Zealand, taking bookings for the company's Canadian service ships and also the transatlantic liners *Queen Elizabeth* (1940, 83,673) and *Queen Mary* (1936, 81,237) which he always described in nautical parlance as the 'biggest bottoms on the Atlantic'! One day Bob was patiently informing a prospective Port Line passenger about the benefits of a nice quiet restful voyage on a Port Line cargo ship carrying 12 passengers. He was explaining how the passengers integrated into the running of the ship and had their meals with the ship's officers and generally became part of the ship's company. The woman continued her pattern of searching questions until she asked Bob 'What happens if you strike a snag on board – a passenger who doesn't get on with the others?' In full Robert E. Parsons style, he replied 'Yes Madam, and it might be you!'

The company's practice of carrying a doctor was very re-assuring for masters even though they were often young men who had recently completed their training and were travelling overseas for further study. Some had experience as surgeons, but generally they were qualified medical practitioners without a wide range of experience. Most voyages were uneventful, but occasionally a serious illness developed which had to be dealt with quickly. In 1926 the second cook of the *Port Bowen* had a serious attack of appendicitis and the surgeon decided an operation was needed immediately. It was performed on a dining saloon table with the chief steward the anaesthetist, and two passengers, who were graduate nurses assisting. The following year a similar circumstance took place on board *Port Auckland* in heavy weather off Cape Horn. Again the patient lay on a dining room table and he also made a good recovery. A third case of appendicitis occurred in 1952 while the *Port Campbell* was crossing the Pacific. Two officers assisted the surgeon, and the only woman passenger on board, who had nursing experience from World War I, administered the anaesthetic. On this occasion additional large lights were brought into the saloon. Another mid-Pacific operation for appendicitis took place in 1966 on board the *Port Nelson*. On this occasion the surgeon was assisted by his wife and the chief engineer's wife, both of whom had trained as nurses. These instances are only a few examples of shipboard 'operations'.

An ACT(A) container ship was on passage from Brisbane to Port Chalmers and some very rough weather was being experienced. The captain suggested to one extremely overweight, and slow moving American passenger, that she might sleep more comfortably if she put her mattress on the floor of the cabin and slept there. The woman absorbed the advice, and after a long pause, asked how she would manage to get upright again!

SUGGESTIONS AND ORDERS

The suggestion boxes on Port Line ships often received some interesting ideas. In 1929 five passengers on the *Port Darwin* urged the company to provide increased supplies of ales and spirits for their use. The request was actioned and no further such requests appeared in later years. In 1931 an enlightened W.A. Stevens, second steward on the *Port Fairy* proposed ship's hatch covers be made of steel and in 1939 apprentice D. Hope made a similar plea, and in this case received a £5 reward from management. It was not until ten years later that steel hatch covers became a reality. Suggestions that everyone on board did 15 minutes of exercises each morning and that a Christian service be led by the master each Sunday were not universally accepted.

STANDING ORDERS FROM THE NIGHT ORDER BOOK *PORT JACKSON* Voy. 4

'The Officer of the watch is not to leave the bridge under any circumstances until he has been relieved by another Officer. Long periods must not be spent in the Chart Room leaving the forepart of the bridge without a lookout. Before taking over charge of the watch, the Officer is to satisfy himself that all is in order, a safe course being steered, lights and lookout attended etc. Before the watch is relieved both watches to muster and report to the Officer, who is to satisfy himself that all are present, before giving the order for relief.

Magnetic and Gyro compasses are to be frequently compared and checked during the watch, and always at the relief by both Officers. Compass errors are to be obtained at least once each watch, and always when course has been changed if possible.

Master to be called if visibility becomes low from any cause, if there is any material change in weather, of for any other reason which would seem to make this advisable. I shall never object to being called at any hour, day or night.

In bad weather, send the Quartermaster round to see that all is in order in parts of the ship not under observation from the bridge.

All officers are required to take a real and active part in the navigation of the ship, and are to submit positions each day at noon. Stellar navigation to be regularly practiced and employed. In circumstances of immediate danger you are to act upon your own initiative and have me called as soon as possible.

Above all the Officer of the watch should realise that he is in sole charge, and that the safety of lives, ship, and cargo is dependent upon his vigilance and activity while on watch.

W. Gilling, Master

Keep the Chart Room tidy
Do not have books and charts which are not in use lying about on the table
Do not disfigure charts by careless use of dividers and pencil
All ship's property such as Instrument Books, Signal Flags, etc should be treated with great care.
The appearance of a ship, and her furnishings and equipment, reflects the character of the people in charge of them.

Bibliography

Primary Sources

PORT LINE AND ASSOCIATED COMPANIES' RECORDS, UNIVERSITY OF THE LIVERPOOL

Directors' minute books

Tyser Line Ltd	1889-1915
Commonwealth & Dominion Line	1914-1937
Port Line Ltd	1937-1952
	1961-1970
Seal Registers	1938-1967
Agreement Books	1914-1950
MANZ Line documents	1937-1944
Ship's wartime experiences/reports	
Negotiations with Blue Star Line	
Various scrap books/loose notes	1913-1949
'Notes of the Month'	1940-1958
Correspondence files/reports	

COMPANIES HOUSE, CARDIFF

Port Line Ltd & Associated Container Transportation (Aust) Ltd files

HOCKEN COLLECTIONS, DUNEDIN

J.M. Ritchie letters, N.M.A. Company of N.Z. Ltd archives

PORT LINE RECORDS HELD BY I.J. FARQUHAR, DUNEDIN

'Notes of the Month' – various issues 1953-8

GWZC CALLING (Port Line House Magazine) Nos 1-48 1959-68

Blue Star Port Lines Journal No. 1 April 1970 – No. 7 October 1971

Blueport Journal No. 8 April 1972 – No. 10 October 1972

Cunarder, selected issues 1974-85

Cunard Line annual reports 1960-70

Trafalgar House Investments Ltd, annual reports 1971-85

41 "Brains Books" with technical details of vessels built between 1918-1968

Particulars of fleet cards 8.1927, 4.1946, 4.1952, 6.1954, 1.1963, 1.1965, 9.1966, 11.1968 and 7.1970.

Port Line Limited – War-time Experiences 1939-45

Equipment and decorations on *Port Brisbane* and *Port Auckland* –March 1949

A Port Line Occasion – Visit of the Queen and Princess Margaret to M.V. Port Brisbane *in London 3.4.1949*

Port Line Story 1914-1964 by A. Stewart McMillan (pub 1964)

Tyser & Company 1820-1969 by H.L. Skinner (pub 1969)

J.R. Rooper, Lecture on history of Commonwealth & Dominion Line, delivered 21.3.1936

Two brochures of passenger accommodation and plans

Sundry newspaper cuttings 1924-1968

Newspapers

The Times, London, 1861-2002
Australasian, Melbourne,1883-89
Sydney Morning Herald, 1883, 1902-3
Otago Daily Times, Dunedin, 1881-1968
Daily Commercial News & Shipping List, 1890-1914
Daily Telegraph & Hawkes Bay Herald, Napier, 1886-91
New Zealand Shipping Gazette, 1951-91

Classification societies/registers

Mercantile Navy Lists, 1889, 1903-37
Lloyd's Confidential Indexes, 1972-98
Lloyd's Register books, 1872-2002
Lloyd's Shipping Indexes, 1976-2005
British Merchant Vessels Lost or Damaged by Enemy Action during World War II
Japanese Naval & Merchant Shipping Losses during World War II

Miscellaneous

Act News, ACT journal 8.1969-Spring 1988
Various ACTA magazines *Act Today* (USA), *Acta News, Contact* (Australia) 1970-87
Sundry brochures published by ACT and ACTA 1970-86
The Compass No 3, 1984, 'Hellfire over Bombay'
IRHACE Journal, June/July and Aug/Sept 1990, 'Refrigerated Exports Over 100 Years'

Secondary Sources

MAJOR REPORTS
'The American Meat Companies: Their International Methods & Aims', paper by J.R., 1916
Exports & Shipping Council, Maritime Policy for New Zealand Forum papers, 1968
Exports & Shipping Council, Focus on Present and Future Shipping Needs papers, 1980
Metra Report, 'The Economics of Container Transport for New Zealand' Vols 1 & 2, 1969
'Report on Shipping Ports & Transport and Other Services' (Streamlining Report),1964
'Report on Container & Cargo Handling' (Molyneux Report), 1967
'Ports and Shipping Reform in New Zealand', New Zealand, Business Roundtable, 1989
'Port Reform in New Zealand: A Mid-Term Update', New Zealand Business Roundtable, 1990
'Report of the Transport Commission: Meat Diversion Scheme', March 1968
'Further Report of the Transport Commission: Meat Diversion Scheme October', 1968
'Report of the Commission of Inquiry into New Zealand Shipping', 1971
The Marine Observer, Quarterly Journal of the Meteorological. Office 1948-1991
N.Z. Apple & Pear Marketing Board Annual Reports 1969-71
N.Z. Dairy Board Annual Reports 1945-61, 1966-2001
N.Z. Meat Producers Board Annual Reports 1931-86
Refrigerated cargoes – Origins and work of Shipping Lines' Research Council 1949
The Shipping & Commerce of Australia – Annual issues 1897, 1899, 1911, 1920-2, 1927, 1947, 1949-53

Shipping journals

Australasian Shipping Record, Australasian Maritime Historical Society 1970-2005
The Belgian Shiplover, Belgian Nautical Research Association 1949-75
Containerisation International 1971-93
The Log, Australian & New Zealand branches of the World Ship Society 1954-67; Nautical Association of Australia Inc., Melbourne 1968-
Marine News, World Ship Society, Kendal & London 1949-
New Zealand Marine News, New Zealand Ship & Marine Society, Wellington, 1949-
Sea Breezes, Journal of Commerce & Shipping, Liverpool, 1948-2005

Books

Alexander, Roy, *The Cruise of the Raider Wolf,* Angus & Robertson, Sydney, 1941
Anderson, Len., *Throughout the East Coast Bays*, Pictorial Publications, Hastings, 1974
Archer, J.F., *A History of Staley, Radford & Co. Ltd, 1875-1975*, author, London, 1975
Bach, John, *A Maritime History of Australia,* Melbourne University Press, Melbourne, 1976
Bakka, Dag, *Speed & Service: Wilhelmsen's First Century in Australia*, Maritime Heritage Press, Sydney, 1995
Barton, R.A., *A Century of Achievement: A Commemoration of the First 100 Years of the New Zealand Meat Industry,* Dunmore Press, Palmerston North, 1984
Beasley, M. *Wharfies, History of the Waterside Workers Federation*, Halstead Press, Rushcutters Bay NSW, 1996
Bowen, Frank C., *The Flag of the Southern Cross 1858-1939*, Shaw Savill & Albion, London, 1939
Brennecke, H.J., *Ghost Cruiser HK 33,* Wm. Kimber, London, 1954
Burley, Kevin, *British Shipping & Australia 1920-39*, Cambridge University Press, Cambridge, 1968
Burrell, David, *Furness Withy* 1891-1991, World Ship Society, Kendall, 1992
Calder, M & Janet Tyson,, *Meat Acts, N.Z. Meat Industry 1972-97*, Meat New Zealand, Wellington, 1999
Cameron, Ian, *Red Duster, White Ensign,* Frederick Muller, London, 1959
Caughey, John, *Seize Then The Hour,* Jas. P. Corry & Co. Ltd, 1974
Cooper, J., A., Kludas and J. Pein, *The Hamburg South America Line,* World Ship Society, Kendall, 1989
Coveney, T.G., *A Venture into Shipping 1912-1972,* Geo. H. Scales Ltd, Wellington, 1972
Critchell, J.T. & J. Raymond, *History of the Frozen Meat Trade,* Constable, London, 1912
Dobson, John, *Fleet List of Shipping Interests of Wm. Milburn*, author, 1990
Elphick, Peter, *Liberty, The Ships that Won the War*, Chatham Publishing, London, 2001
Ennis, John, *The Bombay Explosion,* Cassell, London, 1959
Fagg, Alan, *Westrays: A Record of J.B. Westray & Co Ltd,* J.B. Westray, London, 1957
Farquhar, Ian, *Jack of All Trades, Master of None: The Shipping Corporation of New Zealand Limited 1973 –1989,* N.Z. Ship & Marine Society, Wellington, 1996
Funch, Edye, *A Century of Ship Agency and Brokerage 1847-1947,* Funch, Edye, New York, 1947
Gibson, J.F., *Brocklebanks 1770-1950* 2 Vols., Henry Young & Sons, Liverpool, 1953
Gill, G. Hermon, *Royal Australian Navy, 1939-42,* Australian War Memorial, Canberra, 1957
Gill, G. Hermon, *Royal Australian Navy 1942-45,* Australian War Memorial, Canberra, 1968
Green, Anna, *British Capital, Antipodean Labour,* University of Otago Press, Dunedin, 2001
Gundry, Sheridan, *Making a Killing,* Tairawhiti Museum, Gisborne, 2004

Hague, Arnold, *Convoys to Russia* 1941-45, World Ship Society, Kendall,1992
Harrison, Godfrey, *Borthwicks: A Century in the Meat Trade 1863-1963*, Borthwicks, London, 1963
Haws, Duncan, *Merchant Fleets – Port Line,* TCL Publications, London, 1991
Hayward, Dai, *N.Z.Meat Producers Board-First Fifty Years,* Universal Printers, Wellington, 1972
Heal, S.C., *Conceived in War, Born in Peace,* Cordillera Publishing, Vancouver, 1992
Heal, S.C., *A Great Fleet of Ships – The Canadian Forts & Parks,* Vanwell, Vancouver, 1999
Hereford, P.S.E., *The New Zealand Frozen Meat Trade*, N.Z. Publishing, Wellington, 1932
Hocking, C., *Dictionary of Disasters at Sea during the Age of Steam,* Lloyds, London, 1969
Holman, Gordon, *In the Wake of the Endeavour,* Charles Knight & Co Ltd, London, 1973
Hoyt, Edwin P., *Raider Wolf-Voyage of Captain Nerger 1916-18,* Arthur Barker, London, 1974
Hudspeth, A & Scripps, L., *Capital Port, Marine Board of Hobart*1858-1997, Hobart Port, Hobart, 2000
Hummelchen, G., *Handels Storer,* Mercator Verlag, Munich, 1960
Hurd, Sir Archibald, *The Merchant Navy World War 1* (3 vols), John Murray, London, 1920
Hyde, F.E., *Blue Funnel: A history of Alfred Holt & Co, Liverpool 1865-1914*, Liverpool University Press, Liverpool, 1957
Hyde, F.E., *Cunard and the North Atlantic 1840-1973,* Macmillan Press, London, 1975
Johnson, D.W. & P. Dennerly, *Half a World Away*, Royal N.Z. Navy Museum, Auckland, 1998
Jose, A.W., *The Royal Australian Navy 1914-18 Vol IX*, Angus & Robertson, Sydney, 1928
Kensett, Captain A.W., *All Hands on Deck,* A.W. Kensett, London, 1999
Laird, Dorothy, *Paddy Henderson: The Story of P. Henderson & Co,* George Outram & Co, Glasgow, 1961
Laxon, W.A., I.J., Farquhar, N.J. Kirby, & F: Perry, *Crossed Flags: The Histories Of The New Zealand Shipping Company Federal Steam Navigation Company And Their Subsidiaries,* World Ship Society, Gravesend,1997
Lewis, Glen, *A History of the Ports of Queensland,* University of Queensland Press, Brisbane, 1973
Lind, C.A, *The Keys to Prosperity,* Craigs/Southland Frozen Meat, Invercargill, 1981
Lind, C.A. *A Cut Above: Early History of Alliance Freezing Company (Southland),* Craig's/Alliance Freezing Co, 1985
Loach, Cyril, *New Zealand Refrigerating Co Ltd,* Caxton Press, Christchurch, 1969
Krancke, Admiral T.& H.J. Brennecke, *The Battleship Scheer*, William Kimber, London, 1956
Macdonald, G.R., *Canterbury Frozen Meat Co. Ltd. The First 75 Years*, Whitcombe & Tombs, Christchurch, 1958
McLean, Gavin, *Otago Harbour, Currents of Controversy*, Otago Harbour Board, Dunedin, 1985
McLean, Gavin, *Rocking The Boat: A History of Scales Corporation,* Hazard Press, Christchurch, 2002
Maber, John M., *North Star to Southern Cross,* T. Stephenson & Sons, Prescot, 1967
Maude, W., *Antony Gibbs & Sons, Merchants & Bankers 1808-1958*, Antony Gibbs, London, 1958
Middlebrook, Martin, *Convoy*, Wm. Morrow & Company, New York, 1977
Miller, Harry, *Halls of Dartford 1785-1985,* Hutchinson Benham, London, 1985
Mitchell, W.H. & Sawyer L.A., *Empire Ships of World War 11,* Sea Breezes, Liverpool,1965
Mitchell, W.H. & Sawyer L.A., *The Oceans, The Forts & The Park,s* Sea Breezes, Liverpool, 1966
Mitchell, W.H. & Sawyer L.A., *The Liberty Ships*, David & Charles, Newton Abbot, 1970
Murray, Marischal, *Ships & South Africa*, Oxford University Press, London, 1934
NZSCo., *The Carriage of Cargo in the Steamers of N.Z. Shipping Co/Federal S.N.Co,* London, 1929
Paterson, R.J., *William Nelson of Tomoana, His Legacy to Hawkes Bay*, author, 2001
Phillpot, H.G., *The History of the N. Z. Dairy Industry 1840-1935*, Government Printer, Wellington, 1937

Poolman, Kenneth, *Escort Carrier,* Leo. Cooper, London, 1983
Rohwer, Jurgen, *Axis Submarine Successes of World War II,* Greenhill Books, London, 1999
Rooper, J.R., *The Rooper Story,* S. Straker & Son, London, 1957
Rooper, J.R., *The Uncompleted Journey,* S. Straker & Son, London, 1966
Royden, Sir E.B., *Thos. Royden & Sons, Shipbuilders 1818-93,* author, 1953
Russell, Captain A.G., *Port Line,* privately printed, London, 1985
Sanderson, Basil, Lord of Ayot, *Ships and Sealing Wax: The Memoirs of Lord Sanderson of Ayot,* Heinemann, London, 1967
Scanlan, B.A., *Harbour at the Sugar Loaves,* Taranaki Harbours Board, New Plymouth, 1975
Scott, Dick, *Stock in Trade:, Hellaby's First Hundred Years 1873-1973*, Southern Cross, Auckland, 1973
Scotter, W.H., *A History of Port Lyttelton*, Lyttelton Harbour Board, Christchurch, 1968
Smallpeice, Sir Basil, *Of Comets & Queens,* Airlife Publishing, Shrewsbury, 1981
Spong, H.C., in association with J. Dobson, *Port Line,* World Ship Society, 2004
Stevenson H.K., *Port & People,* Hawke's Bay Harbour Board, Napier, 1977
Stevenson, Jock, *End of an Era: Port & People Supplement,* Hawke's Bay Harbour Board, Napier, 1989
Stewart, I.G., *The Ships that Serve New Zealand Vol 1*, A.H. & A.W. Reed, Wellington, 1964
Strachan, Michael, *The Ben Line* 1825-1982, Michael Russell, Norwich, 1992
Tait, P.S., *In the Chair – The Public Life of Sir John Ormond,* CHB Press, Waipukurau, 1989
Taylor, James, *Ellermans, A Wealth of Shipping,* Wilton House Gentry, London, 1976
Waters, S.D., *Clipper Ship to Motor Liner,* New Zealand Shipping Company, London, 1939
Waters, S.D., *Shaw Savill Line – 100 Years of Trading,* Whitcombe & Tombs, Christchurch, 1961
Watson, John *Savills, A Family and a Firm 1652-1977*, Hutchinson Benham, London, 1977

Shipping Index

Date in brackets after ship's names is the year of build

General Index